JRP|RINGIER & LES PRESSES DU RÉEL

Raymond Bellour

To Nicolas Poussin and Francesco Guardi

Table of Contents

Note for the Century

From one volume of *L'Entre-Images* [Between-the-Images] to the next, from this first book in 1990 to a second (*L'Entre-Images 2*, P.O.L 1999), it was above all a matter of insisting. From one subtitle to the next ("Photography, Cinema, Video," "Words, Images"), the point was to encompass mixtures: those that mixed together "all the images" as such (thus including the painted image), and those that brought these images in contact with their inevitable component of language, as never before in the history of the world, through the use of the computer. It meant tracing out the lines of flight of a protean universe, where the works yet to come seemed to guarantee, in that respect, vitality and a sort of morality.

Since then, nothing has really changed: mixtures appear with ever-increasing speed, mixtures so diverse that sometimes words cannot be found to name them. But maybe something has subtly changed in the awareness we try to have about them.

This nearly global art, this aesthetics of confusion, carries off in its vague, catastrophic whirlwind—catastrophic in the sense of the theory of this name[1]—an art, an industry, a fact of culture and civilization, it is hard to say: cinema, which has encompassed the century like no other art. Early on, at its halfway point (whereas it had come into its own during the sound era) cinema acquired an insinuating enemy, or an alienating friend, from which its destiny could no longer separate itself, essentially for the worse: television. It now has two others: one, that magic called the computer, which will become another name for television, because it is much more immense than TV and is already devouring it. The other enemy, more respectable, friendlier as well, but who can show itself to be much more devious, seems to have settled in: the museum. There, cinema becomes on the one hand really an art, but only an art; on the other hand it transforms itself there into unfamiliar, endlessly mutating *dispositifs*, where it disappears to itself under the guise of reinventing itself under other names.

To such a point that this could increasingly become the paradoxical tension and strain of an activity like this, called "between-the-images": to follow, virtually endlessly, these movements through which so many unprecedented results are invented, while keeping one eye and one eye alone, one privileged eye, on this undivided kingdom, this "impure" art called cinema.

Preface to the second French edition, 2002. Translated in 2011 by Allyn Hardyck.

[1] Catastrophe theory, conceived by René Thom among others [translator's note].

Foreword

Nearly ten years have passed since the previous words were written. The confusion has not stopped growing, with the rise to power of the Internet, virtual access to all images, and an ever-increasing incapacity to differentiate between them. The unprecedented explosion in Biennales and exhibition spaces (galleries and museums) has also encouraged the appearance of countless works where the moving image plays at least a partial role, in varying proportions dependent on the integration of these images into unexpected combinations. Without forgetting, of course—for those works resembling films or videos (now rivaled by the digital image)—the conditions of their projection and occasional presentation. The turning point, if one has to be chosen, coincided with *documenta X*, curated by Catherine David in 1997, and the two Venice Biennales organized by Harald Szeemann in 1999 and 2001. For the first time—perhaps—moving images took the lead over the traditional arts, painting and sculpture. Since then, more than ever, the critic's work has consisted in evaluating, with patience and perseverance, the uniqueness of each of the *dispositifs* presented. In spite of the categories that could be more or less useful in grouping works and classifying them (the wall of screens; the image room/environment; the series of rooms; screens everywhere/the "all-screen"; unadorned frontal projection), it would be pointless to try to bring them together under one unifying term or concept, given that the very variation in *dispositifs* is part and parcel of their principle (among other things, the prosaic term "contemporary art" is at least useful for that).

We can see that such an explosion, with the inventiveness it assumes, was likely to increase the number of connections and contaminations between the various modes of images, as well as between images and words. In addition, more and more filmmakers have been drawn into the making of installations, for several reasons including economic ones, tied to the difficulties in making art films or film-essays, or just for reasons of personal expression. Conversely, many artists (often described somewhat clumsily as "visual artists") have been tempted by film—not to say, too simply, cinema. So we can also imagine that between the works by one group and the other, filmmakers and artists, the points of contagion have grown exponentially, and the ambiguities as well—both when as a result they have tried to remain faithful to their presumed respective roles, and when they have amused themselves by blurring the borders. An unprecedented expansion of intermediate operations has thus found itself affecting—together or separately—both films and visual artworks, each side attracted to the other by subtle yet powerful bonds.

To such an extent that this book, *Between-the-Images*, which was innovative yesterday, has itself become something of a relic. In these times of amnesia and relentless homogenization, this could be one of its virtues. It serves as a reminder, suggesting through the chosen examples how a domain gradually came into existence, for which the term "Between-the-Images" was created in an attempt to sketch out the boundaries. But we should not get the wrong idea about what I had subsequently—in various contexts, a little too simply—decided to call an aesthetics of confusion, concerning all the mediations taking shape between the various modes of images as well as between the *dispositifs* into which they enter. For there are two kinds of confusion. There is the kind that one tries to dispel by attempting to specify in each case how a given work (film, installation) acts upon it. Which means rediscovering, modestly, on the level of the aesthetics of creation, and a taste for viewing artworks and reading, something of the rigor that Michel Foucault assigned to archeology when, in *The Archaeology of Knowledge*, he gave it the imperative of the basic tasks of description. But there is also the confusion that, too often and to an increasing degree, tends to put all the eggs in one basket, for example using the word "cinema" to describe all moving images, and as a result confusing the movement of images with that of cinema, which is a particular kind of movement. For if, thanks especially to the digital image, the contaminations between images that move and those that do not have become more and more fertile—as have those having to do with the degrees of realism of the worlds presented—the *dispositifs* in which these images appear always respect a clear division, in spite of things that may enchant or threaten them: endlessly transformable *dispositifs*, each different and specific in the world of installation art; stubbornly one and the same in the world of cinematic art. For cinema is not only the moving image; it presupposes a particular *dispositif*, determined by a social framework inside of which its images develop in the dark, in silence, and in time, according to a process of unequivocal attention and specific memory. This is the division that the idea of "Between-the-Images" had tried to put aside, in favor of its own operations affecting all of the arts of the visible. This is what should be reconsidered today, via this very idea and its far-reaching spread.

Introduction to the English edition, 2011. Translated by Allyn Hardyck.

Between-the-Images

Alfred Hitchcock, , 1949

You are in darkness. On the small rectangle of the editing table, imagery goes by. Slightly clenched on the control, your hand feels the image. It feels, it knows, it thinks it can control the image. Yes, but for what image? In the name of what image? There were times when the hand forgot, when the image appeared almost of its own accord. A force. A frame. A gaze. Fixity made unbearable. Eyes dilated, mouth on the edge of something that is no longer even fully imaginable, a face has fallen and takes you in its fall. Perhaps you still remember that you are Joan Fontaine in *Suspicion* (1941)—Lina—in this editing room, with a declared goal. Or else nothing. In the time it takes to lower your head and bring your face toward this hole of light, your face that is both too present and absent there, there is a moment of weakness. Fear, to put it simply. Being captured this way within the borderless circle of this ghostly close-up, without origin or destination. As you learn over time, such is the first side of the experience. Its point of anchorage, as well as its flip side in the quite sensible activity, really, of taking your time before the image, stealing its time from it, time that is then sold off for knowledge, research, thirst for ideas. But you also know that there is a second side to the experience. While probably less pure—nothing is more implacable than the cold recognition of the motionless body[1]—the ordeal is no less violent; and in a way it is only the inner lining, the layer beneath the false bottom of the first. You follow Joan Fontaine again, in this story where she has no first name because another woman, a dead woman, has, practically as a preliminary, ingested its substance: *Rebecca* (1940). Hitchcock again. The heroine returns to the Manderley estate in flames. Almost sharing her point of view, we enter Rebecca's room where Mrs Danvers, the housekeeper who set the blaze, stands: a stiff, terrifying figure in the jumble of collapsing beams. It may be that if you paused the image, you would not recognize her, that Mrs Danvers' black silhouette, licked by long white flames, would be nothing but a universe of pure forms. In short, you are for a moment, which could last a lifetime, facing an invented, disfigured image, whose strength comes from its source—a drama—only to offer a forgotten quintessence, a latent energy of lines and spots, of strokes and points, something like an outline [*trame*] extracted from the action underway, but which constitutes its strength.

Why return once again to the experience of the freeze-frame, the induced stillness that obviously just evokes all the others, those that really stop, all the exhibited moments, the flagrant interruptions—not to mention the metamorphoses of the images associated with them? Why? Let us look at the question from two different angles. Why did Serge Daney, one fine day in June 1982, find it necessary to publish in *Libération* eight still frames from *North by Northwest* (1959), taken from the 3,426 images of the scene where Cary Grant and Eva Marie Saint kiss, thereby offering a mirage to the hurried readers of his newspaper, in order to celebrate with them the re-release of a great classic? He comments on this mirage by twice dividing the (English) title to make us see what we only glimpse in this scene where the kiss, the moment that lasts while remaining a moment, obviously represents both bliss and death (thus the harsh beauty of the French title, *La mort aux trousses*[2]). So there is the North toward which the film (let us say the Hollywood film) goes; and there is the Northwest, the direction taken by "the real film, the one you hallucinate, that nurtures your most undaunted dreams," this film then split between the North, where the film as such is headed, and the West, the orientation of "this unknown flesh of the film": the still frames.[3] Second angle: why did Robert Frank write that he would really like to make a film (his "real film"?), which would combine his (private) life and his work, a "photo-film," in order to "work out a dialogue between the movement of the camera and the freezing of the still image, between the present and the past, inside and outside, front and back"?[4] The remarkable thing here has to do with the three last "betweens." They affect the time, the body-soul and the position of the body-gaze, which all find themselves associated with the force that could produce them, or that could at least attest to their visibility: the time between the still and the moving image.

In this way, critical gaze and creative desire come together in a shared gesture which, by encompassing the elliptical space between photograph and still frame, has become one of the chosen gestures of the image's conscience—of its destiny as well as its survival. The VCR has now made it available to everyone, in the same way that television and the film world that accompanies it have ceaselessly trivialized the tormented research (while simultaneously fueling it) through which real filmmakers have attempted to determine their identity.

If the freeze-frame, or the stilled image—what could also be called a snapshot of the film, a pose or pause of the image expressing the capturing power of immobility—if this experience is so strong, it is obviously because it touches upon *l'arrêt de mort*, the finality of death: its vanishing point and in a sense the whole of the real (we all know that the dead become wax figures, a fragment of immobility). But we must grasp what is conjugated in Blanchot's exemplary title,[5] serving as the thread to his narrative: the ruling that pronounces death is also the halt that manages to hold it at bay,[6] turn it around and give it back to life, for a lifetime yet to be determined, and the story endures, in order to replace death with the rapturous force of enigma in its fullness, where there would otherwise be nothing but decay, as if in a *fort und da* of a new kind.

Sauve qui peut (la vie)[7]: rarely has a title been so well chosen. For Godard, returning to cinema after a break devoted to experimentation, it is a matter of noticing that the freeze-frame and the breakdown of movement have become in a way internal to the life of film, and therefore to life itself, and that this means saving them together. This also involves the invention of a new image, which detaches itself (partly, but enough to distinguish itself) from its photographic transparency in order to be open to other matters, to usher in a new physicality. In short, an image that, through disfiguration, becomes open to refiguration. What I have called the second side of the experience. Stretching things a little to express their most active truth, we could say that there is no passage between mobile and immobile (therefore involving the analogy of movement) that does not suppose a formal mutation of the image (therefore of the analogy in its most photographic sense).

It is no accident that the development of the freeze-frame, and of all the forms of "the photographic" that invaded cinema at the beginning of the 1960s, coincided with the transformations that have intensified since then as a result of developments in electronic image processing. One word encompasses this transformation—*video*, a word open on its two sides: television and video art. An improbable word; and it is still not fully understood to what extent it leads the arts of mechanical reproduction that preceded it—photography and cinema—into an unprecedented situation, via the opening of a realm where the question of reproduction is overwhelmed by the as yet barely glimpsed possibilities of the computed image. That is to say a potentiality that is itself unaware of the mutation that the timeless human capacity to create images—and more specifically to define them as art—will discover deep within itself.

This book will not go into such a debate. At least not directly. It has come into being—little by little—from a need to understand what happened to cinema when at some point it became impossible for it to extract itself from the pressure of two forces: one that seemed to rise up from within itself, and another that was modifying it through its collusion (direct or indirect) with video. The difficulty comes from the fact that video art, as external to cinema as it is, cannot be grasped without referring to what it affects—cinema as well as the other arts (plastic arts, music), in short everything it comes from and to which it endlessly returns, to forge itself an identity that eludes it. To be honest, the strength of video art—an art that does exist (it is just 25 years old), and that already has a set of works and masterworks (even if this is still too often overlooked)—the great strength of video has been, is, will be to have opened *passageways*. Video is above all a go-between. Passageways (for my purposes) to the two great levels of experience I have mentioned: between mobile and immobile, between the photographic analogy and that which transforms it. Passageways, corollaries, that traverse without exactly encompassing these "universals" of the image: thus, between *photography*, *cinema*, *video*, a multiplicity of superimpositions, of highly unpredictable configurations, is produced. Finally, passageways, because everything (or almost) is seen on television (or defines itself by putting up a resistance to it). The very nature of a medium capable of incorporating and transforming all the others, connected with the special knack the resulting products have of appearing, at every moment, inside a box that is both intimate and global, has profoundly transformed (this has become obvious to all) our sense of the creation as well as the apprehension of images.

Between-the-images is thus (virtually speaking) the space for all of these passageways. A many-sided place, physically and mentally. Both very visible and secretly immersed in the artworks remodeling the interiors of our bodies in order to prescribe new positions, it functions between images, in the very general and still particular sense of the term. Floating between two still frames and between two screens, between two layers of matter and between two speeds, it is hard to ascribe: it is variation and dispersion incarnate. This is how images now come to us: within the space where we must decide which of them are real images. That is to say a reality of the world, as virtual and abstract as it may be, reality of an image-as-possible-world.

Between-the-images is that space still new enough to be treated as an enigma, and already established enough to have limits. It is not my concern here to write its history (as with all mixtures, that would be hard to envision). Nor is it a matter of coming up with a theory, in the sense of specific concepts that between-the-images evokes and that would constitute the conditions for discussing it. For me, the question has mainly been to try and put into words an experience, such as it has constituted itself little by little, that started when it became clear that we have entered, via video and all its consequences, a new time of the image.

As will be seen, two names come up repeatedly in these pages: Thierry Kuntzel and Jean-Luc Godard. This is because they have had emblematic careers. The first, who came from the world of film theory and was in fact one of its initiators in France, has since become one of the most assured video artists of his generation; and it looks as though this shift that came about via video continues to fuel the same interest through other means. The second, who started out in criticism, later inventing the cinema we all know, was the first filmmaker to seize on video (and television) as fully as he did. He thus made us realize that if something was coming to an end in cinema and with cinema, it was because he was at home between-the-images like no one else, leading cinema (what else could it be called?) toward what was newest within it. Taking all the images along with him, and more as well.

The intent of all this is to help define a twofold movement without which the reality between-the-images would be hard to conceive. The first movement has for some time now led both cinema, and thinking on cinema, toward painting—as though the violence inherent to video (with regard to representation in general) had made the question inevitable (once more), requiring it to be asked more critically of cinema as a whole (and of course of video art, which draws much from painting). The second movement brought the image (cinema and video, and one via the other, but also photography) closer to literature and to language. Literature, for the positions of enunciation, the nature of the creative gesture, the indeterminacy of the works, their reflexive capabilities. Language, in the sense where words are now, more and more, at one with the image (instead of just getting mixed in with it, as was the case with silent film, which had foreseen this tendency). This is the exemplary strength behind Godard's *Puissance de la parole* (1988, and his *Histoire(s) du cinéma*, 1988–1998) for which all his previous work served as preparation.

On the one hand, the texts collected here were written at a particular moment, tied to the discovery of video for instance, as well as to an interest in the relationship between cinema and photography. They were then (starting in 1987 with "The Film Stilled"), though first published in magazines, written as part of an overall plan whose outline established itself. This does not mean that they comprised just so many integral chapters of a book written in one sitting. The proof is in the inevitable repetitions and the returns, to questions and to artists, that I did not want to minimize (some of the works covered were often not well known enough; such treatment could help compensate for that). In addition, I did not rewrite the texts, only making slight alterations for the most part, with some additional notes. On the other hand, the texts are—clearly—like samples taken from within a field impossible to explore fully or even to classify. As such, this collection is nevertheless intended to constitute a sufficient image of the perceivable and logical universe whose emergence I seem to have witnessed.

The three texts grouped together at the start of the book serve as a choice of introductions. The first is a transitional text from "film analysis," my home ground. The second, devoted to Thierry Kuntzel, dates from a close association with his work and with my discovery of video. The third places video art in its unavoidable relationship with television.

The second section is completely devoted to what I have called the first side of the experience. Photography and cinema, if you prefer: the cinema captured by photography (the photographic), then the return journey, with photography as the starting point. But the pages on *Sauve qui peut (la vie)*, for example, suggest that the experience has two sides, and that one does not function without the other.

Subsequently, the third section covers the transformation of the photographic analogy via video, essentially regarding three key transitional works between cinema and video: *La Peinture cubiste* (1981) by Philippe Grandrieux and Thierry Kuntzel, Godard's *Numéro deux* (1975), and

Antonioni's *Il mistero di Oberwald* (*The Mystery of Oberwald*, 1981). But the third analysis, devoted to a single tape (Woody Vasulka's *Art of Memory*, 1987), shows how the two sides of the experience never stop shaping each work.

The fourth section brings together four installations. The installation is the only space in video art that escapes televised broadcast, that belongs to the gallery and the museum. It is also, *par excellence*, the site for a blend of experiences in which this new image body, preordained by the transformations we are undergoing, takes form. The spectator at an installation is a *flâneur*, all the more aware of the passageways between images as his own body sometimes passes into the image, and circulates between the images.

The three final texts, dealing (especially) with video, have one thing in common: in a way they go over everything that preceded them one more time, in order to give evidence of a dimension that video art has helped emphasize. There it coincides with an evolution in cinema, in which it participates, helping cinema transform itself and working to help find a route that until now belonged exclusively to the literary experience: that of the intimate, the subjective, the autobiographical, but also that of a certain kind of reflection, of the essay, that is summed up in the word "self-portrait."

Finally, concerning the three terms that make up the subtitle of this collection—*photography, cinema, video*—I will say this. Photography (only considered in passing as an art form here) appears most of all as both the smallest decomposable unit of the image subjected to *défilement* (in other words as a still frame) and as the emblem of a planetary dispersion of the image that causes it to be, everywhere and always, this fragment of irreducible iconicity connected to every life. It therefore gains ever more significance as the circulation of images grows and accelerates, tirelessly representing the motionless index of this movement. This is what can also be gleaned from the reverie of Robert Frank.[8] In contrast, however, video, mostly considered as an art in itself, must be understood from the point of view of what, in my view, it represents historically above all: a passageway and a system of transformations of images interpenetrating each other. There are the images that preceded it—painting, photography, and cinema; there are those that it produced itself; lastly, there are those that it has brought into being, "the new images," of which it is an integral part and for which it is already a sort of prehistory. Finally, between photography and video, there is film, this already somewhat old art, all the more shaped by photography—which almost returns it to a stage before itself—as video has now captured it, projecting it into a hereafter where it is hard to know what will become of it. It can also choose to keep to what it believes it still inherently is, if only because it has been that way for so long. But even so, hollowed out from within, surrounded by the new forces that irrigate it, it is clear to see that it never stops transforming itself.

1990. Translated in 2011 by Allyn Hardyck.

[1] See Maurice Blanchot, "La ressemblance cadavérique," *L'espace littéraire* (Paris: Gallimard, 1955) 346 ["The Cadaverous Resemblance," *The Space of Literature*, trans. Ann Smock (Lincoln NE: University of Nebraska Press, 1982) 257].

[2] Which could be translated as "Death on His Tail" or "Tracked by Death" [translator's note].

[3] Serge Daney, *Ciné Journal* (Paris: Cahiers du cinéma, 1986) 115–116.

[4] Robert Frank, "I'd like to make a film ... " preface to *Robert Frank* (London: Thames and Hudson, 1985).

[5] Blanchot, *L'arrêt de mort*, Gallimard, 1948 [*Death Sentence*, trans. Lydia Davis (Barrytown NY: Station Hill, 1978)].

[6] "Arrêt" may mean "ruling" as well as "stop." The conventional translation of this phrase is "death sentence," but Blanchot plays with the word-for-word sense: "the stopping of death" [translator's note].

[7] This could be translated as "Save (your life) if you can"—the film was released in English-speaking countries under the titles *Every Man for Himself* (US) and *Slow Motion* (UK), 1980 [translator's note].

[8] "In my film—and because of the very way they float in the current of my normal life—my photographs will become pauses in its flux, breaths of fresh air, windows on another time, on other places." Frank, "I'd like to make a film ... "

Analysis in Flames

Nicolas Poussin, *Le Massacre des Innocents* (*The Massacre of the Innocents*), 1625–1626

Film analysis has finally become an art without a future. The fact is that it has never been, in itself, anything more than an illusory object. That is why, paradoxically, it could appear to be a particular activity endowed with a sort of intransitivity. As it happened, it laid claim to this quality without worrying about the confusions and false divisions that would result from it. At the other end of the chain, this tendency was confirmed by the accumulated bibliographies: useful, but ambiguous, they helped make film analysis a separate theoretical genre, with no justification other than the false sense of plenitude that can derive from the act of analysis itself.

There are two reasons for this misleading effect of analysis: the nature of the "cinematic signifier," which effectively distinguishes film analysis from all other enterprises of the same type; and the coincidence (which was self-evident) between a new interest in films and the general movement in many zones of research that crystallized for a time around the idea of text. Right away, because these two reasons converged, film analysis got to the bodily core of its text. But this seductive body is an elusive one: it cannot really be quoted nor grasped. It is polysemous as well, in an excessive way, and its matter, molded by iconicity and analogy, thwarts language. This irreducibility of the filmic substance, which fascinates and stimulates (as do all such elusive objects), serves to limit analysis: the readings of films have been unable to produce the equivalence brought out in readings of "Les Chats" or in *S/Z*.[1] This does not simply result from the analysts' lack of genius, but primarily from the exceptional resistance put up by the analytic material.[2] This resistance has too often led film analysis to take refuge in its own domain, and thereby to add to the illusions and inevitable developments that are proper to the accumulation and the organization of knowledge a special fascination for the circle within which film analysis, since its beginnings, has not been able to avoid turning. As a result of this it still can happen that film analysis will mistake itself for something it is not.

In truth there are no longer, or should no longer be, any analyses of films. There are just gestures. Free gestures, made possible now because one day a new intellectual practice that had to be called film analysis allowed (then at the cost of great difficulty) for the stopping of films. And for looking at them with a new and, as it were, cleansed eye. An eye at last freely fascinated. These gestures seem to me, today, to be four in number.

First there is this unsurpassable gesture: the freeze-frame. We can never say adequately to what extent it remains the magic gesture *par excellence*. A paradox: the video recorder, the ideal instrument for analysis, is also what has killed it. Via an excessive generalization, a passage to the infinite, we can henceforth possess—freeze—every image. Alone, caught up in one's own thoughts; in bed, touching one's companion, exchanging a knowing look with her and with the image; with one's students, at the moment sought by everyone (the seminar is perhaps the only place where film analysis still exists for itself: covered by the pedagogical alibi, we are enacting an apprenticeship in magic, a collective experience in fascination and dis-fascination, which does more to displace the givens of knowledge than it does to regulate them). The freeze-frame, which moves the film closer to the book, is a turning of pages. But struggling against the "natural" *défilement* of the images, it is also more: a game, a permutation, a diversion [*dérive*] ... A tie-in creation, set adrift [*une création dérivée*].[3]

Quite naturally criticism (good criticism) has emerged from this state of things in a modified condition. If we read the articles of Serge Daney (who today is our most scrupulous and inspired film critic) carefully, we see how certain stops in his sentences correspond with freeze-frames that are projected into the reader's mind. Of course that has always been done to some extent, but not with this determination, acuity, and especially this connivance that assumes we have entered, vis-à-vis moving images, into another era. Their number has grown immensely and will not cease to increase. But they also give the impression of moving more and more and of proliferating because the gaze of the viewer henceforth knows how to freeze them: consequently, how to fix them and make them move in another way.

The third gesture concerns theoretical work, and in the very first place cinematic theory. From now on it will be free of the ghost of film analysis since it can, in the best cases, incorporate it into its processes in an almost natural way. It can do so in spite of the resistance proper to the image, which remains intact. But the impossible element—embracing *the* system of the film as well as the mad desire to touch the film itself—this excessive lack has disintegrated, like a love that dies from no longer repeating its gestures. In addition we have a practically complete inventory of the range of possibilities that allow for playing on the lack or the excess of the absent image (in any case, in the conventional form of the article and the book). So that everyone can determine, then, at each particular point, how to make their analytical strategy comply with their concerns (this is as much an internal calculation as it is a function of the material instruments available). I would say that the work of Jacques Aumont has been, in France, the best example of this process of relaxation. In the small milieu where film theory is produced, it has been impossible not to notice the quite sympathetic skepticism he has insisted on voicing (at the risk of helping canonize the genre) toward "textual analysis of films."[4] This skepticism stems from the simple fact that Aumont chose early on to focus on a general reflection concerning problems of montage and imaging: it was necessary for him to work through certain films that inspired his inquiry, often in a very precise fashion, yet he could not run the risk of seeing his research defined in an excessive manner by this process. In particular he could not allow that perception of his work to gain a foothold. Hence his precautionary measures, which at times may have seemed rather finicky, but which were in the last analysis invaluable. Another example is afforded by the work begun long ago by Marc Vernet concerning *film noir*: today it seems to have escaped from the tension between film and cinema that was sustained too long within the whole of the field,[5] and to have reached, at the same time, the possibility of becoming an organic work. Reading the latest articles by Vernet, we can imagine him from now on passing freely from film to film, as from a concept to a still frame, in order to recount how America was defined, at a certain moment of its history, as much by modes of plot and dramatization as by what he so aptly terms the "flickering of black and white."

Finally there is the encounter, often oblique or indirect, yet so very suggestive, of film analysis with cinema. Its transformation, its dissolution in cinema and video. We can envisage it in three ways. First, as a response by the image to the image. I have spoken often of the possibility of citing, at last, the "unattainable text," of making us aware of this "truth" of the film around which the analysis could only turn in vain. Something there has remained unresolved. A portion of an answer has been given by the best moments of the broadcasts that television has devoted to the cinema: from the unsurpassable *Cinéastes de notre temps*[6] to the magazines of today. But that is very little. Theory has not really been able to arrive at the image—to speak, to hold to, to live by the image; far less than it had been able to retain the image in its words. Perhaps this union of theory and image is an impossible marriage. Yet I continue to believe in the surprises that could arise, at this level, from encounters between the word and the image.[7]

Quite other is the response—a leap in fact—that video has given to a reading of films that has been fixated on the idea of *défilement* in cinema. The most worthy example is that of Thierry Kuntzel. His work in video art, which takes its place beside others that are novel and important, retains the trace of an insight that is its own. Is other. Is marked by the origin it leaves. In his video fictions-reflections, film analysis has literally gone up in flames.

The final encounter is a twofold history, full of holes and unrealizable, yet worthy of being evoked here: between film analysis, which appears, develops, gains a momentary self-confidence and then dissipates into cinema theory; and the history of cinema, which advances by absorbing the emanations from this adventure that it obviously considers unimportant, and that it had in part provoked. Serge Daney recently recalled that Truffaut had ended his first feature film, *Les quatre cents coups* (*The 400 Blows*, 1959) with a freeze-frame (for the first time perhaps in cinema history).[8]

François Truffaut, *Les Quatre Cents Coups* (*The 400 Blows*), 1959

A few years earlier, Truffaut had pushed criticism a notch ahead toward analysis by tracking the development of "two" as a concept in *Shadow of a Doubt* (1943). He had "stopped" on this Hitchcock film as he later would on the final shot of the story he would seek to tell. We see here how the logic piles up, from criticism to directing, from theory to creation. Since then, the cinema has not stopped moving while always looking for more ways to stop, to freeze. Through its own acceleration, triggered by that of all the "new images," it attempts to grasp itself, come back to itself, and thus never cease to reinvent itself. Seen from a distance, that might be the finest result, however minimal, of film analysis: to have burned for the cinema as well.

That said, nothing will prevent a dreamer from one day deciding quite simply to undertake (again) the analysis of a film, in order to understand something never understood. But it would take much foresight to predict whether this move would give rise to a new theoretical proposition or a new form of narrative.

1984. Originally translated in 1985 by Lynne Kirby.

[1] The allusion is to famous analyses of Baudelaire's poem "Les Chats" by Claude Lévi-Strauss, Roman Jakobson, and Michael Riffaterre, as well as to Roland Barthes' book entitled *S/Z* (1970) [translator's note].

[2] For example, I recently received a fascinating manuscript containing both an analysis and a thorough description of Jacques Tourneur's *Cat People*, drawing in some respects from Barthes' procedures in *S/Z*. The author, Dominique Zlatoff, was conscious and rightfully proud of having reached a limit by producing a "mad" work: in its essence very hard to read, and yet often remarkable, if only because of this limit that it made perceptible. A portion has since been published in the special edition of *Caméra Stylo* devoted to Tourneur (no. 6, May 1986) under the title "La Féline." An excellent text, because it is fragmentary, albeit in the form of a long fragment.

[3] Bellour plays with the double meaning of *dérive* as "drift" and as used in the term *produit dérivé*, the French term for "tie-in" [editor's note].

[4] With Michel Marie, he has since written *L'analyse des films* (Paris: Nathan, 1988).

[5] Visible in this distinction is Metz's famous dichotomy—a fine example of the way in which a distinction, however useful it may be, can contribute to forming, at other levels than the one for which it was strictly formulated, a sort of mental block.

[6] A series of documentaries on filmmakers produced for French television by André S. Labarthe and Janine Bazin, later entitled *Cinéma de notre temps* [editor's note].

[7] In this area, Godard's *Histoire(s) du cinéma* (1988–1998) have wiped the slate clean: they show how cinema can think itself, and what thinking directly in words and images can mean.

[8] In an answer given in response to a questionnaire for the festival "Photo et Cinéma" (*Photogénies* 5, 1984).

Thierry Kuntzel and the Return of Writing

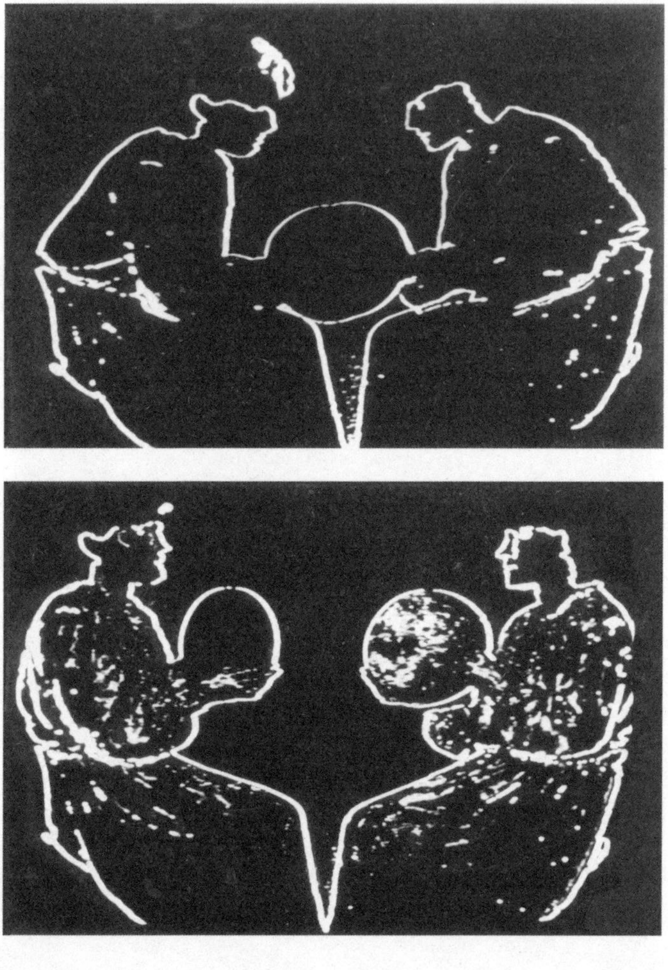

Thierry Kuntzel, *Echolalia*, 1980

It was after this that there was most of a virtue for him, most of a cultivated charm, most of a preposterous secret thrill, in the particular form of surrender to his obsession and of address to what he more and more believed to be his privilege.
—Henry James, "The Jolly Corner"

The cinema has always had trouble analyzing itself. Representing itself, on the other hand, is something it does almost incessantly, its most powerful works haunted by a kind of mirroring and *mise en abyme* which seem to be their favorite form of torment. Lang, Hitchcock. In its purest fiction, the machine even runs away with itself, carried away as if in a hall of mirrors, where in the attempt to see its own image, it no longer knew where to stop. When I say "analyzing itself," I mean pausing and stepping back in a way that displaces and redefines the way we look at a given art form: in the case of literature, for example, Mallarmé, Blanchot, Barthes.

For the cinema, which lacks neither representations nor words (as music does), nor discursive temporality (as painting does), the possibility of analyzing itself is an ever-present temptation and obsession. There are two ways it can do this: from the outside, through writing, and through work on the *défilement* which ensures the cinematic illusion. Eisenstein, Vertov. They combined the two in a way which explains their privileged position in film history and theory. But, for historical and ideological reasons, they remain too concerned with rhetorical effect and didactic purpose. In relation to the machine itself, the example of Michael Snow is altogether move striking; as was that of Mallarmé in his time, and for a long time after. Though I must perhaps step back from history in order to see its objects better. This is why I think Thierry Kuntzel's videotapes are extremely important. In referring to Mallarmé, I am not trying to confer aesthetic value or respectability, but to situate a movement, a change of direction that has taken place and, from another point of view, is being repeated. The slide from film to video may perhaps one day be compared to the move away from the alexandrine and toward free verse in poetry—out of this there emerged a reflection on the literary fate of language, and the same is happening today for the image. Exceptional in this respect is Godard's *Sauve qui peut (la vie)* (*Every Man for Himself*, 1980) and its displacement of the image inside of fiction. The cinema is indeed "truth 24 times a second," but on condition that you decompose it, make it turn back on itself and denaturalize it, so as to reinvent it—which is the work of theory, on the basis of its position outside, what the cinema is trying to do, what video is making possible. And what Thierry Kuntzel's approach illustrates with extraordinary precision.

I.

First of all, then, there is the movement from work on the film, "film-work," to the film itself, and video as a response to that.

Thierry Kuntzel's theoretical writings are unusual in that, unlike those of [Jean-Louis] Baudry and [Christian] Metz for example, they do not concern themselves with the cinema proper—a *dispositif* interposing itself between every film and the spectator—but neither are they really concerned, like so many other analyses, with the films to which they refer. It is more a case of bringing out, each time, the "other film" which the film is hiding, which can define it and which passes unnoticed. But this is not so as to reveal a structure, the exemplary logic of its functioning—even if the texts seem to follow this route, even if they mark it out, and manage to say more than so many others whose purpose this is. For what is at issue, what needs to be specified beyond but also within the object, is a subject-effect, a psychic scene.

That is clear from the outset. Kuntzel *stops* to consider the first 27 shots of Fritz Lang's *M* (1931).[2] He says: the "film-work" can be understood in relation to the "dream-work" whose operations he follows through—a question addressed by the film to cinema. A theoretical position which implies a certain knowledge. But above all a displacement: "This reading of a film's beginning is the '*film*' of a beginning of reading."[3] Between sight and insight, the pause, the slowing down, the putting into words, enable us to glimpse "another film."

The question is addressed to the *défilement*. It is followed through by reference to an animated cartoon by Peter Foldes (*Appétit d'oiseau* [1964]) which allows the problem of the still frame to be posed in different terms: going from the ideality of *signifiance* (Barthes, Sylvie Pierre) toward filmic knowledge.[4] The "other film" appears, between the film stock [*film-pellicule*] and the projected film [*film-projection*], the one you don't see and the one you see or think you see, in relation to what the stopped film, manipulated and reduced to its basic patterns, shows: the most fantasmic transformations, beginning with the bird, between the genital parts of the two sexes. This division is a cleavage which only the animator and the analyst ("the disanimator") can assess, and which the cinema maintains at the cost of an "uncanniness" [*une "inquiétante étrangeté"*]. The repression that is related to it, the guarantee of emotion (of "*l'émouvoir*," the effect linked to motion), is the object of the filmic analysis which *Appétit d'oiseau* brings out. Hence the final statement: "The *filmic*, which will be the object of the filmic analysis, therefore will be found neither on the side of motion nor on the side of stillness, but *between* them, in the generation of the projected film by the [film stock], in the negation of this [film stock] by the projected film […]"[5]

The analysis is therefore undertaken with the "other film" in view (as the "readable" in Barthes opens onto the "writable," and the "work" onto the "text"). Kuntzel analyzes, for example, *The Most Dangerous Game* (1932)[6] The other film is what classical film (especially American) hides best, the expanding secret that it guards, and what the analysis constructs, unfolds, in the concentrated space-time of the opening sequences, of the privileged moments in which everything is programmed: the mad desire of the film (its multiple fantasy to be a film and to portray scenes) and the meaning which takes hold of it, directs it, reduces it, and stretches it out to the set proportions of a drama oriented toward its conclusion.

The classical film thus becomes the "point of departure [from which] another film might be imagined: a film in which the initial figure would not find its place in the flow of a narrative, in which the configuration of events contained in the formal matrix would not form a progressive order, in which the spectator/subject would never be reassured. Lyotard's *acinema*: within the dominant system of production and consumption, this would be a film of sustained *terror*."[7]

In this way, the concept of filmic apparatus [*appareil filmique*] is created.[8] A key concept, quite different from the "basic apparatus" [*appareil de base*] or Baudry's and Metz's concepts of *dispositifs*.[9] The film itself, in-between its physical mass and the psychic density of its *défilement*, becomes the apparatus. Freud's model for the psychic apparatus, reconceived in 1925 along the lines of a writing machine ("the mystic writing-pad"), might well have found a more exact analogy in the filmic apparatus, had he known of it. For the filmic apparatus is indeed a model of the psychic apparatus. In the projection, constant inscription, deletion on the screen; in the film can, the conservation of the traces: this is the very mechanism of the system of perception-consciousness and of accumulation within the unconscious, the process (of misrecognition) whereby they are continually interdependent, as in the film stock and the projected film. "[I]f I [plug] the psychic apparatus [into] the filmic one, I obtain two [similar] mechanisms mirroring each other."[10] And the desire is reformulated, the desire for a theory which would extend toward something other than itself, for a shift from the projected film toward the film stock, beginning in the space between them defined by the analysis and, as it were, beyond the *défilement*. "In this mirroring of machines, while the perception-consciousness system is submitted to this screen-effect, could the unconscious grasp another space, another time, another logic—the film stock to which it is structurally close? [... A] virtual film, the film-beneath-the-film, *the other film*. This other film—to use another image, the strip rolled back up again on a reel, a volume, a film free from temporal constraints—where all the elements would be present at the same time, i.e., without any effect of presence—[screen-effect]—but constantly referring to each other: intersecting, overlapping, regrouping in configurations 'never' seen or heard before in the order of [the *defilement*]."[11]

Functional logic: this text was first written as an introduction to the analysis of a fragment of Chris Marker's *La Jetée*. But an analysis *like no other*: a re-editing of the shots being analyzed (with the aid of video) aiming to conjure, out of a film already struck by a conscious immobility, all the violence of the memory-pad, of the screen memories turned upside down—the unconscious layered with accumulated traces, which the displacements, the condensations, the force of repetition and secondary revision establish as biographical fiction and representability. In this work, *La Rejetée*, video is used, albeit in a fairly basic way, for its plasticity, its ability to transform. The reformulation of a wish, a pointer to future research: "Perhaps it will finally be possible to find a way of writing which is sufficiently labile to render the fluidity of film, its movement, its mixed-ness, and the specificity of its signifying project."[12]

Concurrently, two exhibitions of conceptual or environmental art.[13] There again, it is a case of modifying: space, the conditions of perception, the body that remembers. I can still see, spelled out in neon, "Memory," its illuminated letters standing out across the gallery, imposing an idea of time on the spectator, his own time. "The focus of *Trans* is the subject." "*Trans* reverses the usual relation to the object. *This* is no longer valorized. It only serves as an index; the subject is you." "*Trans* refers the subject back to nothing other than itself, the action in progress, the psychic apparatus."[14]

1978. "The other film" (second section of "A Note upon the Filmic Apparatus") comes to a halt: the interrupted text may be added to the unfinished analyses (*The Man with the Movie Camera* [1929], *King Kong* [1933], *Vampyr* [1932], *Letter from an Unknown Woman* [1948], Werner Nekes' *T-wo-men* [1972], and others in which the same desire is repeated). The other film begins: the other of the other, the real one, born of this impossible recapture.

"It wasn't deliberate, it came and came again: dilated, suspended, a-chronological, contemplative, ecstatic time. It wasn't deliberate: video imposed itself on me—in those long drawn-out images, which are barely images, or which at least are barely images of anything—after a long period of silence, terror, absence, abandonment. The tapes—all of them—bear the mark of that period—those years. The tapes—all of them—have tried to go back over that period—those years—to recount it silently, assigning to the spectator something of my position—the strange position of the watcher."[15]

Over the last two years, and within the framework of the INA (Institut National de l'Audiovisuel), Thierry Kuntzel has made eight tapes (five completed, three in the process of being edited). *Nostos I*, *Still*, *Echolalia*, *La Desserte blanche*, *Time Smoking a Picture*, *La Desserte noire, bleue, rouge*, *La Desserte multiple*, *Nostos II*.[16] To my mind, excessively perhaps, they make up a whole, an initial whole. The fact that they grew out of theory confers no privilege on them, but a clarity of their own—an intense clarity, quite different from anything else I know. They are not intended to be explanatory: theory reflected in practice. They are simply the continuation, by other means, of the same experience, which would have become unbearable to explore any further without this new medium which gives it fresh impetus, which links the subject up to itself more directly, with all the risks that that entails.

On the first of these tapes—marking the shift from the interrogation and tracking down of film to the production of video—Kuntzel wrote, "In 1925, Freud saw in the '*mystic writing pad*' [the '*Wunderblock*'] an almost exact representation of the psychic apparatus, in that it resolved a problem of writing which had hitherto been insoluble: the constant ability of the receptive surface to receive, the permanence of the traces in the wax of the writing pad. But two functions were missing: speed—simultaneous inscription and deletion—and the possibility of making the traces that had disappeared reappear. Does video not constitute the perfect model, the writing pad being no more than an approximation? The working title of *Nostos I* was for a long time *Wunderblock*."[17]

II.

To Represent?

"In *Nostos I* [1979], there is little representation: only as much as will allow one to work under the image and between the images, stopping short of analogy and going beyond it."

It is not a question of wiping out representation. That's too easy, and hardly very new ("*Trans* is not putting representation into crisis: 1926, *ceci n'est déjà plus une pipe*.").

Neither is it a question of aiming directly beyond by postulating between the medium and the psychic (perceptive, affective, neural) body a strictly energetic analogy which would allow the former to express the latter and to act as an extension of it through an interplay of forces, rhythms, intensities, and nothing else.

But rather: of only half representing, of getting past the "gangue of analogy" in order to study not so much representation as the fact that there is representation and that work is going on constantly in the psychic apparatus between perception and the inner image (from the conscious trace to the lost image, the "thing-presentation"). The eye of the spectator is given, since it is through the eye that the unconscious sees, a figuration of figuration: a continuous passage, impossible to fix between the abstract poles of primary and secondary, where the image takes shape while vanishing under the influence of desire and fear. So in these tapes there is some reality, if you like, but only on condition that it disappears.

And so an image is invented which corresponds to this double impossibility of truly representing, and at the same time not representing. It emerges out of a total concentration on light and in relation to the transformations effected by the video synthesizer. When Kuntzel says: "A kind of mad desire to make light visible," he means light as that which permits the appearance of form, itself shaped continuously by mental flux. As if there were a mental light which there, in front of our eyes, became perception,

perception being itself no more than a projection of inner light.

For example, at the beginning of *Nostos I*, on the screen which has changed imperceptibly from blue to white, a form appears, hardly visible, indistinct, and moves upward, disappearing and reappearing all the while, like the beating of a wing perceived, then lost against the sky: soon we realize that this is part of an arm, of a shoulder, taken from a body, lit in such a way that the eye follows it, and sees nothing else. When the body begins to take shape, in the joining together of still disjointed fragments, and a window-frame emerges, the beating becomes more intense, suggesting a flickering effect, but far more meaningful, since it is anchored in the body of the image: an electrical frequency, whose amplitude and speed is modulated, underpins this constant appearance-disappearance, an effect which is no more than variations of light on a body without volume whose very precariousness introduces the possibility of sight.

1

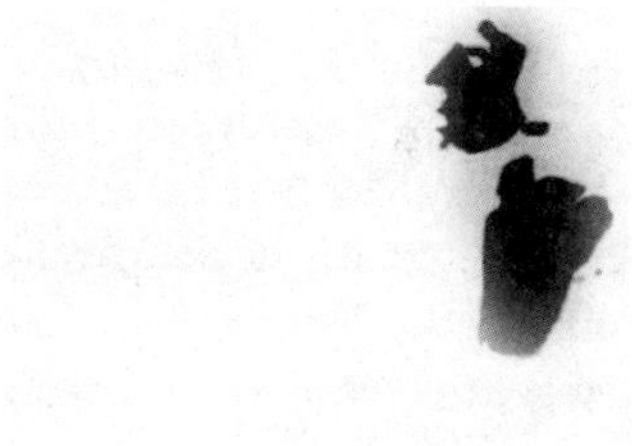

2

3

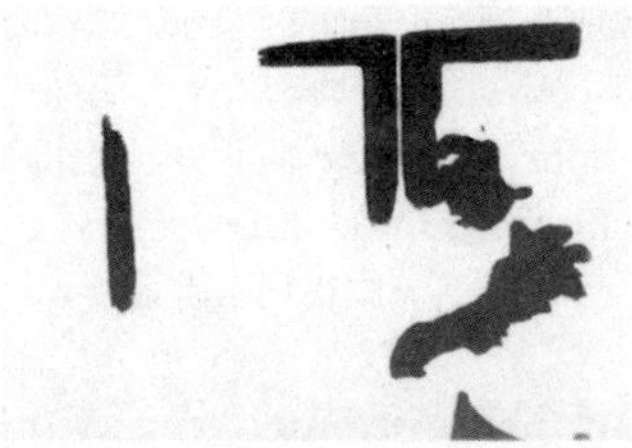

4

5

6

When, later on, a second face appears, also that of a man, the process continues, in a different way: no more wandering forms or flickering light, but modifications within the fleshy mass which is hollowed out to the point of emptiness, invading the frame with its dark surface (this time it is a follow spot, a brush of light which scans a shape, modeling the solid, evanescent form).

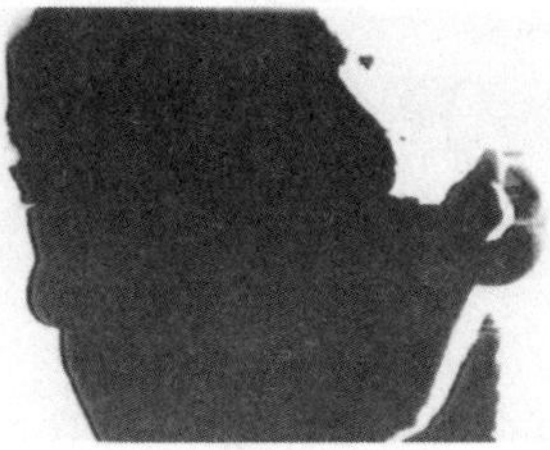

1

2

3

4

5

Later on again, one, then two characters appear, pass through, become lost in the image: no scanning, no modifications of the frequency; their erasure is produced simply by manipulating through lighting what the camera reads as graduated shades of gray (luminance) and which the video synthesizer then sorts into just two visual possibilities, in this case two colors (black and white, blue and black, blue and white)—the synthesizer thus becoming that which modulates this space, this beyond-presence-and-absence.

1

2

3

4

And when the woman on the ground stretches out, it is the combination of this treatment of decomposed values and the way the projector follows the body, which together create the body which can only just be called a body, crumbling away as it takes shape, thc intensified play of light getting caught in the folds of the dress, accelerating the fading and crystallization of the image.

1

2

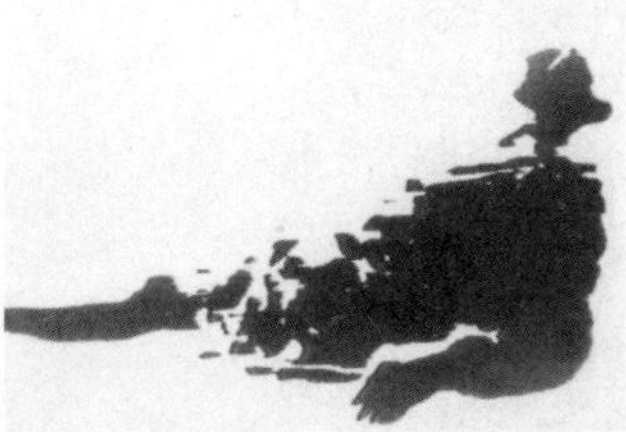

3

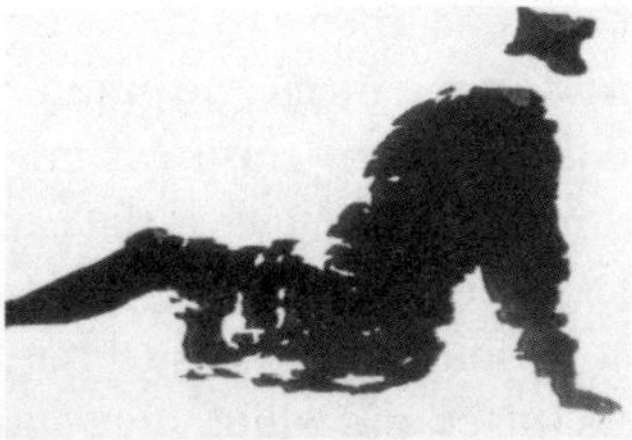

4

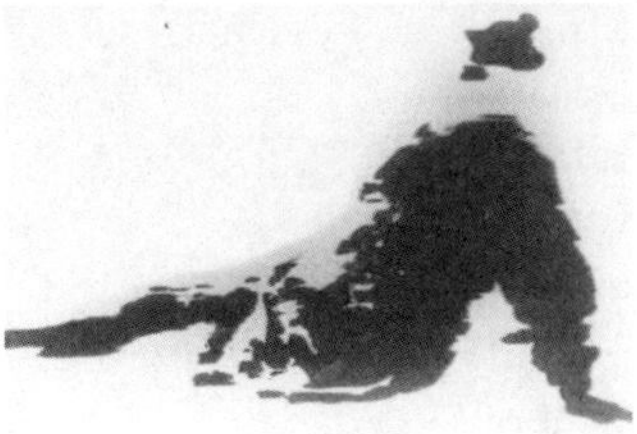

1

2

3

4

5

6

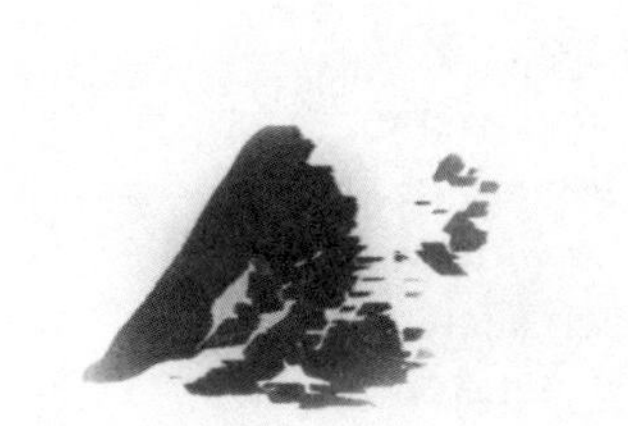

7

8

"Stopping short of analogy and going beyond it, under the image and between the images." That also means producing, in the very continuity of the *défilement*, an ideal equivalent of the singular moment in the analysis when the projected film is converted into the film stock via the study of single images and images in slow motion. Representation stripped of its support opens up a mental space where the image, in trying to be less, aims at more: the fiction of its transformation. This converts its passage into memory: forgetting, coming back again, interminably, the pulse of a thought, its shape, its history.

Fiction(s)

For we are, of course, in fiction. In *Nostos I*, the characters, the man, the second man, and the woman, are involved in some kind of drama, evident in the way the forms are interwoven. For example, the "hero" sitting by the window alternates, as if in a narrative sequence, with the face of the second man, and these two series alternate in their turn with the "hero" walking and the woman moving forward. First of all the hero and the woman appear alone, and then their paths cross as the result of an action which brings them together—but this is not the way to describe surface effects where shapes come together. Their paths do not really cross, or at least, not only.

1

2

They slide into each other, as in a dream image. And so there is fiction, fiction linked to fantasy, if you like, in the sense that a dream is always telling a story about something. But this something has more to do with the form in which it appears than with a stated meaning, or in particular a latent meaning to be formulated: no image ever becomes metaphorical or symbolic, and no interpretation is required. The film—the tape—never aims to be simply a dream, is never simply the wish to be a dream (unlike Maya Deren's *Meshes of the Afternoon* [1943], which does this so well); it tells us something else and more about the dream, the way in which the dream is inscribed in time, is remembered and relived. The banality and elementary character of the gestures are essential to this—"a few minimal actions: turning the pages of a book, sitting or lying down, crossing a space, lighting a cigarette, looking around, opening one's mouth, looking." The fiction relates to a mode of operation, it skirts around, "avoids narrative," becomes fiction about fiction as Mallarmé says in the Preface to his poem "Un coup de dés" ["A Throw of the Dice," 1897]. The initial motif of *Nostos I* embodies a kind of mental destiny: the flickering of the image which pins the hero against the intermittent frame of a double window (it could be a train) presents in the most rigorous way the subject of the *défilement*, of the filmic apparatus as the double of the psychic apparatus, materialized (or immaterialized, it makes no difference) through the video *dispositif.*

Still is this *dispositif.* Still: 1. calm, quiet, silent, immobile; 2. (etc.); 3. static photograph, esp. still frame. "Just imagine: the story comes to a halt, movement ceases, the soundtrack falls silent. You ask yourself: 'What's going on?' For 25 minutes, this: light, color, the slow, irregular building up of a representation—a door opens, on a secret perhaps. Yes, a secret: what the screen could never reveal without modifying the way the monitor usually works: the vibration of light, the pulsation of color, a proliferation of music that has never been heard (before), of words that have fallen silent, of stories that have not (yet) taken place."[18]

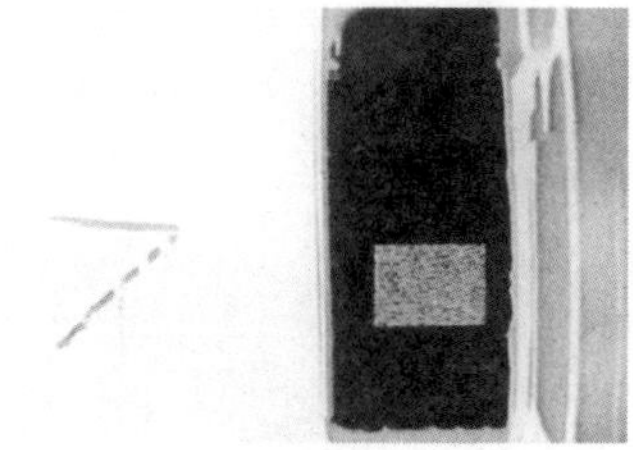

1

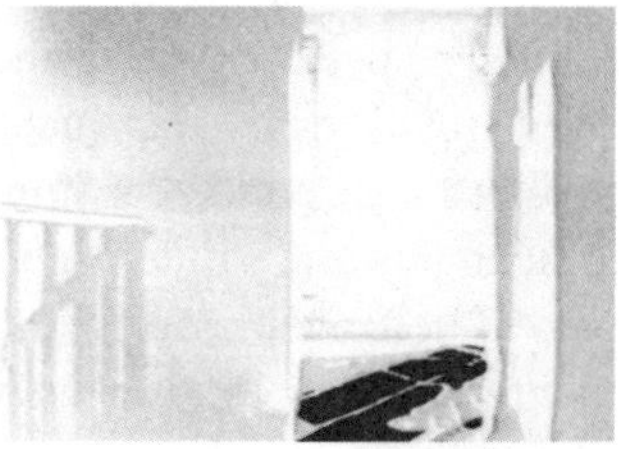

2

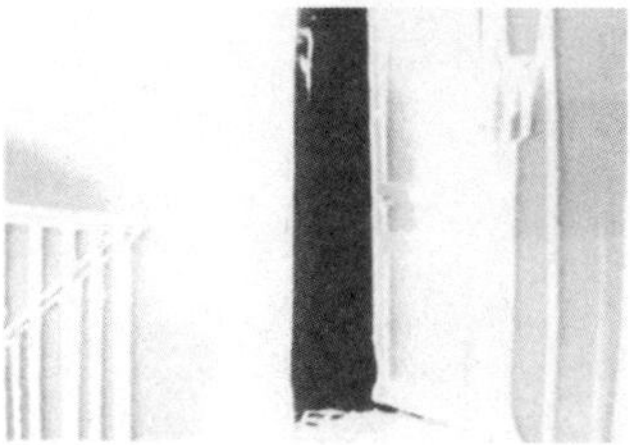

3

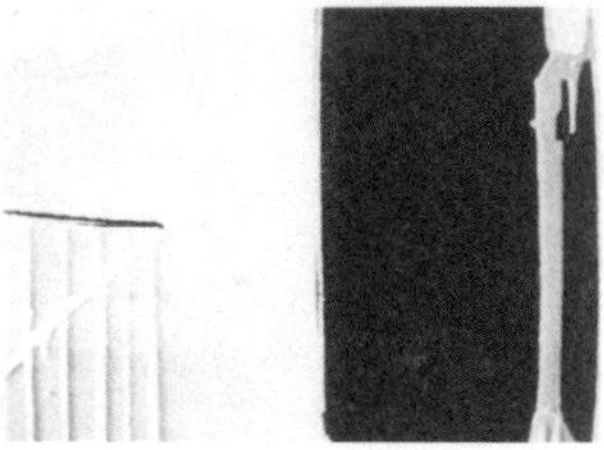

4

Everything is acted out between: first, the image of the doorway, the landing at the top of the stairs which is created and destroyed as it is transformed; second, the keying effect, since the "snow" which vibrates in the small frame to the point of invading the image is the foundation, the organic base, the grain of video (something like the alphabet suddenly appearing as such in a written text); and third, the fiction which is built by these transformations. Take a close look at the second "still frame": the door is closed, but the black trace on the floor (black on white or blue in the tape) suggests an open door. A door can be open *and* closed. Or, or course, half-open. But in the fourth frame there is no longer a door, only a black hole—the fiction is potential for the spectator who, like the hero of "The Jolly Corner," "projected himself all day, in thought […] into the other, the real, the waiting life"[19] until, lingering in the house where he spent his childhood, he is seized by the "intimate conviction" that the door "would have admitted him to the last room of the four, the room without other approach or egress, had it not […] been closed *since* his former visitation, the matter probably of a quarter of an hour before."[20] For the Kuntzel spectator as for the James hero reduced to his essence—in both cases before any elaborations of fantasy—it is a question of "'[cultivating]' his whole perception […] which indeed was but another name for his manner of spending his time."[21] Kuntzel speaks of "the time that time takes to pass."

Time as fiction: that is indeed the subject of these tapes, which are at once so perfectly static and so mobile. *Time Smoking a Picture* (1980): time constructs the image by devouring it, in the way a cigarette is consumed, the one the hero smokes while sitting on the window ledge after crossing the field of the image. There again you have a static frame (made to vibrate merely through an inverted sweep), and

1

2

3

cut into it, another one, distinguishable as a variation of light and color, the color often shifting imperceptibly, but continuously, according to the light, from purple to dark brown, yellow, ochre, white, violet, combining the artifice of the camerawork—the stopping up and down of the lens—with the projection of natural light which, at the end of the tape, in real time, follows the downward curve of a sunset.

The relation between these two frames thus comes as close as possible to representing the unrepresentable: the spatial or temporal in-between created by the disjunction/conjunction between mental representation and perception, surface and depth, back and front, past and present, conscious and unconscious. As the hero—the author and original spectator—establishes his presence, crossing the room in both frames at once, the *dispositif* takes in what representation holds out to fiction: the hero's gaze into the window, where he can see his life slipping past, inside and outside. This recalls the last lines of Roussel's poem, *La vue*, which are quoted at the end of the tape:

> *Mes yeux plongent dans un coin d'azur ; ma pensée*
> *Rêve, absente, perdue, indécise et forcée*
> *D'aller vers le passé ; car c'est l'exhalaison*
> *Des sentiments vécus de toute une saison*
> *Qui pour moi sort avec puissance de la vue,*
> *Grâce à l'intensité subitement accrue*
> *Du souvenir vivace et latent d'un été*
> *Déjà mort, déjà loin de moi, vite emporté.*[22]

Time is in this respect the matte flip side of *Nostos I*: in the broken continuity of space-time, it determines the serialization and eventual return of elements which make "images piled one on top of the other" into a "memory volume."

The Writing Pad, the Book

And so the film, by various means, forms a single unit; is the perpetual unfolding of a condensation that is continually re-forming. The book is the image of this: caught in the fiction because it is at the origin of fiction. First of all on its own in *Nostos I*, then held by the woman; its pages turned faster and faster (like calendars shedding their leaves in films of the 1930s to suggest the passing of time).

Inside the book, images half-glimpsed, which appear and disappear like the human figures. The action of leafing through the book repeats the work of the film, depositing the images one on top of the other, as in memory, in a volume, piling them up, forgetting about them, returning to them.

1

2

3

On the one hand Mallarmé revisited, on the other Freud. The first because the affirmation of the Book, as an absolute of language, aims at the production of a psychic effect in which the writing, the writing on the page, is conceived of as a *mise en scène* ("rather, of prismatic subdivisions of the Idea the instant it appears and while their concurrence lasts, in some exact spiritual '*mise en scène*.'"[23]) Mallarmé can, with the power of ambiguity peculiar to him, refer this effect that "should take place in the reader's mind" to the "cinematograph, whose workings will replace many a volume, to great advantage."[24] The book, thus abstracted, sent back in the tape to its functioning, is a theorized cultural referent: a testing ground of the avant-garde ever since Mallarmé drew out its radical implications, ever since his utopian dream was first revised in the light of historical and technological developments.

And Freud, obviously, who from "A Project for a Scientific Psychology" (1895: two years before "Un Coup de dés," Freud and Mallarmé searching in the same direction in different languages) to "A Note upon the 'Mystic Writing Pad'" (1925) moves from the utopia of science to the reality of the theory he has constructed in his search for a metaphor capable of representing the functioning of the psychic apparatus, somewhere between the optical machine and the writing machine. Freud in Mallarmé, Freud and Mallarmé, fused in the electronic image. The book is not really an image to be interpreted: it is the image of the image at work, the multilayered psychic image of our Western infancy. A book of images, or a picture book, because it has been just that, it facilitates the workings of memory, it is an idealized memory object.

Nostos II comes back to this, but its starting point is a completely different inscription of the trace, of the memory-effect. The tape was shot with a deliberately misadjusted *paluche*, which leaves an afterimage, a luminous trail of forms; this "trailing," brought about by the stopping up and down of the lens, creates a milky substance from which representation seems to emerge, from which it seems to take its energy. Because of this process, the constant camera movement replaces the effects created in *Nostos I* by frequency modulation and the follow spot. The "delayed-action *paluche*" becomes the brush of light which composes an unseen image: in the black and white rushes (which remain black and white in parts) the black and the white, already strongly contrasted thanks to the special qualities of the *paluche*, acquire their separate identities only to merge into each other, in what amounts to a flowing away of representation. At one point, the action of leafing through a book is exposed to this effect and becomes amplified as a result. And later on there are images: photographs thrown down, piled up by the hand of the woman who shows them to the spectator, making a kind of second book or loose-leaf pad. They are clearly taken from a family album (there is nothing to stop us from thinking that they are being dreamed about by the hero whom we have seen with his eyes shut).

1

2

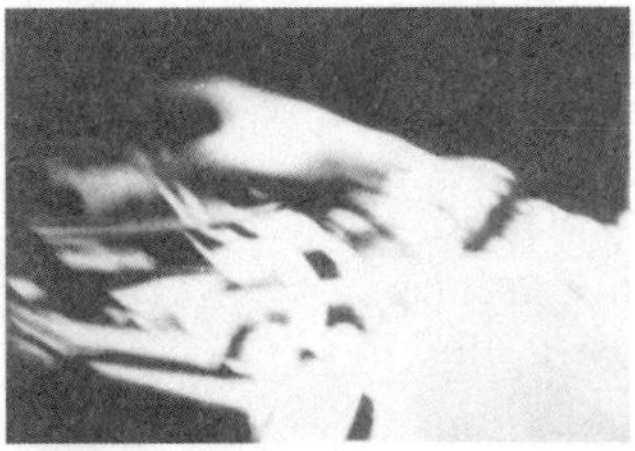
3

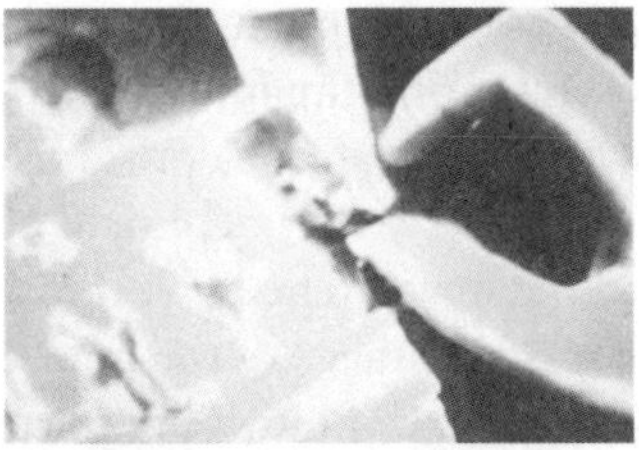
4

5

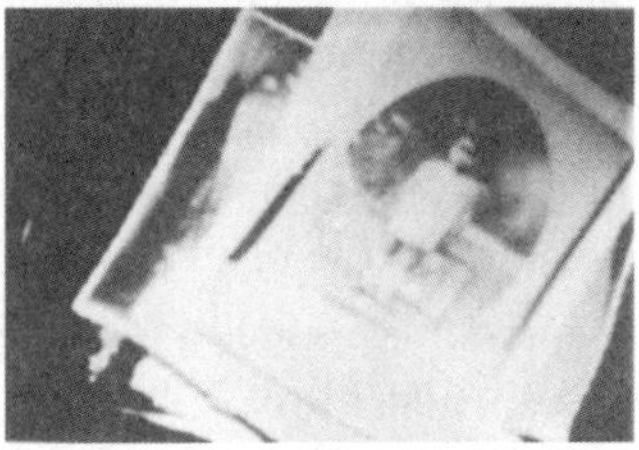
6

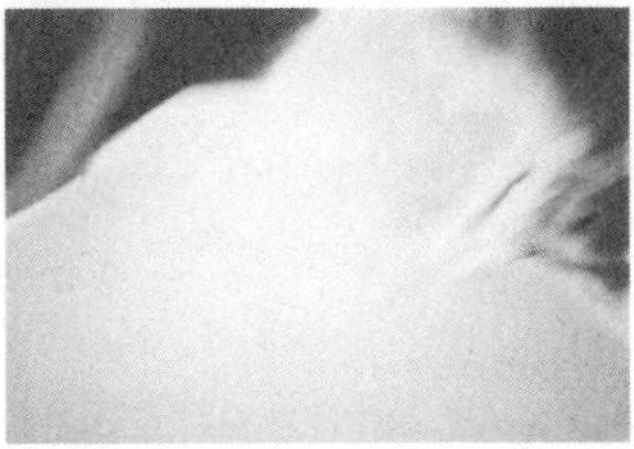
7

But the peculiar strength of this sketch of a family history is that it cannot be pinned down. All it tells us is that this has to do with *a* family history, whose traces form an accumulation of screen memories. The figures you see are linked to the processes of remembering and forgetting that they undergo. You might even go so far as to think that they are at the origin of these processes, that they are subject to the pressure of the image because they are and have been producers of images and that they are still the place where these processes occur and their reference point in time. Yes, you could very well think this, as you look at these photographs that pile up and disappear from view into the white from which they emerge. But this ensnarement via the scenario (the psychoanalytic fiction, its future development, its avatars) has no referent other than the neutral flatness of the appearances and disappearances that mark it; it only exists—when it does—in you, in your response to this structural play. Identification does not go beyond the little that can be identified. The rest is potential; an appeal to the reader-spectator, each according to his own history, to participate in this play on time through "free and individual modulation."[25]

Video-Body

Reverse and complement of this process of abstraction: the body of the image, the corporal effect that makes it so striking. Identification, having eluded us, hits us in another way. In *Nostos I*, the modification of the frequency which composes the hero's movements creates an extremely violent, gasping rhythm: the discontinuity of the trace and its conversion into memory produce a physical pulsation, a breathing in and out which borders on suffocation. The video image reflected in this way introduces something new, already touched upon by the experimental film, but in a manner that is less clear and less immediate.

Take *Echolalia* (1980). A form in which more than one element is brought together, the double body of a woman, in white and black (the outline will change constantly, from white to blue, from blue to white) appears, disappears, against a background which has no depth. Then the two figures face to face. Then the form comes together again to open out in stages. Then it closes in again, to open out this time in one continuous movement, each body being attached to the other by what eventually becomes the same double object (a circle, a mirror) in which various reflections appear.

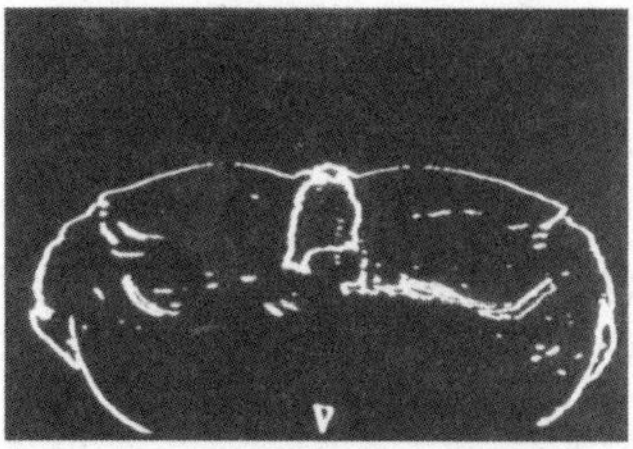

1

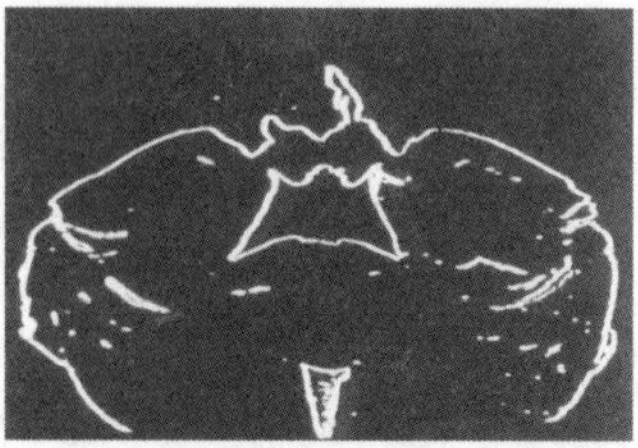

2

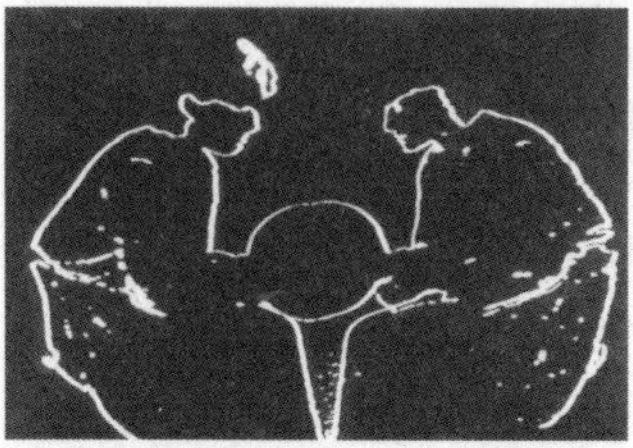

3

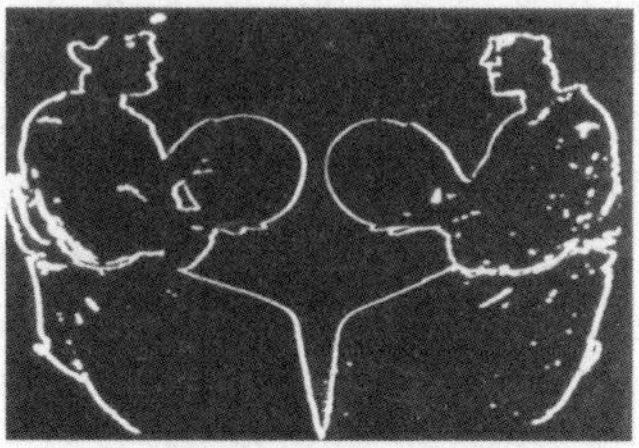

4

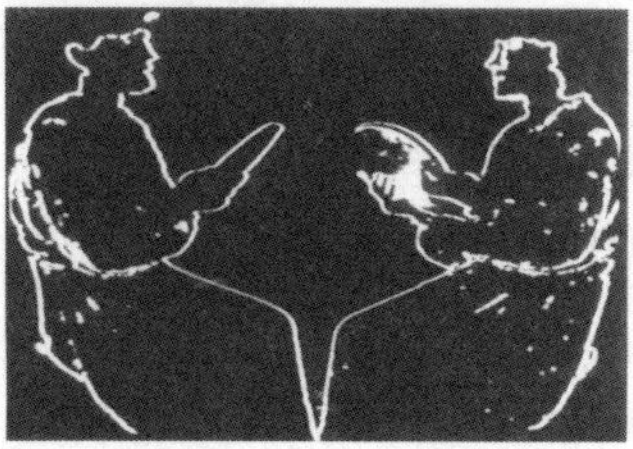

5

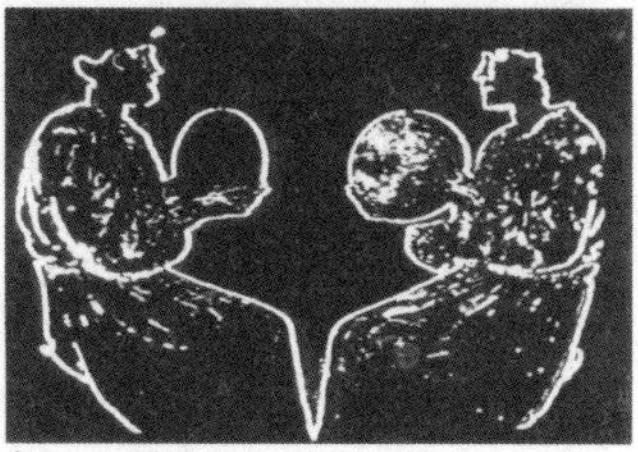

6

Then once more you have the division into two, the two figures face to face, the disappearance of one and then the other, their fusion; bodies which sometimes consist of no more than a single line, which sometimes sparkle like coats of mail or strange, ornate dresses, changing color at the same time. Then once again the original white mass returns, the bodies move upward, separate, lean forward, interpenetrate as if through a kiss, split into two again, holding this weird object which turns in their hands, a double object, one and the same; and finally, after a last, sudden movement, they plunge downward again to become a motionless mass.

Let us say, in terms of a metapsychology of the cinema, that what *Echolalia* does first of all is to articulate the two levels of identification with the figure and the camera (secondary / primary) through which Metz situated the imaginary posture of the cinema-subject, basing his analysis on Lacan's mirror.[26] The symmetry / dissymmetry between the two figures (the same / the other) and the mirror-circle that is created as they unfold leave the spectator free to assume whatever posture he likes. The body-mirror emerges in the images in which the spectator sees his reflection forever deluded, forever divided. Narcissus and Echo coming together, perhaps for the first time. But the work of the image also presents that "more archaic mode of identification," determined by the confusion of hallucination and perception, in which Jean-Louis Baudry, stopping this side of Lacan's mirror, sees the power of the cinema-effect, referring it in Freudian terms to the primordial experience of oral satisfaction.[27] Kristeva speaks of "what remains beyond identification," thereby defining, in the context of other psychoanalytic references closer to the Kleinian theater of terror and aggression, the level of somatic *frayage* (facilitation) of the "unsymbolized drive" which she calls the "semiotic."[28] The fundamental nature of the body, which can scarcely be described in words, and which the cinema brings into view in/under its fascination with the specular, always assuming that not too much of its excess is restored to the symbolic order. She speaks about the "anti-film" in the same way that Lyotard refers to the "acinema," defining as the ideal of the avant-garde this resistance to the symbolic, and this force that brings the invisible into view. "F. is a year old and speaks in nothing but echolalia: rhythm, intonation, variable intensities […]"[29] A first body, made of language before language, a language-body.

That is indeed what Kuntzel's (wordless) tapes show. What the "story" of *Echolalia* is about: the adventure of the body/light traversed by rhythms and intensities, caught in the images of its destiny. What is captured visually and reflected upon re-emerges as physical knowledge and emotion. Never before have I seen a body being created and recreated as in this tape. To the point where it can be seen as a representation of birth itself, of the possibility of birth, linked to its material violence as well as to its imaginary condition. Birth in the image, birth of the image.

To Write Painting

This image is also about painting—painting as its particular temptation, its unfulfilled wish. Of course, video still has a long way to go. It is still feeling its way along. What it has to offer is extremely unrefined and cannot be compared to all the possibilities of the painter's palette. And yet. Today there are usually only seven levels of gray, which the video synthesizer sorts out according to a given color; but Bill Etra is working on a machine that should be able to differentiate 64.[30] The electronic image has immense possibilities not unlike those which painting has always had at its disposal.

In his tapes, Kuntzel is working in this direction, aware of the limits that the medium imposes if it is used seriously, in a way that resists its basic ease of operation (which makes it so like photography). Rather than thinking that his tapes can *already* be identified with painting, or that they go beyond painting through the mechanical use of chains of effects and programmed contrasts that can be obtained by the synthesizer, Kuntzel is trying to go *toward* painting, in a delicate move that involves relations of color, form, and time. In this way it could be said that he does indeed reach beyond painting: in a movement which leads us, through video, to revise our understanding of painting, to reflect on what it is, what it has done, and how it has developed historically.

Consider the three *Dessertes*: *blanche*; *noire, bleue, rouge*; and *multiple*. Matisse's *La Desserte* (1908) serves as an emblem here, as does the thinking of a painter who saw his art as a "kind of perpetual cinema."[31] The earlier effects of remembering and forgetting, appearing and disappearing, perception and hallucination, mental *dispositif* and the influence of the body, all reappear in these three tapes. But the *Dessertes* are addressed more directly to painting, and they lead us to reconsider the biases of the other tapes, to refer them also to painting (the flat forms in *Nostos I*, the drips in *Still* (1980), the sparkling, ever-changing outline in *Echolalia*, the mobile fluidity of *Nostos II* (1984), and in all the tapes, the constant color shifts which culminate in *Time* ...).

First of all there is the fact that these three tapes are elaborated on the basis of a single interior, recalling the way in which, in painting, a motif will often be reworked, or many versions of the same painting created. Monet's *Cathedrals* (1892-1894), for example ("I had nightmares all night long: the cathedral was falling down on top of me; it looked blue or pink or yellow."[32]). Like the *Cathedrals*, the *Dessertes* ought ideally to be seen together, by the same eye—although in different rooms, lit differently to suit the tonalities.

La Desserte blanche. Gestures reduced to their essence—in a black and white stratified by a mixture of positive and negative sensitive to tiny variations of lighting—between a movement and its ending, the shadowy moment when it begins again. The woman who appears in the doorway has thus never really walked through the door, except in our memory of the space, of movements to and fro, of positions imprinted. As time stretches out indefinitely, the gesture in time solidifies through the mental and visual accumulation of instants, producing the overall effect of a moving picture, somewhere between bas-relief and photograph.

1

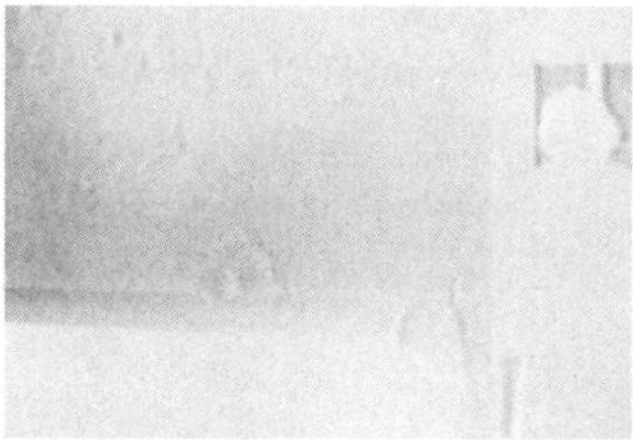
2

3

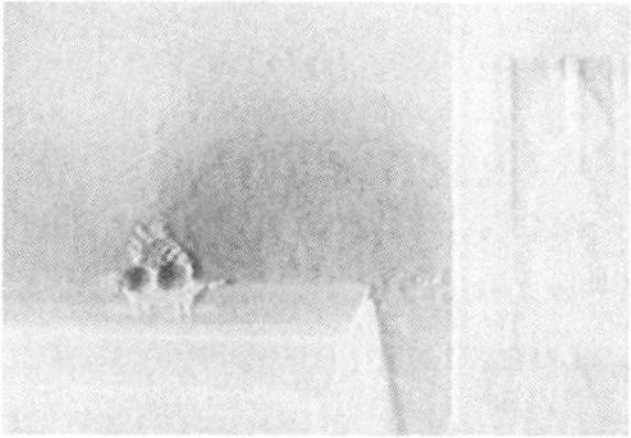
4

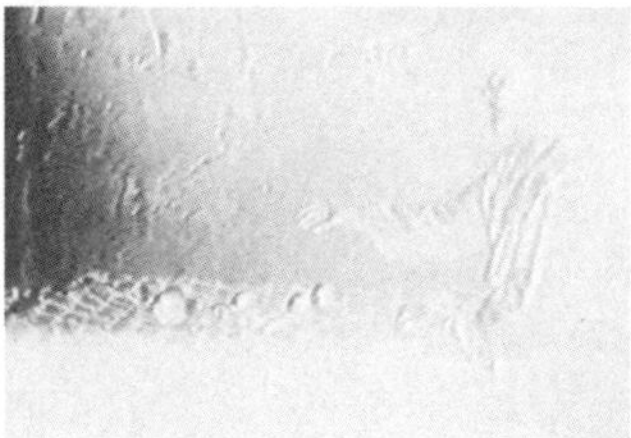
5

6

When suddenly at the end a reddish pink invades the frame from the left, half penetrates the woman's body, melts into the background and begins to spread, the color is an event in its pure state: the coming into being of painting.

 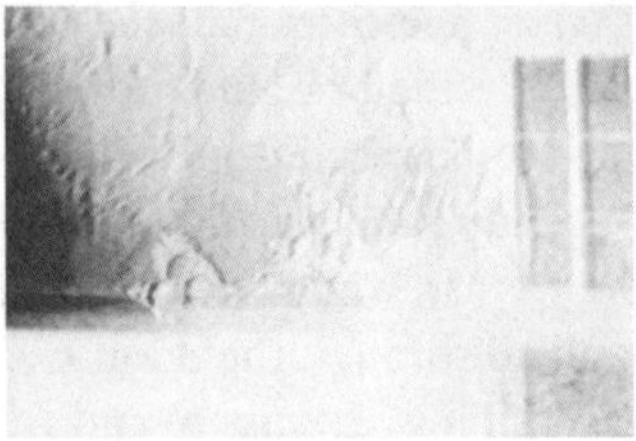

La Desserte noire, bleue, rouge: in different color blocks.

Black: the same image is reshaped by black, and is held apart in shifting forms, mingling with shades of blue, pink, and white under the influence of a very fine "snow" which creates what can surely be called a pointillism of the trace.

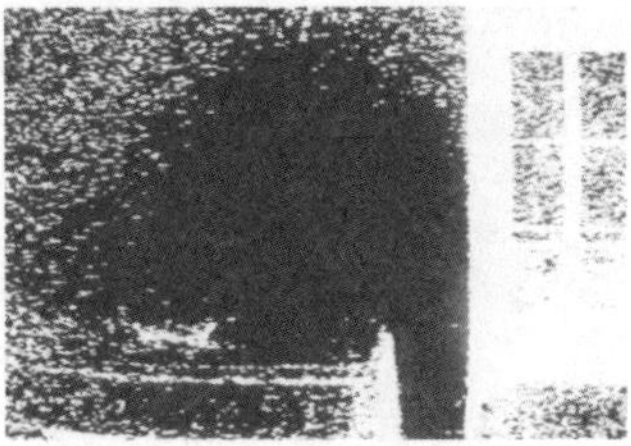 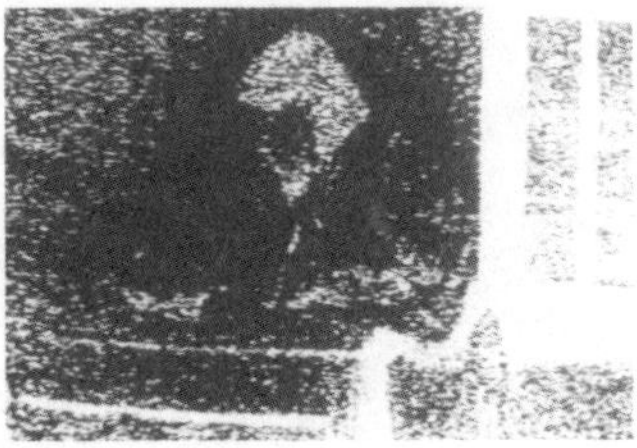

Blue: two *trames* of snow that merge into each other (one very fine, the other more flaky) now cause the substance, which has become heavier and more opaque, to vibrate, effacing and reestablishing the contours of these ghostly postures according to a quite different tempo.

Red: the keying effect allows a form to be isolated (the upper body, the face, the hand moving forward, the bowl of fruit), emphasizing contrasts which have become quite violent (a bright blue medallion against a red/orange/purple background), varied, combined, attenuated by the interplay of the *trames* of "snow" again, and by their transformation, to the point where the medallion is effaced.

1

2

3

4

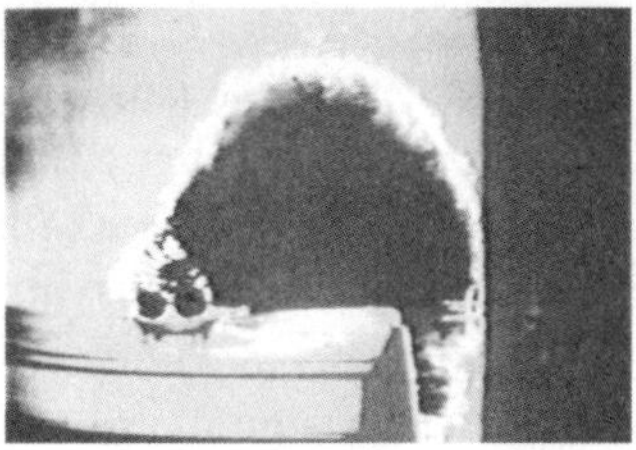
5

La Desserte multiple. In this still unfinished tape, the analysis of light is carried much further, within the same framework, through the variation of color values, and of these gestures recaptured somewhere between the painter and his model. But I was struck especially, in the rushes, by the work done on an isolated motif: the fruit that appears, first one piece, then two, then three, against the initially bare background of the table [*la desserte*], then against a number of decorated backgrounds. Against the first background, they appear to be animated by an inner movement, the result of three cameras placed very close together around the table and changing speed gradually as they turn around it. The variations in lighting are produced by these mini-displacements of the camera (which are linked together by dissolves) and create, in the areas of overlap and through the use of a colorizer, new color possibilities. This process is continued, against decorated backgrounds, by changing the angle of the light.

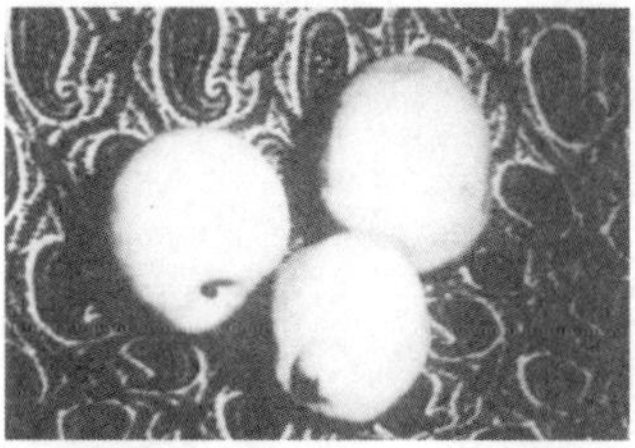

1

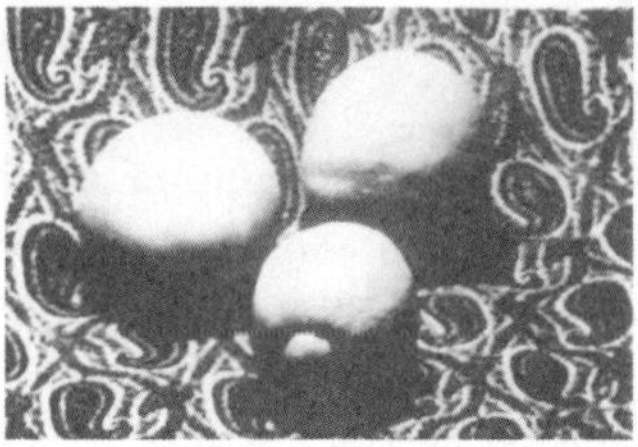

2

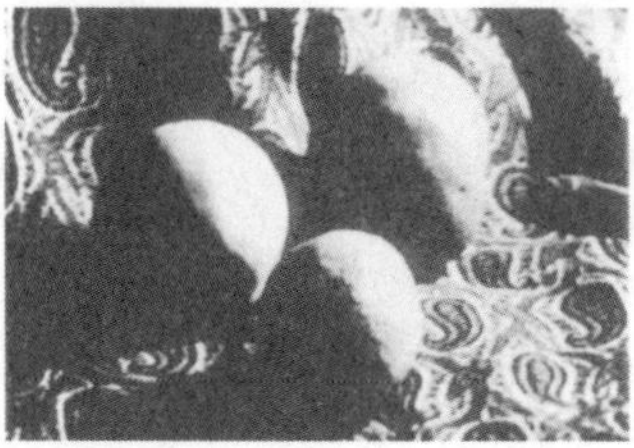

3

Color linked to movement, to its spatio-temporal decomposition, these processes which focus on the still life, the three apples, the "snow" with its *trames* of traces and dots, what more visible way could there be of saying that video, as it meets up with the problems of painting, from Impressionism to Cubism, is leading us on to the *terra incognita* of a new determinism of the visual (to mention only the image), between cinema and painting, toward another body-memory.

To question painting, to reply to cinema. Through the very technology that amplifies it, to work on that evolution of the image which takes shape in the 19th century in the conjunction of techniques for reproducing reality and the new status accorded to subjectivity, whose effects are prescribed and multiplied by psychology (hypnosis, psychoanalysis) in terms of an inner image. Video can of course be thought of in specific terms: the electronic image has a very definite specificity. But it remains to be understood above all in relation to the gestures it permits.

Thierry Kuntzel's gesture is twofold: one of picking up and of displacement. It picks up and displaces through video the more radical experiments of the already long tradition of the experimental cinema: Snow, Frampton, Nekes (whom Kuntzel has followed so closely). But it also picks up what has been learned both theoretically and culturally from an analysis of the cinema. A comparable, although very different, displacement comes to mind: Jean-André Fieschi in his *Nouveaux mystères de New York* (1976). Because the "leap into cinema" at the age of eight was a "search for earlier images,"[33] his attempt at a filmed autobiography goes back over the new images which have subsequently captured his attention, to the point where they become not only the referents but the formal exponents of the images of childhood: the famous matching up of looks in *Nosferatu* (1922) which he is able to reconstruct, thanks to the *paluche*, as Fargier emphasizes, through "unusually varied editing in the shot,"[34] the lost, elusive look in *Vampyr*, and so many other cinematic moments which recur and give body to his fiction because he has also lived through them, handled them, theorized them. In the same way, Kuntzel's tapes, when considered purely in terms of their psychic effect, remind me here and there of the ever-receding scene of the look in *The Most Dangerous Game*, the illusory *défilement* of the fairground train in *Letter from an Unknown Woman*, the camera effects in *The Man with the Movie Camera*, the frozen images in *La Jetée*, the doors and windows in films by Lang and so many others, and this same space, always just beyond, of *Vampyr*, as if saturated with psychic energy. The one closer to Proust, the other to Mallarmé, they find in video the (intellectual, material) force which makes it possible to displace cinema in relation to itself, to give it that supplement that it still lacks and that would ultimately bring it close to writing. Writing not as a privileged endeavor, but rather to allow us to escape its spell by taking away some of its power. Writing as expression, quite simply, freely orchestrated from the essay to the poem, from auto-biography to thought. "An eye at the tips of one's fingers," said Fieschi about the *paluche*.[35] "The eye, a hand," said Manet.[36] To paint and at the same time to link visions (and words) in time is to write, to film. Video, although it is still tentative, too costly, and unrefined, is part of a movement which is gaining ground and making itself felt in a number of ways, giving a new lease on life to an ideal which has accompanied the cinema from the outset. The ideal of "*une écriture inouïe*," of writing never before seen or heard. Go back to the texts assembled in *L'Art du cinéma*:[37] listen to André Beucler, [Antonin] Artaud, [Jean] Epstein, Elie Faure, [Jean] Cocteau, [Alexandre] Astruc. No doubt Astruc was thinking of something else when he spoke about the "*caméra-stylo*" (as his films and references show). And yet: "This is the point we have reached […] a camera in the right-hand pocket of your trousers, the recording on a sound and image tape of the meanderings, of the slow or frenetic unfolding of our imaginary universe, cinema-confession, essay, revelation, message, psychoanalysis, obsession, the machine that will read the words and images of our personal landscape … "

"A language so rigorous that it will enable our thoughts to be transcribed directly onto the film."[38]

It seems to me that given their particular level of abstraction, there is nothing that fulfills this expectation better than the videotapes of Thierry Kuntzel.

1981. Originally translated in 1983 by Annwyl Williams.

[1] *The Complete Tales of Henry James* vol. 12, ed. Leon Edel (London: Rupert Hart-Davis, 1964) 207.
[2] Thierry Kuntzel, "Le travail du film," *Communications* 19 (Paris: Seuil, 1972) ["The Film-Work," trans. Larry Crawford, Kimball Lockhart, and Claudia Tysdal, *enclitic* 2.1 (Spring 1978)].
[3] "Le travail du film" 25 ["The Film-Work" 39].
[4] Kuntzel, "Le Défilement," *Cinéma. Théorie, Lectures*, ed. Dominique Noguez (Paris: Klincksieck, 1973) ["Le Défilement: A View in Close-up," trans. Bertrand Augst, *Apparatus*, ed. Theresa Hak Kyung Cha (New York: Tanam Press, 1980)].
[5] "Le Défilement" 110 ["Le Défilement: A View in Close-up" 241].
[6] Kuntzel, "Le travail du film, 2," *Communications* 23 (Paris: Seuil, 1975) ["The Film-Work, 2," trans. Nancy Huston, *Camera Obscura*, no. 5 (Spring 1980)]. See also "Savoir, Pouvoir, Voir," *Ça Cinéma*, no. 7–8 (May 1975) ["Sight, Insight, and Power: Allegory of a Cave," trans. Nancy Huston, *Camera Obscura*, no. 6 (Fall 1980)].
[7] "Le travail du film, 2" 152 ["The Film-Work, 2" 24–25].
[8] Kuntzel, "A Note Upon the Filmic Apparatus," *Quarterly Review of Film Studies* 1.3 (August 1976) 266–271 (unpublished in French).
[9] Often translated in English as simply "apparatus" [editor's note].
[10] "A Note Upon the Filmic Apparatus" 270.
[11] "A Note Upon the Filmic Apparatus" 271.
[12] "Le travail du film, 2" 183 ["The Film-Work, 2" 56].
[13] In 1976 and 1977, signed "Trans" with Tania Mouraud, and then with Tania Mouraud and Jon Gibson.
[14] "Trans," *tracts* 1 (November 16, 1976) and 2 (January 8, 1977).
[15] *Video About Video, Four French Artists* (bilingual catalogue produced by the Ministère des Affaires Etrangères-Vidéoglyphes, October 1980). [All catalogue translations mine—A.W.]
[16] Since then, *Nostos II* has become an installation. *La Desserte blanche* is also an installation for one monitor, in a white space saturated by the light from neon tubes (it was shown in this environment several times, particularly in *Les Immatériaux*, Centre Georges Pompidou, 1984). *La Desserte noire, bleue, rouge*, and *La Desserte multiple* remain unfinished—see my collection *L'entre-images 2* (Paris: P.O.L., 1999).
[17] *Vidéo: la région centrale, 9 travaux vidéographiques* (catalogue produced by the Ministère des Affaires Etrangères-Vidéoglyphes, July 1980). Citations from Kuntzel without other references come from these two catalogues.
[18] *French Video Art–Art Vidéo Français* (bilingual catalogue produced by the American Center in Paris, 1980).
[19] James 208.
[20] James 216.
[21] James 212.
[22] Raymond Roussel, *La vue* (Paris: Pauvert, 1963) 73. (Literally: My eyes dive into a small patch of blue; my thoughts, absent, lost, indecisive and constrained, dream of going toward the past for it is the exhalation of the feelings and experience of a whole season which for me is coming out with power of sight, thanks to the suddenly increased intensity of the undying and latent memory of a summer already dead, already far from me, quickly borne away [translator's note]).
[23] Stéphane Mallarmé, "Un coup de dés," *Œuvres complètes*, ed. Henri Mondor and G. Jean-Aubry (Paris: Gallimard/Pléiade, 1945) 455 [trans. Daisy Aldan, *Folder* 4 (New York: Tiber Press, 1956)].
[24] Mallarmé, "Enquête sur le livre illustré," *Œuvres complètes* 878. Quoted by Kuntzel among other fragments of texts which were part of the research for *Nostos I*, and which have "trickled into the image" (*Vidéoglyphes* 2 [1979]).
[25] Mallarmé, "Crise de vers," *Œuvres complètes* 363 ["Crisis in Poetry," *Mallarmé. Selected Prose Poems, Essays and Letters*, trans. Bradford Cook (Baltimore: The Johns Hopkins Press, 1956) 38].
[26] Christian Metz, *Le Signifiant imaginaire: psychanalyse et cinéma* (Paris: U.G.E., 10/18, 1977) [*The Imaginary Signifier: Psychoanalysis and Cinema*, trans. Celia Britton and Annwyl Williams (London: Macmillan, 1982)].
[27] Jean-Louis Baudry, "Le dispositif: approches métapsychologiques de l'impression de réalité," *Communications* 23: 67 ["The Apparatus," trans. Jean Andrews and Bertrand Augst, *Apparatus* 54].
[28] Julia Kristeva, "Ellipse sur la frayeur et la séduction spéculaire," *Communications* 23: 73–74 ["Ellipsis on Dread and the Specular Seduction," trans. Dolores Burdick, *Narrative, Apparatus, Ideology: A Film Theory Reader*, ed. Philip Rosen (New York: Columbia University Press, 1986) 236–243].
[29] Kristeva 75 [239].
[30] Cited in Dominique Belloir, *Vidéo, Art, Explorations* (special issue of *Cahiers du Cinéma*, Paris: Editions de l'Etoile, 1981).
[31] Henri Matisse, *Ecrits et propos sur l'art* (Paris: Hermann, 1972) 152.
[32] *Hommage à Claude Monet* (catalogue produced by the Editions des Musées nationaux, 1981) 291.
[33] Jean Paul Fargier, "Le grand écart, rencontre avec un Corse des Carpathes," *Cahiers du Cinéma* 310 (April 1980) 32.
[34] Fargier 28.
[35] Jean-André Fieschi, "Point de vue sur un troisième œil," *Le Monde* (Paris).
[36] Cited by Mallarmé in "Edouard Manet," *Œuvres complètes* 532.
[37] *L'art du cinéma*, ed. Pierre Lherminier (Paris: Seghers, 1960).
[38] *L'art du cinéma* 597, 589.

Thierry Kuntzel, *Nostos I*, 1980

Thierry Kuntzel, *Nostos I*, 1980

Video Utopia

Nam June Paik, *TV Buddha*, 1975

"The power and influence of the press are at their dawn," said Finot. "Journalism is in its infancy, it will grow and grow. Ten years hence everything will be subjected to publicity. Thought will enlighten everything, it –"

–"Will blight everything," interposed Blondet […] "If the press did not exist, we could get along without it; but it's here, so we live on it."

–"You will die of it," said the diplomat.

—Honoré de Balzac[1]

"The electronic image is a marvelous tool for dreaming. I thought I was opening up a path that all of television could take, and I am the lone hero of a lost battle."

—Jean-Christophe Averty[2]

It has been said repeatedly that video art is inextricably intertwined with television, that it in fact derives from television. We know very well that video returns constantly to TV, that it is against, right up against TV, and that this relationship—insufficient on its own as a definition—nonetheless haunts video art to the point that it sees its mirror image in television.[3]

What has seldom been addressed, however, is the question of what is implied by such a negative definition. To this end, I would like to refer back to the late 19th century, to that moment when the literary avant-garde began to define itself, in part, around a conflict it knew how to exploit for its own purposes. As art, as art's conscience, video's relation with television could be seen, then, as a historical parallel to the dialogue between experimental literature and the industrialization of the press.

I am aware of the dangers posed by broad analogies. I know that a hundred years have passed, that modernism and the avant-garde have suffered, after many exalted moments, all the disenchantment, all the dispersal, all the contamination that fosters a belief in postmodernism. I know that the very idea of a utopian model seems absurd, and that the negative relationship itself, with the frictions and fictions it allows—this negative relationship that cannot be reduced to its traditional philosophical sense—no longer really has value. Born of a medium in which, today, the destruction of all reference is consummated, video art is caught up in this same situation. Even so: the very connection linking video art to TV may be, paradoxically, what gives video its particular texture and, by the same token, a privileged place in what one hesitates to call nowadays the avant-garde.

In 19th-century France, where the dialogue between literature and the press is clearest, the point can be summed up in two epochs, two names, two experiences: on the one hand, Alexandre Dumas, Romanticism, and the Newspaper; on the other, Mallarmé, Symbolism, and the work or the Book.

Dumas' relation to the Newspaper is simple, yet excessive. It derives first of all from the sudden growth of the press starting in 1836, a development linked to the name Emile de Girardin. Girardin was the first to launch an inexpensive daily newspaper aimed at a broader audience and supported by advertising. He created the "serial novel" formula that would tempt the best Romantic authors (Balzac, Hugo, Sand, Dumas) and would quickly become a powerful form of the culture industry of the time, prefiguring both the series and the soap opera. For Dumas, the Newspaper served two functions. For one thing, it allowed him to publish his historical novels in serial installments, justified by the both naive and troubled point of view of a God of History onto which the writer's swollen ego is projected: another version of the Ego-Hugo-Ocean or of Michelet's project of the "full resurrection of the past." Dumas also founded his own newspaper-magazines on a number of occasions—more limited in scope than major dailies, and appearing only intermittently, but impressive nonetheless. The entirety of these publications revolved around Dumas even when other authors were invited to publish. Thus, *Le Mois* (1848–1850), "a monthly review of historical and political events, composed entirely by Alexandre Dumas" (*Le Mois*' motto was "God dictates and I write"); *Le Mousquetaire* (1853–1857), "Newspaper of M. Alexandre Dumas"; and *Le Monte-Cristo* (1857–1860), "a weekly newspaper of travel and poetry, published and composed by A. Dumas alone." What Dumas formerly offered to other papers, he now apparently reserved largely for his own, experiencing thereby a doomed but valiant competition between his work as a writer and the social form of a medium that was to become one of the great sources of truth for the 19th century.

We know what happened to the God-Ego-Artwork triad over the course of the century: it came apart under pressure from History, increasingly irreconcilable with itself. Art and History parted company, and from now on their relation would be oblique and/or utopian. This is what Mallarmé's famous twofold distinction confirms—that after him, each would in his or her own way attempt to deny, displace, or reformulate the division. His distinction opposes two modes of speech [*la parole*], and two times of action: general action, i.e., history; and condensed action, i.e. literature, which takes place within history. Even though this opposition assumes a relative autonomy for art, it feeds on the perpetual dislocation between the two modes and two times of action, thereby "revealing the conflict […] in order to elicit their clarity."[4] It is in this context that Mallarmé celebrated the "crisis in poetry" (the rupture of traditional forms of verse), and the liberation of the subjective voice, making it possible to organize the game of literature on the basis of the "twenty-four letters." What is interesting for our purposes is that the consequences that Mallarmé thus brought to light, in *As for the Book*,[5] are directly linked to the extraordinary development of the press under the Second Empire and Third Republic. Mallarmé was obsessed by the Newspaper; for one thing, he must have seen it as an example of "universal reporting": itself hostage to the general action from which literature must protect itself to preserve its identity. But Mallarmé also sensed in the Newspaper a certain logic: the Newspaper, in effect, symbolizes and echoes the boundlessness of the world, in mirroring the essence of events in each of their various instances. It does so by means akin to those of direct, immediate speech, which, no sooner fixed, filtered, and synthesized, is reshaped and redistributed. In this reworking of spoken language and the written page, the Newspaper, as a reflection of the world, is also an image of Mallarmé's Book, which was intended to provide an "orphic explanation of the Earth."[6] The Newspaper thus becomes the negative image of the Book—or rather the Book the negative of the Newspaper. This has the advantage of contextualizing the process of negativity with which poetic language confronts everyday speech in order to "pay for" the arbitrary nature of language in relation to the reality of the physical world. In short, the Book and the Newspaper, as imperfect mirror reflections of each other, work under the same banner. Everything that is social about the Book—the Book as festival, as theater, as new religion (via the transcendence and transformation of subjectivity)—is colored in part by the idea of the Newspaper. In his enthusiasm for the Book, Mallarmé saw within "the current extraordinary over-production" of the press the idea of "a contest for the foundations of modern popular Poetry."[7] Mallarmé himself created early on his own fashion journal, an experience he describes in his short autobiography: "[A]t a certain moment, however, despairing of the despotic book abandoned by Myself, I have […] tried to write completely on my own, including advice on style, jewelry, furniture, even theater reviews and dinner menus, a journal entitled *La Dernière Mode*, the eight or ten issues of which still serve, when I blow the dust off them, to make me dream at length."[8] And of what does Mallarmé dream before this Newspaper he dreamed up by himself, like Dumas had before with his own papers—even if Mallarmé's subject, fashion, and the words *The Latest* in the title underline the extent to which history is reduced to an insubstantial present, continually renewed, yet relative and evanescent? Mallarmé dreams of the Book, of its utopia. He dreams of the "Roll of the Dice" that he dares not yet realize—this "Book-to-come" in which "[the] simultaneous vision of the Page […] taken as a unity as is otherwise the verse or the perfect line," owes much to the multiple, mobile Newspaper page. It then becomes a question of transforming that page, by opposing to it the violence of the idea, the seduction of the word-as-music, the literal spacing of text, the free play of typographic elements—in short, art's utopian provocation.

To simplify, let us focus on the question of time, of a twofold time and of the two types of speech from which it materializes. Let us deliberately ignore the first law of the electronic image, which enables the construction of an instantaneous and virtually infinite duplicate of "reality." Let's also ignore those perverse issues of "life" and "liveness" that surely make video one of the instruments behind our sense that History is disintegrating. Let's even forget about the effects of hyperreality that flow back from the television onto what remains of the physical world (reversions/confusions between the copy and the original). As powerful as these effects may be, they have not closed the breach between the external world and what reiterates it—or at least, as much as some have liked to say. And the increasing speed of media, despite its extreme nature, is not an entirely new phenomenon: this is why the press boom of the 19th century, in the same way as the boom in photography, had such an impact on the definition of art. Here we can draw a comparison to see what it might illuminate: just as there was once the world, the Newspaper, and the poem or the text as the utopia of the Book, there is today the world, television, and video art as the trace of the utopia of art. We should, of course, refine the analogy considerably, in comparing the material components of each. But there remain nonetheless, within the mutation of our time, of our idea of time, two times that are in both cases irreducible and antagonistic in relation to each other.

Let us take as examples three tapes, all American.[9] We will begin with one that turns the institutionalized time *par excellence*—that of the TV newscast—inside out. In 1979, Doug Hall, Chip Lord, and Judy Proctor were invited to Amarillo, Texas, by a local TV station. "Their goal, as artists" (the tape says): to analyze, dissect the news in its context, to mix with professionals and share their experience.

1

2

3

But in order to change it: miming it, mining it, through transgressions both clumsy and subtle, but in any case on target. Through repetition, e.g.: either the pro accomplice (Don Garcia) interrupts his alter-ego, the artist-anchorman (Doug Hall), who stumbles over a word ("apostolic"), in order to teach him the proper rhythm and tempo his role demands (the unrealistic, super-coded voice of the "News"), or shots get repeated, as if by sheer pleasure, to reveal the arbitrariness, the deceptive naturalism, the invisible paranoia of the code. But we are also shown a number of free variations: the TV reporting slides into poetry, scientific reverie and experimental research, by means of improbable images that become autonomous, freezing and turning to black and white. All this is made possible through a look back at the 250 tornados that devastated Texas from 1951 to 1975. The very subtle art of *Amarillo Tapes* resides in maintaining the reality of the newscast while transforming it into unreality, to show the simultaneous lack and surplus of reality.

Media Ecology Ads (1982): both the title and execution say it all. Antoni Muntadas has here chosen the advertisement of the concept as a reversal of publicity, in three shots, three movements.

1

2

3

In *Fuse*, a bright line is stretched horizontally across the dark screen. To the left, a flame lights up and consumes the line. Five minutes and 40 seconds later, when the line has completely disappeared, the ad is over. During that time, a text passes across the screen from left to right in red capital letters: "Beyond all language ... for it there is no ... past ... no present ... no future ... an end ... language is vitally concerned with time ... with tenses ... silence itself is a form of speaking ... just as the blank spaces between the marks of the printing are as much a part of the printing as the letters themselves ... the way is timeless yet it cannot dispense with time ... eternity and time are in love with each other, continually embracing in a union ... yet always separate to the purely human eye ... a beginning ... "
The text is from *Affirming Faith in Mind*, by Jianzhi Sengcan, a sixth-century Zen writer.

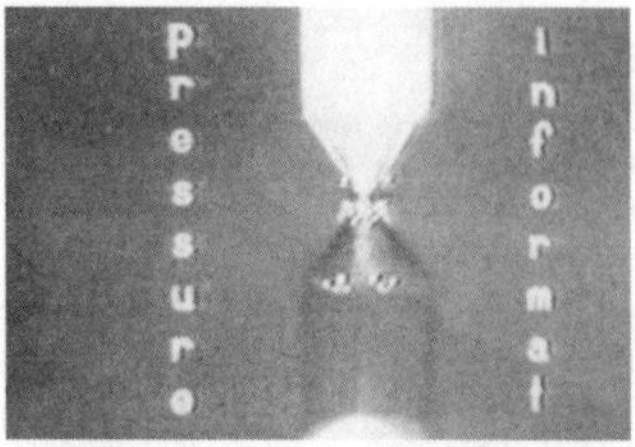

1

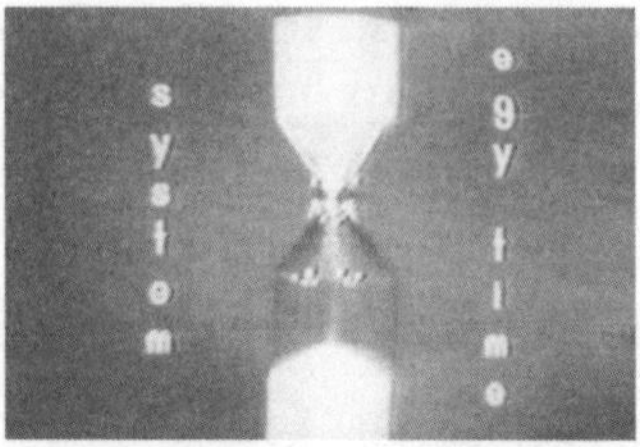

2

3

4

5

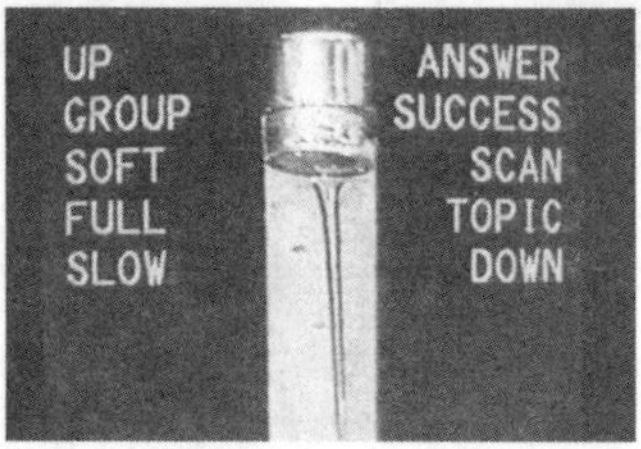

6

The other two pieces, *Timer* and *Slow Down*, employ the same strategy. In the first, figurative concepts composed letter by letter (hence difficult to read) run vertically through an hourglass until it is empty. In the second, words pass at various speeds, either too quickly or too slowly, according to the speed of water that runs; out of a glass tube until it slows to a drip (total running time is 14 minutes).

Reverse Television, by Bill Viola, is not a tape per se, but rather the ghost of a rejected project. Forty-four subjects, ranging in age from 16 to 93, seated facing the camera where they normally watch TV, were intended to appear on public TV for one minute each, in silence, with no presentation by the station (Boston's WGBH). These brief portraits were to be shown hourly, between programs, in spots the station normally reserves for its own publicity, over a period of several weeks. Instead, the portraits were broadcast five times a day, 30 seconds each, during a two-week period (November 14-28, 1983), and signed Bill Viola.[10]

1

2

3

4

What is the reverse of television? It is not merely its audience made visible, the reverse field of an omnipresent shot. It is also, above all, the silence that permeates the shot itself. Viola, not that concerned with such immediate "reversals" of the medium, and focused more than others on the silence of his own work, has for that very reason emphasized the need for this silence in a very sudden, direct fashion. In one of his most beautiful essays, Blanchot wonders what would happen if one day the last writer were to die.[11] One would hear, he says, not an immense silence, but, on the contrary, an incessant murmuring, an inescapable and obsessive noise, an "alien voice." A voice quite close, he adds, to the voices of authority, of control, in short, of dictatorship. It is the writer who silences this voice, approaching it as no one else can, turning it against itself. The video artist could be the one who silences television, as did Viola in *Reverse Television*. For isn't he trying to make us hear silence at the very moment television imposes its will with the greatest force? Just as Muntadas conceptualizes silence by turning the ad-form back on itself; just as Doug Hall and his accomplices play with irony and counterpoint against the News.

However unreal, however modest their efforts, the fantasy of Hall, Proctor, and Lord is clear. If Dumas dreamed, in a "major key," of being the Newspaper itself, these artists try, in a "minor key" both realistic and playful, to take up the position of the News—which is, of course, impossible. Their tape was not aired where it was intended, in place of the news. But later it appeared on another public station, San Francisco Channel 9—not in place of the News, but afterward, in order to delimit the effect of the displacement. The most personal and least parodic elements of the *Amarillo Tapes* have also served as points of departure for Doug Hall's dream-fiction of clouds and tornados in *Prelude to the Tempest* (1985) and his recent *Storm and Stress* (1986).

Like Viola, Muntadas would have liked his *Media Ecology Ads* to be aired in spots usually reserved for advertising on the public channel, or at least to interfere with the regular advertisements. Instead, his tape, shown several times in Canada, Spain, and the US, was always presented in the framework of broadcasts set aside specifically for video art. We can understand the institution's reaction; simply reread the text of *Fuse*. What is this time without beginning or end that flows on but can be reversed, in which emptiness counts as much as fullness, silence as much as sound? This is a (re)figuration of time as pure speculative time, closely approaching that of the televisual flow, in order to invert its tempo, its message, and its values. "There we are ... seeing, believing, marveling, speculating." [12] Mallarmé wrote in the "Roll of the Dice":

watching
doubting
rolling
shining and meditating.

Such is the viewer targeted by Viola during this improbable minute of silence torn from the unending noise of television. A minute intended to be anonymous, just as Mallarmé liked to think of the Book "without an author's name," in order to emphasize the absolute and utopian basis on which the personal work is erected. The ideal spectator of *Reverse Television* is also that of Viola's *Hatsu Yume* (1981), a 60-minute poem on the tension between light and shadow, and on cycles of time. As a work purely about time, *Hatsu Yume* is symbolically inassimilable to television, even if the latter consents to program it, albeit in marginal slots.

Like the newspaper, television seeks to master time, indeed to substitute itself for time. In other words, it aims to be time, instead of just affirming its presence by difference. But how can this difference be situated? It is constructed not solely in relation to the time of life in general, which television transforms and assimilates, but rather in relation to television itself, in the sense that television tends to produce a homogenized time that will barely tolerate difference, if at all.

There are basically only two modes of being for television—even if the formulae, the modes, are more and more multiplied and variable depending on different regulations, countries, assumed audiences, etc. Either television gives in to its own flow, or else it resists it—by every conceivable means. Godard's shot without reverse shot is an example of the latter. Gary Hill's acceleration/deformation of language is another. The slowed-down, cyclical de- and re-composed time of Thierry Kuntzel, another. And the association of images and ideas in Juan Downey's work yet another. And so on. None of these means has an absolute value in itself, even if slowness tends to be today historically privileged in the face of a general speeding up of time. One of television's great powers is its ability to relativize a figure, to recycle and reappropriate it, more or less quickly. But this continuous process is also intrinsically limited. Like the newspaper, television cannot tolerate that which turns against it, cannot really affirm the need for another time. One of the tasks of criticism is to gauge the relation of forces between what the flow assimilates and what resists it.

There are two ways to resist the flow: either by getting inside it, inside television as the institution of flow, or by going outside it. It is striking that nearly all those who resist flow truly from within must also place themselves outside it in order to resist. Installation is for a number of video artists the site of this resistance. Installation creates a simultaneously physical and virtual space where the spectator can reappropriate, at his will, concepts that challenge the institution, opening the path to an interaction as much critical as imaginary. This can also mean, in galleries and museums, screening tapes isolated from the flow and presented under often radically different conditions: why else would Viola and Kuntzel wish to show their tapes in the dark, as at the movies, if not to seek a certain quality of silence? A quality comparable to what the cinema is generally for Godard, insofar as it is opposed, as art, to television. In at least one case, this became the subject of a tape shown on television, when a certain channel (Britain's Channel 4) was prepared to risk it—witness *Soft and Hard* (1985).

There are two ways to conceive relations between video art and television. These two ways oppose each other, despite all their connections in reality, despite all the possible mediations. A particularly clear sign of this opposition is that, in the case of each, one seeks to destroy the other as if, logically or fantastically, the two could not coexist. The first of the two positions resists television in order to (re)affirm the necessity of art, even if hopelessly so. The second, conversely, aims to confound video art and television, as Averty wanted. This is why he never accepted the word "art," nor "video." For him, there was only the electronic image and his aborted dream of absorbing all of television into it. In different terms, this is also what John Sanborn implies when he asks to be considered henceforth a "TV-artist."[13] Today there comes from all sides the demand for an alternative television that would still be television.[14] This position, which pretends to be realistic and suited to the needs of today, is supported, whether its proponents are aware of it or not, and whatever their own motivations, by a rather specific utopia: the utopia of the end of art as utopia. This leads us to hope from television a social redefinition of art, and nothing less.

One would like to believe in it, despite the difficulty. The meeting of art and television runs up against two obstacles. First, obviously, is the logic of profit—when profit, through advertising, becomes the visible form of time. This makes commercial television—American (Italian, etc.) TV, "real" TV—invincible and intolerable, once the resources of humor are exhausted (and they quickly are, unless humor is used as a façade for bottomless despair). And this even if art (advertising art) finds a home on television. This explains why the logic of the lowest common denominator (even the smallest mass audience) yields comparable effects on network or cable TV, where there is more and more promotion, not of products per se, but of programs, channels, flow, the institution itself. So much so that the medium is no longer that which video tried to be(come), as in Fred Barzyk's pioneering broadcast in 1969 (*The Medium is the Medium*): the medium approaching its essence, its potential, through provocation, play, difference, excess, the direct, uncompromising expression of artist's voices. Instead, the medium serves far too often the message. McLuhan's prophecy is fulfilled when, contrary to the myth it pretended to expose, the voices of advertising and programming meet, justifying each other, one entailing the other, as in certain recent broadcasts where artists' works are presented.[15] Television thus risks becoming predominantly what it wished to cease being: noise, a rumbling, an alien voice, the manifestation of an undifferentiated, homogeneous time.

Television as such, in its "universal" American version, will never become our mythology. The American cinema did, and for profit, because it circumscribed its own oneiric space built on an immense, yet delimited capacity for illusion. This is why cinema in and of itself resists television, even when films on TV are subjected to the brutal interruptions of advertising.

Television is no more a structured language than is cinema. But it can claim (dubiously) to have become the universal language that cinema believed itself to be and, early in its history, made it dream of being (in, for example, its Soviet idealist-revolutionary version). This is why television is more *like a language* than cinema ever was. Television has taken up, under the auspices of communication, the succession of language and speech games. This is why, in a time when utopia is faring badly, it can be one of the last refuges of utopia—and of contradictory utopias.

Romanticism is dead, and no one can imagine any longer that he or she alone is a newspaper or a channel, even in Dumas' semi-real way. But the utopia of the Book has been reformulated (via a loopback effect, requiring further analysis, between History as a whole and the history of different arts or media). Paik, the first, dreamed of it in his "Utopian laser TV Station" (from which *Global Groove* was born), and rendered this dream visible in *Tricolor Video* (1982), which, with its 400 monitors, would be its symbol:

"unlimited terminal of all the world's images. Of all past, present and future images."[16] If we have truly entered into post-modernism, then video art is one of the liveliest signs of a postmodernism of resistance—because it has the (hard) luck to have an object it can truly resist.[17] This might suffice to qualify video art as an avant-garde—or, in terms of the dialogue between Habermas and Peter Bürger, as a pointed variant of modernism.[18] Mallarmé said of the utopia of the Book and the temporal difference it opened up: "in view of later or never." He said of the "Roll of the Dice," "without presuming the future that will emerge from now—nothing, or almost an art." Almost an art only. Art as the time of separation and difference, since art integrated into society, under the terms of a "natural" pact, is a "thing of the past" (Hegel). Unless little by little the impossible should happen—the other utopia, which does not even have a name: that television would be able to reinvent the pact in a new form.

1986. Originally translated in 1986 by Florence Dauman and Lynne Kirby.

[1] Honoré de Balzac, *Lost Illusions* vol. 2, trans. G. Burnham Ives (Philadelphia: George Barrie, 1898) 112. Cited in Todd Gitlin, "The Whole World is Watching," *Transmission*, ed. Peter d'Agostino (New York: Tanam Press, 1985).

[2] Jean-Christophe Averty quoted in *Art Vidéo, Rétrospectives et Perspectives* (Charleroi: Lebeer Hossmann, 1983) 59.

[3] Cf. among others: Fargier, "La vidéo, contre (tout contre) la télévision," supplement to *Nordeste* 1 (Montbéliard: Centre d'Action Culturelle, 1982) 4; *Transmission*, especially David Ross' "Nam June Paik's Videotapes"; *New Artists' Video*, ed. Gregory Battcock (New York: Dutton, 1978), especially Douglas Davis' "The End of Video, White Vapor." The term "video art" poses a problem that cannot be resolved by simply eliminating the term, nor by privileging the term "video" alone. Hence, I will stick to "video art."

[4] Maurice Blanchot, *Le Livre à venir* (Paris: Gallimard, 1959) 282 [*The Book to Come*, trans. Charlotte Mandell (Stanford CA: Stanford University Press, 2003) 277].

[5] Stéphane Mallarmé,"Quant au livre," *Œuvres Complètes*, ed. Henri Mondor and G. Jean-Aubry (Paris: Gallimard/Pléiade, 1945) 369-387 ["As for the Book," trans. Mary Ann Caws, *Selected Poetry and Prose*, ed. Mary Ann Caws (New York: New Directions, 1982) 77–84] [editor's note].

[6] Mallarmé, "Autobiographie, Lettre du 16 nov. 1885 à Verlaine," *Œuvres Complètes*, 663 ["Letter to Paul Verlaine (November 16, 1885)," *Selected Letters of Stephane Mallarmé*, ed. and trans. Rosemary Lloyd (Chicago: University of Chicago Press, 1988) 143].

[7] Mallarmé, "Quant au livre—Etalages," *Œuvres Complètes* 376.

[8] Mallarmé, "Autobiographie" 663–664 ["Letter to Paul Verlaine," *Selected Letters of Stephane Mallarmé* 144].

[9] But one might consider equally, for example, *Notes d'un magnétoscopeur* by Jean-Paul Fargier, and *Tout près de la frontière* by Danielle Jaeggi (France), *Passegiate Romane* by Catarina Borelli (Italy), *Der Riese* by Michael Klier (Germany), etc.

[10] Viola has since made a tape in which he explains the project and then shows 15 seconds of each of the 44 portraits.

[11] In *The Book to Come*, immediately before his commentary on Mallarmé, which closes the book.

[12] Robert C. Morgan, "On the Activity of Slowing Down or the Media becomes the Media," *Exposition* (Madrid: Fernando Viganda, 1985) 24, on an installation by Muntadas.

[13] On the occasion of a presentation of his work at the festival of Salsomaggiore (Italy), April 1985.

[14] For example, Beverle Houston's important text "Television and the Video Text: A Crisis of Desire," in *Resolution*, ed. Patti Podesta (Los Angeles: LACE, 1986).

[15] For example *Alive from Off Center*, produced by Melinda Ward for KTCA Minneapolis: Susan Stamberg of NPR's *All Things Considered* handles the segues between the videos, so that they slip more easily into the coarse grain of the advertising voice, and stay there for that very reason (the choice of videos also encourages this).

[16] Fargier, "Un drapeau de moins," *Nam June Paik, Tricolor Video* (Paris: Centre Georges Pompidou, 1982). One may also be reminded of the dream Godard had often mentioned (and pursued, in its most utopian-political form, all the way to Mozambique) of being named head of a TV network.

[17] Taken up by Hal Foster in *The Anti-Aesthetic, Essays on Post-modern Culture*, ed. Hal Foster (Washington: Bay Press, 1983).

[18] See *New German Critique* 22 (1981).

Bill Viola, *Reverse Television*, 1983

When the Photograph of Cinema Is Written

Francesco Guardi, *La Lagune grise* (*The Gray Laguna*), 1790

Roland Barthes would have appreciated this book.[1] Because it deals with Proust, the writer to whom Barthes was ultimately the closest. Because it concerns photography, whose idea constantly haunted him. But especially because in encompassing Proust and photography, Jean-François Chevrier touches on questions that are in a sense internal to Barthes' method, if only because his book attempts to establish a link between the image and the written word that Barthes always rejected, but whose existence and risk he fully acknowledged.

Jean-François Chevrier offers us a fiction: *In Search of Lost Time* as the story of a photographer's vocation as much as a writer's. The Proustian undertaking thus becomes a model for contemporary photographers, driving them to a kind of higher awareness of their art, commensurate with its uncertain, fragile nature (here Chevrier places himself on the flip side of Barthes, or of Barthes' gaze:

the side of the photograph to be taken rather than the one already taken, and thus closer to creation than to interpretation). This means that his essay must take two routes simultaneously, between which he has chosen to maintain a difficult balancing act, as dictated by the seven attitudes that define in his view the realm of photographic imagination (looking, recording, inscribing, reproducing, imitating, revealing, imagining). On the one hand, this involves retracing the genesis of the movement (both real and metaphorical) that in Proust's novel brings together the narrator and photography. On the other, Chevrier constantly fuels this fictional vocation that he attempts to construct by relying on the experience of real photographers (the image plays a part, as in all the volumes of the "Ecrit sur l'image" collection—here through two series of photographs considered exemplary, from Pierre de Fenoyl and Holger Trülzsch).

The fascination that Proust went through with photography comes to life magnificently here. In this he followed many of his contemporaries, as well as writers and painters before him (Baudelaire, Balzac, Delacroix) who recognized its epochal importance. But he had been closer to it than any of them: more than anyone else, he staked his life and his ability to write on a certain relationship between memory and gaze, which in a way is the very subject of photography.

For that very reason, Proust rejects photography. First of all, its mechanical nature makes it inexact (Chevrier quotes the famous example of the narrator arriving by surprise at his grandmother's home and not recognizing her, "for a mere second": "What my eyes did, automatically, in the moment I caught sight of *my grandmother*, was to take a *photograph*"[2]). Next, even if a photograph is a good likeness, it is always only superficially so, and this likeness is itself superficial: photography is a simulacrum. At best a souvenir, with what that implies in lack and separation (such as the actual photograph of the narrator's grandmother taken by Saint-Loup, from which Marcel is unable to recapture the real presence of the dead woman).[3] In short, there is "nothing Proustian in a photograph," says Barthes, summarizing in a phrase[4] the complicated route Chevrier takes, following Proust, between "remembrance" and "involuntary memory." The remembrance has no depth; there is nothing truly present in it. As for the past, the remembrance is only its decomposition. By its nature, the photo is this decomposition; it attacks the forgetfulness from which the revelation of involuntary memory springs. Only this memory—born of chance, of availability—transforms the past into the present and brings them together in the text whose purpose is to conserve what has been captured in perpetuity.

But this movement owes much to photography from which it tries to separate itself. To such a degree that it is no exaggeration to say that photography is the negative of Proustian revelation. It is first of all empirically so: Chevrier thus stresses to what extent the "snapshots of memory" (of which photography is a kind of essence) contribute, in the same way as observational data, to the formation of involuntary memory. Chevrier has made an important discovery in this area: one of Proust's preparatory notebooks for the *Search* shows that he discovered the famous "unevenness of the paving stones"—the phenomenon that in his novel he situated in the courtyard of the Guermantes estate—in a photograph of the baptistery of St. Mark's. Rather than the visual, which he considers too connected to intelligence and voluntary memory, Proust prefers tactile and auditory shocks, more likely to trigger genuine resurgences of the past. But the image is there, lurking in the shadows, from where it is ready to emerge. This makes it clearer why the photographic process (recording and development) also finds itself repeatedly serving as a metaphor for the process of writing. As if by this same chemistry, or alchemy, one went from one order to another; as if writing—by condensing these two steps of the photographic process, and especially by retaining the traces that lead from one to the other—became itself a photograph. Finally, Chevrier effectively shows how much the rejection of photography, as much as the fixation on it, is part of Proust's obsession with the "unique image." The one that in the baptistery of St. Mark's, in the immobile form of a mosaic, represents his mother to him—"the icon of a love like no other"—is the image of which every photograph becomes the lack, but should, could be a tangible sign,[5] like the photograph of the Jardin d'Hiver, which accomplishes for Barthes "the impossible science of the unique being." The one on which he bases his text, because he doesn't show it. Just as Blanchot, in *The Space of Literature* (1955), associates writing in a more abstract and general way with the "fascination of the image," also referring to that fascination with the Mother, and concentrating it in the child's gaze.[6]

The vocation of photographer that Chevrier sees written in *In Search of Lost Time* achieves a sort of utopia of photography. It's an attempt to ground photography as an art, in other words to grant it the scope of a work of the imagination, without denying to what extent its nature forces it, as Barthes says, to be above all "a magic." Whereas for Barthes the photograph divides—irremediably so—the person looking at it, Chevrier, through his fiction, which is also a proposition, tries to recover in the real photograph something of the power that the image-as-absence has (for Proust, as well as for Blanchot and Barthes). This requires separating the photograph from the snapshot (which has probably become its most axiomatic purpose), or discovering a depth in the snapshot that it would never have on its own. So a subtle opposition runs through the book, between Robert Doisneau and Raymond Depardon: the first clearly aims for "the authentication of the imaginary" that the photographs of the second never really attain, although his efforts play a part in it. Thus Chevrier thinks that what he calls a return to the 19th century is possible today: in the very sense in which Baudelaire, in the name of imagination, did not accept being fooled by photography. This is what the photographs of Pierre de Fenoyl and Holger Trülzsch attempt to show, serving as a counterpoint throughout the pages where this reasoning and this desire intertwine.

And this is where there is a strange kind of turning point in this book, illuminating an obstacle inherent to photography. These images (beautiful, powerful ones, incidentally—that is not the issue) only seem to acquire the full force that Chevrier accords them through what he says about them; they play Proust's game because the author speaks to me about them and because, on the opposite page, they are called upon to fill a lack for which they are the sign. In short, they are projective, and not only one by one (submitted to the risky and cruel games of the *studium* and the *punctum*), but overall, as the vehicle for a discourse. The extreme situation of these photographs that are called on as witnesses recalls to what extent photography feeds on words (titles, captions, comments, rumors, interviews, analyses, desires for theory). It thus tries to escape both excessively simple aestheticization and the trivialization that threatens every image; most of all, it responds to the danger (that hangs over every photograph) of materializing what Barthes, at the end of *Camera Lucida*, calls "the wakening of intractable reality." But what, in fact, do all those words do to the photographs they accompany? They endow them with a point of view (dividing itself from the one shown in the photograph); they give indications (biographical, aesthetic, moral, etc.) that the photograph often does not; they organize sequences, relationships, between the photographs; they impart movement to them, with a sort of double depth of field; they temporalize them, as if to escape from this dead, inverted time in which Barthes perceives the "noeme" of photography. In a word, they screenwrite them. I almost want to write: they bring them to life.

I have to say it: reading this book, I was tempted to imagine, like Chevrier, that it spoke of a vocation that Proust does not mention. But instead of the vocation of photographer, what if the intent behind *In Search of Lost Time* was to undertake that of a filmmaker? What if photography, a tenuous art (I do not mean a minor one) as well as a vast phenomenon, was thus able to teach us something essential about cinema? What if in this movement—by which we constantly attempt to bring photography's terrible stillness to life—cinema became able to think about slowing its own?

It is well known that Proust condemned cinema even more harshly than he did photography. Cinema abolishes the unique relationship between sensation and remembrance that forms "reality" and that writing perpetuates as its very purpose.[7] Cinema is inflexible. "And nothing could arrest [its] slow progress": this is how the narrator, at the very beginning of *In Search of Lost Time*, recalls the effects of his magic lantern.[8] This is precisely what Barthes always criticized cinema for, in comparing it to photography: its hysteria, its voracity, its lack of thoughtfulness (this is what drew him to the pleasure of the still frame). Impossible to stop the machine, to live through it, to think through it.

Of course, this is not completely true. With all the great filmmakers of fiction cinema, there have always been examples of breaks during which filmic fascination suddenly seems to turn against itself in order to produce (more or less visible) effects of contemplation and thought. But the *défilement* is strongest when one does not try to stop it. Thus, for some of those people who have wanted for several years to "analyze films," there has been not so much a concern for truth (even though there really has been one) as a desire to experiment subjectively. The work with freeze-frames does in fact create the conditions of another time: it invents, right when the work is carried out, the conditions of reading (I do not mean the texts that result from it—only Thierry Kuntzel's really come close to that experience). It gives rise to a space that encourages both free and controlled associations; in short, it shifts cinema's hysteria by producing what one could call, taking a cue from Hugo, a pensive spectator. In this sense, I would say that this is a Proustian activity; and it is obviously no accident if a whole segment of cinema currently searching for new ideas is moving in the same direction, by developing a passion for the still image and fixity (of which silent film has given—already as though from another time—the most beautiful examples).

"Proustian," when it comes to cinema, means two things (in a much too general way, but just to frame the issue). First, it means shifting the regime of enunciation that belongs to classical fiction—and all true fiction in cinema is immediately, mercilessly classical, as modern as it may be in other ways. It takes shape as soon as one tells a story as if it were obvious, a sort of ideal layer, a second film saturating the space between the eye and the screen: being Proustian means scratching that film, not accepting its mirage. Next, it means attacking the image's substance, its irrepressible tendency toward naturalism, and its mechanical consent to the *dispositif* (there are many ways of going about this, but the voice—words, phrases—is certainly one of the privileged access points: touching the image from the outside, it alters and reconstructs it, modifying its enunciation). Finally this shift is, of course, connected to the conditions of reading. It assumes that the pact so appropriately named "projection" has been broken (at least virtually). Mallarmé described the field of play then recently opened by the appearance of free verse as "free and individual modulation." Free and individual projection is almost like reading, at one's own rhythm (while providing one of the possible responses to the "boredom" and the "excessive" length of films through which a new cinema tries to find itself). It also radically brings cinema and photography closer together (by taking for granted the generalized manipulation of all relationships between words and images). Never have they been as closely linked: working out their differences—which are perhaps intractable, but not as much as one thought—and moving together, especially, with regard to "reality," by relying on the same utopia.

This is what Godard, Snow, Syberberg, Marker, Duras (or equally Fieschi and Kuntzel with video, which takes up the question in its own way) say to me (personally: others will choose different names) through the intermediary of Proust.

1982. Translated in 2011 by Allyn Hardyck.

[1] Jean-François Chevrier, *Proust et la photographie* (Paris: Cahiers du cinéma/Editions de l'Etoile, collection "Ecrit sur l'image," 1982).

[2] Marcel Proust, *A la recherche du temps perdu* vol. II (Paris: Gallimard/Pléiade, 1954) 140–141 [*The Guermantes Way*, trans. Mark Treharne (New York: Viking, 2004) 134].

[3] *A la recherche du temps perdu* vol. II 758–759 [*Sodom and Gomorrah*, trans. C. K. Scott Moncrieff, Terence Kilmartin, and D.J. Enright (New York: Modern Library, 1993) 237].

[4] Roland Barthes, *La chambre claire* (Paris: Cahiers du cinéma-Gallimard-Seuil, 1980) 129 [*Camera Lucida: Reflections on Photography*, trans. Richard Howard (New York: Hill and Wang, 1982) 82].

[5] "The time has now come for me when, on remembering the baptistery, facing the waters of the Jordan where St. John immersed Christ while the gondola awaited us by the Piazzetta, I cannot remain indifferent to the fact that there was by my side in this cool twilight a woman clothed in mourning, whose respectful but enthusiastic fervor matched that of the elderly woman who can be seen in Venice in Carpaccio's *St. Ursula*, and that nothing can ever again remove this red-cheeked, sad-eyed woman, in her black veils, from the softly lit sanctuary of St. Mark's where I am certain to find her, because I have reserved a place there in perpetuity, alongside the mosaics, for her, for my mother." Chevrier 108; Proust, *A la recherche du temps perdu* vol. III 646 [*The Fugitive*, trans. Carol Clark and Peter Collier (London: Penguin Classics, 2003) 610].

[6] "It is because the child is fascinated that the mother is fascinating, and that is also why all the impressions of early childhood have a kind of fixity which comes from fascination." Maurice Blanchot, *L'espace littéraire* (Paris: Gallimard, 1955) 24 [*The Space of Literature*, trans. Ann Smock (Lincoln, Nebraska: University of Nebraska Press, 1989) 33].

[7] "[W]hat we call reality is a certain connection between these immediate sensations and the memories which envelop us simultaneously with them—a connection that is suppressed in a simple cinematographic vision, which just because it professes to confine itself to the truth in fact departs widely from it—a unique connection which the writer has to rediscover in order to link forever in his phrase the two sets of phenomena which reality joins together." Proust, *A la recherche du temps perdu* vol. III 889 [*Time Regained*, trans. Moncrieff, Kilmartin, and Enright (New York: Modern Library, 1993) 289].

[8] Proust, *A la recherche du temps perdu* vol. I 10 [*Swann's Way*, trans. Moncrieff (New York: Vintage, 1982) 10].

The Pensive Spectator

Alfred Hitchcock, *Shadow of a Doubt*, 1943

On one side, there is movement, the present, presence; on the other, immobility, the past, a certain absence. On one side, the consent to illusion; on the other, a quest for hallucination. Here, a fleeting image, one that seizes us in its flight; there, a completely still image that cannot be fully grasped. On this side, time doubles life; on that, time returns to us brushed by death. Such is the line traced by Barthes between cinema and photography.

The spectator of the cinema is idle, yet hurried. He follows a thread that at times seems to move too slowly, but that suddenly goes too fast once one tries to halt it. "Do I add to the images in movies? I don't think so; I don't have time: in front of the screen, I am not free to shut my eyes; otherwise, opening them again I would not discover the same image […]"[1] On the other hand, before a photograph, you always close your eyes, more or less: the time it takes (theoretically infinite, above all repeatable) to produce the "supplement" necessary for the spectator to enter into the image.

What happens when the spectator of film is confronted with a photograph? The photograph becomes first one object among many; like all other elements of a film, the photograph is caught up in the *défilement*. Yet the presence of a photograph on the screen gives rise to a very particular trouble. Without ceasing to advance its own rhythm, the film seems to freeze, to suspend itself, inspiring the spectator to recoil from the image that goes hand in hand with a growing fascination. This curious effect attests to the immense power of photography to hold its own in a situation in which it is not truly itself. The cinema reproduces everything, even the fascination the photograph exercises over us. But in the process, something happens to cinema.

Consider, for example, *Letter from an Unknown Woman* (Max Ophüls, 1948, with Louis Jourdan and Joan Fontaine). Here the power of cinema is at its height. Built on a flashback structure (the pretext is a letter the hero receives in the opening sequence), the film gives us past events in the present tense. The flashback constantly returns to its starting point: we see the hero several times reading the letter from the unknown woman (in reality, the forgotten woman), whose voice-off heard reading the letter ties together most of the scenes. About midway through the film, the hero learns that this woman he has forsaken after one night of love has borne a child he unquestionably fathered. He scrutinizes in close-up, through a magnifying glass, the photographs attached to the letter: three photographs, displayed for the spectator. The first, oval-framed, shows a child about one year old, full face, eyes wide open. In the next, the child has grown taller, and poses with his mother in a hot-air balloon. Finally, the child appears once again, now nearly an adolescent.

What purpose do these photographs serve? A narrative one, to be sure. In the very next sequence, we pick up on the heroine and her son in the middle of everyday life. The photographs act as a hinge between the two major parts of the story; they express the passing of time. Yet, these photographs also seem to resist time. It is not only that they symbolize it, as one might believe. They in fact open up another time: a past of the past, a second, different time. Thus, they freeze for one instant the time of the film, and uprooting us from the film's unfolding, situate us in relation to it. For this there are three reasons. First, the sudden stillness of the image. This has nothing to do with the stillness of those shots where inanimate objects await the arrival of a human being. Rather, it works against the movement of the film, which depends on figures moving. Second, these images look at us, the first one especially, from the depths of a long-lost childhood (photographic time *par excellence*), with the kind of look at the camera almost never seen then in the cinema. Finally, the hero himself confirms the fascination of the photograph in its ability to rivet the gaze. One is tempted to say that, as a character, he adds to the image, even if the film discourages this. What the photographs bear witness to upsets him; he is, at the very thought of what they suggest, petrified. I who identify with him am, like him, petrified. But not in the same way. A division erupts in the filmic illusion: at the same time that I am borne along by the narrative, with the part the photograph plays, I am put into direct contact with the photograph. This does not mean the film permits me to add to the image itself, as I would with a photograph; in any case, it does not afford enough time to do so. But contact with the photograph allows me in retrospect the precious leisure to "add to" the film. And it does this in an unexpected way: by subtraction. The photograph subtracts me from the fiction of the cinema, even if it forms a part of the film, even if it adds to it. Creating a distance, another time, the photograph permits me to reflect on cinema. Permits me, that is, to reflect that I am at the cinema. In short, the presence of the photograph permits me to invest more freely in what I am seeing. It helps me to close my eyes, yet keep them wide open.

The single photograph of *Shadow of a Doubt* (Hitchcock, 1943) creates something of the same effect. This time, the dialogue propagates it like a shock wave.[2] In this film, the photograph is at the heart of the symbolic system: it concentrates within it the film's energy, its meaning; it takes us back to the beginning, to the trauma that (everything in the film strongly suggests) has transformed a precocious child into a psychopath. But we reflect here as well (again, in that curious position evoked above), like Uncle Charlie holding between his fingers this frame embedded many times over within the frame: we reflect on the childhood that, for a second, has looked at us. And the photo-effect spreads from there, to the indeterminate region between child and man, finally coming to the body of the hero, Uncle Charlie, whose face, in the foreground on the left, slowly stiffens, thus contrasting with the two women moving around behind him. This face, around which the camera turns, ultimately becomes nothing more than stone.

The effect of the voice is so strong in its relation to the photograph that a film can often practically forego the image itself. In *Fanny* (Marcel Pagnol, 1932), Marius, returning from the country, tells his old fiancée how, after a long absence, it became impossible for him to conjure up her image. He attempts to describe, as something almost intolerable, the "darkness" that would conceal her face. He decides to write to Fanny and ask her for a photograph. Caught between this black screen and the photograph that replaces it, the lovers' scene veers off for a moment and makes us shudder slightly: this is cinema seized by photography.

Films that take the photograph as their subject (or at least as the linchpin of their *dispositif*) cannot help but parade the effect of those instances where the photograph's material potency radiates in a fleeting moment. Take Antonioni's *Blow-up* (1966), a seminal work. Or the little-known Rossellini film *La Macchina ammazzacattivi* (The Machine that Kills Bad People, 1948). Or Fritz Lang's *Beyond a Reasonable Doubt* (1956). Or the ending of Truffaut's *L'Amour en fuite* (*Love on the Run*, 1979). In these films, on the one hand, the spectator is literally swept up in the narrativization of the photograph. Once past the first shock, he plunges eagerly into the traps laid by the photograph (especially the photograph-as-proof, the index, etc., even if it retains its symbolic value as fetish). Far from arresting the film's temporal flow, the photograph becomes its very instrument: it precipitates, then regulates the suspense. Witness Hathaway's *Call Northside 777* (1948). As soon as the journalist (James Stewart) has figured out that the press photograph he is using for his investigation may contain the sought-after evidence (a newspaper headline date), the implacable suspense of classical cinema is set in motion—and nothing stops it. Except possibly, in the course of the photographic process itself (the photograph is magnified 100 then 200 times), those all too brief moments when the materiality of the photograph leaps to the eye.

But, on the other hand, as soon as the narrative role of the photograph has been sufficiently established, one has the impression of following a fiction divided from itself. This requires strong directors, those who are up to the perversity of the challenge: Lang, Rossellini. In *Beyond a Reasonable Doubt*, under the guise of a debate on the death penalty (there's always the risk of condemning an innocent person), the hero poses for some photographs to be used as evidence so that he can accuse himself without danger of being condemned for the crime of which he is in reality guilty. At the very moment they are to be introduced in the trial, the photographs are destroyed in an automobile accident. Both before and after the accident, they haunt the film, creating a sort of two-way mirror. The photograph, shimmering in memory, plays with the truth of cinema. For his part, Rossellini develops a parable in the form of a fable. Under the spell of a cartoon-like devil, a village photographer discovers that he kills the subjects represented in his photographs each time he rephotographs them. The subject literally dies from a freeze-frame, immobilized in the pose he or she struck in the photograph. This operation is repeated, crescendo, until the spell is broken—and the film ends. More so even than in Lang's film (preoccupied, as it is, with the deceptive truth of appearances), the cinema is here conceived in relation to photography. At the point where the photograph stops time and kills what it sees, the film produces the illusion of life and carries us away in its movement. But this succession of little murders of fiction also illuminates the film's mechanism from within. Think of any film in which the cinema represents itself: such films do not produce this same disquieting strangeness. When film looks at itself, it never sees itself as it does in the photograph.

At the other extreme, the photograph becomes the material support of the film, either in its totality, or in fragments powerful enough to produce an effect all by themselves, as in the beautiful enlargement sequence in in Ridley Scott's *Blade Runner* (1982). In such films, a reversal occurs: immobility becomes the principle (which accounts for the irony, and the force, of the famous shot in Chris Marker's *La Jetée* (1963)—the eye that opens, the only vibration in a completely frozen world). This is why camera movement is often used to supplement the stillness of the image.

But this reversal is in any case much more limited than it would seem, for movement is not what defines cinema most profoundly (Peter Wollen was right to remind us of this recently[3]). Rather, it is time: the concatenation, the *défilement* of images in time, a time the spectator cannot control. Music and voiceover harmonize particularly well in films composed of photographs. It is not simply that the two audio tracks animate such films; it is rather that their respective manifestations [*défilements*] share the character of temporal movement, and that these movements reinforce each other.

What is the difference then in those films in which the substance of the photograph becomes the fiction of the cinema? Quite simply this: their relative stillness tempers the "hysteria" of the film. Such is the secret of their seduction (for whoever is sensitive to it). As we are drawn more deeply into the flow of the film, we are simultaneously able to reflect on it with a maximum of intensity. Within this slight interstice, we can also reflect on cinema.

The presence of the photograph, diverse, diffuse, ambiguous, thus has the effect of uncoupling the spectator from the image, even if only slightly, even if only by virtue of the extra fascination it holds. It pulls the spectator out of this imprecise, yet pregnant force: the ordinary imaginary of the cinema. Photographs are not the only instruments of this uncoupling. In the narrative cinema (leaving aside the question of so-called experimental cinema), what is called "*mise en scène*" can also yield, through its own means, effects of suspension, freezing, reflexivity, effects that enable the spectator to reflect on what he is seeing. It is no doubt this that allows us to recognize the true *auteurs*, and the great films. The photograph transformed into cinema is not always the most powerful of these means. Nor is it especially the most frequently employed, even if its repeated occurrence in film is striking. But it is, in retrospect, the most visible. And the only one that lingers in memory when the film is over thanks to the great, unique materiality of the still image.

Here we touch on the intriguing point that, in terms of a theory of the image, might best permit us to formulate the relation between cinema and photography. As soon as you stop the film, you begin to find the time to add to the image. You start to reflect differently on film, on cinema. You are led toward the still frame—which is itself a step further in the direction of the photograph. In the frozen film (or still frame), the presence of the photograph bursts forth, while other means exploited by *mise en scène* to work against time tend to vanish. The photograph thus becomes a stop within a stop, a freeze-frame within a freeze-frame; between it and the film from which it emerges, two kinds of time blend together, always and inextricable, but without becoming confused. In this, the photograph enjoys a privilege over all other effects that make the spectator of cinema, this hurried spectator, a pensive one as well.

1984. Originally translated in 1987 by Lynne Kirby.

[1] Roland Barthes, *La chambre claire* (Paris: Cahiers du cinéma-Gallimard-Seuil, 1980) 89-90 [*Camera Lucida*: Reflections on Photography, trans. Richard Howard (New York: Hill and Wang, 1982) 55].

[2] The dialogue begins when Emma Newton, Uncle Charlie's sister, asks him to pose for a photograph for a survey on the American family (as a cover story for the police investigation). Charlie Newton (her daughter) is in love with her uncle Charlie, whose behavior is making her somewhat uncomfortable.

Charlie: He'd take your photograph and then we could have it for nothing.

Uncle Charlie: No thank you. I've never been photographed and I don't want to be.

Emma: Oh, Charles, how can you talk that way? I had a photograph of you. I gave it to Charlie.

Uncle Charlie: I tell you, there are none.

Emma: I guess you've forgotten this one. [*to Charlie*] Get it, Charlie. [*to Uncle Charlie*] You sure you don't remember?

Uncle Charlie: Of course I don't ever remember being photographed.

Charlie leaves, returns with the photo, hands it to him. He looks at it.

Uncle Charlie: 46 Burnham Street.

Emma: Mm-hm. It was taken the Christmas you got your bicycle. Just before your accident.

Charlie: Uncle Charlie, you were beautiful.

Emma: Wasn't he, though? And such a quiet boy. Always reading. [*to Uncle Charlie*] Papa shouldn't have got you that bicycle. You didn't know how to handle it. [*to Charlie*] He took it right out on the icy road and skidded into a streetcar. We thought he was going to die.

Charlie: I'm glad he didn't.

Emma: He almost did. He fractured his skull, and he was laid up so long. And then, when he was getting well, there was no holding him. And it was just as though all the rest he had was too much for him [...] He didn't do much reading after that, let me tell you. It was taken the very day he had his accident. A few days later when the pictures came home, how Mama cried. She wondered if he'd ever look the same. She wondered if he'd ever be the same.

[3] Peter Wollen, "Fire and Ice," *Photographies* 4 (April 1984) 118–120.

Chris Marker, *La Jetée*, 1963

Max Ophüls, *Letter From An Unknown Woman*, 1948

Fritz Lang, *Beyond a Reasonable Doubt*, 1956

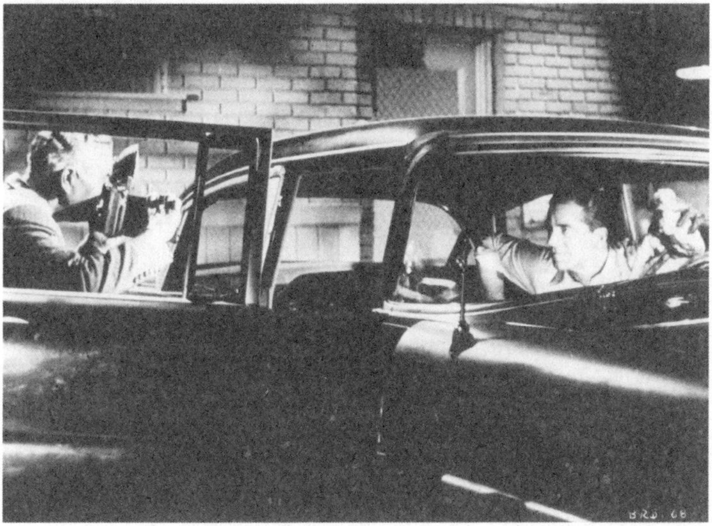

Fritz Lang, *Beyond a Reasonable Doubt*, 1956

The Phantom's Due[I]

William Klein, *La Plage de Saint-Torin* (*Saint-Torin Beach*), 1956

There is magic in motion blur [*le bougé*], the smear of movement, the ghost image [*le filé*]. "I—it—trembles, the infinite incessantly that shudders."[2] Whenever photographs incorporate the trace of visible movement, and give it a place in the image and composition, they succumb to an ambiguous force. There is, on the one hand, a raw, primal quality that brings the photographer face to face with the "real" he or she has chosen to capture. This involves chance, the unforeseen, which cannot be reduced to the essentially imaginary purity of the snapshot and its sharp, all too sharp lines that are all about belief in a transparent vision of life. But, on the other hand, nothing is less natural than these wavy lines, these thick, quivering edges that give the image a sort of second life, irreducible to the simple intent or immediacy of vision. Though it would appear to be impulse itself, motion blur is also one of photography's clearest techniques for pointing to itself as artifice, and appointing itself as art.

As such, motion blur is comparable to lack of focus, for long the extraordinary, phantasmatic aura in which generations of photographers recognized how hard it was for their craft to exist and be able to triumph over the world before it. Today, in the hands of contemporary photographers, who tend to make only relative and partial use of it, lack of focus often serves as an index of the real and the immediate: the snapshot's moral guarantee, in a way. As such, it confirms the photograph as witness, testifying to the haphazard moment that passes, and substantiating a connection to event and evidence. But out-of-focus images also allow us to see better, or rather to see what is clear in a different way. Lack of focus can even serve to illuminate the essence of the photograph, what distinguishes it, its signature—just as the pictorialists of old, faced with the rise of the snapshot, chose lack of focus as a manifest sign and affirmation of art.

If lack of focus and motion blur then affirm both the primitive and the artificial in photographs, it is because the eye as it exists neither sees truly out of focus, nor retains inscribed in itself the materialized trace of movement. The camera lens, however, this false eye, can do so, but only according to how it is used. It is therefore more profound than the eye, on which, however, everything depends. This is what motion blur foregrounds and touches in the photographer and in those who are sensitive to it. It is the eye as body, the eye becoming one (*faisant corps*) with its landscape, the body-eye—what Merleau-Ponty talked about in his last writings and what Deleuze, inspired by Bergson, invokes in his books on cinema: the mind's eye [*l'œil de l'esprit*] sliding into its matter.

Take, for example, Hervé Rabot's large-format landscapes. They seem somehow folded in on themselves, run through with a shudder that transcends the solidity of the object and spills over in a ghostly border, a sort of double of the object. The effect may be carried to abstraction, yet without ever losing a sensory quality. To achieve it, Rabot physically invests his landscapes—for example, the bottom of a pond in Brittany—with his own movements, often timing the exposures by how he jumps, runs, et cetera. He "films" at slow shutter speeds to give the same image several exposures, using 12-exposure rolls of film intended to more fully comprehend the unique image he has intuited each time. Here the body delegates to the eye none of its interior power (though it never truly does, even in the steadiest of portraits); it tries instead to exteriorize it directly, analogically, figured by the movement inscribed in the image.

Certain young photographers have for years now been developing their own strategies based essentially on lengthening exposure time in order to create, they hope, a new relationship with their camera, body, and object. Often movement is literally created, as with Rabot, or with Didier Morin, who waits patiently for the rhythm of his breathing to transmit an impulse to the landscape through the large plate camera he places on his stomach. There is also Eve Morcrette, who turns her camera so as to give her motifs a circular vibration. In some cases, bodily movement finds a relay—for example, in the photographs of Eric Hartmann, who creates images based on the movement of a passing train. In others, the body is ruled by a cold calculation, as in the photosyntheses of Krzysztof Pruszkowski and Yves Lavalette, where movement is created by the superimposition of several images dividing the exposure. More often it is a case of manipulating a preexisting movement, whether real, so to speak, or created to fit the *mise en scène*. And there, too, it can either be captured from the outside, simply allowed to be seen and situated by contrast, or incorporated from within the image in order to merge with its trajectory. Thus, at one extreme we have the massive presences of bodies or objects looming up within a defined frame (like a horse or broom in Steve Murez), and at the other, the construction/dissolution of faces and bodies in an undefined space (as in Martien van Beeck and Didier de Nayer). But in any case, whatever the pretext and the final image, it is clearly about the irruption of what the snapshot conceals. Caught, frozen in the image, movement implies a sort of internal rumbling, and, if not an encounter, at the very least a friction between the body-gaze and the reality that appears in a shudder, in a shutter. William Klein, the great progenitor of motion blur, puts it vividly when he says that the act of photography is for him "a mixture of chance and trance."[3] This speaks to a kind of physical and mental agitation produced by the body as it tries to insert itself directly into the image, in defiance of all technical mediation.

But why motion blur, all of a sudden? Why this obsession with the residue of movement—even if blurred and ghost images have always made symptomatic appearances in the history of photography, as if there had been a need to verify, regularly, that there was indeed a material element at stake, even if only by chance—a chance element that could be provoked? It is important to remember first of all that Klein was a painter before becoming a photographer, and became a filmmaker soon after the publication of his great photo album. And that "shortly before, not long after studying with Fernand Léger, he had produced an album of images made by causing various triangles, circles, and squares to move, in a dark room, on photographic paper."[4] In a brief autobiographical note from 1954, Klein mused: "Following Moholy-Nagy and Kepes, why not do figurative photography alongside abstract painting?"

Twice already in its history the photograph had been explicitly defined in relation to movement as such. The first time, with Muybridge, Marey, et al., the relation was governed by a scientific motive, that of *decomposing* movement. The second time, the motive was artistic, that of creating or *composing* movement—which is what the Bragaglia brothers did with their photo-dynamism. Working in the margins of Futurism, they systematically constructed more or less successive motion blur, endowing the photograph with the powers of abstraction and the material depth of painting. This is, generally speaking, one of the hallmarks of the avant-garde in the first third of this century (consider Dada, Surrealism, Constructivism): the attempt to cross the borders between painting, photography, and cinema, in pursuit of a political, social, and spiritual utopia. It gave rise to figures like Moholy-Nagy, with his prophecy of "cinetism," the name he accorded his photo-essays ("photograms") and the three intertwined subjects of his book: *Painting, Photography, Film* (1925). But when photography intentionally abandoned itself a third time to the passion of movement, with Klein and the photographers who, strangely, years later, are now located more or less in the aesthetic he launched, the problem was and is no longer so much to de-compose or compose movement as to *impress* it. In other words, to let it impress itself on the image, to let it make an impression, without a utopian aim and with few theoretical overtures, but with a pragmatic passion that finds a ready catalyst for new hybrids in the conditions of contemporary art.

There is in the critical conscience of postmodernism at least one thing that is positive, which is that the confrontations, the relations among the different arts occur almost organically. Moreover, the ironic stance that each is supposed to take toward the others produces a sort of positive freedom when it is not caricature, a freshness in the effects of re-working that is not simply cultural recycling. Take, for example, those photographs that I claim let themselves be impressed or imprinted by the movements of the real (or the real of movement). Yves Lavalette's *Arbre en bordure de Seine* (Tree by the Seine) strongly evokes the texture of the most Impressionist of Impressionist paintings, while the facial close-ups of Martien van Beeck urgently recall the tormented swerves of Francis Bacon. An image by Thierry Blandino—a portrait of a woman divided in a ghostly way that conjures up a succession of intermingled impressions—is quite close to certain "painterly" compositions of the Bragaglias.[5] And another of Blandino's photographs points with one of its motifs—a saxophone sliced by rays of light—to Duchamp's mobile stratifications in his *Nude Descending a Staircase* (1912, which is also in an image by Bruno Vereyken). These references—and there are doubtless many others that elude me—suggest that rather than trying to compete with painting, photography can rediscover in its own way something of what painting has already done, and thus open itself up to what it has not yet truly done.

What I love in these "motion-blurred" images, or more exactly what interests me (for I am far from loving them all, and very little truly moves me), is that, for one thing, they restore to the photograph a play with line and depth, as well as a sense of duration that goes beyond the capturing of the look and the reversal of time. They also open themselves up to the indeterminate, yet intransitive force that emanates from silent figures, a force so pregnant in large photographs. Not that such blurred photographs speak; rather, their silence is perhaps less pure, or less whole—less crazy, as Barthes would say, since motion blur draws the photograph magnetically in the direction of art, even if only to permit an essentially primitive nature to emerge.[6] In fact, motion blur condenses for expressive ends proper the drama that all figurative representation presupposes, even that of things. To grasp it, one must start from the zero degree of blur—the *shudder*—such as it appears, for example, in Klein's photograph entitled *Candy Store, Amsterdam Avenue* (1955). A child crouches before a wall composed of black and white squares and half covered with advertisements, while another child stands framed at the waist.[7] The photograph is done in such a way that the shadow of the black squares bleeds into the white squares, becoming diffuse, animating them, and spreading out over the swallowed image in a kind of swirling pattern. An effect like this accentuates, focuses, and develops the invisible shudder that runs more or less through all true photographs and forms, in the very inside of time seized and immobilized, a thin film of time in a pure state. In its own way, motion blur brings out a shudder like that caught by Klein, something between mobile and immobile, and offers up the perception of visible time—in other words, duration. It tends to have two ways of doing this. One leads toward painting, the other toward cinema. But these distinctions become more and more difficult to maintain when painting falls victim to the fascination of both the photograph and the cinema, as in all the forms of hyperrealism; or when photography merges directly with painting while inverting their respective positions (witness the recent work of Duane Michals); or when the cinema, in turn, having already suffered a crisis in story and representation, must contend with the moral and formal influence of painting, without ever failing to emphasize in any case its secret complicities with photography.

The path that leads the photograph to painting also tends to split in two. Either the effect of motion blur spreads across the entire image and affects each motif, like a paint brush grasping within the frame a homogeneous fragment of representation; such is the case with Rabot, Lavalette, Morin, Guillermin, and all those who specialize in landscape. Or the effect is restricted to a part of a motif—but a motif then abstracted from all context, an effect that evokes another tradition of painting in the Baconian portraits of Martien van Beeck and those of Didier de Nayer. In both cases it is the analogical quality of the photographic image (or better yet, its analogical quantity) that comes under fairly sharp attack: the smear of blur confers a strong code upon the "message without a code"—the photograph in its raw state[8]—and thus brings it closer to painting.

But something different happens once motion blur is contained, fragmented, and combined in the context of the entire image with elements defined by photographic analogy. If it is contained and fragmented in a variable proportion, but still limited to a highly recognizable part of the image, it is toward cinema that one tends with a blinding clarity, even if the relation is more enigmatic. Once again an old and magnificent photograph by Klein, *La Plage de Saint-Torin* (*Saint-Torin Beach*, 1956), can serve as an example.[9] A crowd sits on a beach, backs turned to the camera, with certain people turning around to look at the photographer. Closer, in the foreground, are some children. And at the left, right, and center of the image are three blurred patches, on three separate bodies, three quite different points of intensity and homogeneity. Here we witness motion blur's moment of birth, and what happens when the time that belongs to the snapshot collides with the heterogeneous matter that rebels against its realist order: time folds in on itself. It dilates, unravels, becomes divided within itself, only not with the regularity or localized effect experienced before photographs that tend toward painting, but rather with a vertiginous effect. It is as if from this collision an abyss opened up in the image, causing the captured scene to vacillate by each of its two irreconcilable edges. (Similar effects can be found in Klein's fashion photographs, and in the work of Jacques Penom, Bruce Gilden, Eric Hartmann, Claude Caroly, and Jim Bengston.) Again we have to be specific, depending on whether the gap between the two edges is sharp and clear, or, on the contrary, includes transitions that can increase the strangeness, depending on whether motion blur or the ghost image is condensed on one point or covers a larger area. Thus, in a Hartmann photograph, a train station wobbles imperceptibly on its three sides, while the central foreground and vanishing point remain in sharp focus. In the work of Penom and Caroly, by contrast, the effect is that of a hole, of breathing, of bodies inhaling space. In one of Gilden's photographs, we find a twofold scene—sharp foreground/blurred background—with these two otherwise disparate spaces bridged in a small but striking way by a remarkable hat, divided from itself, that one of the figures is wearing. All of these, along with certain photographs in Klein's couturier series, suggest that in multiplying almost impalpably, points of motion blur end up forming a kind of fabric [*trame*], even while remaining discontinuous. They thus interweave closely the effects of cinema and painting.[10]

But, one might well ask, why cinema? We are not talking about an actual material equivalence, as with painting, but rather a mental incidence. This incidence can be found on the one hand in the capacity for narrative, which affects these images insofar as a story, that is to say time, seems ready to develop between their disjointed parts. In Caroly's photographs, for example, the crinkled figure seems to exude a virtual but highly suggestive drama, even as it melts back into the fold of the image. But this cinema-effect derives just as much, I think, from the way film fractures as soon as it is manipulated, slowed down, stopped, and disseminated as still frames or photographs—in short, as soon as its *défilement* is interrupted by processes that fragment its physical and imaginary homogeneity. These processes have increasingly been integrated into the films themselves, made internal to their unfolding, if only in the way that the photograph, as material base and narrative instance, still haunts the cinema that has always fled it (an emblematic film would be Feyder's *L'image* (1923): the photo-woman as quest and odyssey). In short, just as the photo can be animated in spite of its apparent immobility, so can the cinema be interrupted and frozen to reflect its change in condition(s). The question was posed earlier: why motion blur, starting with Klein, and why today with such intensity? Not coincidentally, in the 1950s and then over the last ten years in a major way, the cinema found new ways of twisting its neck around to look at itself, and of transforming itself using elements that apparently went against its nature of illusory spectacle founded on continuity and the illusion of movement. (The use ad nauseam of the freeze-frame is one of the major signs of this.) Coming from photography, or rather from between photography and cinema, the best response would again be from Klein who, for the Centre Pompidou's major retrospective of his work in 1983, opted to project his photos on three screens in the dark, rather than hanging them on walls. This is the same man who in his recent exhibition at the Palais de Tokyo imagined a spiral *dispositif* in which each of his immense photographs could appear as a still frame of a continuous film, with the fashion series, all blurred or ghost images, disturbing the gaze like the point of blur in all photographs.

It is important here to recall how much the video image adds vertiginously to the doubly phantasmatic character of representation. Video's very principle is that of instantly reproduced time, time rendered visible by a redoubling of spaces. The effect is similar to that of persistence of vision, which retains the trace of the object for some time after the body or the camera moves (what is best shown by the use of the *paluche* in the work of both Jean-André Fieschi and Thierry Kuntzel). Video thus contributes to developing the uncertain relation between movement and immobility (like that between the sharp and the out-of-focus). This relation, of which photographic motion blur is a sign, is today the chief attribute of a metamorphosis of the image.

In a wonderful commentary on Raymond Depardon's *Correspondance new-yorkaise* (1981) Alain Bergala distinguishes between two types of photographs and photographers, both historical and structural: those who believe in reality and make the photograph an art of presence (phenomenologists, let us say); and those who only believe in the real as an impossibility and only ever figure its absence (let us call them Lacanians).[11] The photographer of motion blur, of the ghost image, the out-of-focus, does not really count as a third species, but perhaps ought to: regardless of personal tendencies, he or she enjoys the distinction of occupying in principle both positions at once. Whether this is via a physical engagement in the image (and exposure) and/or a particular attention to movement in the elaboration of the work, the photographer connects through motion blur with a matter he or she can only dream of reaching by pure transparence or by the inscription of absence. The act of blurring has a consistency that leads the photographer to believe, if not in the real, at least in some real. After all, motion blur marks the flux of time with a material deviation traced upon the transparent surface of the photographic image. Following Barthes in *Camera Lucida* (1980), one could say that motion blur seeks to specify a *punctum* that would not only be open to the uncertain drive of the spectator, but would be a regulated *punctum*, in spite of the role chance plays in its conception. Motion blur does not say: I am reality, in which you must believe. Nor does it say: I am the flaw in reality. It proposes a reality instantly doubled by a breach in relation to itself: a reconstructed sign, a sign of art that seeks to express a corporeal drive inscribing itself in a time rendered visible. This is the magic of motion blur: to seize an effect of the real, without ever taking itself for reality.

In one of the most inspired chapters in *Le Cousin Pons*, entitled "Treatise on the Occult Sciences," Balzac puts forth the idea that "[if] anyone had come and told Napoleon that a man or a building is incessantly and continuously represented by a picture in the atmosphere, that all existing objects project into it a kind of *spectre* which can be captured and perceived, he would have consigned him to Charenton as a lunatic […] And yet that is what Daguerre's discovery proved!"[12] The 19th century, which believed in ghosts, also believed in this spectral double guaranteed by the unprecedented novelty of photography. The belief was enhanced by what seemed to be the materializing of the spirits or phantoms in the images themselves. In these old photographs, the long exposures produced a dense light suffused with a sort of intermittent vibration that hinted at the movement it was impossible to pin down; this would have been the unique form of the shudder. As soon as the snapshot made it possible to freeze movement, the phantoms disappeared from the image, only to reappear later in a secular form. Through motion blur, lack of focus, and the ghost image, photography continues to pay its due to the phantom, a debt owed from birth that it seeks to settle, often at the risk of appearing forced. As Henri Michaux said, "For want of an aura, let us at least scatter our emanations."[13]

1987. Originally translated in 1995 by Lynne Kirby.

[1] The original title of the article, "La redevance du fantôme," is the French title of the 1876 Henry James story "The Ghostly Rental" [editor's note].

[2] Henri Michaux, "Pensées," *Plume* (Paris: Gallimard, 1963) 88.

[3] *Vanishing Presence*, ed. Adam D. Weinberg (Minneapolis: Walker Art Center; New York: Rizzoli, 1989) 159.

[4] Christian Caujolle, "Le témoin et le hazard," *William Klein* (Paris: Photo-Poche, C.N.P., 1985).

[5] Like "A Turning Face," 1911, in Van Deren Coke, *The Painter and the Photograph* (University of New Mexico Press, 1972) 166, or *Le Salut*, 1911, and *Un pas en avant*, 1928, in Giovanni Lista, *Photographie futuriste* (Paris: Musée d'Art Moderne de la Ville de Paris, 1981) 39 and 20.

[6] Roland Barthes, *La chambre claire* (Paris: Cahiers du cinéma-Gallimard-Seuil, 1980) 180–181 [*Camera Lucida*: Reflections on Photography, trans. Richard Howard (New York: Hill and Wang, 1982) 113–115].

[7] *William Klein*, photograph no. 9.

[8] Barthes, "Le message photographique," *Communications* 1 (1961) 128 ["The Photographic Message," *Image, Music, Text*, trans. Stephen Heath (New York: Hill and Wang, 1977) 17].

[9] *William Klein*, photograph no. 46.

[10] But clearly it is not so simple. The effect of a general vacillation that spreads out over the whole of a Hartmann photograph (for example, trees and landscape) evokes *at the same time* the type of quivering image found in early Danish films and in those of Stiller, as well as in certain French avant-garde films of the 1920s (Delluc and Epstein in particular), and in the paintings of Turner. As for limited effects of motion blur, they obviously recall—even if they are not figuratively significant—the disquieting presence of anamorphosis in painting.

[11] Alain Bergala, *Les absences du photographe* (Paris: Libération/Editions de l'Etoile—"Ecrit sur l'image" collection, 1981) 46–52. [Editor's note: Bergala's text and Depardon's photos and captions were published together in a single volume on facing pages.]

[12] Honoré de Balzac, *Le Cousin Pons* (Paris: Folio, Gallimard, 1973) 146 [*Cousin Pons (Poor Relations, Part 2)*, trans. Herbert J. Hunt (Harmondsworth: Penguin Books, 1968) 131–132].

[13] "Faute d'aura, au moins éparpillons nos effluves." Michaux, "Mouvements," *Face aux verrous* (Paris: Gallimard, 1967) 19.

Bruce Gilden, *New York*, 1983

Jim Bengston, *Slow Motion*, 1977

Didier de Nayer, *Claire*, 1983

Eric Hartmann, *The Train Journey* … , 1979

The Crystal Duration

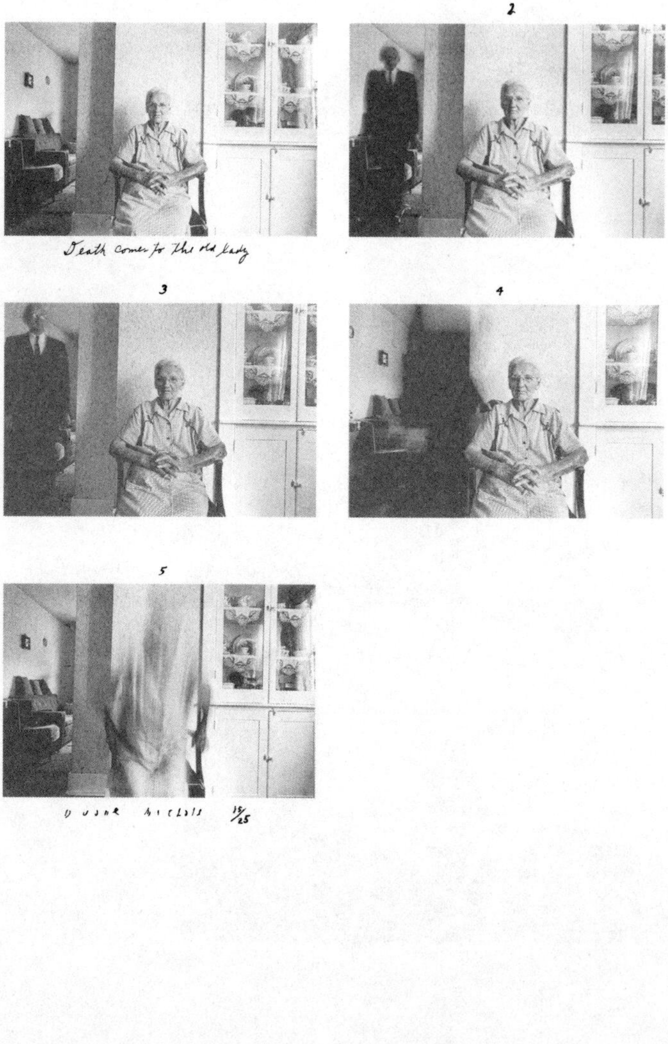

Duane Michals, *Death Comes to the Old Lady*, 1969

The sequence is both the strangest and most natural distortion inflicted upon the supposed essence of photography. Natural because, after all, a roll of film with six, 12, or 36 shots is never anything other than a sort of pre-programmed sequence. [William] Klein—him again—is fully conscious of this when he decides to pass his movie camera over his contact sheets in a falsely nonchalant manner so as to show us the difference between a bad sequence—one that is not sought for its own sake, that is just a series of approximations—and a real photograph (*Contacts*, 1983, 13'). In this sense the photograph, which was initially unique—at the time when there were only plates, not rolls of film—never stops returning to its essence every time it ignores the possibility of several shots of the same event in order to focus on a single image. Klein played around with this paradox again at his last exhibition[1] when he presented a gigantic loop of images whose resemblance to a film was all the greater because it was divided into groups of two, three, or four images taken in one location and connected by a unity of event, in the absence of any stronger relationships of form or narrative. It is clear then that the idea of the photographic sequence, split as it is between the representation of film as a virtually infinite sequence and the search for the unique moment, is not a clear one. This could be the reason why the sequence, after having been relatively absent throughout the already long history of photography (except perhaps when that history coincided with the prehistory of cinema) now arouses more interest, since we are living in a time whose energy comes from confusion, the dissolution of singularities, even when they are still substantiated by a real separation between technical conditions, as is the case between photography and cinema.

The first interest of the movement-sequence is in obliging the sequence to be clearer about what it is: a series of related images that have no reason to be related unless that relation is strong. Take Kertész's seminal sequence. Six images: a horse on the ground, in front of a cart; his harness is removed; when he is once again upright the harness is put back on. Kertész is not interested in movement as such (the fall, and the moment when the horse gets back up), probably to avoid the Marey-Muybridge effect. The realism of his sequence, however, does not keep it from resembling an excerpt of still frames taken from a virtual film: a film of only relative interest that would deprive the scene of the virtue of the snapshot, the truly unique moment, without offering in return a formal or fictional principle that would justify its selection. The photographic sequence—which is precisely not a film, a film that therefore never really has time for it—only tolerates the exception, a plastic one, such as a motion-blurred sequence (Jacques Penom's photographs of staircases come close, but they do not represent a single movement, unlike what Duane Michals does in three images with Warhol's portrait) or a dramatic sequence (except that one needs the heightened drama of logical emotions, and Michals is an accomplished dramatist).

The movement-sequence must be elliptical, intermittent, in other words marking phases that generate massive spaces into which the imagination may penetrate and start functioning, in relation to both a before and an after—unlike what happens with the isolated photograph, which is nothing but a dilated moment, or time turned toward nostalgia and death. Barthes noticed that "the single photograph […] is very rarely (that is, only with much difficulty) comic" because comedy requires movement, because "[t]he sequence (and the sequence alone) offers an effect of comedy which emerges, according to a familiar procedure, from the repetition and variation of the attitudes."[2] And it is true that the movement-sequence on its own tends to be comic: we can see this with someone like Ton Huijbers as well as with Michals. Comic in two ways. First of course because of the intrinsic strength of the idea that is generally concentrated in the final, more or less surprising image, almost inevitably programming a look back at the previous images—for example in Michals' *Chance Meeting* (*Rencontre fortuite*, 1970), where the effect is as discreet as possible, the reversal that in the sixth image suddenly focuses the point of view or rather the point of the gaze, reserved until then for the first character, on the second, inviting us to determine how that became possible, in other words to understand that since the beginning there has been no change in the frame and that this is what gives this doubling its effectiveness. But there is something else, something more subtle about the sequence that makes it comic, or rather comical, which has to do with the effect of gaps in the movement from one image to the other, with both the intellectual and physical rhythm of the jerkiness imposed upon the body. There is therefore a Keaton effect in Michals' work, not so much because he approaches cinematic continuity as because Keaton knew better than anyone how to play with the effects of corporeal discontinuity, both from one shot to another and within a single shot. Through its ability to maintain in this way a virtual timeframe between its phases, a timeframe that neither tends toward illusion nor toward duration, but more toward the logical abstraction of cycles and of metamorphoses (what Deleuze calls "the crystals of time"[3]), the sequence gets its magic strength and its utterly unique rhythm that is so hard to fathom.

But the movement-sequence can also integrate duration as such into the unfolding of logical time, and it is probably never more beautiful than when it manages to do so. Motion blur is what makes it possible. We see it emerging in its unfinished state in the portrait of Warhol, which tells no other story than the pure invasion of the snapshot by the succession of blur. We see it coming like *Death Comes to the Old Lady* (1969), in a paradoxical moment of life. Look how in the fourth image, the man glimpsed in the second at the end of the hall suddenly becomes a shadow that blends into the setting because an event occurs, is ready to occur. And how that event, making itself known through motion blur, changes bodies, pulling the old motionless lady out of her seat, in a movement whose meaning we would never know if the title didn't specify it, as though in contradiction to what we see, since although "death comes to the old lady," we get the feeling that this is the condition under which life comes to photography. As though honoring in every way Blanchot's beautiful title, *L'Arrêt de mort* (1948).[4]

"If Duane Michals has made use of sequences so often, it is not because he sees in them a form capable of reconciling the instantaneous nature of photography with the continuity of time in order to tell a story. It is rather to show through photography that although time and experience never stop their game with each other, they are not of the same world. And though time may well bring changes, aging, death, the emotion-thought is stronger: it alone can make [time's] unseen wrinkles visible."[5]

1987. Translated in 2011 by Allyn Hardyck.

[1] The exhibition referenced here is the one presented in 1985-1986 at the *Centre national de la photographie*, at the time located in the Palais de Tokyo in Paris [editor's note].

[2] Roland Barthes, "Le message photographique" *Communications* 1 (1961) 133 ["The Photographic Message," *Image, Music, Text*, trans. Stephen Heath (New York: Hill and Wang, 1977) 25].

[3] Gilles Deleuze, *L'image-temps* (Paris: Minuit, 1985) 92–128 [*Cinema 2: The Time-Image*, trans. Hugh Tomlinson and Robert Galeta (Minneapolis MN: University of Minnesota, 1989) 68–97]. Deleuze summarizes his idea as follows: "[T]here is a crystalline regime which is that of the time-image. Having only re-connections, it proceeds by irrational divisions and substitutes the power of the false as becoming for the model of truth." "Sur le régime cristallin," *Hors-cadre* 4 (1986) 44–45 ["On the 'Crystalline Regime'," trans. David Rodowick, *Art & Text* 34 (Spring 1989) 21]

[4] Maurice Blanchot, *L'arrêt de mort*, Gallimard, 1948 [*Death Sentence*, trans. Lydia Davis (Barrytown NY: Station Hill, 1978)].

[5] Michel Foucault, "La pensée, l'émotion," preface to the catalogue of the Duane Michals retrospective (Paris: Musée d'Art moderne de la Ville de Paris, 1982) VII.

"I Am an Image"[1]

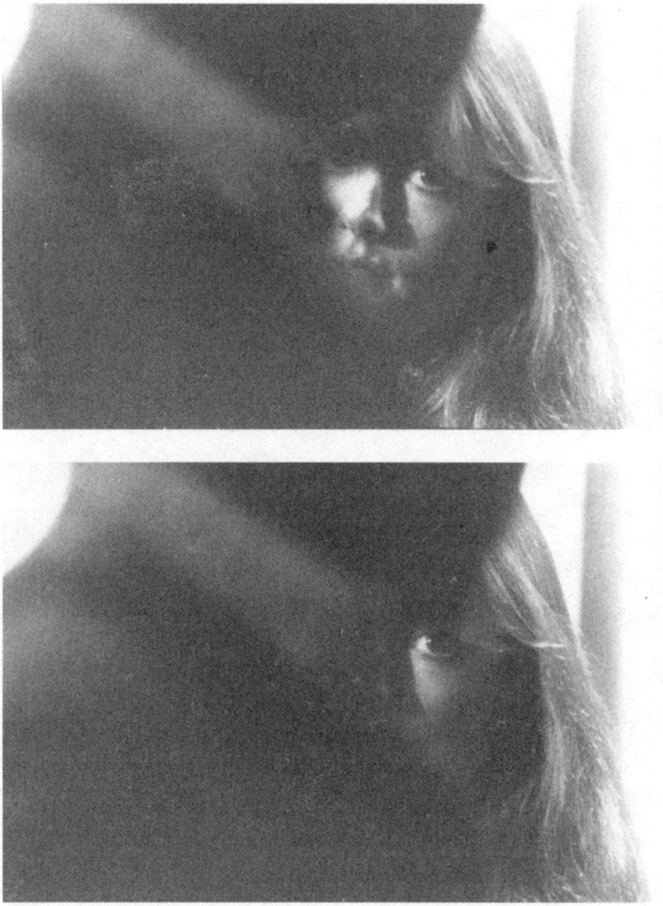

Jean-Luc Godard, *Sauve qui peut (la vie)* (*Every Man for Himself*), 1979

The essential novelty of *Sauve qui peut (la vie)* (*Every Man for Himself*, Godard, 1979) (already suggested in *France/tour/détour/deux/enfants*, 1978) resides in the displacement to which the cinema is subjected. Here, for the first time, the curse of analogy, of the regular reproduction of movement, is brought to an end. Beyond the pure, all too pure division of experimental fiction, the very notion of "truth 24 times per second" attacks itself, destroys itself, recomposes its body born of decomposition, composes a fiction at once different and the same, uncertain not because it hesitates over what road to follow, but because its road constantly teeters over the abyss of a spontaneous perversion of the mechanized illusion of movement.

To create this new kind of fiction, a mere eighteen orchestrated "skids" [variations on stop-action moments] are sufficient. These are sometimes very close to each other, practically forming miniature series: from the first series of shots of Denise on her bicycle to the image of Paul's body as he collapses against the fender of the car, while watching Cecile walk away with her mother. But "shot" is not the right word: the shift toward painting takes place by means of a redistribution, which may now be impossible to analyze, between shot and still frame.

Here, in order, are the 18 stop-action moments—but I may be mistaken, taken in by the excessive naturalness of these breaks which are so much a part of the new nature of the image that soon they will no doubt be impossible to enumerate: Denise riding her bicycle on the mountain road—the Hornussen players on the field during the dialogue between Denise and Piaget—Denise walking away after her talk with Piaget on the field—Piaget's hands as they manipulate the lines of type—Denise on her bicycle once more—the woman slapped by the two motorcyclists as Denise waits for the train—Cecile and her ball on the playing field—Paul and Denise embracing in front of the television building—cars moving on the road at night (after Paul's dinner with Cecile and her mother)—Paul moving toward Isabelle in the line outside the theater—the cars once again (presumably during that same night, when Paul sleeps with Isabelle)—Isabelle cornered by the two pimps who attack her—a man and a woman meeting on the street (while Isabelle does her thing with Monsieur Personne, "Mr. Nobody")—Isabelle and the landscape, when she shows her ass to Monsieur Personne—passing landscape after images of Isabelle driving—Paul's embrace of/assault on Denise in the apartment—Paul meets Cecile and her mother by chance, kissing Cecile—he backs away and falls against a moving car.

The shock-waves produced by the image of that collapsing body are carried by words, by Paul's voice fading away or dying or becoming immemorial, doubly fictive, attributing a meaning to the fiction: "A bit foolishly I began to think... I'm not dying now... my life has not just passed before my eyes... I'm not dying now... since I've seen... nothing..." SEEN NOTHING, at the very instant when we, on the other hand, have seen too much, when the edges of the screen seem to collapse inward under the vibration of space-times internal to the *défilement*, stripped of its mastery. It is when "I" is (am) dying that the images unfold, differently, like the condensed film of an impossible life, like the possibility demanded of cinema that it reinvent life. (Paul) Godard must die from (in) the image so that (Jean-Luc) Godard may be reborn into cinema. A privilege granted, begged from art when all else fails; art conceived once again in relation to death, the transmutation of death warded off by a new form—but at the same time, a thwarting of the illusion that is the hallmark of the religions of art. Cinema dies to itself and transforms itself, doing away with the last refuge that identified it with the realism of representation: no more "cinema is life," guaranteed by the naturalness of movement; at the same time, a refusal of the henceforth all too simple "that's only cinema" (cinema is not life); the reversed alibi of realism, built upon the code of movement; an appeal to "save (your) life, if you can [*sauve qui peut (la vie)*]," by modeling the moving image on the basis of its death, where everything is reborn, between cinema and photography—"real life"—by reconciling the fraternal rivals. "Cain and Abel, cinema and video," cinema always begun anew.

("I exist more as images than as a real human being, since my only life consists in making them. And when I say that cinema is more important than life, that in a way is what those close to me have blamed me for: 'You don't care about food, about sports...' But I say that I care about filming food and that's important to me. And since there's something in life that takes place there, I say I'm a representative of life. It's a life that doesn't exist. When Rimbaud said, 'Real life is elsewhere,' he wasn't just playing with words—that 'elsewhere' is also the beauty of life. Cinema is in the means of communication, it is in this 'also.'"[2])

But that death is also, emphatically, the death of a man: of the hero (or what remains of him). The power of Godard's film, its enormous and violent effect, comes from the way it crosses (among other things, but these two in particular) the battle between images with the battle between the sexes. During that final whirling of instants frozen like an eternity in movement, the voice of his ex-wife takes over as Paul's voice fades away: "What are you looking at? It's none of our business now. Come on, Cecile, let's go."[3] And Cecile goes, fatherless, toward life, where images, as if spontaneously, compose themselves in their decomposition:

on the road, for example, where Denise moves forward, without a man, without any Paul, as if propelled by the force of her own words at last reconquered (her projected book), accompanied by landscape—images, fractured lines and colors.

1

2

3

4

5

6

7

8

9

10

11

12

13

14

15

16

These frames, which are frozen in more or less developed series, are not really determined by any causality. Their power, rhythmic and passionate, comes from their being linked to the quasi-neutrality of the gaze itself—its virtuality. Every image can, could, always stop, fragment itself (Piaget's hands, the ball-players, the cars). But these moments are for the most part united and divided around two possibilities that are indissolubly linked: exaltation of woman and aggression against woman, according to the storyline that opposes Paul to the series of feminine figures—Isabelle, Denise, his ex-wife, Cecile—who are interchangeable and joined in the circuit of dependence-independence, physical and psychic mobility, and historical positivity. (Putting it more precisely, we can say: Isabelle beaten emphasizes, of course, aggression, while Denise on her bicycle emphasizes exaltation; but there is also, in the frame, in the way the actresses play the scene, in the stop-action that works through these moments, an indissociable mixture of aggression and exaltation.) He being a man and they women, they run away, watched and violated by the image, in the image; and he dies of it. As if one were the revenge of the other, the consequence of a socio-historical obsession and guilt: the price to be paid by the one who speaks, the man who directs, desires, and thrashes.

Given all this, one may find surprising at first that the extended prostitution scene escapes this questioning of the *défilement*, this fiction of the stopped image focusing on woman. But one soon realizes that the scene mimes the decomposition of movement by its exaggerated reproduction of the cinema *dispositif*. As Bonitzer has pointed out, all the movements of the film seem to converge in this sexual montage, which becomes the analogue and the emblem of cinema itself.[4] The four linked bodies participate in the production of an image organized by the CEO/"film director" ("You, you put some lipstick on me, but only when he licks your ass... and you, Thierry, you lick her asshole only when the other one sucks you, and you, you suck each time I touch your tits with my foot..."). They produce an image and the sound that goes with it ("Okay, we've got the image, now we'll take care of the sound"). And when they start up again, when the chain functions with image and sound together, the CEO/"film director" tells Isabelle: "And afterwards you'll put some lipstick on me, just once, and if I smile at you, you kiss me." But he doesn't smile. He cannot smile. Death does not smile. What is in question here is the production of an impossible image, one from which cinema has derived its imaginary power ever since Edison's famous close-up of John C. Rice and May Erwin[5]: a kiss, or the image of two bodies reconciled. The decomposition of the image renders the kiss impossible. Save the image, if you can [*Sauve qui peut (l'image)*]: the fragmented stop-action makes it impossible for bodies to come together, as in the fable about Achilles and the tortoise. Paradoxically the stop-action doesn't stop, making impossible the imaginary pause that the image needs in order to satisfy its false plenitude.

The same thing happens when, in counterpoint to the other extended prostitution scene between Isabelle and Monsieur Personne, we see a man and a woman meet on the street: their meeting moves in brief fragments to a near-kiss, to the point of almost achieving the natural and unrealizable contact between bodies and between the sexes. And the same thing happens during Paul and Denise's embrace, so incredibly exacerbated by the fiction of the decomposed shots which never seem to cease being born and reborn one from the other, composing a partition of the space-time of love, panicked by its own indeterminacy. And again, toward the end of the film there is a counterpart to this embrace that almost immediately turns into a confrontation: it is the embrace-assault in the apartment (Paul, sitting at the table, suddenly jumps on Denise), which projects the two bodies onto the ground in breathtaking fragments. "We feel like touching, but we can only do it by hitting each other" (Paul to Isabelle, when she comes into the apartment). In the same way the images seem to hit each other, musically, pictorially, striking each other admirably and thus making impossible any continuity of movement which would produce—when it becomes a matter of bodies and sexes—an imaginary ideality that has simply ceased to exist.

By carrying it to an extreme, Godard explodes the notion dear to Bazin that it is impossible to represent an erotic relationship in cinema.[6] The kiss becomes unrepresentable because at the other extreme the sexual image speaks with a documentary crudeness that Bazin considered contradictory to the imaginary vocation of cinema as he conceived the latter. The impossible mythical kiss of the prostitution sequence is the counterpart of the clinical image that precedes it: the whore Marilyn-Nicole climbing under the table to suck off the man with the "ivory face" and offering her ass to the image like the close-up of an idealized face. (It is not a close-up, for that would come too close to pornography and would kill the effect; but the wider frame, through what it shows, functions as a close-up. It is a sexual appeal, but idealized, concentrated, as for example in the Hollywood tradition of close-ups on the woman's face: the moment of the kiss, or its sadistic counterpart, murder, offered, promised, permitted to the spectator.) An extreme violence inflicted on women, again and always—a violence whose historical critique is provided by the dialogue. ("You know what they called women in the Middle Ages?—Witches.—And what else?—Horizon of the devil, ember of hell.") But it is the violence of a full and continuous image that a stop-action series couldn't interrupt, since in a sense the freeze-frames throughout the film function as a response to it: the response of representation pushed to its extreme by the cold phantasm of excessive power, "an immense and irremediable despair."[7]

The rebirth of the image, this move from the fiction of cinema toward a painting-writing freed from the deceptive plenitude of imagination prescribed by the *défilement* of the machine, thus takes place in the historical gap opened up between two gazes: Cecile's gaze at her father dying in the image, to the image, of the image ("What are you looking at? It's none of our business now"); and the unbearable gaze at that ass, which comes back toward the spectator with all the violence of an overpowering vision and, quite literally, looks at him, at me. Like Isabelle's unblinking eye, isolated by the face of Godard-Dutronc, filling up the frame, when she comes on to him by asking: "Do you feel like going to the movies?"

1982. Originally translated in 1983 by Susan Suleiman.

[1] Jean-Luc Godard, "Propos rompus," *Cahiers du Cinéma* 316 (October 1980) 15.
[2] Godard 15.
[3] "*Qu'est-ce que tu regardes? Ça ne nous regarde plus. Allez, tu viens, Cécile?*" [In French the phrase "Ça ne nous regarde plus" can be translated as "It's none of our business now" or "That doesn't concern us anymore." But in this context, the literal sense alsao seems relevant: "That (thing/corpse/gaze) is no longer looking at us." Editor's note.]
[4] Pascal Bonitzer, "Peur et commerce," *Cahiers du Cinéma* 316: 6.
[5] Lo Duca, *L'érotisme au cinéma* (Paris: Pauvert, 1957) 9.
[6] André Bazin, "En marge de 'L'érotisme au cinéma'," *Qu'est-ce que le cinéma ?* vol. III (Paris: Cerf, 1961) 68–82 ["Marginal Notes on *Eroticism in the Cinema*," *What Is Cinema?* vol. 2, trans. Hugh Gray (Berkeley: University of California Press, 1971) 169–175].
[7] Isabelle's voice, off-screen, at the end of the scene: "I looked at that face of ivory, and I saw there an expression of somber pride, of fierce power, of abject terror, and also of an immense and irremediable despair."

Jean-Luc Godard, *Sauve qui peut (la vie)* (*Every Man for Himself*), 1979

The Film Stilled

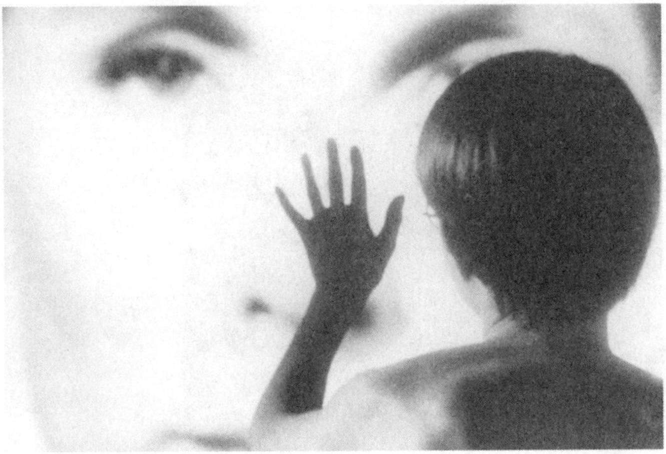

Ingmar Bergman, *Persona*, 1966

If I should ever say to any moment:
Tarry, remain! –you are so fair!
Then you may lay your fetters on me,
Then I will gladly be destroyed!
—Goethe, *Faust* (Faust to Mephistopheles)[1]

[I]t would have been delightful to possess good photographic prints (taken on the spot) of *Joshua Bidding the Sun Stand Still*, for example.
—Auguste Villiers de l'Isle-Adam, *L'Eve Future* (Thomas Alva Edison)[2]

This text is partly born of momentary encounters, and moments of confusion. Drawn by the desire to grasp a mode of presence in some films that could be called (in a word) "photographic," I found myself naturally carried along by what Barthes was able to say or suggest about it, at the risk of occasional indecisiveness: the result of the sort of limits that he himself tried to approach between photography and cinema, between image and language.

At the same time I was reading and rereading Deleuze, fascinated by the extraordinary power of the shift he was bringing about in thinking on cinema. We could say he suddenly tore everything away from cinema, in order to return it to us more whole, more present, transformed. I could also not help but be struck by the way in which he specifically excluded the terms that to me seemed appropriate for translating my impressions of the "photographic." I could have left it at that. Or made it the subject of my own commentary. But through a barely mastered logic, the two things ended up blending together to such a point that, in that separation with Deleuze's wording, I discovered a better way of defining what concerned me. The result was a somewhat strange fusion, which could leave the impression that I am trying to take the opposite tack from those ideas that helped me move forward and better understand myself. So I decided to write these few words in order to dispel, if not the strangeness of the text (I would have had to rewrite it far too much, and almost separate it from itself, which seemed wrong to me), at least those misleading aspects of its effects that remain.

There is one category of time not considered by Gilles Deleuze in his dynamic taxonomy of images: the interruption of movement. The often unique, fugitive, yet perhaps decisive instant when cinema seems to be fighting against its very principle, if this is defined as the movement-image.

Still, we need to distinguish between the two "sides" of movement. First, there is the movement produced inside the image itself, which seems to reproduce at any given moment the conditions of natural perception. In *Creative Evolution*,[3] Bergson calls this false movement, in which he sees only a succession of immobile images (still frames) directed toward the production of an abstract time (the *défilement*).[4] In its earliest stages, says Deleuze, cinema had not yet invented its own time, as it would soon do through editing, the mobile camera, and the advent of multiple takes. So Bergson cannot discern in this the movement-image, whose terms he laid out ten years earlier in *Matter and Memory*[5]: an image that goes beyond both the illusion of divisible space and that of abstract time in order to make of real movement—and thereby of each instant, indivisible in itself—a mobile slice [*coupe*] of a perpetually open and changing entity; that is, the expression of "duration itself, in that this duration continually changes."[6] Such is the second side of movement, which authenticates the first and allows Deleuze to bring Bergson into his attempt to define cinema.

But what happens when the instant, this "immobile slice [*coupe*] of movement," sets itself apart through an interruption of movement—the movement in the image as well as the movement of the image itself (unless this is an interruption of the *défilement* which never stops)? Is there not a contradiction in terms here, a flaw in their circularity? One could reply that such instants always derive from a sort of internal editing; they're still caught in the duration, they're caught in the film as a whole—of which they remain mobile slices [*coupes*]. Of course. But how can their difference be effaced, how can they be collapsed into the very thing from which they derive their difference? Rather, isn't it possible to pull or to lure the film, cinema, toward the point they designate? This leads to bringing the second side of movement back around to the first, which has now become immobile movement. It amounts to modifying the terms used in defining film; or, shifting from movement to time. This is what Peter Wollen does in his discussion of Chris Marker's *La Jetée* (1963) where precisely the opposite happens: a single real movement—the woman half-opening her eyes—breaks the series of photographs. He thus concludes that "movement is not a necessary feature of film," that "in fact, the impression of movement can be created by the jump-cutting of still images."[7]

But isn't this what Deleuze does in his admirable description of the shift from the movement-image to the time-image, the shift from an indirect image of time expressed through movement to the expression of time itself that characterizes modem cinema? Yes and no. Yes, because through this he accounts for the major shift in perspective, which permits Peter Wollen, for example, to redefine cinema around *La Jetée*, and which allows *La Jetée* to exist. No, because in his overall schema of time he is nevertheless conscious of the breach that has been opened by the presence of immobile matter and the interruption of movement. To set up this perspective I will begin with an idea that was already known but was reintroduced by Deleuze to describe cinema as movement-image: the notion of any-instant-whatever. Cinema "is the system which reproduces movement as a function of any-instant-whatever that is, as a function of equidistant instants, selected so as to create an impression of continuity."[8] He immediately remarks, however, that this hasn't stopped cinema from thriving on privileged instants, which Eisenstein aptly called "pathetic." But these privileged instants are in no way poses or postures, general or transcendent, comparable for example to those that characterize the image of a horse's gallop in antiquity. Rather, like Marey and Muybridge's equidistant snapshots, these instants are points immanent to movement; they cannot help but be *remarkable* or *singular* (as opposed to *ordinary* and *regular*) while nonetheless remaining any-instant-whatever. Then isn't the freeze-frame (or freeze inside the image)—with its specific ambiguity that interrupts the apparent movement without breaking up the movement of the *défilement*—one privileged instant among many, that is to say, any-instant-whatever? Or, could it be a privileged instant that would no longer really be any-instant-whatever?

I do not think that there is one set answer to this question. The analysis can only be historical (the history of the freeze-frame remains to be written)[9] or singular (it would then depend on the work or film). The very most one can do, as a preliminary to what follows, is trace the lines of a genealogy. It is obviously very difficult to conceive of the freeze-frame in primitive cinema, which was more concerned with the movement of bodies (if examples do exist, their status would have to be clarified). Conversely, the development of silent film added the freeze-frame to the list of possible tropes. One sees this in Vertov, perhaps the first to use it on a large scale, in *The Man With The Movie Camera* (1929), and in René Clair's famous *Paris qui dort* (*The Crazy Ray*, 1924).[10] These images strike us today because half a century of film has gone by in the meantime. Yet, it seems that the freeze-frame was at the time only one way among many to manage a film-time that was obsessed with conquering its movements. One can see it as a form, admittedly extreme, yet similar to other processes such as slow and fast motion, reverse motion, and so on. Speaking of the decompositions of movement in *Sauve qui peut (la vie)* (*Every Man for Himself*, 1980), Godard pinpointed the possibility, unique to silent film, of varying the speed of the apparent movement of the film. Despite his desire for "other speeds," Godard himself can only slow down the movement and freeze it, whereas cinema, because it was silent and new, was free to vary it.[11]

In sound cinema, where representation is subjected to the homogenizing effects of speech and sound, time unwinds in a more or less linear manner. The freeze-frame is (virtually) foreign to "classical" cinema, which has other ways of managing what fascinates in immobility and reversals of time.[12] At the other end of the spectrum, in advertising, in music videos (and in films that use them as models)—in the era of video-as-transaction and computer graphics [*images de synthèse*]—the stilled image is one form of exchange between images, as vague as it is general, and whose nature remains to be specified. But in the meantime, the stilled image has acted and still does act as a medium for the relentless search for another time, for a break in time into which modern cinema (this cinema of time that came into being after and because of the war, through neorealism and the Nouvelle Vague) has perhaps fallen while searching for its most intimate secret. Serge Daney remarked along these lines that "Truffaut has a great idea when he ends his first film, *Les quatre cents coups* (*The 400 Blows*, 1959) with a freeze-frame of Jean-Pierre Léaud facing the sea [... It is] a way of returning the film to its skeleton of fixed images, like a corpse to the ashes that in any case it is (ashes to ashes, frames to frames ...)."[13] For film theory, among other things, the time opened up here becomes that of film analysis and the question of the still frame (two ways of stopping the film); a time that is also joined with that of photography, to which many have wanted either to compare or contrast film.

It is striking to note that in his description of movement Deleuze has only one idea about photography: as one of the decisive factors in the birth of film, he designates "not merely the photograph, but the snapshot (the long-exposure photograph [*photo de pose*] belongs to the other lineage)."[14] By "other lineage" he is referring to the "poses" or the "general postures" that, in the ancient and classical view of the world, were used to recompose movement " from formal transcendent elements" (once again the example of the horse's gallop). So, historically, but also formally, the long-exposure photograph would be opposed to that of the snapshot which was to become the essential material of cinema. Roland Barthes, for whom every photograph is in the final analysis a pose, thought the very same thing.[15]

The contrast between Barthes' view and Deleuze's theorization is worth reflecting upon. In the chapter from *The Time-Image* that takes up and expands the opening theses of *The Movement-Image*, Deleuze is opposed to anything that tends to immobilize the film. He singles out in particular the semiological gaze that, in likening the film image to an utterance, works like a suspension of movement.[16] More fundamentally, he explains that "a direct presentation of time does not imply the stopping of movement, but rather the promotion of aberrant movement." By this he means a very autonomous movement, one that testifies directly to a time anterior to "all normal movement defined by motivity [*motricité*]."[17] He adds that the movement-image already contains within itself this aberrant movement that is brought to light and worked by modern cinema. In short, Deleuze develops the idea of a flawless meshing of movement and time, where discontinuities and ruptures are integrated into a continuous expansion. He speaks of a modulation, an act of the Real itself that excludes any interruption, any overly privileged instant and any instance that might risk being fixed on transcendent elements.

For his part, Barthes tried to focus on an aberrant movement of another type in film: "the third meaning" (which he compares to the "aberration" that obliged Saussure to hear the enigmatic voice of the anagram in Latin verse).[18] This "obtuse meaning"—as opposed to the "obvious meaning," where signification originates—comes from Barthes' encounter with certain still frames. It is fragmentary, localized, unpredictable and deliberately subjective, and its aim is primarily to be indifferent to and even contradict film movement, in its unfolding [*déroulement*] as well as its *défilement*. It seems that one can reach the obtuse meaning only through the image that is brought to a standstill, even scattered (like the shuffling of cards). And yet the "third meaning" may be said to constitute what Barthes calls the "filmic": a kind of utopic virtuality caught in the very movement of the film, but against the grain. Neither photography nor painting can bring this out because they lack the elements of diegesis. This shows to what extent Barthes is seeking a paradoxical object: a meaning prior to all signification, irreducible to articulated language which is nonetheless its vehicle and to which it is opposed. Barthes leaves open the contradiction that initially led him to seek the "third meaning" outside of film in order then to exhume it from inside.

In *Camera Lucida*, Barthes reformulates a similar opposition, this time concerning photography. Here, the *studium* and the *punctum* take over from the "obvious meaning" and the "obtuse meaning": the first leans toward the meaning of the photograph, its theme, its visible signified; the second designates the irrational, unnamable fragment that fascinates. This essentially scattered affect nevertheless comes together and finally can be said to assume its full meaning in the presence/absence of a single image: that of his dead mother. At this point, ultimate because it is unique to him, Barthes discovers in the singularity of his experience what he had earlier expressed as the fundamental rupture photography introduces into representational arts: a reversal of time that turns it into the tool of the "it has been." The very free and powerful affect elicited by the photograph lies then in its intimacy with death. The snapshot turns back into a pose, a pause of time. The moment it captured, no matter how ordinary, thus takes on an extreme singularity—a transcendence?—that comes from stopping movement, from this interruption of time. In *Camera Lucida* Barthes goes back to his familiar opposition—well prior to his conception of the "third meaning"—between film and photography: one a simple supplier of illusion the other inviting a quest for hallucination. This opposition was fundamental for Barthes. It makes it difficult to relate the freeze-frame, producer of the "third meaning," to the more fundamental stop produced by the photograph itself in relation to film.

It seems to me that one might nonetheless be tempted, in light of these possible formulations, to put forward the idea of film as photography, that is, as grasped through the specter of photography. My question could then be reformulated: what happens to film when the snapshot becomes both the pose and the pause of film? Isn't it the unique privilege of the freeze-frame to bring back, in the film's movement (in the movement of certain films), the photographic, the essence of the still frame [*le photogrammatique*]? Even better: that essence as photographic? Not the still frame torn out of the film, or utopically doubling what the film tells, as Barthes saw it, but the still frame surging up from photography, the overwhelming proof of the photographic immersed in the film, forcing itself into the meaning and the thread of its story. This also means asking: what kinds of instants does the interruption of movement imply? To what kinds of instants is it related?

I.

Let us start with a little-known film by Rossellini, *La macchina ammazzacattivi* (*The Machine that Kills Bad People*, 1948), less poignant yet in a way much more surprising than *Roma, città aperta* (*Rome, Open City*, 1945) or *Viaggio in Italia* (*Journey to Italy*, 1953). Above all, the film invites a reconsideration of those films because, in a way, it is their counterproof: it opens up to cinema the perspective of divided time, rather than that of time as a unifying principle in creation, an idea which André Bazin helped to establish. Although it seems to have been a minor film for Rossellini (he didn't even finish the shooting), it has no less resonance for his subsequent reflections on cinema.[19] The decor is literally put in place by hand: the hand of artifice, emphatically theatrical, serious yet playful, so that one knows what to expect, as if to foil in advance the too great credit given to any belief in reality, given to anything that leads to cinema being taken for real life.

The action takes place in a small fishing village in southern Italy, where the Americans landed during the war. The mayor, backed up by an Italian-American who returned there a few years earlier, has real estate plans: he would like to use a possible ministerial endowment to buy the "castle" overlooking the sea, and turn it into a tourist complex. The project is not well received by the people of the village: everyone has different plans for the money. As for Donna Maria, owner of the castle, she wants to give her money to the poor. The castle also serves as a place of worship: the ashes of the dead are stored there after a brief stay at the cemetery, which is too small to accommodate them.

Into this situation comes a strange old man who asks the photographer Celestino for a night's lodgings. Celestino is the (living) memory of the village; linked with Donna Maria, he is conservative, pious, superstitious. He shows the

1

2

3

4

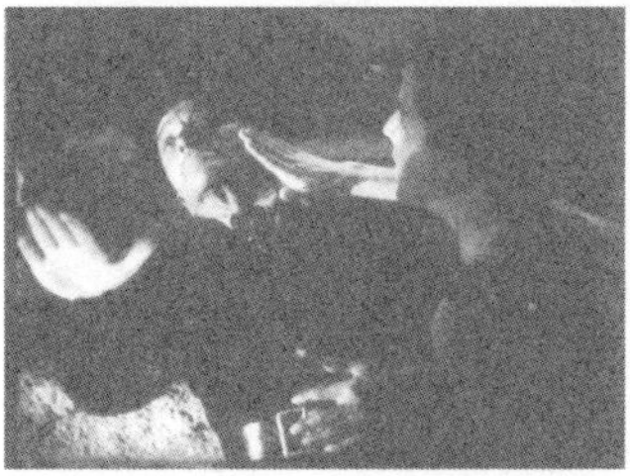

5

6

7

8

9

10

Roberto Rosselini, *La macchina ammazzacattivi (The Machine that Kills Bad People)*, 1948 old man "the photographs of two generations" that cover the walls of his studio and rails against Agostino, the policeman, who tried that very afternoon to stop him from photographing the procession honoring St. Andrew, patron saint of the village. The old man asks: "Do you have a picture of him? We're going to make him keep his peace." Celestino pins the photograph to the wall, and the old man adds: "You have to photograph this picture." Celestino does just this and the old man concludes: "My goal is to destroy the wicked." We immediately hear noises, murmuring. Celestino runs outside: he sees Agostino on a terrace, his arm raised in the fascist salute, in exactly the same position as in the photograph. When touched, he falls dead to the ground. Celestino returns to his studio. The old man is gone. He takes down the photographs, hides it; and finding on the ground a negative of the photograph he had taken of St. Andrew during the procession the day before, he recognizes the old man and cries out: "Jesus! It was him! I've seen St. Andrew!"

This strange principle of rephotographing the photograph permeates the film. First, Celestino experiments with a donkey, surreptitiously photographed, in order to assure himself of his new power. As conflict stirs up the community, he "kills" four people in succession. Giving in to the madness that overcomes the village he gets ready to photograph everybody and anybody as he comes across them in his archives, without sparing himself, preparing for an unheard-of form of suicide. Still, he wants first to destroy the one who gave him this fatal power. But, when he tacks the photograph to the wall, the old man reappears; and when Celestino presses the shutter, St. Andrew turns into the Devil. A modern devil, unarmed and playful, one who can leisurely bring his victims back to life and turn back into the false saint that he was. But this return of the "real" signals the end of the film: the giant hand seen at the beginning returns and places its cardboard characters into a miniature set before disappearing into the clouds from which it emerged to tell this story.

So, rephotographing a photograph stops the movement of the shot. This reproduces the effect of a freeze-frame, but focused on a detail from the shot (for example at the funeral of one of the victims, a man comes to a standstill, transfixed by the effect, his two hands in the pockets of his vest, while behind him the funeral procession files by and disappears). The exact position of the bodies in the photograph is also repeated in the stilled image (until it is taken to the absurd when the mayor is caught in a pose in wich he was photographed as a child, nude on a fur rug). The paradox is that this effect does "stop" the film and even brings to mind the physical gesture of stopping the film on an editing table. But it can't be captured by bringing the film to a standstill, because the effect vanishes. One has the feeling that something impossible is trying to manifest itself here. Nothing less than a photograph that would appear as a moment of the shot or as a still frame, one of the frames comprising it. This frame is obviously virtual, but its effect is nonetheless real: it inscribes in the depth and duration of the shot an equivalent of what would be its almost zero value as an immobile image, impossible to grasp in the *défilement* of the film. Transformed into fragments of film-images, these photographs produce a back and forth effect between long-exposure photograph and snapshot. Themselves images within the image, on which the camera lingers for a varying amount of time, they already oscillate from one to the other: in general, the subject is depicted in a pose (Agostino doing the fascist salute, Donna Maria reigning like a smug middle-class bride) rather than being caught in the dialectic between any-instant-whatever and the decisive moment. As a result of being incorporated into the image, of which they become an aberrant motif (in spite of the fable that justifies them), these photographs attack that much more the integrity of film movement based on the linking of snapshots and the equal distance between them. Agostino's burial produces this effect in an ironic way: one side of the coffin is shaped to accommodate the dead man's implacably outstretched arm. The photographic body is thus displaced in the body of the film and causes it to vacillate.

One could say that when film is penetrated by photography these instants become its pregnant moments. For Gotthold Ephraim Lessing, the pregnant moment [*l'instant prégnant*] in painting is the significant instant, the one that supposedly represents both the average and the acme of a dramatic action, thus expressing the painting in its entirety. In a painting the pregnant moment doesn't refer to anything real, it is a fiction, a kind of synthetic image [*image de synthèse*].[20] On the contrary, the photographic instant—no matter how poignant or close to the pose, as Barthes thought—is always by the force of circumstance a "decisive instant" torn from reality. It can only be called pregnant in relation to the reversal of time and the generality of death, of which it is the trace; it is the trauma, the secret subject that doubles the apparent one. Otherwise, it is at best the sublimated but immanent form of any-instant-whatever.

So there wouldn't be in the literal sense a pregnant moment in cinema because, as one can see, the privileged instant can only spring from any-instant-whatever, from the photograph reduced, in terms of its movement, to its quality as pure snapshot. Yet where does my desire to qualify these moments as pregnant come from, these moments that suspend the time of movement and open up, inside of time, another time? First, it is because they make cinema lean in the direction of photography, toward its power to inscribe death. All the more so when they are directly supported, as in Rossellini's film, by a re-representation of photography, and when the significant effect of the stilled image is stipulated by the scenario or its theme. But perhaps, above all, it is because these instants possess a quality of abstraction and of irreality that seems to introduce a kind of paralysis—comparable to one that strikes (in) painting—into film. Of course, these instants are basically fugitive, while the painting's pregnant moment occupies the entirety of its time, if you will, since it is conceived so as to give to space the feeling of time. But in another way, the instant that stills the film bears a relation to the film as a whole. It goes way beyond its purely material inscription, reverting the film back onto itself, capturing its singular drama, emphasizing the fact that it cannot be reduced to the overly natural time of illusion, inducing a space-time at the juncture of the visible and the invisible. The characterization of film's pregnant moment, linked to the overall conditions of each particular film, is thus found to be both broad and limited, diffuse and localized. But it always echoes, in a time that is by definition spread out, the unsettling of perception, the tingling of the unreal that the eye experiences at the sight of the fictive movements of bodies in painting.

Let us take as a (magnifying) example Holbein's *The Ambassadors* (1533) The anamorphic death's head—

in which the painting's meaning is completed and which gives logic and significance [*prégnance*] to the pose of the two men—this skull is only clearly visible if a certain course is followed: it first assumes a spectator who is at an angle to the painting, identifying the skull and already making out the bodies and the objects that he will plainly see when facing the canvas. From this position in front of the painting, the floating object at the bottom of the picture appears unrecognizable but remains nevertheless knowable because of his memory of it. This *dispositif* helped Pascal Bonitzer show that if painting moves more than is believed, cinema likewise might move less than one would expect, and so the relation between the two may be much closer than it might appear.[21] But above all, the example of Holbein has the advantage of showing us, in the extreme, what really happens in front of any painting: an unsettling of perception in relation to itself, a superimposition of images which remains in the background between the significance of the instant that is sought and the verisimilitude of the intended representation. Such is the visual (mental) process that is displaced, fractured, modified by the film, but which constitutes the basic process: the projection of one image onto another, of one state of the image onto another. And so of a movement (of emotion or of the intellect) produced in immobility. This is the reason why the freeze-frame has an effect that is, in varying degrees, close to painting, but also why today so many paintings seem to be freeze-frames.

This wavering between stillness and movement, which is at the heart of *La macchina ammazzacattivi*, is inscribed in the narrative in such a way that it puts into play all of the dualities on which the film thrives: tradition and modernism, America and Italy, the good and the wicked, good and evil, heaven and hell, God and the Devil, the light that creates and the one that destroys, life and death. (Celestino, the hero of these transitions, of this confusion, says in fact: "I don't know anymore if I'm dead or alive.") Without ever being able to reduce film or photography to corresponding strictly to one or the other of these opposing terms, without organizing all of the terms themselves into a flawless credo, it is clear that photography holds the power of death throughout the film. Celestino photographs, then photographs again, killing animals, men, women; and in doing this he attacks the very movement of the film. He can do this because St. Andrew, protector of the village and representative of God, is also the Devil. So film can be a gift from heaven (as is the case with that hand that pierces the clouds) only on condition that its intimacy with death is recognized, an intimacy that threatens its movement—what one believed was the plenitude of its movement. Here, death is a figure of both the real and of style: that is, playing as much on the idea of real death as on the idea of putting to death the art (or one of the dimensions of the art) that choose to make this its subject.

Let us remember that in *Viaggio in Italia* a distraught couple arrives in front of an excavation site in Pompeii from which, after an injection of plaster, there emerges the form of a couple clasped in an embrace, like a photographic image appears in the developer. Thus, a photograph is formed from the real itself. This embrace (stopping only in death) becomes the necessary passage to the kiss, until then impossible, which is finally exchanged by the husband and wife in the middle of the procession where they seem—with a mad, sudden movement—to come to a standstill in the image. This deeply moving privileged moment was made possible because earlier, as always, an image came to a standstill for them, an image that becomes for the film a pregnant moment as much because it contains in itself the entire film as because it creates movement and affinities between some of these moments.

This image of immobile embrace condenses the two great series of images which before that moment had caught the heroine's eye: on the one hand, pregnant moments of art and of the cult of the dead (museum sculptures, a wall of skulls and bones in the church); on the other hand, the pregnant women she follows with her gaze. Three terms and three times are thus linked in a single instant: pleasure, birth, and death.

II.

There is a famous image in *Persona* (1966): a barechested youth reaches out, as if in vain, to touch a woman's face. What is singular about this face, whose features seen in an extreme close-up barely stand out from a milky white background, is that it appears at the same time very close and very far away, still and yet animated with a type of movement that is difficult to pinpoint. It finally changes, as if this was not really the same woman that the youth was trying to reach at the beginning and at the end of the shot. A closer look, one that anticipates the rest of the film, will discern that the film's two heroines are presented here one after the other, both chosen because of a latent similarity in their features. Most likely, there are two photographs or still frames kept under glass, which would explain the effect of fixity. But a very slow dissolve assures the passage from one image to the other, producing a near-movement, accentuated by the variations from blurred to focus. All of this ascribes the strange impression of fixed movement to the only subject who really does move in the image, and thus to the spectator.

It is easy to see in this image an illustration (but it is obviously the theory that illustrates the film) of Jean-Louis Baudry's interpretation of the ultimate power of the cinema *dispositif.* Its effect comes from its production of a representation that oscillates between hallucination and perception; and, as in dreams (whose desires are renewed in film) this representation reproduces for the child the pleasure of satisfaction (but also the drama of its loss) experienced in the relation with the maternal body (in particular in the activity of nursing, where the "dream screen" turned into a film screen would reproduce the image).[22]

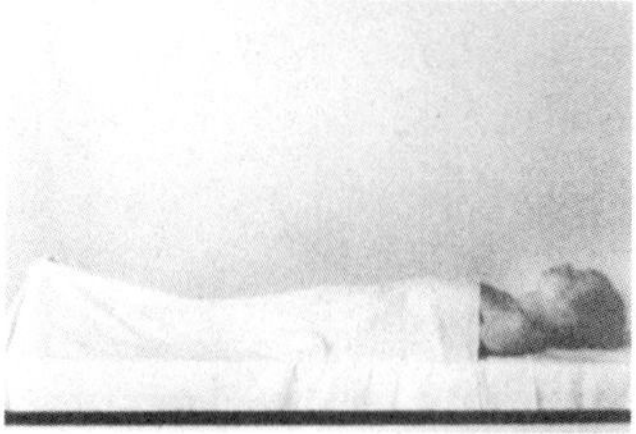

1

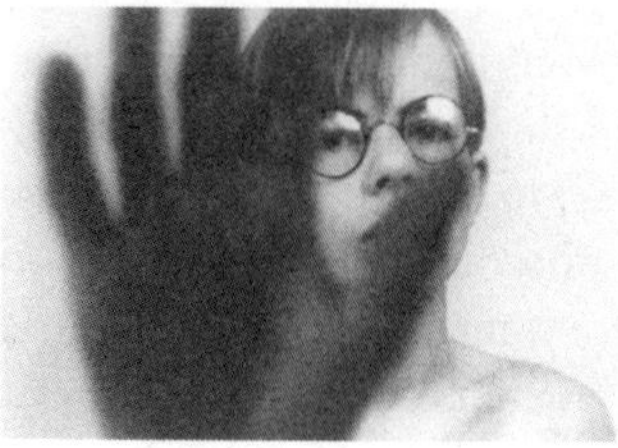

2

3

This would not mean much (or very little) if this shot did not come at the end of a particularly striking scene before the credits, which have no apparent relation to the film and are composed of an extremely rapid series of obsessional representations, themselves centered for the most part on a physical and historical decomposition of the cinema *dispositif*'s phases. It concerns the mechanisms of a (or several) projection(s), as well as the mechanisms of the images that compose them. They are characterized by two important features. On one hand, an oscillation between a moving and a stilled image: whether it is a simple matter of a petrified representation, or a real freeze-frame (as in the inverted shot of a cartoon image that comes from the early days of film).

There is, on the other hand, a very lively thematization of death: for example, the chase scenes from a sketch in "primitive" film. But at any rate, neither life nor death is sure, no more so than the immobile (or immobilized) picture and the moving picture are sure. Let us take for example the close-up of an inverted head of a woman whose closed eyes open, for a fraction of a second, stunning the spectator, making perception tip just that much more into hallucination. From all of this it becomes clear that the shot of the child of the women [*l'enfant aux femmes*] (as one says *The Virgin of the Rocks* [*La Vierge aux rochers*]) is in fact the living synthesis of a cinema *dispositif* that is haunted by death, and in particular by its own death.

Again this would not be enough if this fantasy-child were not projected throughout the narrative (from which he is physically absent) in the form best fitted to dealing with his appearance: a photograph torn to pieces by his mother, which launches the multiple-entry fantasy that is developed throughout the film. This becomes clear in the end when the two women, face to face, play the same scene twice, and once again their faces intermingle, and the two halves of the ripped-apart photograph are joined. This fantasy implies that the mother has a pent-up desire for her son that she cannot accept, either during her pregnancy or after his birth. This hampered desire then echoes the child's impossible desire for the mother and the woman, symbolized in the film's opening. This alternation between the two women affects the second heroine as well. The long story told by

Bibi Andersson to Liv Ullmann is centered around two instants/images that are both dispersed and elided: her sexual pleasure (in the mini-scene of the orgy on the beach followed by sex with her fiancé) and her abortion. Between these two desires that intersect through the use of improbable images, the subject's desire (director and spectator) for the work is formed: the divided, fractured, torn apart film, tormented by its nature, its history and its prehistory.

For there is a second photograph in the film: the image (an emblematic and very well-known one) of a Jewish child with a hunted look, his hands raised, alone in the crowd on a platform in a train station. The photograph is detailed, fragmented and endlessly worked by a camera looking for a secret impossible to pinpoint. This horror is comparable to the television image transmitted live, showing a Buddhist monk who sets himself on fire, an image that grips the speechless heroine in her hospital room. Between these two pictures cinema burns and is reborn (at the very beginning of the pre-credit sequence, light surges forth between the two electrodes of an electric arc); it becomes postwar cinema, where movement is not guaranteed any more than is speech, subject to a paralysis that can at any moment condemn them to come to a standstill.

III.

Curiously enough, it is in relation to *Numéro deux* (1975), a film that has practically no still images, that Serge Daney defined the vanishing point of "Godard's pedagogy." This pedagogy "has as its horizon, its limit, the enigma of enigmas, the sphinx of the still photograph: it is what defies the intelligence that can never exhaust it, what holds the look and the meaning, what fixes the scopic desire: actively retains it."[23]

From *Les Carabiniers* (*The Riflemen*, 1963) to *Photo et cie* (part 5b of *Six fois deux / Sur et sous la communication*, 1976), via *Ici et ailleurs* (*Here and Elsewhere*, 1976) and *Comment ça va* (1975), Godard gave a literal and dizzying rundown of the state of photography in the contemporary world, and thus in film as well. But it is in *Sauve qui peut (la vie)* and *Je vous salue Marie* (*Hail Mary*, 1985) that the questions opened up by Rossellini and Bergman re-emerge in a more direct fashion, as an interruption of movement and a search for the instant.

The cascading decompositions of movement in *Sauve qui peut (la vie)*, as those before in *France/tour/détour/deux/enfants* (1978), are just so many freeze-frames that never really stop because they recompose a movement. It is another kind of movement, another kind of speed, which attacks the *défilement*, yet it is no more able than the freeze-frame to escape it. So at first glance cinema indeed remains, as Deleuze says, "the system which reproduces movement *as a function of any-instant-whatever*"; but this is no longer "as a function of equidistant instants, selected so as to create an impression of continuity." On the contrary, the moments of the shot subjected to the effect of decomposition are selected so as to produce an impression of discontinuity, or a continuity of another nature. For Deleuze, they turn into mobile, as well as immobile, slices [*coupes*] of movement (but remain visible as such). So can one really say that they are conceived as a function of any-instant-whatever? And, conversely, what would be the "not just any" instant, the modern equivalent of the pose or of the transcendent posture, as a function of which the moments of the shot would be isolated as over-privileged instants?

I can begin to answer by saying (like Daney): the photograph. No longer the photograph in its facticity, its materiality, its integrity. But instead, the photograph as an absolute limit, the inner body of the film that, by its very difference, it virtually constitutes and reconstitutes. And so the photograph again manifests itself as an impossible still frame, yet in a way that differs from Rossellini's apologue. These stilled moments (which nevertheless leave the impression that they are bound together as a whole) designate a vanishing point: this point emerges from the inherent divisibility of space once the continuity and the illusion of its "natural" movement are attacked. In a sense, this divisibility goes well beyond the still frame because it implies that there is a space *in-between* the frames—even though this divisibility finds its material limit in the frame—on the condition that one goes outside of the film and the time of its projection. When one remains inside the film it becomes a sort of mental, virtual frame which is then projected, an image of an image left to the spectator, even though each and every second of it has been programmed by the film.

But this is not enough. One cannot limit oneself to the abstract form of these moments; what they designate must also be considered. Paradoxically, the strength of these moments lies in having been extracted from something neutral, from run-of-the-mill life and time, and in being any-instant-whatevers. And yet at the same time, they designate a space impossible to isolate: the moment of contact between bodies, between the sexes, in love (and in the violence that is its flip side) in the scenes between Paul and Denise (the embrace in front of the TV studio; the embrace-assault at breakfast), and when the anonymous man and woman brush lightly against each other in the street (during the scene between Isabelle and Mr. Nobody). This is also true of the final scene when Paul runs into his ex-wife and his daughter at the very moment of his hypothetical death, which is suspended and made unreal precisely by this stop-action that is never stopped, the sign of a film that would never be stilled, because it has broken the pact that links its movement to the spectator. A virtual kiss also comes to mind. Projected, predicted, and yet never exchanged (between Isabelle and the CEO/"film director"), it serves as a moment-act asymptotic to the extended porn scene where Godard outlines, with a cruel stroke, the fate of the cinema *dispositif*.

He has no need to go back to the decomposition of the image because he has literally put it into action in the continuity of the representation that is internally crippled by the impossibility of the bodies ever coming together. So the "neutral" moments of the decomposition are related, if only through the work of the gaze that they require, to the privileged instants when this decomposition is thematized around certain gestures and around certain moments (in the same way that a scattered gaze refocuses on whatever catches its attention). Everything is crystallized in this manner around two instants that have become unrepresentable from the moment that film can no longer avoid bringing them together as such, in their pure value as interruption: the instant of sexual pleasure (of which the film kiss has always been the image) and the instant of death.[24]

It is to these (pregnant) moments that *Sauve qui peut (la vie)* refers. They cannot be defined except by default, but they are nonetheless projected and reprojected over and over and endlessly made virtual. This is where *Passion* (1982) takes over: this time involving painting directly, assuming the paradoxical task of representing shots from film as *tableaux vivants*, thus stealing pregnant moments from high art, and showing that this way of redirecting them is a (new) concern in film.

One comes across these moments again in *Je vous salue Marie*. Here they have a purer vocation as present-absent instants, shedding light on the course of film, shaping the spectator's mental journey. This time it is about the relation between two instants. On one hand there is the instant as it took place, but off-screen and outside of the film, an immaterial, transcendent instant if ever there was one: the moment of an elided pleasure (it is miraculous that Mary, the unique one, full of grace, was impregnated by God). On the other hand, there is the instant that cannot come to pass, the instant when Joseph would touch Mary, when this touch would equal the gaze of God. The leitmotif runs throughout the film ("I want to kiss you," "Let me touch you," and so on).

The famous sequence where Joseph tries to touch Mary is a direct sequel to the scenes of embrace and combat in *Sauve qui peut (la vie)*.[25] There is no need for Godard to resort to the decomposition of movement and time to close in on an image impossible to reach, because the act takes place within the content of the shot, in the gestures of the characters. Similarly, he no longer needs painting, no longer needs to reconstitute this exemplary pregnant moment that is the Annunciation in a (fake) painting, because it is integrated into the story of his new narrative. Joseph's hand reaches out toward Mary's stomach and at the same moment he says the words this gesture implies: "I love you." Mary cries "no" when for the first and only time the hand does touch her, "no" again when the hand reaches forward a second time. She says "yes" as soon as the hand pulls back, until the moment when Joseph can almost touch her stomach. Everything is in this "almost"—beginning with the withdrawal she has imposed which moves to the rhythm of this new kind of "*fort und da*." This repetition of retreat, which symbolizes the forbidden (of incest, as Alain Bergala insists), imitates a decomposition of time defined by the impossible image of the Conception of Christ. It designates (Philippe Dubois saw this very clearly) the utopia of a virgin image, an image yet to be exposed that would permit the gaze to touch in all innocence the body of a woman. Just an image, says Godard, one that would at last become a just image. But what does "just an image" really mean? Couldn't this just as well be a still frame, a photograph, a detachable fragment, unique, ideal, pointing to an instant already past, yet always virtual, and from which it derives what it can reveal? This image was used on the poster for the film, for example, where it is no longer clear if Joseph's hand is going to touch Mary's stomach, has already touched it, or will never

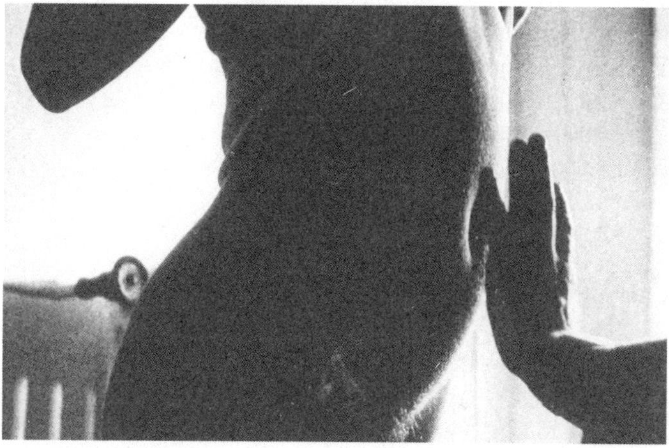

touch it. Any-instant-whatever, the privileged or decisive instant and the pregnant moment have perhaps never been confused to this extent—the pregnant moment that has never so rightly deserved its name.[26] The confusion between them, at a point that is both designated and dispersed, is the subject or rather the motif of the film.

This motif was already outlined in *Die Marquise von O* (*The Marquise of O*, 1976). Following Kleist to the letter, Rohmer was confronted with an ellipsis-instant that held the secret of the narrative: the rape of the marquise by the Russian officer, her savior. This elided act takes place between two shots. The first follows the marquise's point of view as she is threatened by the abusive soldiers. She sees the count—dressed all in white, surrounded by an aura of almost superhuman brightness—as if he were falling from the sky and flinging himself at her (this is the shot referred to in the final words: "You wouldn't have seemed like a devil to me if I hadn't taken you for an angel when you first appeared!"). The second shot shows the sleeping marquise, being attacked by this "devil" that the spectator obviously doesn't see. Rohmer introduces an image that is not in the novella, which imitates a famous painting by Füssli. He took care to leave out the demon(s) that suggest(s) the highly elusive significance [*prégnance*] of the nightmare that wavers between the desire for love and the fear of death. He does this because the film's dramatic climax—haunted by the plasticity of painting, the ability of the frame to capture gestures that, by holding back time, express the pathos and the depth of the drama—this climactic moment is situated *in-between* the two shots I have just mentioned, within their alternation. The film prolongs the effect of this alternation until the final embrace of the husband and wife who are at long last reunited, capturing and interiorizing this invisible image that streaks through the film like a bolt

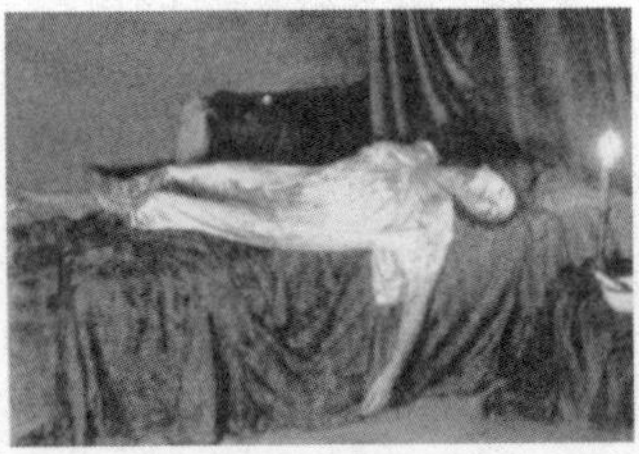

of lightning, and around which time—one day—came to a standstill for them, in reality as in a dream.[27]

As for time itself, the instant as such, it was Rohmer who, in a very Rossellinian way, gave us the shivers. There are two ways of going about it, in the same way that there are (at least) two Rossellinis: one, dear to Bazin, used reality as a unifying principle; the other was one of the first to consider its discontinuity. The green ray—in *Le rayon vert*[28] (1986)—and the blue hour—in the first story of *Quatre aventures de Reinette et Mirabelle* (*Four Adventures of Reinette and Mirabelle*, 1988)—present unique and rare moments when time is suspended in an event that the characters and the camera would like to fix in the present, in order not to be left with only its virtuality or its memory. This is probably why these moments are so rarely present on Rohmer's screen, ever faithful to the obligations of reality, even in its ellipses. They are much more obvious and meaningful in the text (in the dialogues) than in the image. And so even when one watches the sun as it sets on the ocean, or the day as it breaks, one has the feeling that these are freeze-frames that don't really take place, because the appearance of reality has not been attacked. But at the same time, one cannot quite grasp this moment for what it is—as a photograph that would last, a still frame spread out in time—because this moment, that is so fair, cannot be stilled.

I was about to finish this text when I saw *L'ami de mon amie* (*Boyfriends and Girlfriends*, 1987). Here, everything seemed so simple, so clear, smooth and continuous. The obsession with the instant seemed to have been melted down to a pure algebra of feelings that counted on the film's ending to solve all of its equations. For just one moment in the forest, the fragile mental state of Blanche (one of the heroines of this four-sided story) let a Murnau-like affect hang over the scene, as in *Reinette et Mirabelle*. And suddenly the ending comes in the lakeside restaurant where the couples are reconciled. Alexandre and Léa walk off into the background to the right; Blanche and Fabien, framed in a medium shot, turn to watch them leave. And without warning the image comes to a standstill, as in so many films where this has no (real) consequence. I've seldom experienced such a feeling of brutality at the sight of a shot: the characters—so concrete a fraction of a second before—seemed dislocated, pinned down like butterflies. While nothing had hinted at this (save a certain difficulty Rohmer has in filming and, perhaps, in believing in his film), one finds oneself thrown back 30 years, facing the prophetic image at the end of *Les quatre cents coups*, announcing that it was over, that never again could cinema be filmed as before.

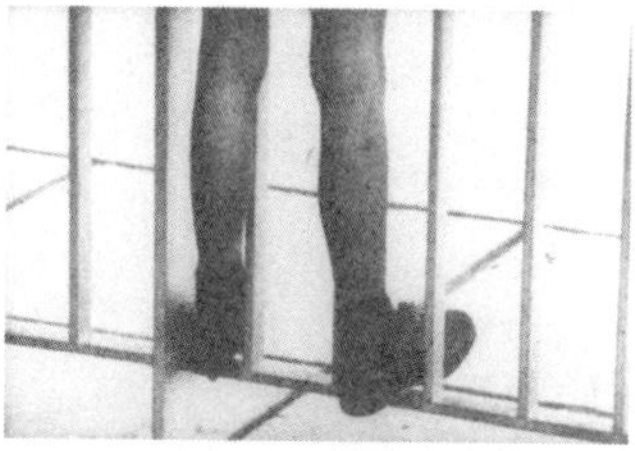

1

2

3

4

5

6

For the overly still image, the far too visible suspension of time, leads irremediably to loss and death. This is the lesson of *La Jetée*. If there are so many stilled images composing an entire film, even a short one, it is because they all come together around a single image: the image of the main character's death. To bring this out, a decomposed series of images is needed which makes this single image virtually indiscernible—as in the ending of *Sauve qui peut (la vie)*—yet one recognizes it by its unique type of movement. Peter Wollen saw how this photograph reproduces a famous snapshot by Capa turned into, as he says, a "'pregnant moment' after Diderot or Greuze" (so the images have varying destinies, from the quality of pregnancy that is or can be attributed to them).[29] And the text isolates this moment, in order to capture its violence as a decisive instant. ("He understood that one does not escape Time, and that this moment that he been shown in his childhood, which had continued to haunt him ever since, was the moment of his own death.") In the journey that takes place in this way between all of the photographs that tell this story and *the* photograph (that is the image that traverses the film in each direction, returning from its end to its beginning: "This is the story of a man, marked by an image from his childhood"), *La Jetée* alone seems to cover the entire breach opened up in cinema from its beginnings (if not from its origin) by the immobile presence of the photograph (both as body and as idea). The photograph has always designated, as in Feyder's eloquently titled film *L'Image* (*The Image*, 1923–1925, dedicated to woman-as-image), the object of the strongest desire, the sign of the most poignant reality.

It might be asked what I wanted to say by using a few privileged films to link these variable figures: the freeze-frame and the freeze in the image, the presence and treatment of the photograph, such and such an instant, this or that gesture. One can see that this concerns diverse forms that interrupt movement: the image or the body that comes to a stop, the gesture that stops in midair or touches without touching, the already immobile photograph. It is clear, then, that these forms are related to acts, to exceptional or fundamental moments: the green ray, the blue hour, birth, death, the kiss, sexual pleasure, incest, the Annunciation, the shot (photographic and cinematic). It could be argued that acts such as these (most of them at least) occur every day in films and are not dealt with in such a formal way. Of course. But the opposite is not true, at least not in the films I have been talking about, every one of which testifies to a certain state of film that is historical and at the same time always contemporary. Here, the forms that immobilize movement are related precisely to these acts and moments (even if their range happens to be much larger, with multiple perspectives, as in *Sauve qui peut (la vie)* or *La Jetée*).

What seems to me to be very strong and worth emphasizing is the connection between these forms and these moments, which one can see is very diverse yet is also repeated time and again. It forms a constellation that is, I believe, only the most visible part of dealing with the immobility of this art of movement that is cinema—this is something that has not yet been considered carefully enough, in its various aspects: stylistic, aesthetic, psychological, historical.

It will no doubt be asked why Deleuze was brought into this debate, given that he is unaware of it, even puts it aside, and develops in completely different terms the aspects of the time-image that could be connected to the ones I have spoken of here. It is because, as we have seen, he took up these difficult questions of movement and time at their very foundations, and because he spoke better than anyone else of the formal and historical breaks that little by little composed a cinema of visible time and one particular destiny of modern and contemporary film. But perhaps I should be more specific. In his two books on film, Deleuze both borrows from others and draws them in to his way of thinking. Some are currently divided between the view he offers them and the one that until then had supported their approach to film: either an ideological view (today very quickly buried in the rubble of history), or more profoundly, a view that can be called psychoanalytic in the broad sense of the term—Freudian, Lacanian. It is clear that Deleuze's conception dissolves the footholds (explicit or not) implied by a psychoanalytic perspective. Let us briefly describe film in the following way: a psychological subject, a spectator defined in relation to a *dispositif*, a putting into play of sexual difference, and above all the vision of time connected to it. This vision of time comprises points of anchorage characterized essentially by their anteriority, their fixity, and the possibility of reversal that they produce; whence in this perspective, the existence of the privileged instants, privileged by what must be called a kind of transcendence, because if they don't master time they orient it by means of their very existence. But above all they make it vectorial (pointing from the present toward the past, from the graspable to the ungraspable), and this vector itself creates a tonality that is somewhere between nostalgia and melancholy. Deleuze's thought opposes all of this to a Time that is unitary and global, even though it is infinitely stratified and dispersed. A time both material and abstract, on which neither the future of any utopia nor the past of any regression has a hold. A time in which the film never comes to a standstill, is oblivious to the mirages of the instant, the points of emptiness and lack, the trace of the negative and the specter of photography. One finds oneself faced with two opposing conceptions of time and of memory (one could just as easily say two ways of reading Proust): on one hand, Freud and everything linked to him; on the other hand, Bergson revisited. On one hand, there is Deleuze's energetic, objectivizing view (with everything that it excludes); on the other, there is a subjectivizing, nostalgic, melancholy view (with everything that it perpetuates). Benjamin, for example, is divided between the projection of a return of the aura and his tendency to repeat tirelessly "Joshua's gesture."[30] Then there is Barthes' twofold gesture, placing his trust in the utopia of the still frame only to surrender univocally to the fascination of the photograph.

If I had to give a film-image of this disparity, I would gladly project it in the breach between two films by Michael Snow. The first would be *La région centrale* (1971), with its endlessly turning movement, open like a pure and limitless positivity, deploying on an uninhabited terrain a point of view outside of all interiority. In the second, *Wavelength* (1966–1967), a forward movement, both continuous and discontinuous, takes shape through repeated pulsations of sound and light, and travels through enigmatic events, for example a man's death. It ends up at the point that has oriented it, without our knowing it, from the beginning: on a wall, a photograph of the ocean, animated by immobile waves, into which the camera enters and freezes.

But one must also consider this photograph as do those who see photography as a capturing and a reversal of time; in the same way that I was only able to bring to the films that "stopped" me a gaze captivated by the strength of their desire to interrupt. There is for example in the "angelism" of contemporary movies, of which Rossellini's film seems to have been a forerunner—whether heaven is named Hollywood (again Godard, *Soft and Hard*, 1986), the 19th century (*Die Marquise von O*), a woman's face (*Persona*) or the Christian Western world (*Je vous salue Marie*)—a mix of desperate utopia and regression that makes it difficult for me to see them in any other perspective besides that of a divided time. A time that can be related to the instants that ground it, as points of transcendence that are known, repeated in the ellipses, decompositions and immobilizations that run through them.

1987. Originally translated in 1991 by Alison Rowe with Elisabeth Lyon.

[1] Goethe, *Faust I & II* (1808–1832), ed. and trans. Stuart Atkins (Princeton: Princeton University Press, 1994) 44.

[2] Auguste Villiers de l'Isle-Adam, *Tomorrow's Eve* (1886), trans. Robert Martin Adams (Urbana: University of Illinois Press, 2001) 22.

[3] Henri Bergson, *L'évolution créatrice* (Paris: F. Alcan, 1907) [*Creative Evolution*, trans. Arthur Mitchell (New York: Modern Library, 1944)].

[4] For more information, see Gilles Deleuze, "Thèses sur le mouvement (premier commentaire de Bergson)," *L'image-mouvement* (Paris: Minuit, 1983) 9–22 ["Theses on Movement, First Commentary on Bergson," *Cinema 1: The Movement-Image*, trans. Hugh Tomlinson and Barbara Habberjam (Minneapolis: University of Minnesota, 1986) 1–11].

[5] Bergson, *Matière et mémoire* (Paris: F. Alcan, 1896) [*Matter and Memory*, trans. N.M. Paul and W.S. Palmer (New York: Macmillan, 1911)].

[6] Deleuze, *L'image-mouvement* 21 [*Cinema 1* 11].

[7] Peter Wollen "Feu et Glace," *Photographies*, vol. 4 (March 1984) ["Fire and Ice," *Other Than Itself: Writing Photography*, ed. John X. Berger and Olivier Richon (Manchester: Cornerhouse Gallery, 1989)] 120.

[8] Deleuze, *L'image-mouvement* 14 [*Cinema 1* 5].

[9] As is finally being done in the United States in a recent book on the flashback by Maureen Turim, *Flashbacks in Film: Memory and History* (New York: Routledge, 1989); and one on trains in early film: Lynne Kirby, *Parallel Tracks: The Railroad and Silent Cinema* (Durham: Duke University Press, 1997). Philippe Dubois gave a paper along these lines at the colloquium at Chantilly, *Cinéma et peinture* (June 1986) titled "Ralenti et arrêt sur image" on the freeze-frame in three films: *The Man with the Movie Camera*, Marcel Carné's *Les Visiteurs du Soir*, and *Sauve qui peut (la vie)*.

[10] See Annette Michelson, "*The Man with the Movie Camera*: From Magician to Epistemologist," *Artforum* (February 1971). In this article she establishes a connection between Clair and Vertov.

[11] *Jean-Luc Godard par Jean-Luc Godard* (Paris: Editions Cahiers du cinéma, 1986) 461–465. Perhaps this is the same thing that Vertov made us aware of, prophetically, in *Three Songs of Lenin* (1934): the stop in movement and the slide toward immobility that shape the film are not only the inner figures of the mourning that starts with the death of Lenin (and of the Revolution), but are already the figures of the initial "death" of cinema.

[12] Four examples came to me subsequently, spread across two periods of classical cinema. In Lang's films *Liliom* (1934) and *Fury* (1936), two newsreels projected in two courtrooms—one in heaven, one on earth—justify two freeze-frames of the same sort: in both cases the stopping of movement guarantees a supplement of truth (as to the innocence or guilt of the hero). In particular, it makes commentary on the image possible, thus marking a sort of intrusion of documentary into the fiction. In Capra's *It's a Wonderful Life* (1946), the freeze-frame on James Stewart/George Bailey—captured in a medium shot right in the midst of an everyday gesture—definitely has that element of distance inherent in all freeze-frames (the voiceover stresses this: "I want you to take a good look at that face"). But this shot also gets the fiction in gear: it enables the acceleration of the passage from childhood to adulthood, and the introduction of an element of suspense, which the return to movement hastens to make the most of. Finally, in Mankiewicz's *All About Eve* (1950), two appearances of the same freeze-frame—once at the beginning when the image freezes (the freeze-frame then briefly reappears), then once near the end when the stilled image comes back to life—underline the moment when Eve receives the Sarah Siddons Society Award, honoring her talents as an actress. The image is ambiguous, especially at the beginning. Alternating with a shot of George Sanders whose voice-over sets the scene of the story and transforms it twice over into a flashback, the freeze-frame can thus have the status of a mental image of the narrator/

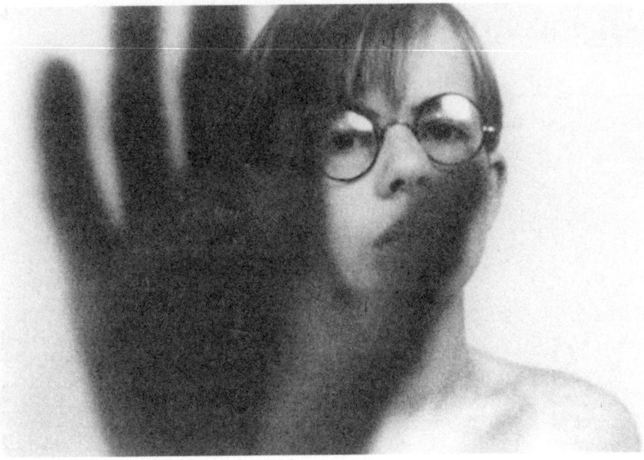

Ingmar Bergman, *Persona*, 1966

intermediary. It could also represent a photograph immortalizing the moment. In any case, it underlines the moment that may give the film its meaning, to the extent that it allows for the retroactive justification of Eve's character and behavior (which is why it is both repeated and "restarted").

[13] Responses to "3 Questions sur: Photo et Cinéma," *Photogénies* 5 (1985). "Ashes to ashes, frames to frames" is in English in the original text.

[14] Deleuze, *L'image-mouvement* 14 [*Cinema 1* 5].

[15] Peter Wollen quite rightly emphasized this point in "Feu et Glace."

[16] Deleuze, *L'image-temps* 40–41 [*Cinema 2* 27].

[17] Deleuze, *L'image-temps* 53 [*Cinema 2* 37].

[18] Roland Barthes, "Le troisième sens," *Cahiers du cinéma* 222 (July 1970) ["The Third Meaning," *Image, Music, Text*, trans. Stephen Heath (New York: Hill and Wang, 1977)].

[19] *Roberto Rossellini*, BFI dossier 8, ed. Don Ranvaud (London: British Film Institute, 1981) 12.

[20] Gotthold Ephraim Lessing, *Laocoön* (New York: Dutton, 1961). Jacques Aumont discusses this idea in his book *L'Œil interminable (cinéma et peinture)* (Paris: Librairie Seguier, 1989).

[21] Bonitzer, *Décadrages: peinture et cinéma* (Paris: Cahiers du cinéma / Editions de l'Etoile, 1985).

[22] Baudry, "Le dispositif" 67 ["The Apparatus" 54].

[23] Serge Daney, "Le thérrorisé (pédagogie godardienne)," *Cahiers du cinéma* 262–263 (January 1976) 32–40 ["Theorize/Terrorize," trans. Annwyl Williams, *Cahiers du cinéma: Volume Four, 1973–1978: History, Ideology, Cultural Struggle*, ed. David Wilson (London, New York: Routledge, 2000) 120].

[24] For more information on this articulation between the different stop-action moments in *Sauve qui peut (la vie)* and the rest of the film, see "'I Am an Image'" in this book.

[25] The repercussions of this for the future of filmmaking and of film were analyzed very well by Alain Bergala and Philippe Dubois. See Alain Bergala, "Si près du secret," *Cahiers du cinéma* 367 (January 1985); "Qu'est-ce que faire un plan pour Jean-Luc Godard," paper given at the colloquium *Jean-Luc Godard, le cinéma*, Brussels, April 1986 (published in the expanded edition of the special issue on Godard of *Revue belge du cinéma*); Philippe Dubois, "La Passion, la douleur et la grâce," *L'Epoque, la mode, la morale, la passion* (Paris: Centre Georges Pompidou, 1987).

[26] Jacques Aumont emphasizes this in *L'Œil interminable.*

[27] It's interesting to recall that Barthes initially wanted to use the short story by Kleist as the "tutor text" for his grand attempt at "pausing the text" before finally replacing it with Balzac's *Sarrasine*. Likewise, just to tie up loose ends, we might add that the motif of incest (brother/sister, mother/son), which runs throughout Balzac's narrative, is also at the center of Kleist's (in the form of an excessive bond between the father and the daughter at the moment when the father grants forgiveness, a bond which the film has more difficulty showing than the text has saying). This same motif of incest (father/daughter) runs just beneath the surface in *Sauve qui peut (la vie)*, and haunts Godard to such an extent that its counterpart (mother/son incest) can be seen as a displacement of it, via a return to the great figure of origins, in *Je vous salue Marie* (Bergala has pursued this, particularly in the Godard/Sollers video interview by Jean-Paul Fargier, *Le trou de la vierge*).

[28] The film was released as *Summer* in the US and *The Green Ray* in the UK [editor's note].

[29] Wollen 119.

[30] As Pierre Missac clearly showed in one of the chapters of *Passage de Walter Benjamin* (Paris: Seuil, 1987) [*Walter Benjamin's Passages*, trans. Shierry Weber Nicholsen (Cambridge: MIT Press, 1995)].

Six Films (In Passing)

Winston Link, *NW 1103 August 2, 1956 Hot Shot East Bound at Laeger West Virginia*, 1956

Contacts, William Klein (1983) [1]

"A contact sheet, a roll of 36 exposures, six strips of six photographs, taken one after the other. You read them from left to right, like a text; it's the photographer's diary. You rarely see a photographer's contacts, you only see the chosen photograph. You don't see the before and the after." We see some contact sheets; the camera moves forward to isolate a frame, and starts a movement which only finishes with the film: a panoramic journey miming the movement of the eye, the contact sheets "like a text," stopping only from time to time, in just so many privileged stations, until "the" photograph, the right photograph appears.

The conditions that let it appear are varied. But each time eloquent, irrefutable. The narrowing of space, the dramatization of the bodies, the direction of the looks, the creation of a fiction, the perspectives, a poignant detail (Barthes' *punctum*).

"A pose from a family album, lines of flight, the kid from earlier on near the back door, and above all the handkerchief behind the sexton. Chance makes a photograph." We have seen, from one frame to another, the body becoming frozen in the half-open back door, the two children really posing, the sexton slightly opening the door on the left and beginning to disappear, leaving behind him the white mark of the handkerchief he is holding in his hand. "I take a photograph of a woman wearing a flowered cardigan. It is not photograph, but a reflex, a detail. Later on she is still there, but everything has changed, everything has become organized. The light, the stairs, the actors: it is a photograph." Especially because, in the meantime, a woman has appeared on the right, exposing her body to the shot in a kind of offered, ecstatic attitude. But "chance" can also be reworked, hastened. Out of the famous *Candy Store, Amsterdam Avenue* (1954–1955) which shows two children in front of a wall of black and white squares in New York, Klein produces an image divided from itself: "I put the negative in the enlarger, I play with the focusing, the whites move, I let the blacks bleed. It is another photograph."

1

2

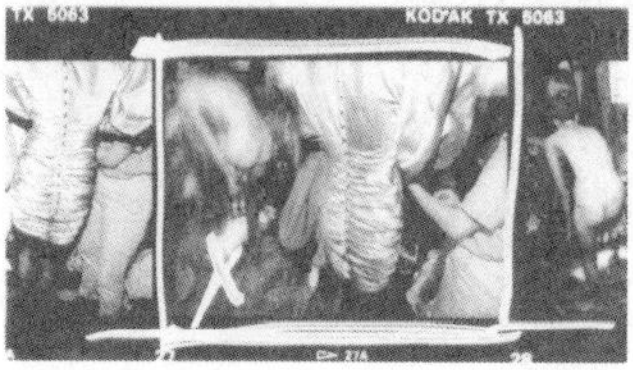

3

In this way we can see what is almost never seen: decisive moments. These moments seem all the more taken out of the imaginary continuity of filmic imagery that we find ourselves precisely at the cinema (or in a cinema situation) when Klein proposes we should capture (encircle) their apparition: that is, in the time the picture flashes by and we cannot stop it (unless we have a VCR) or manipulate it.

While it is flashing by, we often see the mark of the felt-tip pen that separates the frames and whose separation line we step across: a way of reminding us that we are in the photograph—within photography—when the camera suddenly shows the improbable object that looks like two overlapping still frames but which is merely the indication that two snapshots follow each other, only more distant from each other than in a film (as is especially true of Klein who never uses a motor winder to load, in order to give the "real" the opportunity to reorganize itself and have an even better chance of capturing an instant).

Thus we are in a time which is a little mad, at the same time very constrained (the tracking movement which looks as if it will never stop) and unsteady, because of all the interruptions, the changes provoked: in short, as close to being *between* photography and cinema as we can get. Klein has taken the measurements of this temporal paradox in his stride, at the very beginning of the film saying "A photograph taken in 1/125 second. What does one know of the work of a photographer? About a hundred photographs, perhaps 125 [...] That makes one second in all. Maybe 250 photographs. This would be quite an important body of work and it would make two seconds. The life of a photographer—even, as we say, a great one—two seconds." He comes back to this at the end to tell us what we have seen: "That's it. Twenty or so photographs, a hundred non-photographs. A few contact sheets, a few seconds." Between the instant and the eternity of the photo-image, 13 minutes of cinema construct a sort of implosive time that haunts the memory long afterward.

Les photos d'Alix (Alix's Photographs), Jean Eustache (1980)

"Alix Cléo Roubaud passed away at 5 am on January 28th, 1983. She died from a pulmonary embolism. She had been seriously ill with asthma since childhood. She had just turned 31."[2]

The young woman is the heroine of this short film made in 1980 by Jean Eustache. The photographer who is looking at us and is speaking to us is therefore a dead woman filmed by a dead man, the only real filmmaker who has ever chosen to kill himself. A unique coincidence of destinies, which weighs upon this film and makes it even more unique than it already is because of what it says about photography and pictures.

From the beginning, the stakes are clear: two photographs against a wall, he enters from the right (he is Martin—Boris in real life—Eustache's son, an adolescent, a little shy), she from the left (she is Alix, her voice is strong, almost indiscreet as it is so full of presence, but we get used to it; we would like it if this voice never left us). To something he says to her, she replies: "This is an old negative that I took back from my mother. It's a childhood photograph she took of me. That's me there. Don't you recognize me?" On the photograph on the left, one sees a little spot between the trees, vague patterns, scattered, drowned in the white. On the photograph on the right, there are only patterns.

The strategy of this breathtaking film becomes manifest: the division between what one recognizes and what one does not, because a picture is not identical to itself depending on what one says about it. This is what this woman says, this woman who takes these photographs, touches them up, often makes them indeterminable in order to force us to see what we could not see without her, but also to encourage us to see other things, all the things we are not capable of seeing or imagining. For example how "a photograph can be personally pornographic while being publicly decent."

Shot: Alix and Martin, sitting (after the opening and the credits), commenting upon each photograph they are looking at. Reverse shot: the photograph in question. There will be 18 of them. The art will be in the drifting, the variation in the drift. To Martin's questions, Alix responds by explaining the circumstances of the shot, the nature of the transformations that have been carried out, the point of view adopted. But as early as photograph three, doubt creeps in surreptitiously, and with it a drama both subtle and light, about a detail: a man in the background framed at the waist, whom we suppose naked, whom Martin believes to be part of a painting, but who was really present for the shooting and who, Alix says, "was not naked, contrary to what the photograph may suggest: he is perfect there, isn't he?" Then, brutally, in photograph four, and afterward—but not always, that would be too simple—a more or less wide breach forms between what is said and what we see, without either of the two observers worrying about it, but in such a way that within oneself one starts feeling disquiet compounded by fascination.

This very strong impression is twofold, even if it is hard to determine the divide. It firstly relates to the cinema: between the shot and the reverse shot, the gaze and the object, the spectator and the screen, the body and its image in the mirror, there is a break. They can be at the same time fused together and irreconcilable, as if they were disconnected. A narcissistic wound. The truth of the cinema is no longer what it was. It is undermined, emblematically, by photography, itself affected: it is the second side of the operation. Photography is affected not as an art form but because its art is too violent, too intimate, to be anything else but a backdrop for projection (as Hanna Schygulla says in Godard's *Passion* (1982), to her director-lover who wanted to see her naked, as a reconstituted element of a painting: "what you are asking me is too close to love"). The photograph is too close to childhood ("the only true photographs are childhood photographs"), to feelings ("all photographs are sentimental"), to death ("every photograph struggles against death") and to pictures and events of oneself ("all photographs are me"); photography is too much all this not to compel everyone to speak. This is the strongest point of Alix's photographs, so close in this to all the language strategies that Eustache has excelled in assembling: they make us understand that any true discourse on photography is condemned to be—for an essential part of it, and despite everything—chatter.

News from Home, Chantal Akerman (1977)

There is no photograph(y) in *News from Home*, but there is the photographic. This means that most of the shots are like fixed and often very long photographic exposures in which movement may take place, but it is a kind of uncertain, open, documentary movement, something like the development of what a snapshot captures. The rare camera movements are pans that sweep the surface without entering the real body of the city, New York, where the heroine/auteur of the film lives, far from her native Belgium. We could, for example, make a comparison with the famous forward tracking shots of Resnais in *Hiroshima mon amour* (1959) to underline what a genuinely cinematographic incarnation of a city (or rather two: Nevers, Hiroshima) might resemble, as opposed to what in Chantal Akerman's film becomes its photographic capturing. But that's already considering it in an old-fashioned way, out of a need to establish distinctions: her film is no less a film than is Resnais'. Quite simply, it is a moment of cinema captured from now on by photography.

This impression grows stronger because we do not see the auteur but only her eye, which we assume is identified with this camera that sits and waits, with a marvelous sense of framing and of time, for something real to happen—even if it must wait a long time, and in the dull indifference broken by sudden jolts that is so specific to photographic activity. There is for example an extraordinary, very long shot, in the subway: on the platform, five pillars that are irregularly laid out delimit three terrace-like spaces for the two train tracks, the double platform that separates them (unlike the layout of the Paris metro), and the two platforms bordering them on both sides. The strength of the spatial dimension of the shot is directly related to the fact that everything seems flat, as if squashed onto a single level, despite the levels of depth one can make out: these levels only come back to life during events (people walking around, trains coming into the station), before evaporating again. To such an extent that this interminable shot looks like a series of prolonged snapshots, interrupted by brief moments when life returns.

1

2

3

4

5

The impression of photography comes from the very subject of the film, its principle: a mother, in Brussels, diligently sends banal letters to her daughter who has left the family home to try to live and work in New York. The daughter reads the mother's letters, in a singsong, monotonous, and detached voice, these letters in which the mother gently complains that her daughter writes so little. She also demands photographs, naturally, and this again emphasizes the photographic effect of the letter, this conversation immobilized in time, this sort of "freeze-text."

Between the image and the text, therefore, a strange frozen circulation sets in. A division. On the one hand, there is the capturing, fragmented, silent, elliptic gaze of the daughter—an eye in its natural state so to speak—that strives to observe itself while discovering the city; on the other, there is her voice. One gets the feeling that she only reveals her absent mother's words in this way in order to give them over more effectively, via a kind of calculated sadism, to their undivided solitude.

The Sphinx, Thierry Knauff (1986)

The camera moves along the bushes, on a terrace in a French-style garden; it discovers the statue of a sphinx slightly overlooking the park, at the top of some steps; it starts turning and freezes. The camera is now facing the sphinx, centering it in an utterly static shot. Then there is a series of closer shots, all totally static. "A photograph has two dimensions, so does a television screen; neither can be walked through. From one wall of the street to the other, bent or arched, with their feet pushing against one wall and their heads pressing against the other, the black and bloated corpses that I had to step over were all Palestinian and Lebanese."[3] Flies can be heard.

"The first corpse I saw was that of a man 50 or 60 years old."[4] A man of the same age is now standing in front of the sphinx. The shot is strangely still, just like the many closer shots and close-ups that follow, always of the same man. It is almost impossible to know if these are photographs or still frames that have been filmed again (later on, the strangeness of some postures lead us to opt for this second solution; however, it is not the right one). But the only thing that matters, in either the "natural" stillness of the sphinx or the frozen poses/movements of the various figures, is the presence of the photographic. Produced as though beyond photography or before arriving at it, it testifies to photography's powerlessness to truly embody death in this context, even though it is its symptom, its mark, and its instinctive sign. This is why we do not see real photographs in this film, any more than we see real corpses: instead we see their incarnate, commented principle. "A photograph doesn't show the flies nor the thick white smell of death. Neither does it show how you must jump over bodies as you walk along from one corpse to the next."[5]

This solemn and pure film expresses this principle with a literalness that does not exclude several shifts, when it goes from one series of shots to another, from one image to another, showing for example—after a gray-haired woman, who could be illustrating what the text expresses, fictively representing, again, one of the chosen victims—a couple of lovers with deeply affecting bodies, sitting at the feet of the sphinx, no longer having anything to do with the "body of a man of 30 to 35 […] lying face down."[6] Toward the end, a long sequence with children creates an especially powerful moment: a little girl covering the sphinx's already ineffably closed eyes; the head or parts of the animal appearing by themselves amid the a crowd of children gathered as though for a class photograph. In this way the idea of something stiller than stillness is introduced: degrees of stillness, as there are degrees of death, of the perception of death, the terrible photographic rigidity of death. The director conceived the idea of interrupting, five or six times, this tense dialogue between motionless forces with a few shots of nature—trees, sky—still or moving shots that approach the most intimate point of the tension between what is moving and what is motionless, to an intolerable extent.

1

2

3

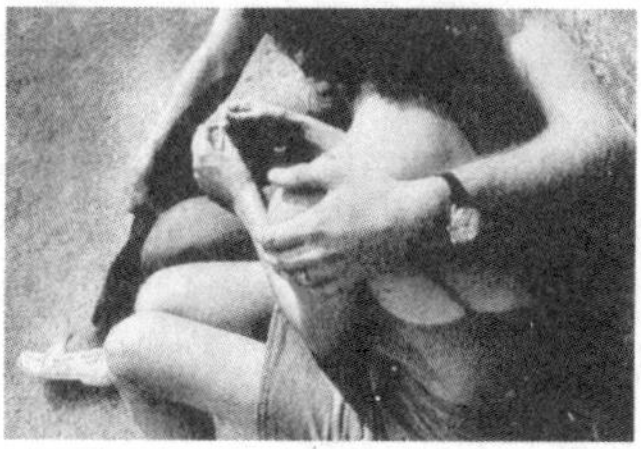
4

5

"I had spent four hours in Shatila," Jean Genet finally says. "About 40 bodies remained in my memory. All of them—and I mean all—had been tortured, probably against a backdrop of drunkenness, song, laughter, the smell of gunpowder, and of already of decaying flesh. I was [alone] with a few old Palestinian women [and] a few young unarmed Fedayeen, but if these five or six human beings had not been there and I had discovered this butchered city, black and swollen Palestinians lying there, I would have gone crazy [...] That city lying in smithereens which I saw or thought I saw, which I walked through, felt, and whose death stench I wore, had all that taken place? I had explored, and poorly at that, only a 20th of Shatila and Sabra [...]"[7]

Ici et ailleurs (Here and Elsewhere), Jean-Luc Godard & Anne-Marie Miéville (1976)

Ici et ailleurs signals two breaks. The first is the end of militant politics, of the exportation of concepts and of their credo: it is no longer the privilege of Here (France) to tell the truth about Elsewhere (Palestine), and even to be able to abide by words and pictures which would be responsible for expressing some truth about politics, politics as truth. The second break, its consequence (at least for Godard who lives it and expresses it in this way), is that of the cinema with itself; it can no longer be one with its *défilement*.

Hence photography: "the truth" which comes to both interrupt and fulfill the being of cinema, "truth 24 times per second" (Michel Subor to Anna Karina in *Le petit soldat* [*The Little Soldier*, 1960]). Godard, who leaves militant films to arrive at a type of cinema he senses but that he still does not know, does not (just) question photography (as he did in *Letter to Jane*, 1972, or as he will in *Comment ça va?*, 1978, and *Photo et Cie*, 1969, part 5b of *Six fois deux*). He redefines cinema, starting from photography and also from the still frame, in a sufficiently exemplary sequence to make him feel the need to produce a second version of this 12 years later, much more voluptuous, and nostalgic, putting cinema to the question of both photography *and* video (*Grandeur et décadence d'un petit commerce de cinéma*[8]).

So, in this symbolic sequence, five extras gathered around a camera, each holding a photograph, turn toward the wall and pin up the photographs while declaiming a slogan: "The will of the people," "Armed struggle," "Political work," "The extension of war," "Till victory." Then they turn to us, each one underneath his or her photograph. Godard comments: “Here you can see all the photographs together, in the cinema you can’t, you have to see them separately, one after the other, and this is what you get”—that is, a projection, at first shown as such (the projector in the lower left corner, the mini-screen on the wall in the top right), through which, in a full-screen image, we then penetrate inside five photographs, in five successive shots (each time separated by black). Godard’s voice returns: “But that’s what you get, because actually, when you make a film, things happen like that. Each time a picture comes to replace another, each time the next picture chases away the one before, takes its place, while of course keeping it in mind more or less. This is possible because the film moves and the images are not being recorded together, but separately, one after the other, on their support.” While he is saying this, the extras, still holding their photographs, walk one after the other toward the camera, which is filming them.

1

2

3

4

5

Two things are striking here. The photographs first projected on the wall and "edited" are nevertheless separated by black: this is a way to both protect the autonomy of each photograph and to materialize the separation between the frames on the film stock, which projection prohibits us from seeing. This means projecting, in linear time, the separation visible in spatial terms between the photographs pinned on the wall or held up (in a second phase) by the extras lined up and moving toward the camera, thus forming a broken/ unbroken line (a continual sound replaces the discontinuity of the five slogans). So it is then this space-time relationship on which Godard comments (third phase), with an exacting patience that well expresses to what extent it intends to capture and restore to us an elementary, irrevocable truth: the reversion of space into time (of each extra-slogan-photo-space into extra-slogan-photo-time) is truly a metamorphosis, but remains current and visible throughout; such that the filmed space yielded to the time of projection subsists within this time and inescapably leaves its mark there. The second striking thing is that each of these photographs is represented by a body. In this way, Godard translates—depending on the whims of his pedagogy—the connection between film and movement ("the film moves," like bodies move), only to melt it down immediately into fixed images entrusted with expressing some fundamental truth about it (consequently, the film is regularly stopped, as bodies can be; and these bodies standing as one are as inescapably separated from each other as the frames are). "And the film—that is, in sum, images on the assembly line [*la chaîne*]—gives through this series of images a good impression of my double identity: space and time chained to each other like two workers on the assembly line, where each is both the copy and the original of the other."

This is what shifts and deepens with the two questions that Godard subsequently asks (himself). *First question*: "How is a chain organized?" First of all he lets some pictures flash by, photographs—a real car assembly line, a war scene, a concentration camp, an advertisement for Jacques Borel hotels, the structure of DNA, a nuclear family—images that fill the screen. Some of them, however, still incorporate the black bar between television frames, the sign of their *défilement*: the continuity that impels them is thus correlated both with their stillness and their separation.

1

2

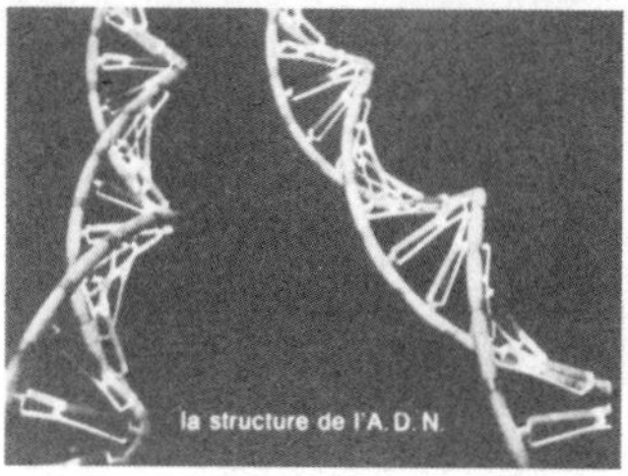

3

4

He then displays three photographs on one screen simul-taneously: in this way, a horizontal interval replaces the interval implied by the black bar. These photographs appear and disappear, transform themselves, punctuated by the noisy clicking of a slide projector into which a barely glimpsed hand inserts them: as a result, they are again identified as photographs, each given its own sound.

Second question: "How do you find your own image amid the order and disorder of the others, with the agreement or disagreement of the others? And to do so, how can you make your own image? Your public image, your trademark, an image that leaves a mark?" You have to emphasize move-ment: to no longer have three mini-screens within the screen, but nine (monitors), and to have them take the place of each other following the same principle, thus intensifying the redistribution of time in the space that is itself borne away into time after a new "deal" of images. All it takes is to borrow the effect of the black bar while intensifying it, and to relate the whole process in the end to the lens of a still camera (that we see and hear "and that becomes you, and will become you or me, you and me"): a lens entrusted with representing the gaze that we have "when we look at this image."

Thus, cinema is the truth 24 times per second only because photography—the photography within cinema, in other words the still frame—is endowed with its paradoxical truth: both fixed (in space) and moving (in time).

La Jetée, Chris Marker (1963)

Almost everything has been said about Marker's film over the last 25 years, as its extreme singularity, which now seems obvious, had been so striking. It has also been used, especially by theoreticians, to redefine a certain state of cinema. To show, for example, how the soundtrack can give back to fiction film what photography tends to take away.[9] To understand that movement is not what is most internal to cinema, but time.[10] To capture a level of "monstrosity" which, through the use of fades to black and especially of dissolves, reveals the madness of the "pictogram," a sort of primordial instance of the unrepresentable.[11] Nor am I forgetting that in trying to analyze *La Jetée*—first through words, then through a rearrangement of the film's images, thus pushing an already extreme critical undertaking to the limit (although his project, *La Rejetée*, had to be abandoned)—Thierry Kuntzel has gone from an unparalleled theoretical approach to the conception of a body of work through which video shifts and renews the conditions of the cinema-image.

To this we should add that this film condenses, in 29 minutes, a love story, a journey toward childhood, boundless fascination for a single image (the uniqueness of the image), a combined representation of war, the nuclear threat, concentration camps, an homage to cinema (Hitchcock, Langlois, Jacques Ledoux, etc.), to photography (Capa), an approach to memory, a passion for museums, an attraction to animals, and amid all this an extraordinary sense of the moment.

But I would especially like to say why this fiction film, indeed this science-fiction film, seemed absolutely essential within a selection of films essentially documentary in nature (this also applies to Raoul Ruiz's *Colloque de chiens* [*Dog's Dialogue*, 1977]). The reason is simple, although strange: it is quite simply that the photograph—in itself, but also because of its difference with film, and all the more, probably, if the film is a fiction film—the photograph has an unavoidable documentary dimension. It does not shadow time, as film does: it suspends it, breaks it, freezes it, and in this way "documents" it. It constitutes, in a way, a kind of absolute truth about each of the instants it captures. "Photography is truth" (as Godard had Michel Subor say while stalking Anna Karina with his camera in *Le petit soldat*). But what does his next statement really mean: "Cinema is the truth 24 times per second"? Something impossible, since cinema hides what photography shows: each picture for itself, in its naked truth, overcome by the *défilement*. Unless cinema could, through this very *défilement*, get near this truth through various means, the safest and in any case the most striking being, one would imagine, to tell a story made of frozen moments, as soon as they have been shot, whatever may be "the life" with which they find themselves endowed through the montage, the music, the words, and the voice. This is what *La Jetée* does, two years after "The Little Soldier" of the cinema revolution issued his call. It is by the same token a way (again not the only one, but one of the most radical and probably the most striking, both abstractly and materially) to check a second proposition Godard made, which must be linked to the first one as they shed some light upon each other: a film must always be the documentary of its own making.

1989. Originally translated in 1989 by Sylvie Osmond.

[1] *Contacts* was a series of short programs produced by Klein for the French TV network La Sept in the 1980s, consisting of voice-overs from well-known photographers (Cartier-Bresson, Nan Goldin) commenting on their work. The quoted text in this article comes from the episode on Klein himself, which he also directed [editor's note].

[2] So begins the text written by Jacques Roubaud that appears on the back cover of the *Diary of Alix Cléo Roubaud*, his wife (Editions du Seuil, 1984).

[3] Jean Genet, "Four Hours in Shatila," trans. Daniel R. Dupêcher and Martha Perrigaud, *Journal of Palestine Studies* 12.3 (Spring 1983) 4.

[4] Genet 5.

[5] Genet 5.

[6] Genet 5.

[7] Genet 21.

[8] An episode of the TV series *Série noire*, broadcast in 1986. Literally "Rise and Fall of a Small Film Company" [editor's note].

[9] Roger Odin, "Le film de fiction saisi par la photographie et sauvé par la bande-son. A propos de *La Jetée* de Chris Marker," in *Cinémas de la modernité, films, théories* (Paris: Klincksieck, 1981).

[10] Peter Wollen "Feu et Glace," *Photographies*, vol. 4 (March 1984) ["Fire and Ice," *Other Than Itself: Writing Photography*, ed. John X. Berger and Olivier Richon (Manchester: Cornerhouse Gallery, 1989)] 120.

[11] Réda Bensmaïa, "Du photogramme au pictogramme: A propos de *La Jetée* de Chris Marker," *Iris* 8 (1988).

Chris Marker, *La Jetée*, 1963

The Limits of Fiction

Bill Viola, *Chott-el-Djerid. A Portrait in Light and Heat*, 1982

Orson Welles, *Citizen Kane*, 1940

When I began to reflect upon the complex issue of video-fiction and its relationship to cinema and television, two images (or sequences of images) immediately came to mind: in both cases, images of snow—one from a videotape, the other from a film.

The video is Bill Viola's *Chott-el-Djerid (A Portrait in Light and Heat)* (1979). In the opening sequence, we see a snow-white screen and a tiny black dot moving ever so slightly. It continues to move and approach the camera (the sequence lasts four minutes), until it gradually assumes human form.[1] The film is Orson Welles' *Citizen Kane* (1941). The scene: a child playing in the snow who, at his mother's call, comes to greet a man who tells him he will become one of the richest men in America.[2]

Could these two images, separated by such radically opposed artistic and cultural codes, be combined in a single film or videotape, could they become compatible elements sharing a single medium? I asked Bill Viola this question, in so many words, in a conversation. My question was: "What would happen if this character continued to approach us, and instead of simply assuming human form, actually became a real human being and started talking to us, like a character in a story, about some situation he was involved in, something about life or death or sex or whatever?" Bill Viola evaded the question, as one could only evade it by bringing up the subject—as has been done so many times in the past—of two separate modes of fictions, whose distinctions are so blurred they can only be described in their most extreme forms: on the one hand, zero-degree fiction; and on the other, narration.

Let us say then that fiction has two centers: one abstract, the other concrete. The abstract center (which is sometimes considered the most concrete) or starting point is a sort of minimalist drama that establishes a situational relationship between at least two elements, for example a point on a surface. The concrete center (which often seems more abstract, or in any event, more illusive), wherein the situation becomes a story involving characters in a specific time and place, is portrayed with a reality that seems completely natural, which always has and always will seem completely natural, in spite of everything, even if it is strictly a cultural construct. To a greater or lesser degree, fiction in cinema (at least most cinema) has been and continues to be defined in terms of this second center. The opening scene of Viola's tape is an example of the first center, even though—as he himself reminded me—this very long sequence does provide an essential reference point for the viewer, enabling him to define his own position and establish his own identity in relationship to the fiction.

At this point, I cannot resist complicating the issue by recalling a third image: once again, an image of snow, from Hollis Frampton's experimental film *Zorns Lemma* (1970). In this case, the image occurs in the last sequence, after a prolonged series of paradoxical juxtapositions of words, formed by changing one or more letters in their spelling, and the objects they represent. After this rather disconcerting but carefully thought-out synchronization of words and images, which clearly exposes the disparities between language and image, we suddenly see a man, a woman, and a dog in a field of snow. As they move off into the distance, a confusion of words and snatches of conversations on the soundtrack seems to condense, transpose, and distort all the words and sounds we have read and heard in the preceding sequence.

All my efforts to explain why these three images are associated in my mind, and to determine what they might have in common, led to an analysis of the image of snow as the zero-degree state of the electronic *trame*, from which all other images proceed. The more I tried to put this idea out of my mind, the more I became convinced that this was the crux of the problem and that I should examine it in greater detail.

"Experimental" or "avant-garde" film (neither term is really adequate) and video art (again for want of a better word) both use every means at their disposal to transcend the limits imposed by photographic analogy, realistic representation, and convincing plot development. As has often been suggested, this tends to create stronger links between them and visual art and poetry than with cinema, the medium with which they are so closely identified. The procedures, techniques and modes of expression that have resulted in this development can be described in two words, addition and subtraction, despite the fact that this vastly oversimplifies the matter. In most experimental films and videotapes, there is no longer a "natural contract" between image and sound. Instead, there is always subtraction, and addition: acceleration and deceleration, multiplication and elimination of effects, countless disturbances that lead to a complete breakdown of the century-old contract between cinema fiction and the spectator. But it should be noted that the techniques of resistance and separation used to create a different order of time and space, and thus a specific art form or level of art, are in fact quite distinct in experimental film and video. In spite of the many—often underestimated—similarities between the two, the essential distinctions between them are very significant. Yet it almost seems as if video artists and critics had chosen to ignore this major difference. The most important major difference is that experimental film has been defined in terms of its relationship to cinema, whereas video, as Jean-Paul Fargier has insistently pointed out, is more closely related to television (although this is debatable, particularly for the best in French video art.)

But what does it really mean to suggest that video has its origins in television and is defined in terms of its relationship to television? Television has become the modern world's most important purveyor of images, including cinematic images, which constitutes such an important—and, as far as the TV audience is concerned, popular part of its programming. Let us just stop for a moment and try to imagine the proportion of cinematic images we see on television (not merely images on film), with all the overlapping and blurring of ethics and aesthetics this entails. To mention but one example, of major importance at the present time: the overwhelming number of promotional videos that are shot on 35mm film, which are seen, recognized, and acknowledged as television/video productions.

This seems to imply a major shift in the relationship between video and television. Initially video art considered itself as an autonomous *dispositif* in relation to television: an anti-*dispositif* in the prevailing spirit of dissent, taking a cue from the visual arts. Now, however, video artists must contend with the fact that television has become the most important source of fiction in society: of cinematic fiction especially. Because of this profound change in the role of television itself, as the largest producer and distributor of images, video by artists has acquired virtually unlimited power, far surpassing that of experimental film vis-à-vis commercial cinema.

This brings us back to the image of snow—the essential nature of the electronic image. On the one hand, electronic images can easily create the illusion of reality, as do the majority of film images; the medium and even the nature of the image may differ, but there is really not that much difference between the film image and video image when analogy and representation come into play. But on the other hand, the electronic image can be manipulated (what's more, simultaneously or live) so that the illusion of reality is relative: no longer simply undermined (as in experimental film), but in a constant state of flux. As video becomes ever more closely identified with fiction (which seems inevitable as long as it remains one of the major elements in the contract of fiction every society establishes with its individual members), this facet of the electronic image becomes increasingly problematic.

At this point, it would be appropriate to make the distinction between what might be called "fiction as system" and "fiction as body." Gary Hill's tapes constitute a good example of the first type. Their intellectual and formal abstraction desen-sitizes them to the issue of representation and the unease it can produce. Adhering strictly to their own system of logic, they create a sort of permanent meta-fiction. One might suggest, by analogy, that in his tapes, Gary Hill approaches the question of fiction similarly to the way in which Raymond Roussel dealt with narrative literature in his books. This technique of adopting "fiction as system" *a priori* is in complete contrast what happens when fiction presents itself as a body, that is when one takes on the *mise en scène*, materialization, and dramatization of bodies.

I will briefly consider two examples—simple but eloquent in their very simplicity—taken from tapes by Danielle Jaeggi: *Tout près de la frontière* (Right Near the Border, 1982) and *Mon tout premier baiser* (My Very First Kiss, 1984). In the first tape, the scenario seems to suggest (via the careful framing of the images and the way the heroine/actress delivers her lines) that the person we see is assuming the role of a TV newscaster. She addresses us as an audience for such a program, but she tells us about her own personal life. The tape itself is in many ways edited like a film and the opening credits (passing trains, long tracking shots of landscapes going by) create the distinct impression that we are watching a film. One sequence interests me, as it contributes to what Jean-Paul Fargier has called the "*aventures de la trame*." The heroine falls asleep after watching the news, and her voice accompanies three images (the last is a TV image): "In the final cut, you don't have to show the images I see before I fall asleep." When she wakes up, a doubled, processed image, furrowed with lines and colors, turns toward us, before we see the "real" image of her face reconstitute itself at the end of its movement (the voice returns: "I had a nightmare last night.")

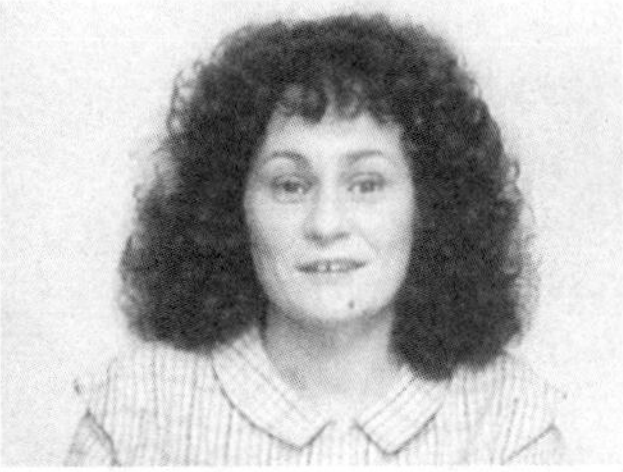

1

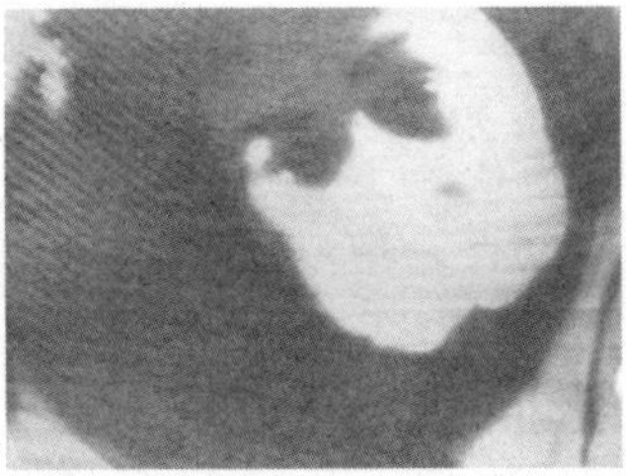

2

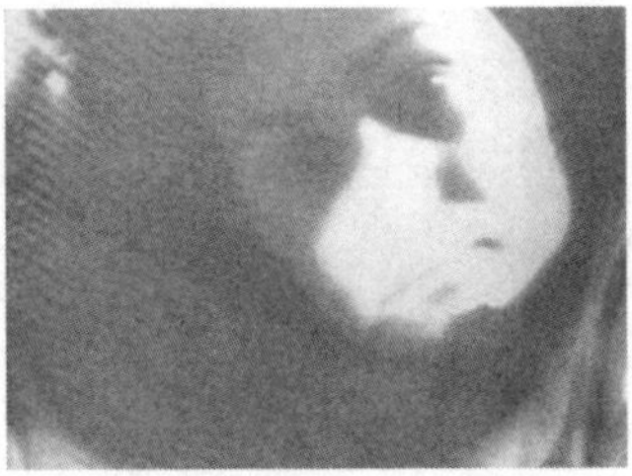

3

In *Mon tout premier baiser*, Danielle Jaeggi also uses the image of her own face to create a very subtle and highly sophisticated series of transitions and counterpoints between the "real" and manipulated electronic image. This time we see the artist conducting an interview. (A brief synopsis of the tape seems in order here: a woman, Danielle Jaeggi herself, decides to meet the man who kissed her for the first time some 20 years previously. As a young woman she had even recorded this in great detail in her diary. She arranges an interview with the man—who has since become a nuclear physicist—ostensibly to talk about his work. But after the first question, she drops all pretenses and asks him if he remembers the woman—i.e. herself—who remembers him so well.)

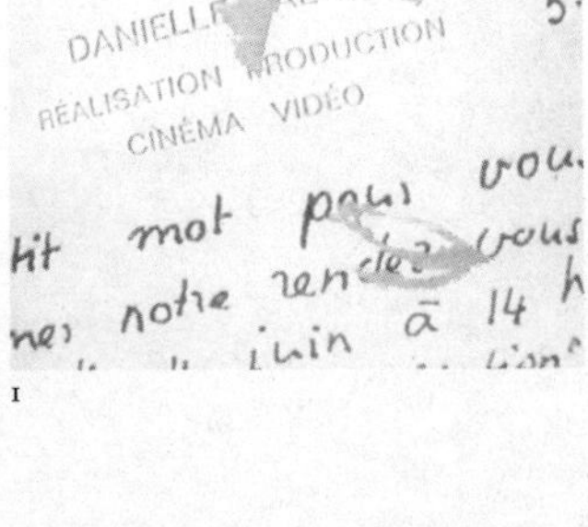

1

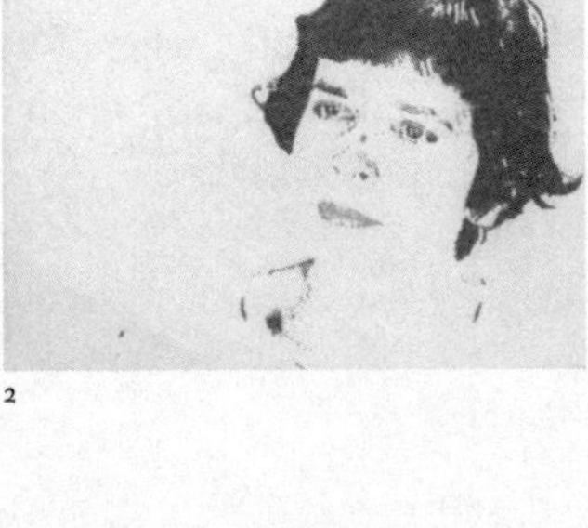

2

1

2

3

The striking thing here is that the technique of using red lines to create a "real" image which takes shape and dissolves before our eyes, especially in the opening sequence, also recalls the subject of the tape itself: the kiss, the red lips kissing. In this way the video image experiments with the "image of the first man who kissed me."

It seems to me that these two examples raise a fundamental issue that enables us to place in their proper perspective two questions raised by Fargier as reference points in these discussions. According to Fargier, experience to date has proven that the answers to both of these questions are in the negative. Fargier asks: 1. Is it formally possible for video to become more oriented toward fiction without developing these "*aventures de la trame*"? and 2. Can video fiction find themes and subjects outside the realm of video itself (as it becomes more and more identified as the generic and rather all-inclusive term used to describe new media: i.e. television, computer imagery, music videos, etc.)? In this context, I would like to ask another question, which might serve as a response, however conditional, to this question. Is this reference to a recognized medium (i.e. television) perhaps necessary to guarantee that the effect of the *trame* on bodies can avoid seeming unreal and ridiculous (perhaps they are one and the same) once they become part of a narrative or plot that makes them believable as bodies?

In other words, isn't the reference to the medium what creates an illusion of reality that lends credibility to unreal bodies produced by the effect of the *trame*? This raises the basic problem, I believe, of video fiction as it relates to cinema and television: at a certain level, fiction as narrative will inevitably become video's permanent temptation, just as it has always been and continues to be the "natural" vocation of cinema. This is why I have reservations about the term "science fiction" which has been used to describe the evolution of video fiction as a genre. It seems that the problem we are dealing with here is much more basic than the question of genre; it is part of the whole process of re-defining the importance of image versus narrative taking place at the present time (even though, it must be admitted, this problem is as old as cinema itself, as witnessed in experimental film and the upheavals of the silent movie era.)

With these ideas in mind, I would like to make a few brief comments that might help define the problem or, at least, see it in a different light. For example, think of how difficult it is to return to a more or less realistic image once the image is no longer associated with the "reality" of photographic representation. Let us also suppose for a moment that the television *dispositif* no longer serves as the token framework, medium, or mediator that somehow guarantees the image will not be perceived as totally unrealistic, and facilitates the transition between different levels of imagery. (The same problem arises when it comes to maintaining the credibility of the narrative—although here, the difficulties are of a different order; naturally enough, the two problems most often occur simultaneously.) Once one is within the domain of the *trame*, once a "new image" has been invented, how can one ignore the possibilities of further mutation and manipulation that may be inherent in the very logic of the image itself? Is it possible or even conceivable to regenerate (more or less) the imaginary body such as the (generally) familiar photographic illusion of cinema has presented it? I am reminded here of Thierry Kuntzel's work: his tapes are effective precisely because they make this transition impossible and reflect the desire to go beyond cinema, not only on the level of the visual material itself, but in the way they transcend the notion of fiction as dramatization and *mise en scène*. One very arresting example of this is Kuntzel's tape-film or film-tape on Cubism (co-signed by Philippe Grandrieux). In what appears to be a quasi-symbolic gesture (even though technical considerations do come into play), the film sequences create a minimalist scenario that constitutes the framework of the piece—a man, a couple thrust into the realm of Cubist painting. The video segments explore the more abstract and at the same time more material dimensions of this scenario—the purely cubist elements that create a type of space and image quite different from photographic realism. In this case, painting and art history serve as the reference points that the television *dispositif* usually constitutes in the majority of video productions, thus adding yet another level of abstraction to the work.

I am also reminded of the famous controversy, initiated by Bazin and particularly relevant at the present time, over the problem of portraying eroticism in cinema. While he always maintained certain reservations about his theory, Bazin proposed that "cinema can say everything, but not show everything"; and further, that in order to evoke the passion of bodies, "the image [must] never [take] on a documentary quality." He then arrived at the problematic conclusion: "the one critical censorship that the cinema cannot dispense with is imposed by the image itself."[3] In other words, it is not due to notions of morality, but because of the very nature of the illusion and the convincing reality of the photographic image that, beyond a certain point, one runs the risk of violating the contract of fiction established by the image itself. With this in mind, I find it moving that in *Sauve qui peut (la vie)* (*Every Man for Himself*, 1980), the impossibility of filming a kiss leads to the disruption, decomposition, and distortion of the image—techniques ultimately suited best to video. This raises the question of whether the film image, subjected to video manipulation, might one day be capable of portraying a kiss while sustaining the illusion of corporeal reality that film has presented too often but that video has not presented often enough. We are dealing here with a very difficult and obscure issue that involves the relationship between the subject and the body, all images of the body. Furthermore, the very foundations of cinema, from its ideals to its prac-tical reality, are called into question as soon as the actors' bodies themselves become the primary focus of our attention.

Let us now take a great, purely theoretical, leap and try to examine the problem on several levels at once—*mise en scène*, production techniques, construction of meaning, collective imagination. I am reminded here of one of my favorite tapes—Max Almy's *Modern Times*. In a segment entitled "Modern Communication" we see a woman talking to her friend about a (romantic) experience she has just had. The first woman appears seated facing the camera, talking to her friend whom we cannot see. However, we do see the lips of this person, within a square that is then superimposed in four different places on the body of the woman on the screen. This effect is heightened by the fact that the distribution of the speaking parts makes it hard to tell if one single woman is playing both parts or if, in fact, two different women are involved (as if one became one of the interior voices of the other). Now let us imagine what would happen if these two women—instead of being the artist herself, one of her friends, a performance artist, or any other person she might use, like me or you, the way it usually happens in video art—were in fact Isabelle Huppert and Isabelle Adjani.

1

2

3

What would happen if these disembodied lips—isolated, impossible to identify as belonging to a particular body—were the only sign of Isabelle Adjani's presence on the screen? This would obviously suggest that our whole system of representation (not to mention society itself) had undergone some profound and definitive changes, and that video and cinema, as we know them, no longer existed as such. While this seems hardly likely, unfortunately, it is nevertheless very interesting to think along these lines. All of which brings me back to my opening remarks about the images of snow in the two works I mentioned by Bill Viola and Orson Welles: if we adopt the point of view I have described, it seems entirely possible that one day these two images might be combined in a single work, or at least be conceptually perceived as congruous images.

1983. Originally translated in 1986 by Jean-Luc Svoboda.

[1] This example—quoted from memory after three or four viewings of the tape—is incorrect: this error shows just how difficult it is to remember sequences of images (video makes this even more difficult than usual). I decided it would be better to admit my error while retaining the example as mentioned in the text, for its metaphorical value. In fact, the first seven sequences of *Chott-el-Djerid* are images of snow, in which a hamlet gradually appears. The shot I am talking about is the first shot of the desert after the snow sequences; this is what seems to have caused my confusion, especially if one takes into account the very slight change of hue in the images themselves—in this case, the image seems to be uniformly pink, with a faint line dividing the dunes from the horizon at the top of the frame.

[2] This sequence lasts for six shots and combines close-ups and long shots of Kane who is first seen in a medium long shot and then in the famous long shot framed by the window during the discussion between Thatcher, the mother and the father; the sequence concludes with a shot of the sleigh gradually disappearing into the snow.

[3] André Bazin, "En marge de 'L'érotisme au cinéma'" 252 ["Marginal Notes on *Eroticism in the Cinema*" 172].

From In-Between the Bodies

Jean-Luc Godard, *Scénario du film* Passion (Scenario for the film *Passion*), 1982

There are and there have been numerous ways to say: cinema, the art of movement and of analogous images, comes from or moves toward painting, a presence which is immobile and yet is so much freer in its relation to any represented reality.

It was possible, as Elie Faure had done in the days of silent films, to initially experience cinema as an "animation" of painting. But he sensed very quickly in "cineplastics"[1] (in spite of what the word itself seeks to designate) "a phenomenon too radically new for us to even think [...] of painting."[2] It was also possible to look for "the origins of *mise en scène*" in painting, to turn Giotto, Michelangelo, or Brueghel into the heroes of a pre-cinema attentive to the quality of movement and detail, to the off-screen space. J.G. Auriol did just that, while immediately limiting (and complicating) his analogy with the following proposition: "The absolute filmmaker, until the day when the direct recording of the imagination's productions is made possible by the harnessing of mental waves, the filmmaker who alone can show his film as he saw and created it in his mind, is perhaps the creator of 'cartoons': the man who has the means to take his images still moving from his head, a studio of magic, and to arrange, to harmonize, to animate and to punctuate them according to his intentions."[3] Finally, like André Bazin taking the question up once again, the two arts could be opposed by tracing between them a dividing line that has caused much ink to flow, the line between the frame and the mask, between the centripetal screen and the centrifugal painting.[4]

Lately, in an opposite move, we have seen Pascal Bonitzer, bolstered by the transformations of modern cinema, devote himself primarily to showing that if cinema moves less than is believed, painting likewise moves more than one might expect. This is the clue to a proximity (new and at the same time old) that is based as much on a common passion for seeing, as it is on comparable ways of approaching the image's components.[5] This perspective is also adopted by Jacques Aumont when he situates painting and cinema in his history of the visible, in which they together form what he refers to as the "endless eye."[6] He does this following a genealogical view, systematically distinguishing the different aspects (frame, space, light and color, form and expression) through which a more or less lively contamination operates between the two arts. This contamination obviously testifies as much to the current crisis of their specificity as it does to the retrospective truth regarding the nature of their respective media.

I find something striking in these two essays. In limiting themselves (it is in their interest) to fiction cinema—that is to cinema that works with actions and with visible bodies—they do not envision (or only to a limited extent) the way in which cinema, in transforming itself through video, draws closer than it has ever before been to painting. And, more precisely, to painting (ancient or modern, ancient and modern) in the way that it approaches bodies and their settings through means other than those of the photographic analogy (and of what replaces it in painting). Neither essay really touches the matter at hand, "the body of the body" as it were, the matter of the bodies and of their surroundings in their relation to the real-unreal of representation. Bonitzer can be seen to waver on this point in an interesting manner (my reading pushes him closer to the problems as I see it). First (in a previous book), he attacks with concentrated violence what he calls the "video surface": the image without reality or distance, without shadow, without history.[7] Next (this time in *Décadrages*), inspired by a moment in *L'avventura* (1960) when the hero spills a bottle of ink on the design of a young architect, he praises the "spot" in Antonioni: "The spot expresses entropy, degradation, the irreversibility of events; but it also marks the creation of a remarkable figure, even if it remains shapeless and unnamed."[8] Is this not precisely what is done, what can be done, by video? Does it not seek to design in the figure (the figure of bodies, of objects and of landscapes) that which is (still) shapeless and unnamed? Video is not only a surface, even if it does contribute to the removal of some of the image's (in particular the film image's) former depth. It also bestows on cinema a new depth, difficult to name. As if by magic, video allows bodies to appear and to disappear, which has been from time immemorial one of the (traumatic) dreams of the image. But above all it stretches, as if to infinity, the register of what until then had been permitted in cinema essentially by lighting and by a limited number of special effects (this will always be the wonderful part of silent films). In short video makes the truth (or the illusion, the madness) of the image well up *from in-between the bodies*.

This should come to light in the three films (or three tapes) I have juxtaposed here, because they seem to me to form a picture, to prefigure together this new state. Let us say: how video apprehends cinema as painting.

I. "Seul dans la nuit"

Why start with this tape (this film), *La Peinture cubiste* (*Cubist Painting*, 1981, 49'), in attempting to outline the effect of a passage between painting and cinema? The approach, adopted by Thierry Kuntzel and Philippe Grandrieux on the basis of Jean Paulhan's text, is as fictional as it is discursive or documentary. These two authors have imagined a division, an alternation between cinema and video (Philippe Grandrieux taking charge of the film portions and Thierry

Kuntzel the video portions), which has the merit of permitting a coherent interpretation of the text while also using it as a pretext. In this way, the relating of two classical terms, painting and cinema, opens up a three-legged (three-termed) race from which emerges (through this painting or this text, and beyond them) the very question of the relation—actual and virtual at the same time—between cinema and video.

This is what the story of the art lover (a Paulhan as real as he is imaginary) suggests, when coming home to his studio one night he decides to leave the lights out so as not to disturb his sleeping wife, and finds himself having an experience in his familiar environment that he sums up at the end of the film in this way: "Then, at the very instant when two o'clock sounded on a third clock, a strange feeling came over me, the feeling that I had crossed through the space of a Cubist painting."

As a result, the question of the genealogy of image media necessarily follows. The close alternation between the film and the video segments in fact supposes that video (processed this way thanks to a video synthesizer) performs a transgression—in relation to (more or less) implicit norms of the film image—that is comparable to Cubist painting fracturing what remained of classical pictorial space at the turn of the century. We might wonder to what extent it is correct to say that the overstepping of realistic representation, radicalized in the image animated by video, repeats or reproduces the image which progressively invaded painting from the moment when photography and then cinema became more "real" than painting had ever been. In the same vein, but staying much closer to the work itself, it would be possible to attempt to define how the components of the video segments respond to the rationalizations of the text (the narrator's voice, and the voice of the pictorial "*doxa*" which comes from a radio); through this we might understand to what extent the video image, worked in this way, corresponds (more or less) to the mutation of the vision projected in the past by Cubism. But we can also question the way in which film and video are invited to cohabit in a common space. Each is attracted there by the other, but at the same time they exclude and repel one another along their mutual edges. It is always following this principle of alternation, as we have just seen, that video succeeds film. The distribution is very clear: it proceeds by groupings of shots, autonomous blocks of varying amplitude—let us (cautiously) say "sequences"—that have no carefully planned transitions between them. But this alternation never moves from shot to shot (which would be like going toward more or less unified sequences, as in classical narration), and in any case it is never resolved within a single shot. As if this were a prerequisite for thinking about the relation between cinema and video (and for rediscovering, from a different point of view, the idea of cinema revisited by painting). It is this third aspect that interests me, even though it appears only by means of the other two.

What is at stake here is clear. On one hand, we find ourselves before a "normal," realistic image, in which the objects are laid out in their usual three dimensions—with their visible and hidden sides, their vanishing lines and their relations of tone—in accordance with the laws set down since the Renaissance and subject to the rationalization that optics operate in the conditions of natural vision. Confronting this sensible image is another, which no longer has a visible eye. It has neither surface nor depth; it is immaterial to say that the surfaces sink back into it, or that its depth is shrunk to that of a layer of film. Nor can we really make the distinction between light and darkness (in which fiction finds its pretext); it is more a stratification of blackness and of colored vibrations, as if they were lit or darkened from within, inside the mass of form and lines. This image is multi-layered, mobile, translucent; it is made up of superimposed layers, of disassociating strata. We could just as easily say: there is no body in this image. Or on the contrary: this image is only that, body. And the real body, the lost hero's body, blends with it until they flow one through the other.

The spectator notices very quickly that the two authors were astute enough to avoid having the video segments spring systematically from the film images, of which they would only be a reinterpretation. On the contrary, the authors often first introduce into the floating image of the video an object that is later rediscovered in the stillness of the film frame. (For example, the mandolin, the chessboard, or the book essential to their purpose, *The History of Painting*, which the hero leafs through on several occasions.) This approach allows them to steer away from didactic cinema. In theory

1

2

3

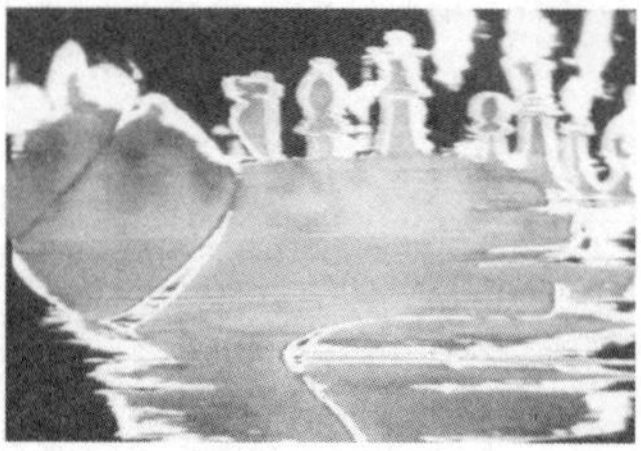
4

5

6

7

8

9

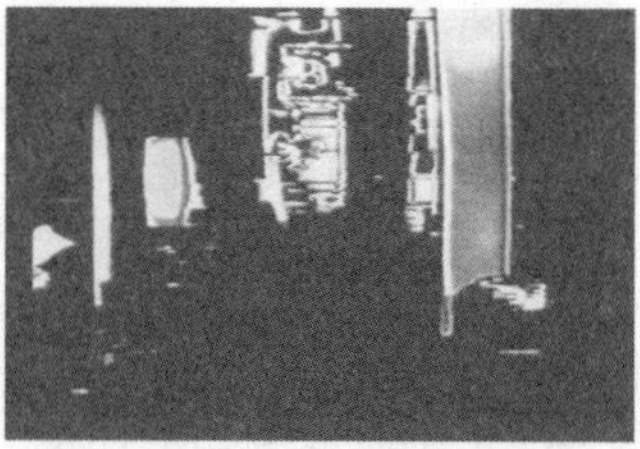
10

11

12

13

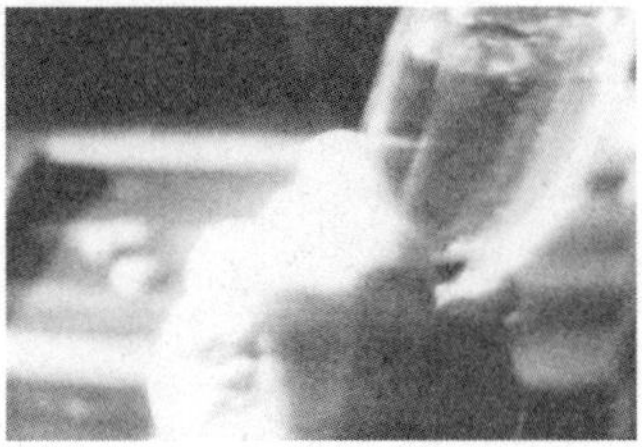

14

15

16

17

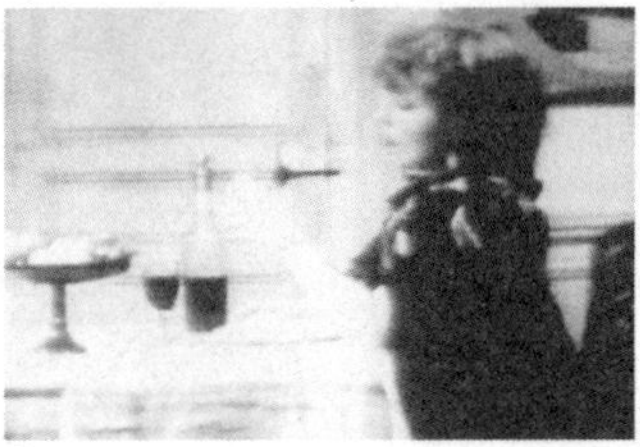

18

19

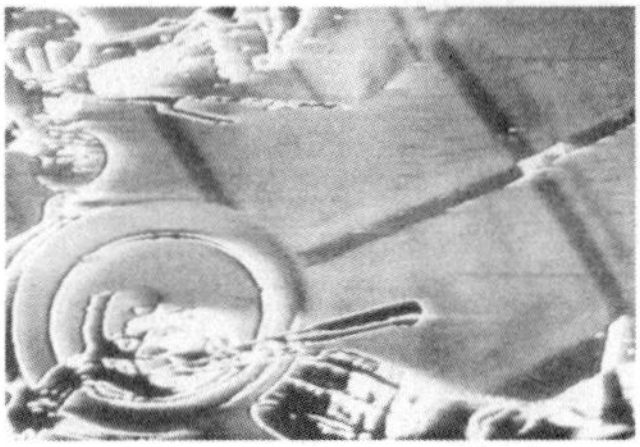

20

21

22

23

24

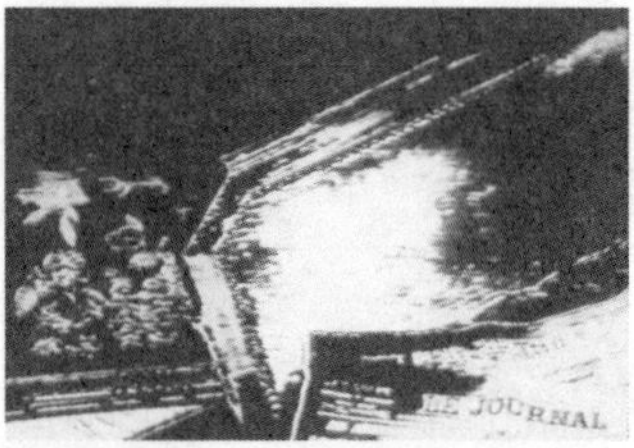

25

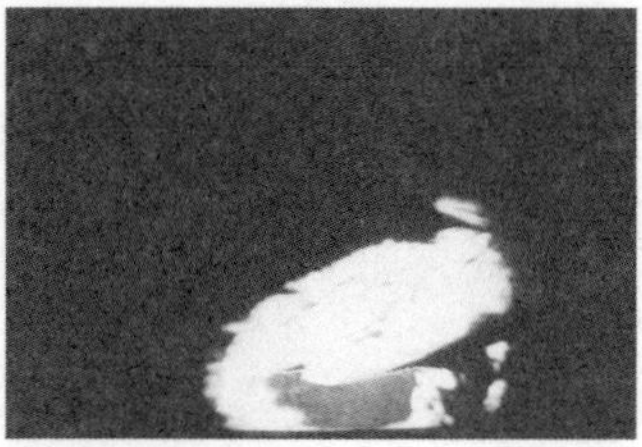

26

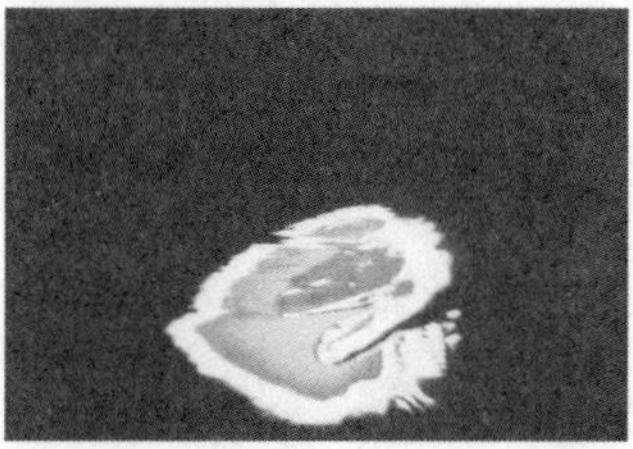

27

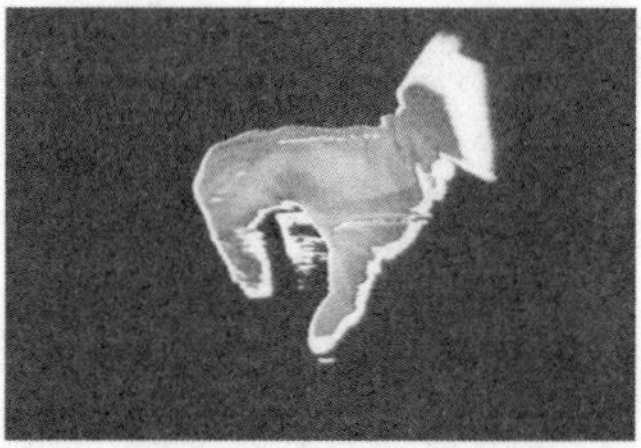

28

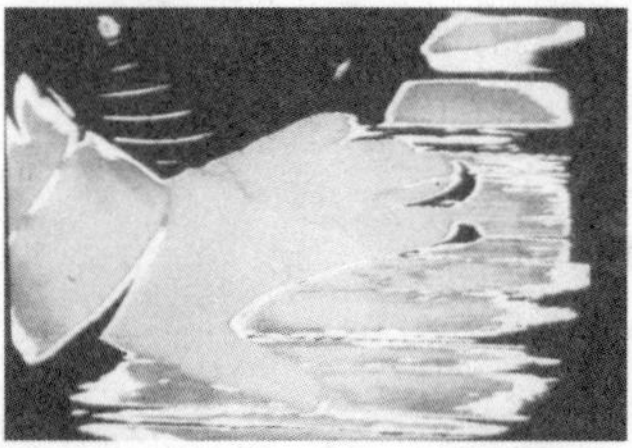

29

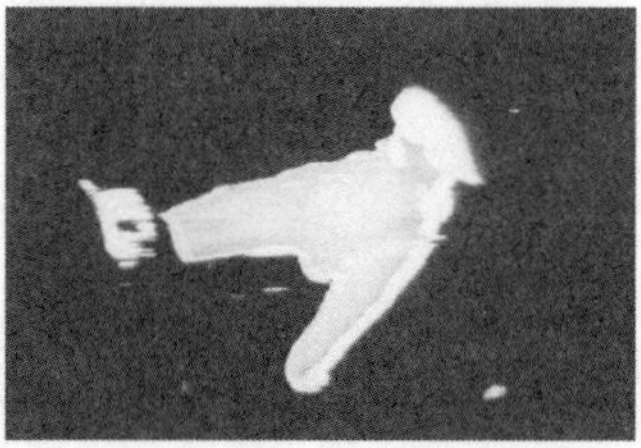

30

it grants equality to the video image, which initially appears only as a secondary image (as historically it is). In the end it is a way to link the two spaces, visually and narratively, and to close in on what separates them more effectively.

And thus, the question of the passage arises: how to go from one type of image to another? How can this passage be justified, authenticated? Or more to the point: under what conditions is this passage possible, desirable, even bearable? Through painting, (and more precisely through Cubist painting), a question is put to film representation. This representation faces at the same time a possibility and an impossibility, something in the order of a virtuality: how can the *represented* body and the *dis-represented* body be linked in the same (both concrete and psychic) space?

In his desire to uncover flaws—vision's points of resistance in classical cinema—Stephen Heath cites an example taken from *Suspicion* (1941) that enables him to turn Hitchcock into the hero of a "skewed vision."[9] When two policemen arrive at Cary Grant's home to question him about a shady affair, the gaze of one of them suddenly lights and lingers unreasonably long on a painting hung in the hallway, "a post-Cubist painting," says Heath, something like Picasso's *Pitcher and Bowl of Fruit* (1931). This insertion of a frame within a frame, of the painting within the film image, maintains of course a theoretical exteriority between them; but in the fleeting moment that it links them this gaze emphasizes the fact that in stumbling across something that is (by convention or by nature) foreign to it, reality also slips out of its own reach.

"Reality": everyone knows what it is, even if we choose to ignore it. Even if all that is ever seen in cinema is an illusion or an impression (for want of sensations, such as internal feelings, which video could very well hope to give it). Quite simply, reality is the part of vision that most closely resembles natural perception, and the analogous image that frames and accompanies it. It is the represented. The dis-represented troubles it, provoking either the deepest emotion—genuine seduction—or hilarity, uneasiness, even ridicule, given the violence of anything affecting the integrity of the human body, or the material world surrounding it.

There is then a difficulty in representing and in dis-representing within a single space: in the same film, in the flow of a sequence, in the succession of its shots, and even in the same shot. This is true whether or not the transitions in question, depending on the inflections of the scenario, are motivated by a mutation of vision, by a welling up of emotion, a change of heart, a search for the symbolic, or a desire for abstraction.

If we keep (for the moment) to video itself, and in video to works opening onto fiction (for example those that J.P. Fargier once assembled under the banner "*de la trame au drame*"[10]), we notice that most of these works have no trouble at all in dis-representing. Yet this is subject to numerous requirements. Firstly, it is understood that the degree of fictional reality must remain minimal, thanks to various means that could easily be compiled into a list. (One of the most obvious is the absence of dialogue, which renders the incarnation tenuous. This is also one of the most interesting characteristics, one that revives the particularities of silent film, as many works of experimental cinema were already doing.) By simply establishing the dis-representation from the onset, it will subsequently impose itself as the general rule. This is one way to avoid the problems of transition—this is not in any way a value judgment—and in particular to avoid the risk of an overly brutal repudiation of the belief in the body's image. (Staying with Kuntzel's work, let us take for example *Nostos I* (1979): the unconscious body, perforated, pulverized, decomposed, is at the same time the only body which can call itself into being here.) As to the passages themselves (quite frequent all the same) from one image level to another, they seem to always depend on two modes. The first is a(n) (omnipresent) reference to the technological *dispositif* (television, the monitor, the *trame*, etc.). This is much more than a mere quotation: it allows the reinstatement of the belief factor, insofar as the *dispositif* itself is endowed with the capability of metamorphosis produced at the very same time by the image; the *dispositif* motivates and assists it, ensures that it is accepted. The second mode, less stable, is linked to particular situations that possess in themselves an incentive value; whether they have an effect on psychological states (sleep, dreams, etc.) of which the *dispositif* is more or less an emanation (since it is the material equivalent of a psychic scene); or whether they possess a symbolic value, or a value of fantasy that can be isolated in a figure (the sexual act, for example). Here again, we come up against the problem that has haunted cinema (in particular in the guise of the trick shot). In this respect *Liquid Sky*, Slava Tsukerman's 1982 film, could serve as a mediating example between cinema and video: the heroine's putting to death of her numerous sexual partners is underlined in the film by a complex figure that is reiterated throughout (a process shot obtained either by using a video synthesizer, or by the processing of digital images), which transforms the bodies, the real bodies, into a pure vibration of colors, lines, and light.

The question then must be asked: how, in a work of fiction (in cinema or video, cinema and video), can reality be treated, varied or transformed on the level of the body itself, on the level of the surroundings that frame it? This obviously means: in proportion to the degree of reality that has been obtained, all the more so if this degree remains high—as at any rate is the case as long as this is based on the omnipotence of the photographic analogy (or on its equivalent in electronic reproduction). This amounts to asking, for example: how to operate, for the matter and the figure of bodies, in a manner comparable to Godard controlling the speed of movement in *Sauve qui peut (la vie)* (*Every Man for Himself*, 1980). That is, by intervening in the very flow of a story subjected to a series of breaks, by lingering on random or secondary moments in the narration as well as on its strong moments and its watersheds.

I believe that the very strong suggestive value of *La Peinture cubiste* lies in this. Admittedly, the passages are only leaps made from one state to another. There is no dialogue between the characters, and the belief in their incarnations is accordingly minimized. Here, it is painting in particular that plays the role given to the tele-video *dispositif* in most of the other works. It does this in two ways. By its abstraction (the ideas that it serves and supposes), and by its materiality (the bodies and the painted objects that constitute it), Cubist painting (and through it all painting) becomes the mediation which makes possible and natural these passages from the "real" image to the "derealizing" image. So this tape (this film) will only dis-represent under certain conditions.

And still it is immensely unsettling. In my own case, this uneasiness goes far beyond mere disturbance.

For a start, the character's off-screen voice (played with extraordinary accuracy by Constantin Jelenski) confers on his living double (actually his double twice over: in each of the two images) a true dimension of experience; even more so as this voice comes and goes freely (nothing is more free than a voice) between the film and video sequences. Moreover, as the tape advances (it is relatively long for the little it seems to say, but its slowness, its reiterations, and its dreamy tone are all part of a strategy), the spectator increasingly lets himself go, as the effects of the impression and the psychic reversion between the two images and the two spaces become more pronounced. Directed by the hero's voice, subjected to the rather crazy vacillation that continues to come from the apparently sober and regulated figure of the alternation, the mind begins to project the two types of images—placed so meticulously back to back—over each other. The distribution of the fading (fades to black and dissolves) accentuates this confusion. Initially it seems that they are performed this way in order to isolate the film sections from the video sections. Little by little they also divide up each segment itself, to such a degree that these fades end up drawing closer the very segments they were supposedly driving apart.

This works all the better because there are here and there privileged moments that favor this mental passage, this virtuality. I have chosen two of them. One with a limited scope, the other more developed. And I'm doing this knowing full well that I am asking the reader to imagine an almost impalpable (and yet very real) process.

The first is situated near the end of the eighth segment. From its beginning the hero's hand, as if following the voice, retraces his journey in the studio's nocturnal space. The hand's movement obeys the modulations of the video image, dark and yet translucent, which doubles each line with a ring of vibratile light. Paulhan's story theorizes this experience in which he rediscovers Cubist painting, but his terms also anticipate what video produces, especially the effect of the *paluche*, this camera that becomes "an eye on the fingertips," with which Thierry Kuntzel (like Jean-André Fieschi) conceived almost all of his work. "It would seem then, that touch overrides sight, that the tactile space overrides the visual space. Everything happens as if our gaze were nothing more than an extension of our fingers, an antenna on our forehead." Then the camera abandons the hero's hand, lingering for a long while on the mingled, stratified, liquefied objects that his body-gaze discovers, coming back to his hand only at the end of the segment. This is when, in its final movement, the hand goes around the edge of a piece of furniture: still this hand of crude light that resembles a wave. But suddenly the effect is diluted (at least we believe it is), the way a lamp dims. For an instant—at the very end of the shot before everything sinks into a fade to black—a "real" hand appears, entirely "analog": a movie hand, that can see only when it is seen, without its tactile and inner gaze.

The second moment immediately follows the first (in the ninth film segment). In a medium close-up the hero, lying on his bed, looks around himself into the air. We see with him (in three shots that alternate with his worried face) what he sees: three spaces composed of curtains and of pleated cloth that trace sharp lines in the frame, as if taking note of the gaze's bounds. His eyes close. Dissolve. And we cut back (segment ten) to video. A (very beautiful) effects shot shows his wife Germaine's face in close-up; it turns in the bed in a linked series of phases whose *trame* seems to stay printed in the memory of the image as the movement unfolds. Same thing in the next two shots, with a glass and a small cube (already seen) that turn in the hero's hand. And then the three subjective shots of the preceding segment are repeated, very quickly, in succession and in a different order. But above all else—and this is the most interesting part—they are almost identical to the preceding shots (they are not subjected to any perceptible effect). Only the lighting changes: here dull, flat; there mottled, slightly shimmering. At this moment, through this interference effect, the video image and the film image draw close, attracting each other, making use (both actually and virtually) of their smallest differences to express slight lapses: physical, psychological, affective. The hero's voice seems to speak from a dream, linking through fiction wake and sleep, states of "normal" perception and of tactile-mental sensation. The voice reintroduces—by identifying at the same time the tape's game and what is at stake in it—the distance that at this very moment is almost warded off by the image: "I was moving forward through a space that was a riddle to me, and it would have remained just that had I not remembered, by chance, just as I was falling asleep, modern painting."

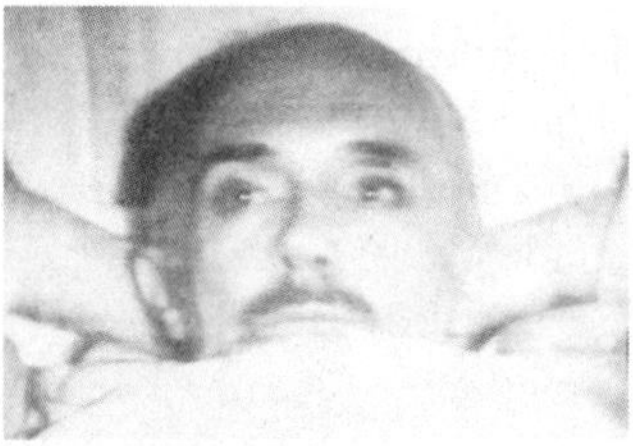
1

2

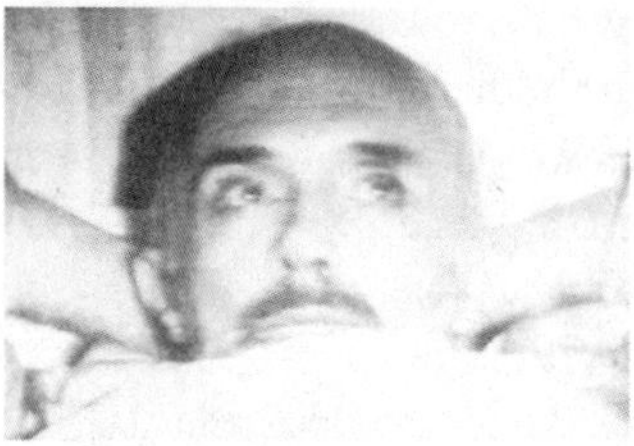
3

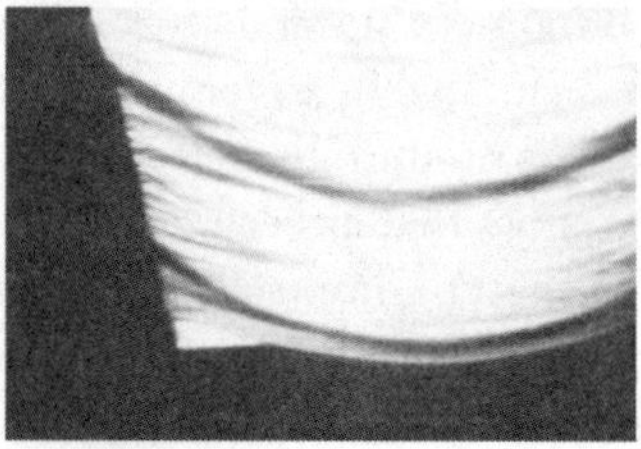
4

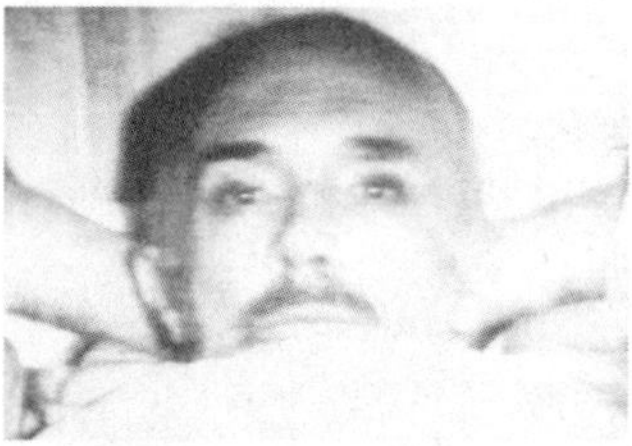
5

6

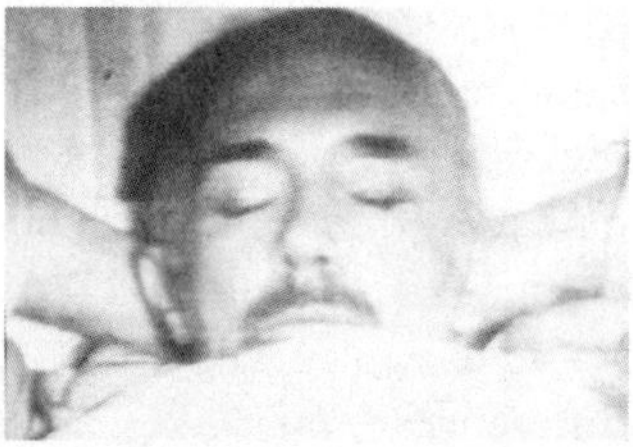
7

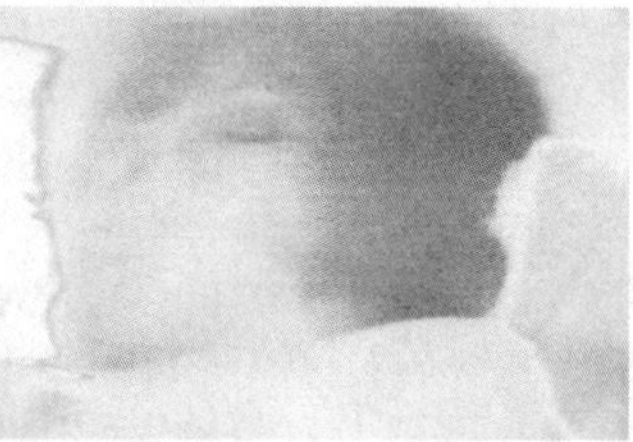
8

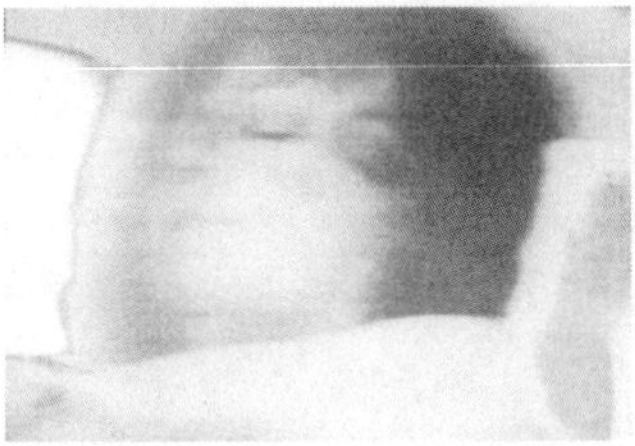

9

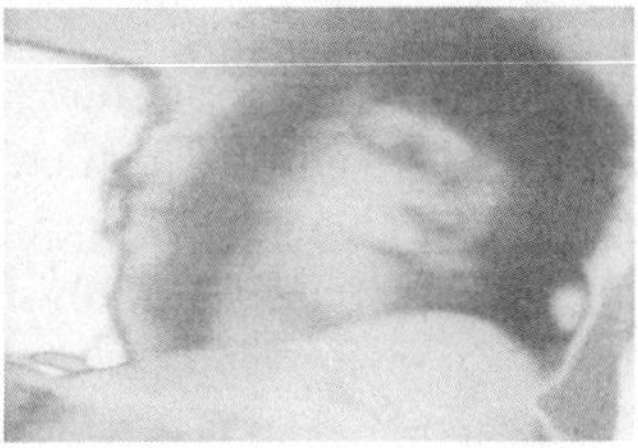

10

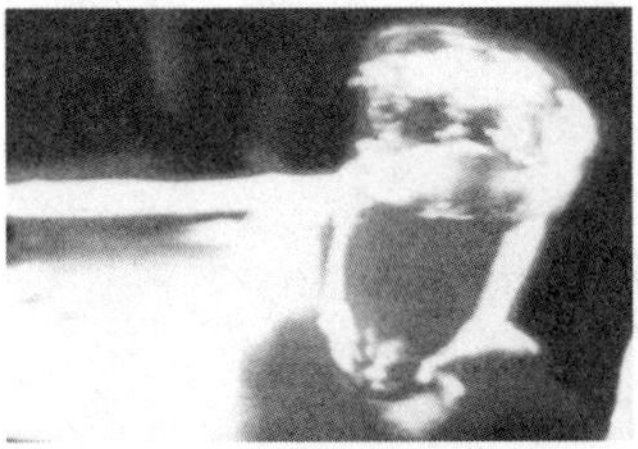

11

12

13

14

15

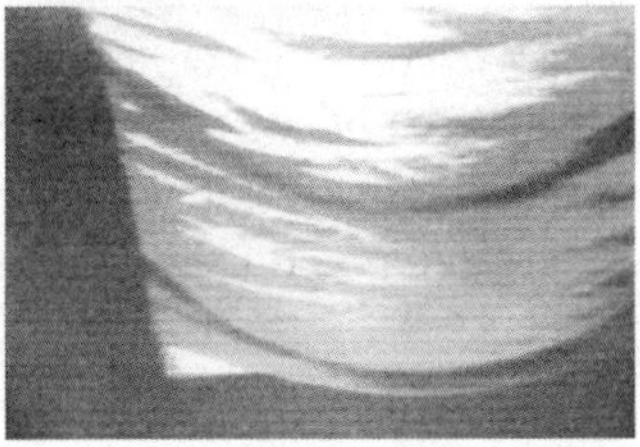

16

17

18

It must be emphasized that this effect of attraction and interference (the effect of the non-effect) lasts, unchanged, in three shots of paintings (which come after the three shots of cloth). In this way, from their very function as *dispositif* (they are images of Cubist paintings), they take on a paradoxical reality effect (they are objects among many). In fact, there is even less reason to process these shots with a video synthesizer in order to express the idea (the sensation) of a multifaceted reality, since the paintings accomplish by themselves what the video image can do in another way. The video image does this at the risk of seeming, like the paintings, to generate another "surface": that is to say at the risk of transforming into aberrant volume the illusory volume (this particular kind of surface) that the enigmatic volume of the living space has been reduced to when it is subjected by the tape to a purely perceptive dimension, to the codes of perspective that isolate it and bring it into focus.

In this way a turnabout is performed between these two segments, following a variable curve, until the identical emerges, between surfaces (or thicknesses) and depths: between cinema and video. In what they represent, both materially and historically, the paintings presented here serve as physical supports and as metaphors for this undertaking, which allows the film image to be confronted with the video image that doubles and transforms it.

Painting does indeed remain the agent and the motor of the confrontation, even if the game goes beyond it. This is what Godard sensed so keenly in *Passion* (strangely enough, the same year). In the part of the film concerning painting, he takes on only the pose of the bodies in their surroundings (he does this through cinema alone, but he too relies on the surface depth of video to conceive the project, then augmenting it with a postscript on the surface depth of video). He works in this manner to produce—between movement and stillness, life and death, the pregnant moment and the any-instant-whatever, representation and re-representation—a confusion extending the one he had already introduced (this time more directly through video) in *Sauve qui peut (la vie)*. In each case he pursues in a different manner the dis-representation that he once achieved, perhaps most vividly, by penetrating inside the bodies.

II. The Intermittences of the Body

After leaving the movie theater that day, he walked down the street without understanding what was happening to him. Pushing open his apartment door he heard cries and noises, stumbled onto bodies and conflicts. In that instant he understood that he had not left his home—as he usually did—in order to lose himself somewhere else, in the space of a film; but that the uniqueness of the film he had just seen was that it forced him to find himself at home, always and forever, in the film.

In the first place it must be remembered that *Numéro deux*—which has neither been rereleased in movie theaters nor rebroadcast on television since its release in 1975—is one of the works that most clearly inaugurates the transition from "cinema" toward something else. It prefigures Godard's series of television works as well as the films of his third period, with all of the new gestures that accompany them.[11]

Almost always one, two, three frames on a black background: a shattered, plural, unstable and unpredictable image. Such is the law of this story, which is not a story but becomes the matrix of possible stories—between men and women, parents and children, the young and the old, image and sound, cinema and television. In the beginning, at the end, in two long sequences (the only two full frame sequences, even if the monitors-as-screens do cut holes in them), there is the insistent presence of the master of ceremonies: he who receives the images and the sounds and redistributes them, at once the master and the slave of the *dispositifs*. Words regularly turn into images, screen-letters in this "screen film," representing Godard's voice which is already present in the voice of the characters: active, associative, uncontrollable, irritating pedagogy, which sends all meanings spinning and prevents us from choosing only one, finally forcing us to instead observe ourselves.

Four times in this scattered journey, in four love (or sex) scenes, the image changes in nature (three times toward the beginning, the fourth near the end). No longer only an image unburdened by, or loaded down with, the fact that it is always the image of an image—or the fragment of an image—but the image in its very body. This change bears on its materiality, opening up new possibilities of representation through dis-representation. This story races forward through a blending of forms and colors, as the innermost reality of family life is approached, reinvented. This reality—so deeply attached to the fluidity of the flow, to the transitions of tonality—is particularly delicate to render in words or in still images. But the stakes are high enough for us to try, even in an unsatisfying manner, to sketch its outline. Knowing full well that its importance is also seen in our incapacity to reproduce it.

1.

The film has been running for about ten minutes. The image preceding the scene shows the *dispositif*: projectors, editing table, two monitors with images flowing by. At the bottom left, the nightly news, the commentator inlaid on crowd scenes. Above it, a porn film that calls to mind an unclad Mizoguchi or a fragment of *In the Realm of the Senses* (1976): a woman climaxes, her body convulsed in the space, her face offered to the spectator.

We do not have enough time to make out the pretext-image, Pierrot taking Sandrine from behind. It has already become cloudy, invaded by a patch of blackness (coming from the right, as though bursting out from the black edge of the frame), when in it materializes a face; a woman's face, or rather a child's.

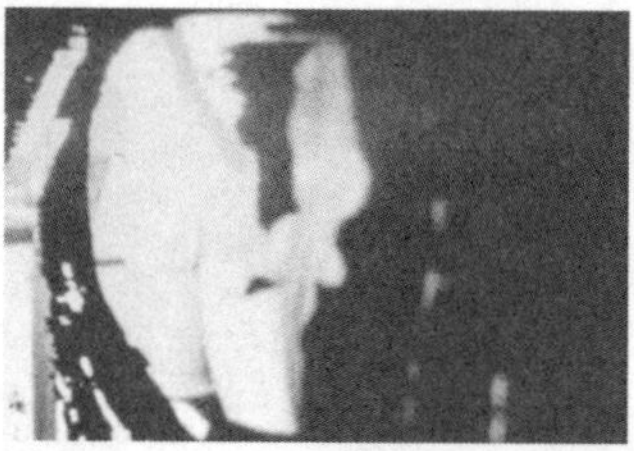
1

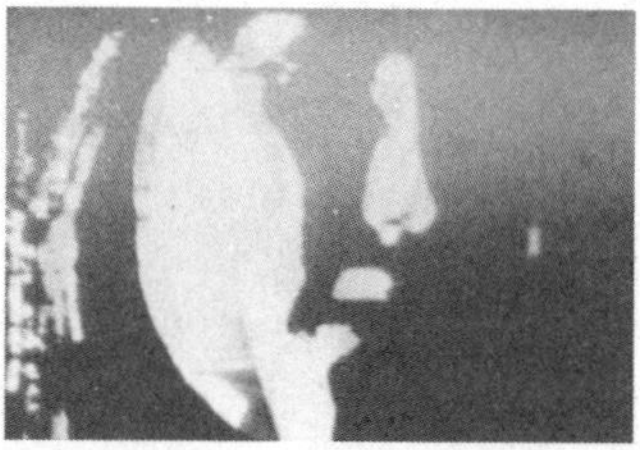
2

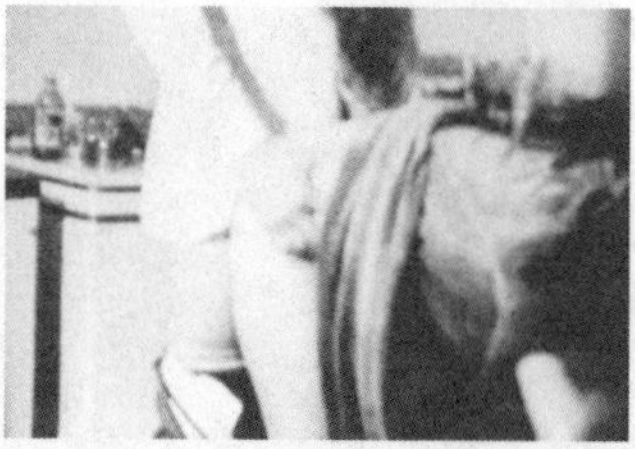
3

This face is not constituted in part, as the still frame might make us believe, by the bright white of a form that covered the bodies of the two partners. It is composed by a video synthesizer with the help of their modulated bodies, and by the distribution of blacks in such a manner that the second image introduced through the first literally seems to be its emanation (the left part of the face, the cheek, is in part formed by Sandrine's buttock and thigh). It is a face made up of their headless bodies. Its eye intermittently stares at us, an eye moving between life and death, taking the place (Medusa, paralyzing/paralyzed) of the supposed climax. In a sense a voyeuristic face, since it introduces a gaze that is substituted for our own in relation to the scene, and thus accompanies it. But at the same time it takes us beyond voyeurism, since it is made up of the internal substance of that which does not see and cannot see itself, of what it would observe for us while hiding it from us (actually as well as metaphorically).

This extraordinary impression stays behind after the effect has dissolved and all that remains is a patch of black to the right of the frame, in the place where Sandrine's truncated head would have been. A way of underlining that the effect can reappear, that in its brevity (around 15 seconds) it is only that much closer to hallucination, like the scene itself.

The image of the *dispositif* returns. The porn film and the news. Then nothing more than snow goes by, and the bar that demarcates the images. Virtual imagery. It could be a glimpse of the image. The film image inserted between the television images: through video it has become an enigmatic image that renovates and metamorphoses the former magical virtues of double exposure, by making from the mix of bodies an alloy that emerges from in-between the bodies.

2.

Again, the same image: Pierrot taking Sandrine from behind. An intertitle precedes it: MONTAGE. Again from the beginning, coming into view under the pale blue/dark green image of the parents (even if we can't see it clearly in the still frame) is their little girl Vanessa, pink sweater and blond hair. She imperceptibly gains in brightness until almost

1

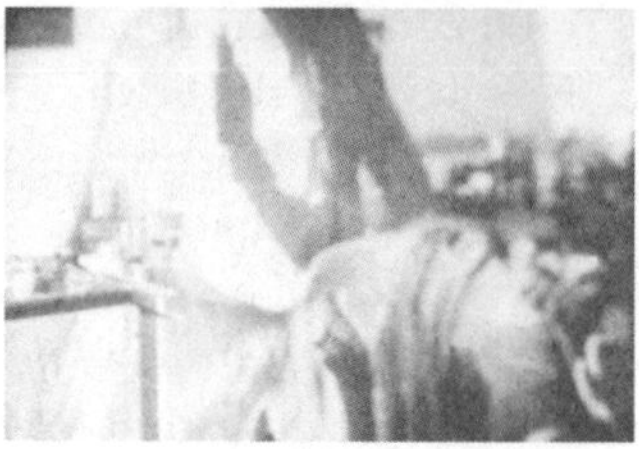

2

3

making them disappear, then the interplay is reversed in order to reestablish the first image. In this way, in a much more direct fashion, the child's gaze is asserted (she says: "Sometimes, I think what Mama and Papa do is pretty, and sometimes I think it's yukky.") Here, apparently, we are dealing with a more classical effect of double exposure, equivalent to an "edit" between two or three shots. But is this is due only to the combination of video processing with superimposition (in particular by the treatment of the colors that run one into the other); in fact, we have the startling feeling of finding ourselves in front of anatomical charts showing skinned body parts. We are no longer only at the exterior surface of the bodies; we also slide into their interiors, we think we penetrate them in the same way they penetrate each other both sexually and in the gaze that sees them while imagining them. In this way an uncommon depth, one that cinema could never achieve by itself, wells up from the "video surface."

The effect is even stronger since the scene is immediately relayed by the intertitle that follows it, this time MONTAGE enters into a series of transformations: "MONTAGE / UONTAGE / USITAGE / USNTAGE / USINAGE / USINEGE / USINEE / USINE." We recognize one of Godard's fondest ideas, the overlapping between production (cinema/industry) and pleasure. You only make love on the production line; you mount a woman like you mount a film. The body is a factory. But the metaphor holds—I mean to say exists—embodied for the mind as well as the eye, because at the heart of the editing process (here superimposition + video processing) we see or think we see the workings of this factory, in the same way that one of Bacon's paintings shows the interiors of a face and of a body in the unfolding of its exterior movement. Moreover, in the progression that leads from "*montage*" to "*usine*" (factory) on the electronic keyboard, we travel through words or para-words, portmanteau words that have meaning and at the same time hinder it ("*usntage*") by multiplying it ("*usinege*" where, under "*usinage*" in which there is already "*usine*" and also "*montage*," we also hear or rather we see "*neige*" (snow), the video snow.[12] It is in this, in the word treated as figure, that an effect of the "third sense" augments, prolongs what has just been born of the image: these fragments from in-between the bodies that defy all attribution and induce a reverie in the spectator that is both sur-signifying and inexhaustible, because it is limitless.

3.

"Something horrible happened. Sandrine had slept with another guy and she didn't want to tell me who. I felt like raping her. She didn't put up a fight, and finally I fucked her up the ass. And then she started screaming. We realized afterward that Vanessa had watched the whole thing. Maybe that's what 'family matters' are."

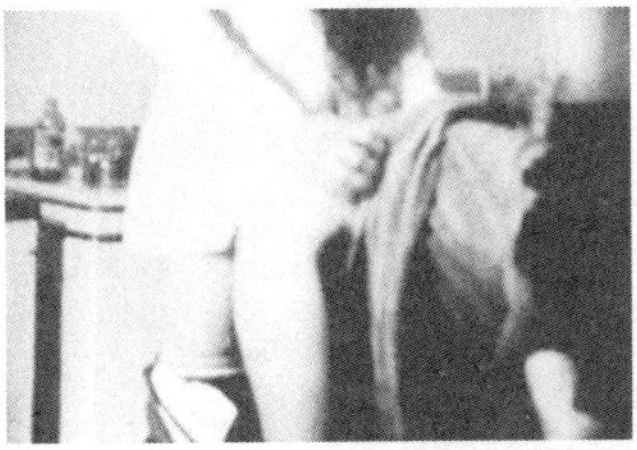

1

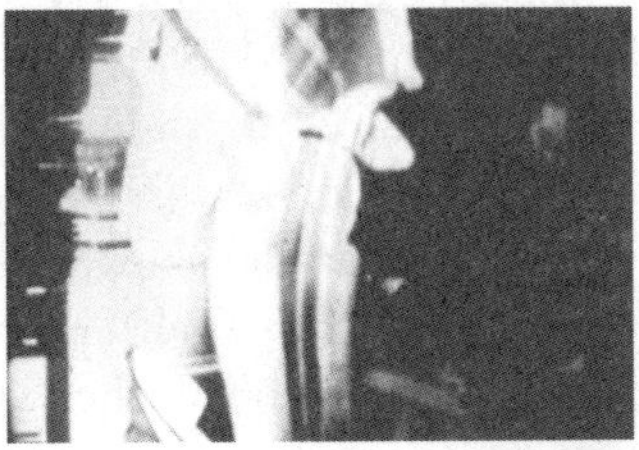

2

3

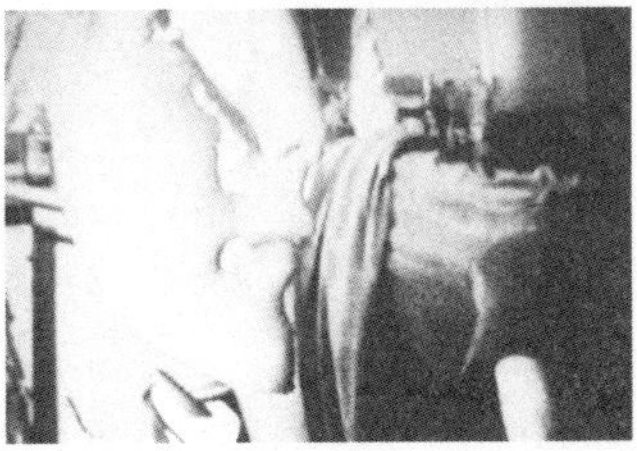

4

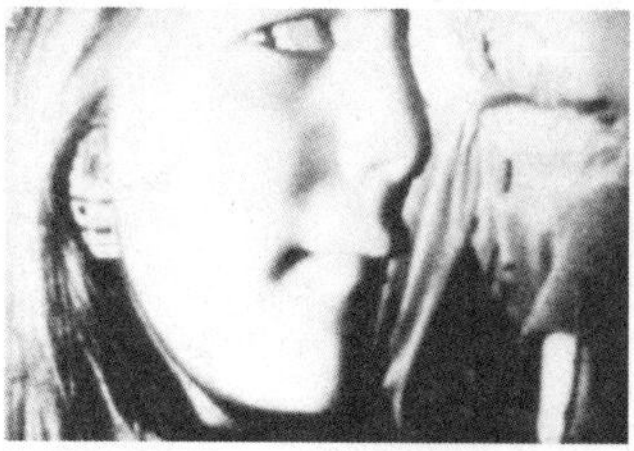
5

6

The same shot comes back again. But this time Pierrot's commentary clarifies it, gives it an added violence that rebounds onto the two previous scenes and shows through in the processing of the image. Here again, what matters are the face and the eye. The face is made up of the matter of the bodies; it may seem real but it is a profile that is being hollowed out, the silhouette of a face whose eye has a hard time taking, becoming gaze. And suddenly the face is there, almost a material presence, with a fixed gaze that seems to see beyond what is possible. But the face is still moving, stretches again toward this profile of features that compose it by decomposing it; until the climax (fleeting but wide open, toward which the scene seems to stretch in its game of almost unbounded transformations): the moment when the eye—in the still carnal profile that is already threatened by abstraction—looks straight at you and then fades away, while in its place only a hole remains, through which the visible-invisible takes place.

In this way, Godard shows us what no other photographic image can directly express (even in expressionism's most extreme lighting schemes); what film can articulate only through several shots (in *Psycho*, 1960, for example: Norman's dilated eye, pushed up against the hole drilled in the wall; then Marion seen in the shower; and later the hollow eye sockets of the mother's skull). He reveals that the seeing eye is a hole, like the hole of the vagina or the ass, when it sees what we cannot see and we want to know what is going on there.

4.
The fourth moment contrasts with the other two. For the first time the image changes, even changes twice, as if exhausted after Vanessa's wild gaze and the confession of sodomy and rape. At the beginning it is again Pierrot and Sandrine, nude; Pierrot's gaze plunges between Sandrine's legs spread wide over his shoulders. Next we find them talking in the bathroom; Sandrine does most of the talking (as in almost all of the film).

"You know, I've realized that I don't really know how to do anything. Well, maybe I'm overdoing it. Sure, I know how to churn out tenderness, I can cook, I also, well yeah, I can do Nicolas' homework, and I know how to suck cock."

From one scene to the next, the same principle of transformation, although it is much more developed in the second scene. This time it is Sandrine's face that is formed out of the blackness that invades the image, that doubles or obscures the representation, substitutes for it and beckons to us with its eyes.

The partial arbitrariness of the choice of the two still frames must be accepted in order to attempt to get a handle on the first scene. We should be aware of the resulting fact that they tend to exaggerate what is happening here, that they don't give us a clear idea of the overall picture: this is the price to be paid for any written version of a visual experience that doesn't limit itself to general ideas.

The blotch of black that moves into the left of the image—still from the funerary edge that bands the restricted frame of the visible image—this blackness seems to move toward the blackness of the genitals, as does the thin black fringe that brings them together with the lower part of Pierrot's face. Here, in a manner as direct as it is metaphorical, we have a twofold male gaze turned toward Sandrine's crotch: Pierrot's gaze, and through him, within him, the gaze of enunciator/effects man Godard. In the second image we see the face of Sandrine (not shown in the first image) lying down. It appears in superimposition, like a real, photographic face (though formed in part by the curve of Pierrot's arm and by her own legs, following the principle of the first and third moments). But the face is also simultaneously divided from itself, sketched in rough lines, redesigned by the video effects.

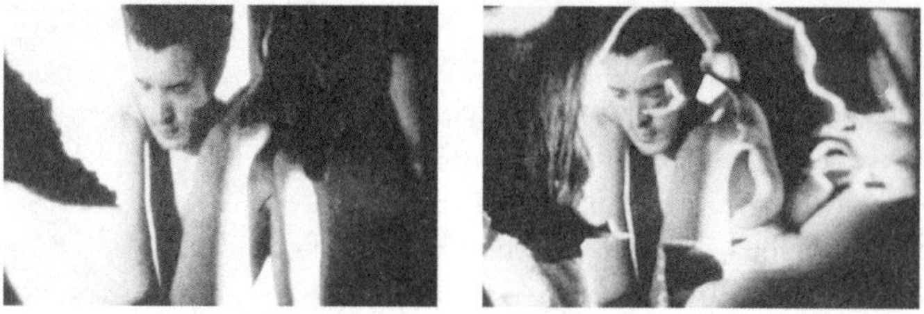

In this intertwining, this superimposing of heterogeneous forms and lines—through which Pierrot's head is lodged in Sandrine's—Sandrine's left eye is hidden by Pierrot's right eye, and at the same time is reproduced in it by the video "brush stroke." This is done so well that we read the image doubly, projecting a double gaze from the same eye. Pierrot's gaze toward the genitals. And Sandrine's gaze, on- and off-screen at the same time, which answers without answering, abstract, facing nowhere in particular, except toward us who remain stricken by it.

In the extreme beauty of its transformations, the second scene revives this gaze. At first it is purely an inner gaze, or is experienced as such, following the variations of Sandrine's face, in close-up, in profile, covering or uncovering the scene with its black mass that shrinks and swells. A scene of which she is both judge and participant. The most surprising thing here is the fact that these variations seem to be the plastic expression of the words pronounced by Sandrine. As if she were twice present in this space, the sound of her voice in her first (real) body modulating the appearance of the (virtual) second one. But Sandrine's gaze also becomes, in the moments when her face is undone in the blackness, an eye. As with the previous scene, an eye that appears to be, both in profile and frontally, like a Cubist eye; that appears to encompass the entire scene, of which it is nonetheless only a fragment. With the disturbing effect of a look given to the camera, all the more aimed toward the spectator as he continually receives the scene through and around this interposed eye.

These four scenes or moments—the only ones wherein the image changes in nature—are also four love and sex scenes. They are not, for all that, the only scenes of sexual relations (or non-relations) between Sandrine and Pierrot: far from it. There is the "riverbank" scene, where

Sandrine squats over Pierrot who is laying down and looking up at her ass. There is the one where she goes down on him (we only see, in a miniscule screen, Pierrot's lower body and Sandrine's head). The scene, in bed, where she gives him a handjob (Pierrot's head is off-screen). The one where she masturbates in her room after returning from the market, and throws Pierrot out when he tries to join in the game. And the scene where the two parents, lying in bed, teach their two children (a girl and a boy) the illustrated ABC's of desire.

As a general rule there is sex and there is body, heavily sexed body, throughout the entire film (in the dialogues and the monologues when it is not in the image). There is Vanessa in the bathtub, asking her mother if all little girls have holes. There is Sandrine's clogged ass, when she can't shit. There is the grandfather, giving one of the morals of the story: "Sometimes, yeah, I look at my dick... there are times when everything is channeled through the dick..." There are the porn films, their unbearable and fascinating monotony.

1

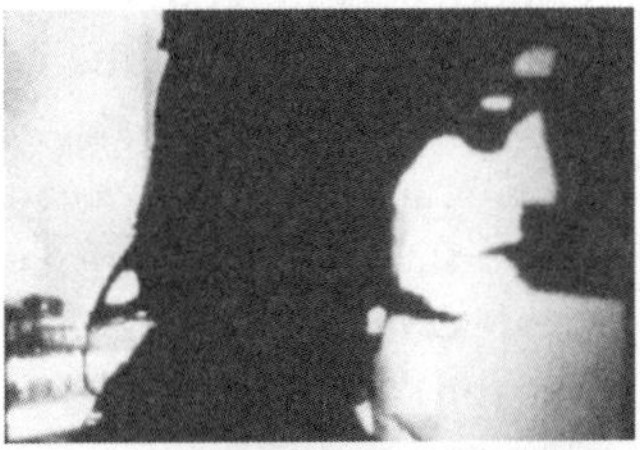
2

3

4

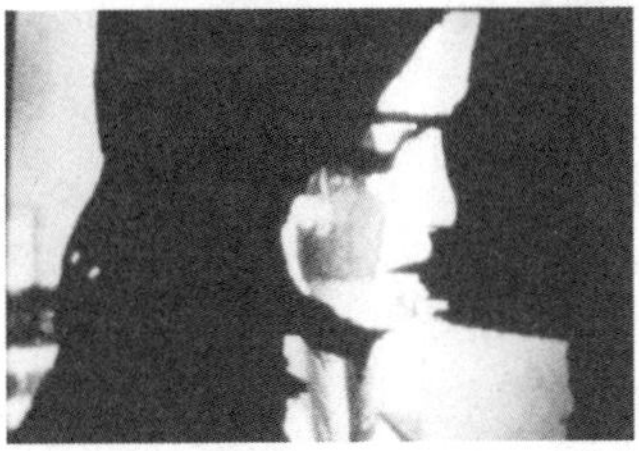
5

6

All of these scenes have one thing in common, especially those that bring Pierrot and Sandrine together. In the bodies there is always—in the idea we have of them—something missing, something that hinders, something that we cannot see and that we do not know. In short: in sex, between the sexes, there is a difference, an attack of vertigo, a black hole. Granted, a trite idea. But it is less trite when it is said, in every possible way, with a relentlessness that casts about desperately for metaphors. And it is anything but trite when it is shown in such a new and overwhelming manner that it shatters the well-known difficulty of representing eroticism and sexual life on the screen.[13] Firstly, this is translated by the work on the frame (increased tenfold by the play between the frames, the multiple screens and the black border that surrounds the image). The bodies are always sectioned in a way that physically inscribes the presence, the relation between what is missing and what is unknowable, between (not) seeing and (not) knowing. Next—this has been emphasized—the very strength of the video effects is to be able to capture, in the moving matter of bodies, this moment wherein the insatiable, the inscrutable, and thus the unfilmable reside.

We notice that Godard, in a subtle manner, seems to have initially reserved these effects for what we could call the traumatic or primal scene of the film, and in this, for what is said there (for him) about the cinema *dispositif*. But this fourth scene is interesting in that it spreads this effect to the sex scene as a whole, and above all to the domestic dispute where desire and/or sex, certainly never missing, melt back into the disturbing triviality of everyday life. This gives even that much more strength to the effect in relation to the rest of the film, of which it thus becomes a point of crystallization. It is a little like the decompositions of *Sauve qui peut (la vie)*, which will orchestrate even more subtly the relations of tension between the sexes, the impossibility of bodies joining together; while also zooming in on the most exemplary "any-instant-whatevers" of life, in such a way that their effect is propagated, virtually, throughout the entire film.[14]

By modulating the representation of bodies through their dis-representation, by working on their interpenetration to the point of giving the illusion at times of reaching all the way into the body's interior, in short by boring into the photographic surface in order to double it with a material depth that brings it close to the depth of painting—of the body's adventure in painting—Godard proposes a new form of editing in fiction. In this manner he reinterprets the earlier principles of the (Eisensteinian) montage of attractions by putting the accent on the relation between elements. (The didactic dimension is taken up by a visual pedagogy that is, in a way, Godard's pedagogy in tactile form.) Above all, he invents or reinvents a new form of long take, which permits an advance in the always problematic expression of the relationship between the seeing and the seen.

Classically, there are only two ways of expressing this: either by a change of shots (exemplified by the shot-reverse shot—monopolizing, tiresome, and clumsy all at once); or by a camera movement that handles the connection and disconnection between the elements according to another continuity. But with great filmmakers the film always more or less tends to cancel this distance between the shots (or shot moments), as if to inscribe everything on a single surface (a single volume), ultimately transgressing the position that imposes upon the spectator, as an integral part of the *dispositif*, the role of mirror to the film screen: the primordial "shot-reverse shot."

Taking once again the example of *Psycho*, we clearly see that Hitchcock went as far as was possible in this direction, given the limits of his filmmaking. What happens in the shower scene? In his fetish-room where he is watched over by the motionless eyes of stuffed birds, we recall that Norman Bates slides a painting across the wall, one of the countless versions of *Susanna and the Elders* (thus situating the film in the filiation of painting as a scene for the eyes, the founding place of voyeurism in Western culture). Underneath the painting there is a hole, and putting his eye up against it he sees, as do we, in another field of vision (many other shots), Marion in the shower. Marion filmed in such a way that the sight of a woman's (imaginary) climax is projected (for Norman and for the spectator). It is (into) this image that Norman-the-mother will penetrate with his-her huge tragicomic knife, in order to possess and to do away with her. So that—coming full circle—the dead eye of Marion, lying on the floor, echoes Norman's dilated eye against the hole in the wall. And so that—full circle once again—these two eyes cancel each other out in the empty eye socket of the mother's skull (at the time of the third murder, and at the end of the film).

Does Godard not succeed in filming an equivalent of this, four times, but each time within a single shot? Through video, the painting effect as referent (historical and material) is this time inscribed in the very shot, of which it becomes the formative and the transformative agent. The different shots combine into a single optic mass, inside of which the variation of lines and tonalities obstinately keeps trying to grasp the same story of the gaze-as-sex and its transformations. But the story also changes, in its content as well as in its form. And not only because the sex "scene" becomes explicit, but indeed because a gender reversal is carried out here, to an impossible degree.

In his lengthy footnote to "Le thérrorisé," Serge Daney made the following proposition: "Sound (her). Image (him)/Voice (her). Eye (him)."[15] This is a way of saying that facing the classical phallic position (which makes man the eternal hero of the scopic drive, a "bulging eye"), there is in Godard a woman's voice (in *Numéro deux* and elsewhere) which intervenes and lays down the law, which disentangles itself and us from the image, becoming the heroine of Godard's pedagogy. "Cruel mothering," Daney says, which gives Godard pleasure and where he reaps the benefit of masochism: for it is the woman, in this strange feminism, who takes up "the reasoning of the rod."[16] I think that this proposition, an accurate and forceful one, is contradicted (to say the least) in the four essential moments wherein the film crystallizes its representations of sex, of the sexes and of their difference, around the video-painting effect. Godard's masochism might well be even more vivid than Daney imagines, and the inversion that he touches upon that much more extreme.

In the moments when the man's desire-gaze sets the sexual scene (in the three first scenes and in the first part of the fourth), or becomes what is being talked about (in the second part of the fourth), there is constantly the face and the eye of a woman: doubling this first image, blending into it, judging it, veiling it, going through it, boring into it. Whether it be the daughter or the mother, Vanessa or

Sandrine. The problematic feminine eye. The woman's eye that sees. The gaping eye that supports all the metaphors for the inscription and the turning away of the gaze. The virtual eye through which the impossible mission is carried out that would allow us to escape the cinema *dispositif*'s realm of imagination in order to find ourselves at last not facing the image, but inside the image itself.

Onto this eye—used as symptom, sign, and concern of the film and of its transgressions—a double gaze can in fact be projected. It can be made into an eye-discourse that, like language, would be on the side of the law (assuming that Godard does not put language to use in another way). Woman becomes its medium, through an inversion that affects the roles and the representation of the symbolic without disturbing its logic. It could be said from this perspective that the video effect becomes the agent of this supplement of discourse, in that it goes beyond the photographic analogy and therefore constitutes a type of meta-image. But on the other hand, we can sense that the image stands (we want to say withstands) before its phenomenological realism and the effects of discursivity linked to it. It thus gives access to an infra-image, into which the eye slides like a matter-eye—at the same time a visible, seeing and unseeing fragment of matter—rather than stopping short at its separating function. An eye from in-between the bodies as much as an eye between the bodies. Underneath the symbolic eye, in sum, a semiotic eye.[17]

In this way we can discern—and in fact this is what interests me the most—the necessary principle of a vacillation in these moments. This vacillation is all the more relevant for the representational supports as it concerns the representation of sex and the sexes, expressing one through the other, as questions addressed to cinema and to the image.

This, among other things, is what makes this obsessional documentary on "wise Pierrot's" family life—as well as on the gaze of his witness, on the Godard who rambles at the beginning of the film about the "*machins et les machines*"[18] before finally turning his head dreamily toward his *dispositif*—a film that marks a turning point, a watershed film that may very well be much crazier than the one that preceded it.[19]

III. Induced Color

Antonioni's endeavor is completely different. Kuntzel opposes two image systems (two states of the body and of the world) in an alternation that winds up producing a virtual effect of generalized interference, and at times an actual moment of fleeting contact. Godard riddles his film with moments of extreme violence in order to intermittently make a supplement of being burst out from inside the bodies themselves. Antonioni, on the other hand, chooses to induce the image through an arrangement, an atomization, a denaturation, perhaps even a symbolization of color.

He does this with artifice. An expressly conceded artifice, accepting with detached enthusiasm to film a story he does not like, which at the same time is his only film situated outside of the immediately contemporary world of which he was such an unwavering witness ("this is not a 'film by,' this is a 'film directed by'").[20] Clearly, the story itself (Cocteau's *L'aigle à deux têtes*, 1943) allows him to stand aside: it serves as a mediating *dispositif* and becomes an equivalent (a weaker, indirect one) of what Cubist painting was for Kuntzel/Grandrieux, and what the tele-video machinery was for Godard. Nonetheless, what Antonioni projects onto his screen is of profound consequence; it is directly along the lines of earlier intuitions.

Antonioni has often said that there is too much reality in the image, that it is too safe in its analogical depiction.[21] This is how the "vertigo of the spot," which so thoroughly seduces Bonitzer in the black and white of *L'avventura*, must be considered. There is all the more reality in the color image, too much fidelity, since its rendition has gained in subtlety, since "the colors have become more refined." We thus see Antonioni musing, asking himself concerning color: how can you go back to making silent films in a modern cinema that is trying to reinvent itself? How can color be manipulated in a narrative sense, as was done almost by natural inclination in the "colored" silent films? (He says almost passionately: "I think that I've seen every color silent film. I've even seen the very first movie filmed in color […] It was a very strange short that dated from 1906–1907. Its effects were heavy and very violent, but interesting for the period."[22]) How can you film the way

1

2

3

4

5

6

Piero della Francesca—his favorite painter—paints? The word Antonioni uses is "violence" (he comes back to it often). How can you do violence to the image? How can it be made to express (instead of admit) a supplement of truth or of being that would no longer rely only on bringing exterior circumstances together in front of the lens in order to capture an inner emotion, but that might emerge from within itself as a direct emanation of inner life?

Red Desert (1964) comes to mind. Already, with his first color film, color as title and obsession, from its most motivated to its most arbitrary use. The painted sets (Giuliana's store). The painted vegetables and fruit (the street merchant). Even painted landscapes: the small, "white" grove, which was removed from the final cut. Antonioni wrote several pages about this grove that make it a perfect example. In his text, one clearly sees the mix of demiurgic reason and derision that exists in wanting to "actually" reinvent nature: all night long the workers painted the trees, in the morning the rain washed everything away.[23]

Blow-Up (1966) also comes to mind. "I took the trees, the grass where it was a little dry, a bit burnt, and I made them *green*. Then I wanted a white spot, so I built those houses whose facades you see in the very back. For the photographer's studio I wanted clear, violent colors that were to define the character's rather rude temperament. Certain blacks, certain yellows; I'm the one who created them. They seem to be realistic colors, because a studio can in fact be like that. But it wasn't, I did it. Same thing for the color of the large pieces of paper."[24]

There is a problem here that comes from what Antonioni says about *Zabriskie Point* (1970), then about *Identification of a Woman* (1982). For the first of the two films he chooses "intentional but real" colors; he is not the one who forces them "onto reality," even though, he says, the result might seem close to what he did in *Red Desert*. The second is a "normal" film, in which "there is no pursuit of color effects." This has not stopped Sylvie Blum from writing (in a short and admirable text that seems to have been half-dreamed, which gives it a profound suggestive quality) that in this film "each feeling has its light, each emotion its color, or rather, to each sensation corresponds a shade or a half-tone."[25] As if there were a gradation that could be obtained without effect, thus making it possible, as she says, to go from photography to painting without losing at the same time the completeness of reality that despite everything prevails in this film about the very desire to elude it. The problem is that in arranging deliberately chosen tonalities in front of the lens—the lens that we are trying not to disconcert too much, after all—we fall short of the violence wished for by Antonioni, and in relation to which he is not sure if it is better to paint reality rather than to depict it, to render it convincingly abstract rather than unconvincingly figurative. We owe some of the most beautiful films in existence to this tension. But it leaves unchanged the desire to take on the illusion of reality that endlesslyimposes itself, with what it gives but also with what it forbids (even if, in *Identification of a Woman*, the director of photography's account clearly indicates that an attempt was made to eliminate color, which means: the possibility of asserting color).[26]

Antonioni's response to this problem is the temptation of video. Which is in essence—in the way he expresses it—the temptation of virtuality. But this virtuality is essential, as seen in his interviews published at the time of *Identification of a Woman*'s release (some three years after *Il mistero di Oberwald* [*The Mystery of Oberwald*, 1981]). He recalls (with a joy common to very few filmmakers) that "with electronic equipment, you get exactly what you want: the color of the image, or of a section of it, can be added, taken away or modified. In short, the 'tele-camera' permits us to make reality much more malleable." It is a question, he says, of individualizing this matter. "You can film takes—it has already been done—by making the characters lose their 'corporality,' by leaving only the contours, luminous signs in a real context." In this context he recalls a project conceived after *The Passenger* (1975), entitled "Jealousy" or "The Color of Feelings." On the way to meet his mistress a man obsessed by jealousy undertakes a voyage that crosses through three levels: reality, memory, and imagination. "This structure gave me the possibility of coloring, so to speak, the events with colors that varied according to the level they belonged to: the color of a scene we imagine changes depending on how we feel while imagining it."

It is clear what is at stake in a proposition of this kind. Without mediation of any sort, without a safety net, it means, on the one hand, retaining reality, the story, the character(s), the bodies, subjectivity, feelings; but on the other, inventing (as in the most beautiful days of silent film, but much more radically) a way to interpret them that will suggest their inner mode. In other words, it means inventing a way of reaching a level of materiality (physical and psychological) that is situated at the same time before and beyond the contour of reality imposed by photographic capturing. A vision that would be both discrete (in its linguistic sense) and imperious (because it is marked, with all the risks this implies) would take the place of photography's inescapably massive character (no matter how subtle we are). Antonioni put it very well: if for the moment video is only a technical factor, it "does allow the possibility of a different *impact* than matter, the possibility of being even more violent than the matter that is treated." This violence, provided it is developed, may well permit "things about which we don't have the slightest idea with film." It implies "a new relation between author and reality, between author and images." Antonioni once illustrated, in a prophetic and indirect fashion, the violence that one must be strong enough to do to the image. He borrowed words from Oppenheimer (which Oppenheimer had used to defend those colleagues of his who had constructed the first atomic bomb), and from them he made the title of one of his movies (never filmed). He made the following comments about it, refusing to clarify the meaning of a choice that he prefers to keep obscure; the focus of this choice, however, is the risk of explosion to which sooner or later he will have to subject the image. "Everything that constitutes a step forward toward the knowledge of truth, a scientific truth, whatever it may be, is justifiable precisely because it is technically sweet, irresistible."[27]

And then there is *Oberwald*. This story he doesn't believe in, this story he could treat violently (probably with less difficulty than other ones). We should point out that while Antonioni does not believe in this story, 20 years earlier Rossellini filmed *Vanina Vanini* (1961) on a similar subject (19th century, politics, emotions, fatality, Romanticism). The undertaking thus seems marked by two contrary risks for Antonioni, between which a decision is impossible: either it is the dated, conventional plot that, like him, we can't believe in, in spite of the image work to which he subjects it; or it is the image work itself that we can accuse of keeping us from believing in this period tragedy. And it is true that it gets in our way, that the "truth" of the bodies eludes us. It is true that at times it seems to slip away precisely when the effect appears. But in its place there also emerges something very difficult to name. One less, one more truth, if you like; but certainly something completely different. A rare and strong feeling, the effects of which we can try to put under several headings. I see five of them: *Ridicule*, *Dullness*, *Excitement*, *Stupor*, *Rapture*.

It is impossible to isolate these five groups. Not only do they overlap with the occurrence of this or that effect, but they are virtually always present (more or less), throughout the film. In this way, they define a possible position for the spectator. Their proportions, like their distribution, are very subjective, depending on the degree of each spectator's acceptance or rejection of what has been attempted.

Ridicule comes from the very irruption of denaturation. Why, as early the prologue, are the exaggerated greens of the forest suddenly pierced by pink clouds? Why does the landscape, through which the hero (Sebastian, the young anarchist who wants to assassinate the queen, and will end up loving and being loved by her) walks up to the castle, suddenly become mauve, then change to blue, when at first it was presented in an almost "normal" fashion? Why does the image, until then in gray-green-brown tones (one of the "natural" dominant characteristics of this costume film), turn completely to green when Edith de Berg opens the window in the queen's chambers? Could it be that green designates the "window" element, or the "queen" element, as a second occurrence of green seems to indicate later when the queen (played by Monica Vitti) opens a window herself? But then why is the queen pervaded by blue when she falls asleep in her chair, and why on another occasion does a mauve and blue light enter by the same window? The problem becomes this: arbitrariness or motivation. Antonioni put it in these terms: "When someone is angry, we say that he sees 'red': but he could just as well see 'yellow' if the circumstances suggested that color to him." Antonioni does not seem to have given himself any fixed rule here, but rather let himself be guided by the circumstances in order to try colors, to experience different modes of transition and of usage that end up expressing his feeling of the color as well as (if not more than) translating "the color of feelings." We find ourselves faced with a dynamic, with a rush of color as emotion, with the rhythm, the pulse of the film as a body of color; instead of being faced with the search for a term by term correspondence, or even a highlighting of privileged moments. And so it is striking that the only slightly sensual love scene (in the park, between Sebastian and the queen) is filmed without any special effects. Antonioni avoided the ridicule of an overly literal translation. He prefers an arbitrary one, which in fact is never more than half-arbitrary. It suffices to put one's faith in the spectator's innate sense for creating a surplus of meaning, for associating a feeling to the proposed color on his own (if he accepts the risky game).

It may happen that the spectator is not able, or does not care to do this. *Dullness* is this indifference. It goes just as well with the flow of meaning as it does with its absence. I couldn't get interested in the shot in the castle courtyard, where the blood that flows from the neck of the decapitated chickens turns to dark red. Excess of meaning? Maybe. But the blue smoke that ends Sebastian's ascent, without any obvious reason, leaves me just as indifferent. Could it be that I don't yet know the character well enough and that the color would have to be linked, if not to a recognizable feeling, at least to a possible emotion that is addressed to, or goes through someone? Not even. An abrupt, very vivid bleaching—carried out on the landscape when a previously unseen young farm girl moves—suddenly grips me. And yet the chromatic variations—beautiful nevertheless (bright green to blue to mauve), which seem to surge from the queen's telescope pointed at the garden—leave me rather cold. The alchemy of colors seems to be all the more mysterious as its effects are detached and visible, calling on unformulated feelings.

And yet, it is clear that *Excitement* is more likely to come out of those scenes where the color generates system. Not meaning, but system, produced by the effects developed over time in such a way that they act upon the figures the (more or less rhetorical) figures, unique to cinema itself. In contrast to Aldo Tassone, I have a hard time seeing in the "violet" halo (in fact blue in the first scene, mauve in the second, which tends already to desubstantialize it) that accompanies the Count of Foehn, the chief of police, a translation of the "character's deceitful nature." But the manner in which the color announces him (the blue door that stands out, even before we catch sight of him, in the first scene with the queen)—the way it follows him, moves about with him, spreads itself out and retracts, filling the entire frame or only a part of it, varying according to his movements and those of the person he speaks with (the queen in the first scene, Sebastian in the second)—all of this gives to the color the role of showing, as a visible influence, the mysteriousness of the body's aura within the space of the shot and in the shot relations. There is a particularly exciting motif: the moments when there remains in the image of the Count (uniformly bluish) or of the queen (a relatively realistic yellow-brown-green tone) only a fringe of color from the other's image, an edge of the tone, for signaling his or her presence off-screen. From the absent other emanates, within the frame itself, what usually comes from the immediate memory of the image supported by dialogue. It is impossible to say exactly what such a variation translates, any more than a given body movement within the frame would. But the "plus" that this variation expresses—in becoming color that invades, repels the color of the other—gives the idea of a materialized inner space, even if we do not know how to name it. Antonioni knew how to make use of this situation, how to prolong its excitement. For example he used the Count's passing in front of the window to puncture the uniform blue that surrounds him with a striking green (in this way he creates an improbable image, a mental collage). And at the end of the sequence, this mass of blue is suddenly reduced to the silhouette of the minister, as if to mark his disappearance, without really doing it, because the blue is again lightly diffused around him when he crosses through the door of the chambers.

These variations underline the virtual, polemic, almost conceptual character of such effects: in the scene with Sebastian, the two men are at first posed for several shots in the same color (that then becomes a near-absence-of-color) before the pinkish mauve again takes hold of the Count according to the principle of the earlier scene. But together the two men will be thrust, for a few shots, into color—then into the lack of it—before an acid blue, introduced through the top of a door, acts in turn on the whole image, then fades away. It could be said: there is no rhyme or reason to what Antonioni does. No: he is trying out various solutions, opening but also limiting a composition principle that could just as well be a matter of rigorous motivation as one of complete arbitrariness. And this is what is exciting, for the eye as well as the mind.

Stupor does not leave much time for reflection; this way it has a chance of overcoming *Ridicule*. The green that overruns the screen when Edith de Berg opens the window is of this nature; as is the beautiful blue-mauve that suddenly appears when the queen, later, simply draws close to the same window. These two examples are taken from the side of the arbitrary. On the other hand, the variations of color intensity within the same tone are tied to the meaning of the story and to the destinies of its characters. When the pale pink flowers (isolated in close-up) darken to red, this marks a swelling of the desire between Sebastian and the queen; when the Count of Foehn seizes a purplish flower and—passing to the interior of Sebastian's field of vision (in the scene already mentioned)—its color disappears, this is a sign of coming death.

If *stupor* persists, and holds firm, it then becomes *rapture*. As during the queen's horseback ride. A meadow that is too green. A forest that turns blue as the horse advances, as the camera follows its movement, emerging against a green sky. This green floats on the horse's mane.

1

2

3

4

The foliage and the fields change to pastel pink and to mauve. Very close shots. Distant shots. Streaks of yellow on the horse's rump move forward toward a sky of yellow clouds. There is an overwhelming audacity here in the linking of the colors, in their progression, their rhythm. This way of using color to convey the relations of distance between the shots takes one's breath away. Now and then this mad rapture receives a response from a gentle one. Then the realistic color plunges into a pale blue shaded with pink: a kind of pastel, a coloring-by-bleaching of sorts that harmonizes with the suspension of gestures. A semi-motivation makes way for the semi-arbitrary: the contrast of bright colors brought forth by the ride is followed by a moment of amorous illusion for the queen, of tender melancholy for her lover. The scene continues, taking the route of a varied shot breakdown that anchors the attempt little by little; the color's return to reality, delimiting the effect, reinforces its intensity. If the spectator has not remained aloof, he is submerged in something never before seen, or in any case that had never before been designated so directly: variations of color searching for those of feeling.

Antonioni insisted on making it clear that his reference was painting, and at the most opportune moment: in the final scene where the death of the lovers is the object of a constant shifting between natural and interpreted color, at times blurring the border between the two. The queen passes in front of a tapestry from which we retain only the motionless faces (but the impression is very strong); then she draws close to a painting that I have not been able to identify, but in which we recognize the frenzied pathos of the bodies in old paintings (a woman threatens a man prostate on the ground with her brandished sword). The queen turns,

1

2

3

following the stairway, turns back and looks for a long while at the painting; in the right section of the frame the position of her body echoes the position of the motif, which itself refers to the framework [*trame*] of the film. "*Trame pour trame, drame pour drame.*"

And yet painting is insufficient to describe the shifting that video thus allows cinema. It was also insufficient in the cases of *La Peinture cubiste* and *Numéro deux*. The problem, as we have seen, is that of the *passage*, which each of the three works handles in its own fashion. How can we go from an image that "represents" (considering the implicit norm of natural perception relayed by that of the lens) to an image that "dis-represents" (in other words, that works against this norm, even if it is only a vague one)? Elie Faure's reverie comes to mind: this "animation of painting" that cineplastics would appear to achieve, seemed to him to be a phenomenon too radically new for us to "even think of painting." He invoked architecture, in which he saw the main expression of this new world's particular form of "plastic civilization" (cinema is thus "an architecture in motion"). But cineplastics seems to tend toward music above all. This is how Elie Faure reintroduces into painting, reconsidered from cinema's point of view, a time that is never its own: a time that poses a problem to cinema—revisited by painting as it is today—that painting does not really know. This is because painting only produces fragments of space (in spite of all that can be said to the contrary), and because its relation to analogy is different (even if modern art has in part consisted in perverting this frontier). On both of these accounts, painting ignores the question of the passage between heterogeneous levels of reality arranged in time. And so the desire suddenly arises to look for a response within the only art form that maintains an absolutely free relation with these levels of reality and with their temporal development, because its matter is a volatile substance: literature.

It would seem that the three works brought together here do indeed strive toward a possibility of this order: they emancipate themselves from the excessive reality of the image in order to invent ties of a different order between the actual and the virtual, between the material and the immaterial. Obviously, this analogy cannot be taken literally. But when cinema goes beyond the frontiers of bodies in order to reanimate them, either from within (as do Kuntzel and Godard) or by external chromatic pressure (as does Antonioni), it seems to postulate a capacity for variation that literature has freely put to use, because it can do this naturally, as soon as it insistently asks itself (perhaps under the influence of photography and cinema) questions about the representation of the body, about its image and about the image itself. In this respect it must be noted that Antonioni had thought of having Barthes participate in his research on "the color of feelings," and that eventually he did this by trying to support his project with excerpts from a book that is dedicated to the body-image: *A Lover's Discourse* (1977).

I will look at three examples very briefly. Each attempts to outline, in the literary process, a moment or a posture of transformation that cinema can today express with more clarity and freedom than before, when it is, thanks mostly to video, revisited by painting. At one point in Henry James' "The Jolly Corner," the hero—after wandering at length through the large house of his childhood and seeing (with a gaze that goes beyond gaze) what his image would have become had he never left this town or this house—finally sees something take form in the texture of his perception. "The penumbra, dense and dark, was the virtual screen of a figure which stood in it as still as some image erect in a niche or as some black-visored sentinel guarding a treasure. Brydon was to know afterward, was to recall and make out, the particular thing he had believed during the rest of his descent. He saw, in its gray glimmering margin the central vagueness diminish, and he felt it to be taking the very form toward which, for so many days, the passion of his curiosity had yearned. It gloomed, it loomed, it was something, it was somebody, the prodigy of a personal presence."[28] It will be said that such effects irresistibly evoke those that the cinema of the fantastic has cultivated for so long. And that today Raul Ruiz, or David Lynch, or Philippe Garrel … Of course. But it cannot be ignored that if this exemplary moment is made to travel—if its pressure inside the work is increased, and above all if attention is paid to its way of affecting the body itself and, through it, the very core of the image—that this moment represents the point where video, encroaching upon cinema, allows cinema to enter into the image as its explicit point of vibration and of metamorphosis.

I am borrowing the second example from Deleuze's evocation (in *Anti-Oedipus*, 1972) of the slow process that leads the Proustian narrator, through dozens of pages, toward Albertine's cheek, which he is trying to kiss for the very first time: "Albertine's face is at first a nebula, barely extracted from the collective of girls. Then her person disengages itself, through a series of views that are like distinct personalities, with Albertine's face jumping from one plane to another as the narrator's lips draw nearer her cheek. At last, within the magnified proximity, everything falls apart like a face drawn in sand, Albertine's face shatters into molecular partial objects [...]"[29] Is this not the explosion of too much analogy? Does it not mark the necessity of a passage beyond, in order to define the infra-world of a sharpened perception that makes the seer's inner projection the condition for the formation of a new image?

And then, as vanishing line, there is the "in-between world" of Michaux. A universe of transformations of states of the "I." The "I" has the consistency of the author's first double (and from this unsteady point, of an infinite string of doubles). But its materiality goes well beyond the contours of the person: it becomes translucent, dissolves, is absorbed by the color or melted down to a line, as seen in his watercolors or his ink sketches. And so he carries us to the limit of the story, where (in the multiplication and the infinite disintegration of the stories) fiction hangs only by a thread (this would be for example the story of "*les hommes en fil*"). But this thread is strong, a figure of the future.

I believe that the day when cinema will have truly tamed painting, through video (and beyond, through what extends it, the computer-generated image whose name alone is virtuality itself), it will be able to do what until then could only be achieved by literature, albeit through other means entirely (if it does not lose the skill it has acquired of dealing with time by telling stories). This requires maintaining a hold on both the narrative aspect (the plot) and on the pure dimension of affect, expressed from within one's body. This should not be interpreted as the desire for a program or a norm. Jean-Georges Auriol (carried along by one of the numerous waves, appearing since the silent era, that laid the basis for the "auteur theory") had no such desire either when he recognized in the creator of cartoons "the absolute filmmaker, until the day comes when the direct recording of what the imagination produces is made possible by the capturing of mental waves." Neither did Antonioni when he foresaw "a new relation between author and reality, between author and images." At the most, it is a question of reckoning (once again) with a virtuality that has become more and more necessary, since we now know that the image, also, cannot help but go elsewhere. We know that the image is no longer, as was the case in the past, one that fights against itself. In principle this aspiration does not contradict a cinema of the transparent, of the visible. It is rather a way of realizing, once and for all, that this art was not any less "abstract" because it was supported by the photographic analogy. This is also the opportunity to see the analogue image become more and more valuable now that it is truly threatened. As if this threat held a "violence" that was positive both for analogy itself and for what can be glimpsed through it of a cinema visited by forces perhaps even more extreme than those which have carried it along until now.

1987. Translated in 2011 by Allyn Hardyck.

[1] Walter Pach's translation of Faure's "cinéplastique" [editor's note].
[2] Elie Faure, *L'arbre d'Eden*, 1922, quoted by Pierre Lherminier in *L'art du cinéma* 75–77.
[3] Jean-Georges Auriol, "Faire des films, 1. Les origines de la mise en scène," *Revue du cinéma* 1 (October 1946).
[4] André Bazin, "Peinture et cinéma," *Qu'est-ce que le cinéma ?* (Paris: Cerf, 1959) ["Painting and Cinema," *What is Cinema?* vol. 1, trans. Hugh Gray (Berkeley: University of California Press, 1967)].
[5] Pascal Bonitzer, *Décadrages* (Paris: Seuil 1985).
[6] Jacques Aumont, *L'Œil interminable* (Paris: Librairie Séguie 1989).
[7] Bonitzer, "La surface-vidéo," *Le Champ aveugle* (Paris: Cahiers du Cinéma/Gallimard, 1982).
[8] Bonitzer, *Décadrages* 101.
[9] Stephen Heath, "Droit de regard," *Le Cinéma américain*, II, ed. Raymond Bellour (Paris: Flammarion, 1980) 90–91.
[10] On the occasion of the Montbéliard conference, "Vidéo, fiction et Cie," C.A.C. Montbéliard, 1983.
[11] See the excellent dossier in issue 262–263 of *Cahiers du Cinéma* (January 1976), the only critique that measured up to the event and has not dated, with texts by Serge Le Péron, Serge Toubiana, Thérèse Giraud, Louis Skorecki, and most importantly Serge Daney's "Le thérrorisé (pédagogie godardienne)," with this remarkable note; "Sound (her). Image (him)/Voice (her). Eye (him)."
[12] In fact, *montage*, which introduces this scene, is already a transformation of *réglage* (adjustment), which ends the preceding scene where Vanessa asks Sandrine: "Will I have blood between my legs when I grow up?" ["She has her period" is translated in French as "*elle a ses règles*"—editor's note].
[13] Cf. Bazin, "En marge de 'L'érotisme au cinéma,'" in particular pages 73–74 ["Marginal Notes on *Eroticism in the Cinema*" 174]: "[The] cinema can say everything, but not show everything [...] but only on condition that one resorts to the capacity for abstraction in the language of cinema, so that the image never takes on a documentary quality." Video would thus be—as will be seen in Godard's response to Bazin—that which allows us to show as well as to hide: it embodies the possibility of abstraction in cinema versus the tendency of its images, especially those of sex, to always become more documentary.
[14] See the chapter "I Am an Image" in this book.
[15] Daney, "Le thérrorisé" 40.
[16] Translation of the Lacanian concept of "la pensée du manche," which Jean Allouch associates with Lacan's notion of "the master's discourse" (see http://www.cairn.info/revue-cites-2003-4-page-71.htm, 25-09-2010). As with "rod," "manche" can have both utilitarian and phallic connotations. Rendered as "the winning thought" in the translation of Lacan's *Encore* by Bruce Fink, *On Feminine Sexuality: the Limits of Love and Knowledge* (New York: W.W. Norton, 1998) 109 [editor's note].
[17] In Julia Kristeva's terms. See in particular "Ellipsis on Dread and the Specular Seduction (1975)," in Philip Rosen (ed.), *Narrative, Apparatus, Ideology: A Film Theory Reader* (New York: Columbia University Press, 1987).
[18] Possible connotations of the pun: thingamajigs and machines; what's-his-names and what's-her-names; things and things (in reference to the sexual organs) [translator's note].
[19] Bellour is speaking here of *Ici et ailleurs* (*Here and Elsewhere*, 1976) [editor's note].
[20] Discussion with Serge Daney and Serge Toubiana, *Cahiers du cinéma* 342 (December 1982).
[21] Except when otherwise indicated, the remarks by Antonioni that follow are taken from an interview by Aldo Tassone in *Le cinéma italien parle* (Paris: Edilig, 1982).
[22] François Cuel and Bruno Villien, "Michelangelo Antonioni" (interview), *Cinématographe* 72 (November 1981) 5.
[23] Michelangelo Antonioni, "Le bosquet blanc," *Caméra-Stylo* 3 (November 1982).
[24] Cuel and Villien 5.
[25] Sylvie Blum, "La couleur de l'identification," *Caméra-Stylo* 3.
[26] It is interesting to see how the tension between artifice and reality (taken up by Sylvie Blum: she is the one who quotes Antonioni's cameraman) has been tempered (even if the terms really are not contradictory) by Alain Bergala when he writes: "If there is one modern film where not a single trace remains of the stiffness of a filmmaker straining with his project, it is indeed *Identification of a Woman*."
[27] Antonioni, *Techniquement douce* (Paris: Albatros, 1978), quoted by Tassone 28–29.
[28] Henry James "The Jolly Corner," *The Complete Tales of Henry James* vol. 12, ed. Leon Edel (London: Rupert Hart-Davis, 1964) 224.
[29] Gilles Deleuze and Félix Guattari, *L'anti-Œdipe* (Paris: Editions de Minuit, 1972) 82 [*Anti-Oedipus: Capitalism and Schizophrenia*, trans. Robert Hurley, Mark Seem, and Helen R. Lane (London: Continuum, 2004) 77].

Jean-Luc Godard, *Scénario du film* Passion (Scenario for the film *Passion*), 1982

Images of the World

Raoul Walsh, *Battle Cry*, 1955

Richard Fleisher, *Between Heaven and Hell*, 1962

The images of the world have returned, every one of them. Those of history and of legend. Like those of the machine-body that receives and emits them. They arrive with a violence that heightens our sense of urgency. We need to know what these images have become, and how they come back to us—today when the world has disappeared, vanished, has been swallowed inside itself and devoured by its own expansion. Today when, as Gilles Deleuze says, we no longer believe in this world because the bond with man has been broken, how can we believe in belief, our only link, how can we believe, in spite of everything, in a world in which we find ourselves "as if in a pure optical and sound situation"?[1]

In Woody Vasulka's videotape *Art of Memory* (1987), at least four levels of memory are presented. Let us examine each level of memory separately.

First is the memory of the artist as a child returning insistently through a memory: it is the end of the war, he is ten years old, he lives near a military airport that has become a cemetery of planes; in the German fighters, he finds ultra-perfected war machines in pieces, which he takes apart and reassembles, subjecting them to an endless autopsy. "Europe was a huge junkyard after the war. You could find everything from weapons to human fingers in the dump."[2]

The next memory level is that of the grown-up Vasulka, who remembers the power these war machines had on him as a child. He has since become an amazing creator of vision-producing machines, in his search for new images. For years, with Steina, he has gathered, constructed, and deconstructed the basic elements of a language that he sometimes envisions as a new "natural language": a "vocabulary" capable of establishing, then developing, the immaterial physicality of images created in real time both from simple reality and from the video signal, through the machines' half-blind, half-visionary power.[3] Jean-Paul Fargier has demonstrated how this basic research grew into an oeuvre, for Woody, through the "selection of a subject matter" that accorded the "story" a particular "destiny" entirely contained within its mode of processing (for example, the decline and death of a virtuoso musician in *The Commission* [1983]); for Steina, the subject matter is the "West," understood as a vanishing of limits.[4] Paganini's life, decline, and death in *The Commission* are depicted by his body being subjected to a perpetual motion, undergoing a figuration-disfigurement (like that of Berlioz, who also plays a part in the violinist's fall). "There are always two images on the screen: a virtually complete image, and one of the partial and transitory states presented by its constant mobility."[5] This is *The Commission*'s great novelty: it creates new states of the images for a fictionalization that both employs and reinterprets the high-contrast lighting of German Expressionist cinema (in its lines and image fields), as well as the diffused lighting of Impressionist or Fauvist painting (in its strokes and pointillist touches). *The Commission*, which displays a filmic aspiration to opera, thus lends unsuspected vitality to the narrative archetypes of Romantic subjectivity (death, the contract, guilt, castration, and so on) that, to my knowledge, video has never before attempted to return to so directly.

Art of Memory departs from the concerns of *The Commission* toward another subject matter, which itself has a dual aspect: its own particular mode of processing and experience of the world. This proceeds by incorporating the medium that historically has been entrusted with conveying and instilling memory in the child and the teenager born out of war: cinema, as witness to all wars of this century, whose memory video seeks to extend and renew here. A twofold memory, that of war, and that of cinema as passageway between an old and a new way of waging war—projecting images as well as missiles, projecting missile-images—a way that leads to disappearance, as Paul Virilio has shown.[6]

The third memory level in *Art of Memory*, which plunges us deeper into the work, is that of the performer/character[7] that Vasulka has assigned to be his alter ego. He is the man with deeply etched features who appears at the beginning of the second section to challenge the enigmatic
creature—angel, devil, sphinx, Spirit of History, Icarus, 14
or Superman—standing in the landscape; the man whose wrinkled face bears the mark of experience that in itself is the subject of the tape. Later, in a powerful image at the start of the third section, the man is faced with his doppelgänger, all wrinkles, who speaks to him from behind with Oppenheimer's voice, as if from the inside of a materialized brain/consciousness: he is made of pure *trame*, through which electronic memory is suddenly, exemplarily, blended
with the web [*trame*] of history.[8] 19

It is between these two extreme points of representation (photographic and processed imagery) that the actor's body oscillates—in a more direct way than in *The Commission*. Here, the man is either one or the other in order to be one and the other for the spectator. Similarly, the tape as a whole is determined by the double, vertiginous use of cinema and
video. At the start of the second section, in the foreground, 14
the protagonist faces the mythical creature; suddenly, the sky 15
in the background changes, turning an abstract gray split into particles, while a kind of metallic rain comes down like a heavy curtain. The following shot is edited with a very rapid matching cut: the protagonist, up to this point seen from behind in three-quarter profile, is reframed in a side
close-up, throwing himself to the ground amid the bushes 16
to escape the threat of a flying object that darts across

the screen. Here is a truly filmic shot, without any video processing—a shot one might imagine coming straight out of Spielberg's *Close Encounters of the Third Kind* (1977). This is followed by the effect Vasulka uses again and again in the tape—splitting each of the shots in the middle—which governs the transition from one shot to the next. From the start, then, the character in this fiction/opera stands out: the strategy that makes him the conscience of the drama is made clear in terms of both shot construction and the substance of the image, so that conflicts and changes that affect the shot construction also become elements at stake in the narrative and in what it suggests.

Finally, there is the spectator, whose memory is put to the test because, as a moral subject, he must mentally go back over the terrifying space opened up by the metaphysical upheaval of modern war from World War I to the end of World War II that is condensed into the image of nuclear apocalypse. This is true particularly because, as a psycho-physical subject, he has to try to memorize what is presented to him as a particular reading of the event. In Vasulka's work, the ungraspable or just graspable aspect of what is shown becomes very acute. The vertigo thus created is less subtle than in *The Commission*; but it becomes more interesting conceptually (albeit at the cost, sometimes, of a certain heavy-handed didacticism) because the spectator is led to a more active consciousness in order to maintain the visible coherence of everything he sees. Echoing the tension that occurs between "real" bodies and bodies made of *trame*, we attempt to grasp the two levels of the circular dialogue that is set up between cinema and video, as well as between analog and digital representation. The first level denotes a tendency toward the shot (and the segment, as well); the shot, while imploding and redefining itself in the act, still forms narrative and dramatic units whose perceptible divisions give expression to the ungraspable character of the event. The second level—internal to the first, yet quite specific in itself—lays out a "theory" of the still frame, and of the photographic, as the most intimate part of the relationship between video and cinema.

Art of Memory is divided into seven clearly defined acts or sections. Sections three to six each correspond to a particular theme: nuclear holocaust, the Spanish Civil War, the Russian Revolution, the Pacific theater in World War II. The first section is an overture of sorts; the second introduces the performer/character (who returns in sections three and four, then disappears); the last section reintroduces him, changing his status as part of an epilogue.[9]

The effect used to pass from one shot to the next (for all but one shot) is a sort of sinusoidally shaped "wipe" that opens up (and closes) from the center of the frame, lending new versatility to the ancient "wipes" of silent 8, 10, 11, 17
cinema (the same "wipe," without motifs and in a solid gray, marks off the different sections). From the fifth section on, this transition process is doubly complicated: either only the top part of the image seems to change, because the bottom part of the two images is identical, or, most frequently, the top part of the image, when pushed away, instead of moving off the top of the frame, narrows and becomes a sort of scarf that seems to wave within the frame before moving off (or reentering—special effects always work both ways) on the left. This second variation is very disturbing for the eye of memory because it adds to the confusion between the two separated shots, thus increasing the time the image lasts even as it is already being "drained away." This, however, is nothing as compared with the process that permeates the sixth section: an image strip, frayed at the edges, enters sideways, passes through, breaks up the shot, and then expands, imposing the new image in combination with the dividing "wipe"—so that we witness a sort of dilation of the space-time the two shots share, like the very long dissolves that stunned the spectator's gaze in the early cinema. Thus this kind of effect tends toward the shot, as such effects have always done in cinema—marking the limits of the shot at the same time that it challenges them: "video" is one of the names for the passageway that leads from the marking out of the shot to the vanishing of its limits. As one might guess, however, the strongest challenge created by the effect arises from within the shot, attacking its unity by multiplying it—thus opening the perspective to two connected levels: the still frame and the *dispositif*.

Nearly all of the shots are divided between two motifs. The New Mexico landscape—mountains and desert—makes 6, 7
up the background, the context: this image is wholly

photographic, even if its color is often a processed one.
Inscribed against this are large digitally created *gray shapes*
whose complexity comes from their relationship with analog
representation—they either redouble it by mimicking its
motifs or they capture and redistribute it.[10] In the first
instance, the first shot (over which the opening credits are
shown) simultaneously shows a background of red mountain 1
and yellow sky, and in the foreground a series of gray waves
are propelled with a slight rotating motion that evokes
the mountain shapes. The simultaneous appearance of these
motifs sets up a reversibility between nature and artifice,
form/figure and background, while the breach between them
remains highly conspicuous. In the second instance, which
comes up as early as the second shot, a gray, geometric shape,
like a double folded screen, stands out against a background
of rocky desert; on one of its sides, one can make out an 2, 3
obscure, fascist-revolutionary sign,[11] on the other, a spinning
globe of the Earth on which the shadow of the sign is
projected (to the accompaniment of sounds of wars, of
the language and words that punctuate them: "Stalingrad...
Africa...").

The primary interest of the tape comes from the
activity of the large gray shapes. Their role is either to
represent something—animate or inanimate—or to serve
as a kind of medium. Or both. In the first instance, they
create a certain confusion, allowing for alloys, ensuring
transitions between various levels (of ideas, of categories,
or matter). In the second and more profound instance, these
shapes involve the functioning of memory, of the memory-
image, at the core of the experience comprised both by the 5, 9, 12, 13
vision of the tape and the dual history displayed in it: the
history of this century and the history of media. This second
history involves the transition from cinema to video and
the digital image, and what passes between them: the
photographic. As an example, I will analyze one previously
mentioned shot, in which, at the very beginning of the
second section, the protagonist faces the devil-angel, casts
a stone at him, and then photographs him five times. At this 14, 15
point, the sky, which formed the background, changes into
a gray shape (the only case in this tape, I believe, of a clear
transformation of the analog into the digital, of the figurative
into the abstract). The sky becomes a screen of metallic

rain whose imaginary drops, propelled by a constant motion (upward, then downward), are actually many solid micro-fragments, juxtaposed and welded together. It is as if each fragment of this artificial section of the image, born out of the act of taking a still photograph, is reduced to the equivalent of a still frame—as if that whole is a simultaneous image of the shot itself, a sum of individual frames (or, by analogy, of the tape insofar as it is the sum of all the shots). These frames, rendered two-dimensional although in motion, both construct and represent the screen that contains them.
Thus, we can then pass on to the only shot of the tape 16
that is purely filmic. The gray shape—because it penetrates the film from within it, jogging and reviving its memory—is charged with representing film mutation.

With the third gray shape of the first section, the die is cast: the elbow-like "bachelor machine" that straddles the landscape is composed of unequal parts that appear
to be welded together; onto this entire surface, however, 9
film is projected, modulated by the cuts, recomposing so many shots and/or still frames, both real and virtual. Eight (out of 13) shapes of this sort can be counted in the first
section. The images that throng and follow on each other 5, 9, 12, 13
constantly reach the limit of visibility and legibility, mostly because they match up with the most unexpected compositions of the gray shapes: thus they become moments of a sort of global phenomenal body, mutating, conspicuous, external/internal—as well as fragments of perception, originating from an autonomous vision. They are at once propelled by a constant motion and ceaselessly interrupted, one might say, by moments or points of fixity that imply barriers from one scene to the other and images "lifted" within the same scene. Finally, one does not know if the scene (minimally) changes or is (merely) reproduced from one shot, from one still frame to the other, if it is sheer repetition or constant difference. (Rather, one has the feeling of going beyond, as if toward a possible image, a visible beyond the divisible yet made of it, close to repetition, as Deleuze defines it, as difference within concept.)[12] Nothing is really decipherable, not even for the analyst-spectator who struggles against this decomposition of memory in order to see how it is composed. Everything happens too rapidly, or too obscurely, or too indefinably, even if one guesses

or "sees" the totality of what escapes vision: army movements,
cities on fire, aircraft carriers, charges, assaults, rocket
launches, flights, takeoffs, silhouettes, frightened faces.

Thus, the gray shape seems to harbor the body
of the film, its purely material substance, making the film
beneath the film, "the other film,"[13] appear; however,
the variations of figures, rhythms, and frequencies are also
in themselves possible echoes of the content of the scenes.
The gray shape materializes the thousand and one shapes
of this simultaneously real and virtual body—the film—only
to the extent that it functions at the same time as a screen.
This takes place in the third section, just after a section that 15
engenders the most beautiful of imaginable shapes: a machine 18
worthy of Kafka's *The Penal Colony* crosses the desert like
a rake or a mad insect, while scenes of extreme violence
seem to vanish and rebound against the edge of the receptor
panels, where they may be halted yet may also pass through.
The effect is enhanced by a movement sweeping the land-
scape that serves as a background to the machine, which
appears to be followed by a tracking shot (this is an extremely
rare occurrence in the tape, where movement almost
invariably arises from within the image).[14]

In the third section, the screen is first placed behind
the actor, as a memory toward which he turns back: a huge
concave Cinemascope screen, spread over the landscape
like a Richard Serra sculpture that has finally found its
natural surroundings. The solid gray is gradually disturbed; 21
clouds float by; the light rises, gathers, and vanishes. The
atom bomb explodes. All the world's memory. All the energy
of a single movement in a huge still frame.

The screen thus returns as a leitmotiv for the entire
third section, with or without the protagonist or the spectator
interposed. The interest of this section, however, lies mostly 23
in the other gray shapes, which appear in ambiguous yet
powerful alternation. Nearly all these shapes are spinning,
spiraling, and most are prismatic, composed of micro-elements 22
arranged in curves and shattered with intense vibrations
that recall the steel curtain-screen originating in the sky.
The atomic explosion, commented upon by Oppenheimer's
voice and digitized face, is represented both on the screen 20
and by the infinite division of abstract cells conveying pure
energy on shapes that serves as screens. These all function

1

2

3

4

5

6

7

8

9

10

11

12

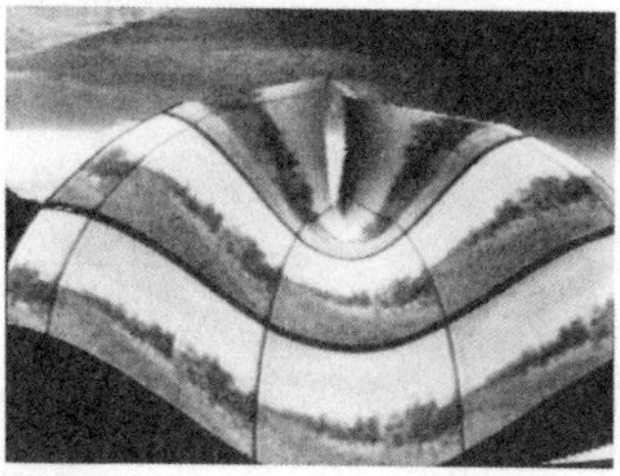
13

14

15

16

17

18

19

20

21

22

23

24

25

26

27

28

29

30

31

32

33

34

35

36

37

38

39

40

together as a revival, an amplification of the gray shapes/
projection backdrops presented in the first section.

Up until this point (roughly in the middle of the tape)
one can find three main kinds of gray shapes:

– the undivided screen, with the single event that
seems to boil down to the shot / still frame; 23

– the myriad form, whose own "empty" event is the
processing of the screen, fluctuating from the pure pulsing
and twisting of light to a nearly infinite division of cells 22
(these cells, produced along a model of geometric progres-
sion, are nevertheless largely unequal because of the form
of the gray shapes; each of them is therefore unique);

– the gray form with a divisible screen (an average of
ten unequal screens, themselves dependent on the variations 5, 9, 12, 13
of each form) onto which historical scenes are projected,
in an extremely broad range of speeds stilled by brief
motionless moments.

Thus, the attentive viewer will appreciate what is
being carried out around the still frame/screen: a frame per
24th or 30th of a second, one screen per frame. This is what
should be visible. For example, in the Spanish sequence (IV)
the photograph (or the frame?) of a man's face glides upward 26
and downward: the chain of images, which is interrupted
by dark spaces (like black leader on a film reel), goes by in
such a way that one image seems to occupy the whole screen,
even though its connection with the other images is
perceptible (every occurrence of the image is, in addition,
underlined, mechanically punctuated by a voice that repeats,
like a broken record, "Por la Revolución, Durruti!"). The
same thing happens in the Soviet sequence (V). Here, the
gray shape first consists of two identical images (of Lenin,
Trotsky, and so on) spinning around. These fragments
of film stock coiling and uncoiling, these series that begin 29, 30
then limit themselves to dividing an image from itself,
are situated precisely in the interstice between the (unique)
photograph and the (individual or multiple) still frame.
This feeling grows even stronger in the fifth section when the
mode of *défilement* used in the Spanish sequence reappears,
in a more significant way: moving horizontally now, the
images take up nearly the whole screen (one only catches
a glimpse of the colored desert landscape) and assume the
shape of a screen themselves. Two women's faces glide by,

from right to left: somewhere between still frames and photographs, they alone nearly fill the shot, which they set 31, 32
in undulating motion. This "parade"[15] ends with the image of a book, which has become emblematic of the psychic browsing produced by the filmic apparatus; this image, long inscribed by cinema, has been recognized in film theory (by Thierry Kuntzel among others) and reworked by video as an after-product of cinema (by Vito Acconci, Kuntzel, and others).

Earlier, by way of introducing the transformation affecting the gray shapes, I used the phrase "from the still frame to the *dispositif*." The still frame/screen is at the heart of this transformation, but only because the screen is in itself reworked as a variable of the photo-cinema-video
dispositif. Recall, if you will, the two-sided screen on which, 2, 3
at the very beginning of the tape, the fascist-revolutionary sign and globe of the earth were inscribed. This effect is not only connected with the *défilement* and stratification of the images, but also with their spatialization within the *dispositif*, that is, the virtual position of the spectator's eye. When the screen is only (and variously) double—instead of becoming polymorphic (as in the gray shapes with multiple images, where the gaze confronts a sort of tactile multiplicity)—what is directly designated is the mirroring structure of vision within the *dispositif*. What, then, happens to my mirror-body (facing the screen), which continues to function, even if my eye has already become a polymorphic body? The sixth section (war in the Pacific) tackles this problem by setting up two double screens (and showing these screens together). On the left side, there is the bifacial screen, closely resembling its first appearance (although with multiple size variations between its two parts); but in the middle, there
is an even stranger double screen. The part of the image 35, 36
this latter screen covers is split in two and folded at a right angle: its top portion appears in frontal view like a normal movie screen, while its bottom part, much larger, stretches down slantwise to the bottom of the image. As a result, the action—here, mainly bombers taking off—occurs twice: the second time partly as a mirror and partly as a ghostly, excessive prolongation of the first one. Meanwhile, on the other pair of double screens, the action embodies other motifs (the soldier's dirty work). Thus, the gaze is constantly

relayed from a crossing or breaking of the mirror it continues to face.

Each section, in effect, advances one step further in the systematic exploration of a virtuality of images as an extension of the theater of war. The seventh and last section takes a decisive leap: it draws the character/actor back within the field of memory and casts him, as a being made of pure *trame*, within the gray shapes. He is enclosed in a split screen, with one of the two images lagging behind the 37, 38
other. He suffers within this frame and, as his younger, former self, turns back into his own spectacle, a bygone image.

This tortured double face is subjected to two other divisions from itself—which is all I am left with, what I could see or make out in this section that borders on the enigmatic, where the divided screens are vibrating over themselves, multiplied, and substituted for one another, and are inhabited by exchangeable figures with exchangeable features. The first division shows the protagonist, half recog- 39
nizable, half made of fiber and folds, abandoning himself to a performance/dance that leads the images of the world back to video art and its origins, to the exertion of one's body, triumphant inside its screen-cage. The second division turns this standing body into a sitting body, making it a spectator, its own spectator. One cannot say that these three same figures—metamorphosing and gliding under one another—form a closed loop, for none of the images here have the power to prescribe an overall meaning. Nevertheless, one has the feeling that the images of the world are hostage to a memory designated within the very art that calls them forth.

To further convey the complexity of the work and conclude this analysis, which is partly a description, I offer a few additional remarks, if only to convey how hard it is for mere words to render some of the new states of the image, given the extent to which, in this work, a truly "unattainable" text is composed.[16] The word text no longer makes any sense, except as a reminder that language's sole prerogative is still its ability to try to say something, to remonstrate against anything. The first striking fact is the interdependence created, with the gray shapes, between figure and backdrop; what exists as figure, or moves toward the figure, may also

be backdrop. Some of the most disturbing moments of the tape are caused by the way the screens/media become in themselves objects that seize some meaning, some possible meanings, such as the several gray shapes that are loaded
with films and still frames. In the Spanish section, a huge 24
stratified mass on which a still projection that could be mistaken for a fresco is inscribed, as though on an immense cenotaph. A comparable mass appears at the end, as a false backdrop for the credits. It is hollowed this time, however, as though frayed from within and laden, so to speak, with all the undone memory that has accumulated throughout the tape, for the spectator as well as for the protagonist and the author he represents. This mass might be—and this is where its power lies—tomb, monument, brain, rock, face,
a mass of undifferentiated memory. 40

Next comes the very substance of the shapes—particularly of the shapes that are also projection backdrops. I depicted them as being both full and flat (in spite of the strange profiles that can be seen in the illustrations). Yet, part of their power comes from their malleability, their transformability. A gray shape can become thick like a wall, the screen a mass that accumulates memory, seemingly one of
the real things of the world, even if it is a mere mirror for its 34
images. A gray shape can be translucent, like a silhouette cutout. Curiously then, the shape is no longer really gray but gradually takes on color, having a less clear-cut relationship with the natural background than the other gray shapes in the tape.

Finally, a gray shape can be frayed, cloudy, perforated. In the Spanish sequence (where the backgrounds for multiscreen projection powerfully reappear), these different occurrences of the gray shapes are combined in the most
extraordinary way: images are projected onto false decom- 25
posed screens where representation seems to collapse within the very space-time in which it is presented. This process grows more vertiginous when the actions of the bodies contradict the nature of the medium that holds them: soldiers charging with guns and bayonets, or digging up the moving ground of this screen, which is always on the verge of splitting open under the weight of its own lightness. There
is as well an extraordinary moment in the Soviet sequence: 31, 32, 33
shots or photographs of women glide by, from right to left,

nearly filling up the entire screen; they are followed by the image of a man that moves past, multiplying itself, in a similar fashion, except that the gray shape has now become both thicker (like a wall or screen) and perforated, distended, with its lines of memory left agape. In this image, volume and surface compete and verge on disappearance; in turn the image spawns a series of screens-words-images-books: the very image of the stratified and layered[17] cultural memory that could be emblematic of the entire "art of memory."

Those who have not seen the tape (or may have forgotten it somewhat) will have to imagine how the transformations I just described are combined with those I mentioned earlier, and especially how this continuous mutation of the gray shapes within their own space, as within the entire screen, is ceaselessly combined with the constant yet variable special effects that establish transitions 8, 11, 17, 18
between shots or moments. A continuous mobility results, one of unceasing intersections and crossings and one that would seem to defy any drawing of distinctions. Nonetheless—and such is the power of the tape—the feeling of the shot, although fractured, divided from itself and, as it were, vaporized, still endures. The shot remains the site of découpage and of memory, for the spectator whose mind scans the history of wars captured by cinema in this century, which has become a history of cinema itself. The effort to maintain the shot as a unit of comprehension is quite close (yet with extremely different applications) to Marcel Odenbach's work on the strip-form[18]: there is the same repossession, the same distancing of the world, proceeding from a formal rearticulation of major works from the past via video—Hitchcock for Odenbach, Eisenstein and Vertov for Vasulka. Destroying, then reconstructing the shot, then making this work visible: this, too, is the art of recognizing the memory of and within cinema.

There is, however, within this very movement, a more profound way to reach cinema while projecting oneself beyond it. I have spoken of the structure of the cinema *dispositif*—as screen, staging area, solid memory—as constantly renewed with the aim of materializing the filmic apparatus and thereby capturing the still frame, both actually and virtually. More precisely, that frame is shown in its infinitude, multiplicity, *and* singularity, but primarily in both its immobility *and* movement—one overlapping the other without completely encompassing it. One comes to realize, as in Vertov's work, how this immobility itself creates movement, and also how, at the very moment this movement (here infinitely accelerated) speeds up, motionlessness might at any point fall back on itself. The photographic emerges as an element both visible *and* invisible, but always divisible, of the transformation process that carries it to infinity. This is fundamental. The whole of Woody Vasulka's art is directed toward a processing of the image that aims at determining its substance and modes at every point, beyond the "natural" dictates of photography and its corollary, analogy. It is directed, in effect, toward a cameraless art. The power of this work, which allows us to glimpse a possible mastery of abstract time—time devoid of all connection to a preexisting visible world—is that it simultaneously maintains a relationship to that visible world, thus restoring to us, in real time, the conditions of memory. One might say, as long as lines and points bear the mark of the photographic that preceded them, memory is still matter for a (hi)story, and cinema is still captured in the course of its own development.

1988. Originally translated in 1996 by David Jacobson and Bérénice Reynaud.

[1] Gilles Deleuze, *L'image-temps* 223 [*Cinema 2* 172].

[2] Woody Vasulka, quoted in Ken Ausubel, "Woody Vasulka: Experimenting with Visual Narrative," *News and Review* (May 11, 1983) 8.

[3] Untranslatable pun: Bellour uses *extra-lucide* (visionary), an allusion to *voyante extra-lucide*, the French version of "readers and advisers" [translator's note].

[4] Jean-Paul Fargier, "Steina et Woody Vasulka: Zéro un," in *Où va la vidéo ?* (Paris: Cahiers du Cinema/Editions de l'Etoile, 1986) 76–82.

[5] Jean-Paul Fargier, "Steina et Woody Vasulka: Zéro un," *Où va la vidéo* (Paris: Cahiers du cinéma, hors-série, 1986) 79.

[6] See Paul Virilio's *War and Cinema: The Logistics of Perception* (London, New York: Verso, 1989) and *The Aesthetics of Disappearance* (New York: Semiotext(e), 1991) [editor's note].

[7] The character was portrayed by the American choreographer Daniel Nagrin (1917–2008) [editor's note].

[8] Perhaps this face that speaks with Oppenheimer's voice is just his own, which reappears later on in the tape. But in this shot, seen in this form, it physically parallels the actor's face to such an extent that it seems to be its double.

[9] I have deliberately "cheated" on the découpage. Syntagmatically, there are, strictly speaking, eight sections, if one follows the logic of segmentation demonstrated in the demarcation device—the gray "wipe" that closes shut (with a clapping noise that heightens the image-effect). From the point of view of the theme, however, section 3 and what would hypothetically be section 3a or 4 are homogeneous, since both deal with nuclear holocaust and are based on comparable elements. We find here, in an amusing but significant way, the basic problems of segmentation of classical cinema.

[10] There are exceptions to this omnipresence of the gray shape: the single "filmic" shot; several shots with the devil-angel in the landscape (for example, six in the first section), two shots of Oppenheimer in the third section (a third shot turns Oppenheimer into the gray shape), and a few colored solarizations behind the protagonist in the same third section.

[11] In fact, the sign bears the letters "UFA"—the initials of the biggest producer of German movies, which later became the producer of propaganda films for the Nazis.

[12] This is the emblematic formula used by Deleuze in *Différence et répétition* (Paris: PUF, 1968) [*Difference and Repetition*, trans. Paul Patton (London: Continuum, 2004)].

[13] By "filmic apparatus" Thierry Kuntzel designates a space both material and mental, between the "projected film" and the "film stock." See Kuntzel, "A Note upon the Filmic Apparatus," *Quarterly Review of Film Studies* 1 (August 1976) 266–271.

[14] This shows the extent to which this quite short third section, involving three singular shots (the conflict between the protagonist and the mythical figure, with the steel rain coming down; the "filmic" shot of the protagonist; and this gray shape), constitutes the heart of the tape, its turning point, underlining most of the points of tension between cinema and video.

[15] Untranslatable pun. Bellour uses the verb *défiler* (to glide, to glide by) for the images; the beginning of this sentence reads *cet album-défilé*: in this sense, *défilé* means fashion parade (hence the connection with religious procession and, more significantly, military march) [translator's note].

[16] See Raymond Bellour, "The Unattainable Text," *Screen* 16.3 (1975) 19–27.

[17] Untranslatable pun: *feuilleter* means both to layer and to leaf through, so the past participle *feuilleté* connotes both books and "stratification" [translator's note].

[18] See the text entitled "The Form My Gaze Goes Through" in this book.

Burning Memory

Hollis Frampton, *Nostalgia*, 1971

Thierry Kuntzel, *Nostos II*, 1984

There are images that burn. Already in Hollis Frampton's *Nostalgia* (1971) one sees photographs consumed one by one in front of the lens, traces of a life recaptured by the voice-over speaking of photographs destined to disappear. In *Nostos II* (1984) the image burns in its very essence, the return of the return of nostalgia, to an unbearable degree. In *Nostos I* (1979) Thierry Kuntzel began his work on the traces that memory leaves behind, wipes out, and recaptures. Now he shows us how a memory burns. This is the unique effect of his installation. The mental image, the true image that consumes the body, builds itself there in time, yet still retains its instantaneity.

Nostos II tells a story. But the only subject of that story is time. Four parts, four times, four aspects or functions of time. The woman, unknown, smokes a cigarette: pure time that passes, time consumed. More and more photographs are accumulated, piled up, they

Thierry Kuntzel, *Nostos II*, 1984

disappear return: the time of memory, the anamnesis of lost time. Pages of a book turning incessantly: time leafed through, the conjugated time of culture and idleness. The unknown throws letters into the fire, into the fireplace, the image which serves as the leitmotiv of the four parts: through this action, which unites present and past, as in the time of the photographs and the book, we again enter, in a different way, the time consumed.

How does this story of time become a spectacle of our mental activity? How does the spectator, projected outside himself, come to experience the functioning of his own mind? First of all there is the "drag" of the misadjusted *paluche*, which gives the black and white image a material of its own, sluggish light tracing round each movement (of the camera, of the actress's body, of the objects manipulated) contours of a ghostly character. This white material divides all the elements in the representation from themselves while binding them together: it accentuates what one sees, but at the same time it makes it unreal, while making one believe all the more in that very unreality. Strictly speaking, there is never an image in the frame, but layers of images, each level with its own internal time, which does not correspond exactly with its duration, but rather with the mixing of the layers of material. In the sequence of photographs for example: substituted for one another, piled on top of each other, they also flow into each other. There are moments when this reaches the point of vertigo, when this fusion takes place against a window frame that appears to come from another image but is, nonetheless, part of the same one: this mobile, fluctuating, fugitive, but nonetheless present framework is the open space, the material and psychic screen on which all the images deposit themselves and from which they spring.

The light is sluggish, but it also irradiates. The smoke of the cigarette, the flames in the fireplace, for example, grow inside the frame, invade it, and die there, making time into a material of which the energy rises and falls, from too much white to its vanishing into black. This time—of traces, of layers, of impressions—is full of intensities.

But these layers, these intensities, this time that will not pass or finish its transformations; all this has the violence and brilliance of a snapshot. Or rather, starting with the snapshot, an elusive and indefinable time is created. Nine scenes: the image appears here or there, here and there, just as the reminiscence arises in the memory logically or, equally, arbitrarily. There are 1, 2, 3, 4, 5, 6, 7, 8, or 9 images, always more or less different and playing on those degrees of difference (with the sole exception of an identical leitmotiv shot of the fireplace seen four times)—images that supplement each other, cross each other, react to each other, spin around on this screen of screens. A block of images that fill it completely (sometimes: the fireplace again, or the turning pages of a book), because emptiness regulates their circulation. The black, the blacks, are fundamental, largely preserved: blacks from which the images can be born, a bit more, a bit less, always unexpectedly. Thus the montage of the nine tapes is the patient, skilled, and implacable operation whereby the explosion of psychic time installs itself in space, in all the excess and arbitrariness of its insistence.

This makes *Nostos II* one of the most direct expressions of the "mystic writing pad," posited by Freud in his attempt to represent the psychic apparatus. A few years ago Thierry Kuntzel asked himself whether the "filmic apparatus" (the "unconscious" of the film, the displaced, condensed, immobilized, analyzed film, the film of the film, the "other" film) might not be this mystic writing pad that Freud was not able to discover in cinema itself? From his first tape onward (the working title of *Nostos I* was "Wunderblock" for a long time) Kuntzel has thrown all his energy into making visible this question through which video gives a renewed impetus to the image machine, fulfilling cinema's destiny. But he has never quite hit the mark until now, in this installation. That is why cinema can draw on it.

The last section of *Nostos II*: cinema as memory and quotation. And with unbelievable violence: the call of fiction. All that is needed, at the beginning and end of the film, is a bit of music and a voice (and on the leitmotif image a few short rising scales). Anyone who has not recognized the film will, I think, get from this a confused, but very vivid impression of *déjà vu*. As if by some hypnotic trigger, he will at once enter a space from the past: the fantasy on which classic American cinema is based. The spectator familiar with *Letter from an Unknown Woman* (1984) will experience something more piercing: he will remember with a shudder that in that film (along with *Vertigo*, 1958, perhaps the cruelest ever made in America) a dying woman—the unknown one—is writing an immensely long letter out of which the film flows. A letter addressed to a man who could not love her and who could even end up not recognizing her because he had never seen her as anything but an image.

1984. Originally translated in 1990 by Alison Rowe.

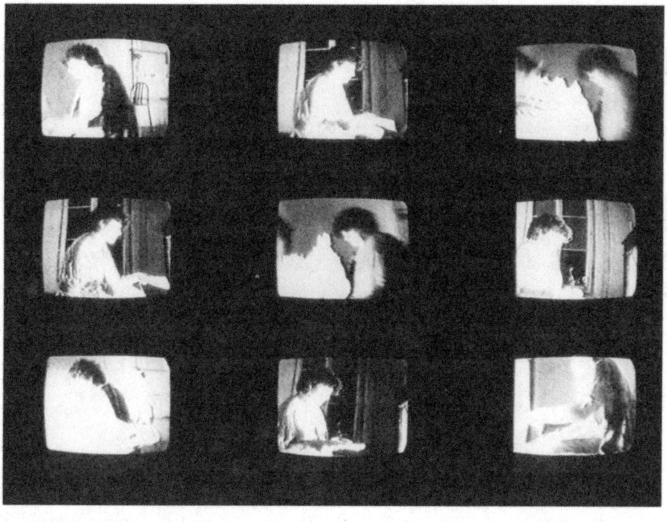

Thierry Kuntzel, *Nostos II*, 1984

Video According to Saint John

Bill Viola, *Room for St. John of the Cross*, 1983

The room is completely dark (or almost), immense. On a large screen half covering the back wall, black and white pictures of mountains file by one after the other, moving in an unsteady, rapid, never-ending rhythm. The wind blows, the noise is deafening. In the middle of the room a cube, just barely as tall as a person, reproduces the cell where Saint John of the Cross was shut away for nine months in 1577 (abducted by monks who could not stand his excess of godliness, of asceticism, his pretension in drawing too close to divinity). The gaze of the intrigued spectator passes through—if he bends down—a small opening, standing in for an imaginary window, into the interior of the poorly lit cube: a table, a glass, a pitcher of water, a minuscule color monitor. He sees a mountain, filmed in a still shot and in real time. It comes from *Ancient of Days* (1979–1981), one of Bill Viola's strongest tapes, one where the metamorphosis of time that so obsesses him is in its purest state: the passage from the time of sight and then recording, to the time of imagination in the final edit. This editing tries to retrieve in perception itself the condition of memory and the condition of the anticipation of mental images, in order to enter into the absolute, global time of sensory-conceptual affect. We can barely make out the movement that stirs the trees and the bushes in this image, the slow, very slow mutation of the clouds. Still in the cell, a voice that seems to rise up from the floor recites poetry in Spanish, fragments of the *Spiritual Canticle* written by Saint John during his long reclusion: a voice just barely audible if we make the effort to bend down just a little more, but always covered over by the howling of the wind that blows outside.

All of this, we realize, is about the relation between two spaces. In the same way that we hear the wind in the cell, we cannot see the entire image on the large screen without difficulty, without being "bothered" by one of the angles of the central cube. Unless we cross to the other side of the cube, and then are too close to the overly large image, which we leave behind in order to find a feeling of unity, in order to decompose and reconstruct a route along the various "stations." A route whose quality as tangible mass is in no way diminished, because it concerns perception, the body and memory all at same time, and presents a virtual conception of their relations. Everything depends on the position (physical and psychological) that the spectator comes to invent, divided throughout these wanderings between an inside and an outside, numerous insides and numerous outsides.

But why Saint John of the Cross? Let us say: to try to express what has taken the place of God in our day. We suppose that in his windowless cell, which he leaves only to go to the refectory where he is subjected to psychological and corporal trials, Saint John has kept the memory of a landscape: he keeps deep inside himself the image of a perception. This, above all, is what the presence of the small color monitor can suggest, if only in an overly realistic manner: what remains of the world, unshakable, when there is no more world, when it has been reduced to a still (almost still) image that acts as an inner ascension toward the light. This is the point from which Saint John would depart to plunge into the "Dark Night," there to meet God. Metamorphosis of image into poem, of any overly visible image into an indirect image of breath and of verb, once all organic mass has been abolished.

Haunted by the "irresistible power of the landscape," Bill Viola strives to invent a relation of the same order through video. By putting the small monitor in the cell and the cell in an enormous black box, Viola is constructing a *dispositif* that attempts to represent the functioning of imagination and inspiration, like the functioning of the video tool that simulates and produces them. Viola reminds us in this way that video is itself a permanent double of the landscape, of everything that the camera—which has become the potential eye of the new mystic—looks at in real time. This is the second thing suggested by the small color picture of the mountain. Viola then tells us that this continual perception is connected to an inner rumbling: a kind of organic furor, an uninterrupted flow of images-sounds. Out of the live, raw image, as it were, comes a type of body-image without which not a single transmutation would be possible. In welcoming this force, video-perception undergoes a metamorphosis, is transformed into a poem. Through this process we go back and forth from the inside to the outside of the image; we transform its theoretical exteriority into a form of visionary vitality.

This is what is implied by the continuity made up of such clear contrast between the organic, black and white image (founded on a kind of breathless panting, as if it were always just about to overflow the frame of a screen to which it doesn't really seem destined) and the color image (framed, placated, immobile and silent, almost too simple, displayed on the monitor, on the table, in the cell).

The confusion experienced by the spectator-stroller, if he takes the time to think about it, comes from the respective position of the two images, which cannot be seen at the same time and are, nevertheless, received as a whole; most importantly, such that one is received in the place of the other. But this only happens in one direction, when we go from the large image to the small one, from the immense *camera obscura* to the lighted cell. Obviously the archaic, nocturnal image gives a more direct material representation of the inner turmoil that resolves itself into a mystical poem than the miniature with its technological attributes. In this sense the external image occupies the place of God, or rather fulfills the function of the image (and body) state that leads to God. This is why the sound of the wind, which enters with the spectator inside the cell, is so important. It allows him to experience the two images at the same time. He is haunted by the memory of the large one, carried by the sound, at the very moment he looks at the small image and confuses this twofold vision with the murmur of the poem, which seems to rise up from the ground. But for the analogy to work, the image on the monitor in the cell must appear to be simultaneously a calm relaying of the large image and a television image. Only then will the journey that leads to the poem's "Dark Night" be credited to video, capable of reproducing this experience because its ability to simulate it almost offers a guarantee that it can be relived and metamorphosed. This is exactly what happens when the spectator exits the cell, without however leaving it behind: from this moment on, its memory haunts him. And facing this immense, vibratile and dark image, in the installation's second (yet for the spectator previous) night, he finds both the obscurity of Saint John's cell and a psychological freedom (translated by his freedom of movement). And thus it is a tumultuous version, before and after, of the Kantian adage, without any (moral) law but that of potential ecstasy, the star-studded sky transformed into a sky of images above our heads.

1984-1989. Originally translated in 1990 by Alison Rowe.

The Last Man on the Cross

Gary Hill, *In Situ*, 1986

Why Blanchot? Why *Thomas the Obscure* (1941)? Because in the first chapters of this book—in the chapters read by the hero, the actor-author of *In Situ* (1986)—there is an extraordinarily violent clash between sight and language. Thomas—and this is perhaps where he gets the name Obscure—Thomas loses himself, disappears, in the intimacy of his own gaze, which he experiences as coming not from his body, but from outside, from the night, from the very silence of things. And the words—because Thomas is also a reader—the words enter into this triumphant and threatening gaze; they radiate from it like the eyes of living beings, of animals ("a giant rat [...] with piercing eyes and pure teeth"),[1] exercising a hold over him that is like the hold of a fight to the death. It is understandable that Gary Hill, so haunted by the materiality of language that for years now he has made it the principal tool of his compositions, was tempted by a work of fiction that he opposes here, here, in both a metaphorical and real manner, to the fiction and the *dispositif* of television.

What does the implied spectator, to whom Gary Hill offers a comfortable chair, see in the tape that appears and disappears, in short sequences, on the single monitor of *In Situ*? First the ocean. Then the eyes of the man we will call the hero: the left eye and the right eye, in turn, in extreme close-up, wide open, yet twice closing violently, too violently, as if to nullify an intolerable sight that must nonetheless be tolerated. A zoom-in pictures a fragment of a page from *Thomas the Obscure*, the words "staring into the ..." can be made out. Then again, the ocean, the sky. And close-ups of the hero's forehead and his feverish hands, which are suddenly interrupted by an inaudible voice on the soundtrack playing backward. This sound introduces the tape's second series of images: television images, on the Irangate crisis, the sale of arms to the Contras, we see Reagan, and so on. Twice these images intertwine with those of the first series: first in a long series of superimpositions and dissolves, then in parallel editing (i.e. the two great implication principles of any narrative told in images). In-between these two interventions of television, the hero, seated at a table, eats while reading *Thomas the Obscure*. And twice he collapses in his chair and falls back. The first time, he begins reading again while lying on the floor. But the second time he shoots back up as if surfacing from an underwater dive and then swims with difficulty for a long, long time (this is when parallel editing is used).

It is obviously very simple, too simple, to see in this montage a criticism of information, of televised disinformation, skillfully set up by the elements of the overall *dispositif*. In this room that reproduces the proportions of the monitor, the carpet (a stylish gray) is lined with stripes that bring to mind the lines of the video *trame*, and the armchair (covered in gray velour) is so comfortable that its occupant slides naturally toward the TV set, collapsing into the image. To underline this, Hill thought of modifying the monitor and the armchair in the same way, by reducing the size of the cushion in the armchair and by placing the monitor in a frame that exceeds it in exact proportion. From this comes the reinforced effect of the TV images themselves, most often reduced to a partial frame in the center of the image. In addition, they move backward in this frame, with the same movement that makes Blanchot's reader fall back. It is done so thoroughly that when the hero swims, and seems about to drown, he swims in information: it is information that lures and then smothers him. But it is also (this is where the criticism is really interesting, that is, intelligent) Blanchot's text that he crosses, in which he swims and floats. *Thomas the Obscure*'s reader will not have forgotten that Thomas, in the first chapter of the book, is so wrapped up in his effort to resist the swell of the ocean that there is a moment when he almost lets himself be killed. And a very careful reader of Hill might have made out, in the numerous pages of the book that are centered and wavering in such a way that we cannot really read the text, part of the story's first line: "(Thomas sat down) and looked at the ocean." The ocean that appears in the tape's very first shot and comes back several times (already, in 1980, the first line of *Processual Video*: "He knew the ocean well").

And so there are two deaths at work here, both metaphorical yet, nonetheless, full of significance: one comes from television (here Gary Hill puts himself in a well-known position that has been developed at length by American artists); the other comes out of Blanchot's text. The second is much more original, reproducing in a very exacting manner (I do not know to what extent Hill was familiar with this or even aware of it) the way in which Blanchot introduces the relation between the literary word and something he calls the "rumor" or the "foreign voice" into his essays. He opposes the two, obviously, in the same way this has been done since the 19th century in the name of the specificity and autonomy of art. But he introduces the idea that from this point on literature comes into its own and can show its difference only when it confronts—head on and even excessively—this rumor and even risks being confused with it. Because the two are cut from the same cloth, their difference being that the literary word exists only to oppose this rumor, to oppose all forms of dictatorship contained within it, by confronting it with the only force it has left: its silence. From this comes its power to withdraw, its special intimacy with death.

Gary Hill knew how to give direct expression to this intimacy in an installation whose elaboration went on before and after the creation of *In Situ*. In *Crux* (1983–1987), in a desolate island landscape featuring a castle in ruins, five monitors reproduce the partial images from five cameras attached to the author-actor's body: two on his feet, two on his hands and one at his waist, aimed toward his face. The text that accompanies the gait of this disconnected body is itself a "blank" text: it does not have the essentially machinic quality of most of Hill's other tapes. It is a text of desperation and of wandering, close to some of the writings of the *nouveau roman*, and in particular to those of Blanchot, whose dislocating and decentering force is captured by Hill.[2] From this solitary destiny, that in fact is not a destiny at all because it has neither beginning nor end, the hero bears the cross, alone (a cross marked out in the installation by the five monitors). He becomes one of many possible Christs (there are *Four Hundred Men on the Cross*) whom Michaux made into one of the mainstays of the domain of modern literary imagination, and Blanchot's *Last Man* who is his counterpart. Christ as the last man. The last two shots of *In Situ*, seemingly detached from the rest, have this same erratic quality: a quick—I almost want to say running—forward tracking shot, in a park where the ground is covered with dead leaves; followed by the resumption of a similar movement, this time on the contrary showing the trees, and centered on the character's back, which seems to carry the weight of the world. Things become clearer when he turns around, pressing the remote control, and the image disappears: his cross is at once his mad dash, the equivalent of his wandering word taken over by Blanchot, and television.

This is what comes out of the very subtle confusion brought about between the acts and the positions that bring these two series of opposing images together. But Hill, in order to arrive at the conceptualization that he wants to produce in this manner, placed this first *dispositif* within a second one without which it would have only a limited meaning and through which it expresses something that Blanchot cannot say in the same manner, because it has to do with seeing and touching. Hill has, in fact, arranged in his space four pillars that can suggest the cardinal points of the field of information. But above all, each of these pillars has a ventilator, which is tied to another, stronger one, which intervenes between the spectator and the TV set. Their main function is the dispersal of the sheets of paper that fall in regular intervals from a machine and are strewn little by little over the ground, spinning haphazardly around the spectator. These sheets—and this is the installation's true stroke of genius—these sheets reproduce the images (and the texts) of the tape that is playing at the same moment on the screen.

I prefer to leave to the imagination all that can be said about the way the cinema—or video—*dispositif* (here it is all the same, with the difference that video, once again, is able to say or to show better than cinema itself what cinema is, and what it becomes through video) is illustrated by this intensifying effect. These swirling sheets are still frames, the successive impressions of the "mystic writing pad" in which Freud saw the truest representation of the unconscious: they are the strata of the "filmic apparatus" made visible, the layers in which Thierry Kuntzel so clearly saw a more exact replica of what Freud was trying to imagine. They are also the pages of the Book (all books and any book) in its uncertain fall, its dispersal, its cast of the die. But above all, I would like to express the jubilation that comes over the spectator/guinea pig when he understands that these sheets, which are more or less falling on his head, are the images that are entering into his brain, something like the layers of skin on the skull. Gary Hill told me that during the creation of *In Situ* in Los Angeles, the eye that is the first image reproduced on paper became stuck, in falling, on the eye that appeared at the same moment in the monitor. It stayed there until the spectator got up to take it off. A matter of not letting his perceptions wreak too much havoc on his ideas. Or maybe the opposite.

1987. Originally translated in 1990 by Alison Rowe.

[1] Maurice Blanchot, *Thomas the Obscure*, trans. Robert Lamberton (Barrytown NY: Station Hill Press, 1988) 69.

[2] Hill later removed this text from *Crux*, which is now silent. It reappeared as a voice in his tape *Site Recite (a prologue)* (1989).

The Art of Demonstration

Antoni Muntadas, *The Board Room*, 1987

The art of demonstration has its own kind of sensual pleasure. It is all in the way of doing it, in the choice of the material. Demonstration is then the art of living, of surviving among the monsters. An art of defense and of (de)monstration. The art put into practice for example by Godard in *France/tour/détour/deux/enfants* (1978). Here he travels regularly among monsters: among those who have forgotten the very meaning of words, the meaning of the most elementary questions, adults, television viewers; this is what he and the two children demonstrate. Everything depends on the way in which it is done. On the material. These monsters cannot be underestimated. The demonstration is accurate, that is to say effective, only if it is sensual and generous, able to compete with what it deals with, to use seduction to go beyond the appeal of monstrosity itself. In Godard it is the art of colors. Also, a great lesson from Brecht: the dialectic of conflict will be all the clearer if the poor really seem to be poor; and so their costumes have to be made from the richest fabrics, as rich as the clothing of the rich, perfectly catching the light.

The Board Room (1987) relies from the start on the sensual pleasure of pedagogy. A luxurious and calm atmosphere envelops the visitor who wanders into this dimness lit up by a warm, shimmering light. Lit from underneath by an invisible red light, a long oval table seems to float. Like a large mirror, its surface reflects the blurred images of the 13 portraits that surround it. The glow from the portraits reflects off the metallic structures of the 13 chairs arranged around the table. An attentive spectator will notice (thanks to the central portrait, in the background, the only one placed exactly in line with the seat at the end of the table) that the backs of the chairs were designed in proportion to the size of the portraits. As if a board of directors, mythically called together in absentia in this room, would have liked to endow themselves, in their own eyes, with a maximum of symbolic efficiency.

The second movement goes toward these portraits, collectively and then one by one. The brightest light radiates from them. Its two sources: a small lamp, hooked onto the top of each image that gives out a constant glow; and the varying flame bursting forth from each of the micro-monitors that take the place of each speaker's mouth. A well-ordered gaze should cross through three stages, thus passing through the three most important (historical) modes of representation and portraiture. First it comes to rest on the gilded frame of a painting. Next it enters into the "real" image of a photograph. But everything has been set up here so that the emblems linked to the portrait since the Middle Ages and the Renaissance are represented (and so that painting then continues in photography): clouds, red velvet drapery, blurred landscapes, inscriptions, images within the image, a few uniform backgrounds. Finally, the spectator enters television. Displaced in this manner, it becomes paradoxically one more pictorial element inside the photo-painting: the art of video art, of mixing the different levels of representation and turning them back onto themselves.

In television, on each of the small monitors, the spectator initially sees light. A bluish white that flashes and leaps out from the screen, in contrast to its surroundings.

A very attentive spectator will next make out acts: scenarios, lessons, appeals, strategies of seduction. Each one seems even more incredible than the last, and at the same time oddly natural. The 13 charismatic leaders brought together by Muntadas to represent a board of directors, a sort of central committee of politico-religious delirium and of audio-visual communication, are engaged in their great maneuvers. Two of them are included here to widen the scope, to extend it from America to the rest of the world and to make us wonder about this projection: Khomeini, John Paul II. The eleven others are American evangelists who have become remarkable businessmen, holders of an immense power that comes mainly from television. In these tapes edited in loops (of varying length: from five to 45 seconds), we feel the shock of advertising strategy in its purest form (several of the tapes were conceived by the leaders themselves, they can be purchased or rented). Here we come across the persuasive force of a proven rhetorical style, oscillating between mythical autobiography and the lives of famous men. The power is distributed here in couples, in descendants, in families (Billy Graham and Schuller have sons already prepared to take over the helm). We marvel at the mix of races (the Maharishi comes straight from India, the Reverend Ike is black, Rabbi Schneerson is Jewish, Moon is Korean). It goes from California cool (Schuller) to intellectualized manipulation (Erhard), from all-purpose prophecy (Graham) to the strong-arm right (Falwell, Robertson, Swaggart). We hear enormous budgets being set forth by a new type of corporation, one that owns television stations, hospitals, and universities (Roberts has an annual budget of $50 million to $70 million; Falwell, $100 million). In fact, the things we see here are inconceivable. Swaggart in overflowing stadiums, attracting up to 90,000 people. Moon marrying 4,000 couples at one time. Falwell, fully dressed and up to his knees in water, blessing the letters from his followers, preparing small bags of water that they can use to rebaptize themselves in front of their TV sets, and his son blessing his father's wallet. The Reverend Ike sending out handkerchiefs to be left overnight under a pillow and sent back to him the next day (preferably with a check). Pat Robertson, candidate for the presidency of the United States, head of the country's fourth largest network (Christian Broadcasting

Network) is there, improvising on a board (or pretending to) an advertisement/beginners' lesson on the origins of the Creation, God, and the greatness of man, of which the almost sublime stupidity fulfills in one fell swoop the dreams of Flaubert and of Godard's pedagogy.

But above all, in all of these tapes that pass by like waking micro-nightmares, the truly attentive spectator will discover bodies. Real bodies at work. Believing, active, hysterical bodies. Bodies full of violence, of hatred, uncultivated bodies. Bodies greedy for visible power, for crude manipulations, for short-term profit. Look closely at Roberts in his baptismal waters. Watch Swaggart, striding across the stage, stopping, howling, handling his microphone like a rocker (he is incidentally a cousin of Jerry Lee Lewis). Listen to all of them, putting new garb on the oldest ideologies in the world. God. Jesus. The prophets. Morals. Purity. Power. Money. It brings back old memories. Very recent ones, too. Le Pen's body is made of the same matter. The two Serges of *Libération* (July and Daney) repeated it at leisure during the French presidential campaign: this man pleases, he believes in the sensuality of the word, he hits you in the guts; his success is not only due to the real conflicts that are poisoning French society, but comes from his knowing how to play with them, to play them, directly, with a disarming vulgarity, a deep understanding of the body-as-show, by using television like a sexual caress. The voluptuousness of horror. We may also soon have a new school of preachers (we have recently started to have our own apostolic Christians). This is what strikes us if we draw close enough to these little screens, if we stay around long enough. We cannot help but notice, each time we again step back to set out on our way, the effect produced by these so tranquilly obscene images in relation to the entire image, the paintings that they puncture: they are the natural complement to idealized poses, with their eyes fixed either on our own or along the thin blue line of sky that they promise. The image in movement is at the service of the still image, the stereotype, the icon image that hides in it (in that the second receives from the first its body, its true grain of reality), which accordingly founds its (illusory) values of exchange and communication.

Finally, the spectator will see words appear on these screens. In capitals, keywords, proper names, abstract terms, in a varying rhythm (REPENTANCE, MONEY, FINANCIAL, POLITICAL POWER, TELEVISION, GIFT, EDUCATION, DEGREE, PROPHECY, RESOURCE, PACKAGE, for Falwell, for example; others have more; Khomeini has only one: REVOLUTION). These words have an analytical, catalytic function. They speed up the associations between moments of discourse, the production of effects of discourse on the bodies of the actors. In this way the words inscribe the moments and effects in our imagination on the bodies of the spectators, those tens of millions of unfulfilled Americans who regularly send to their gurus the money necessary to their prosperity. These words have their own efficiency, their own sensuality. They prove once again to what extent video's function of inversion passes through writing. Writing is conceived here as a particular type of image, fragmented, intermittent, a network of raw significations that allows the image to become unstuck from itself without, for all that, causing it to lose its seductive force. A minimal critical discourse that holds together an overall *dispositif*, itself entirely conceived as an intensifier.

In *Monkey Business* (1952), Howard Hawks found a gentle way of taking a caustic view of the falsely majestic setting of the boardroom of an American company specializing in the pursuit of dreams and illusions. In this room he united Cary Grant and Ginger Rogers—returned to childhood through the properties of a rejuvenating potion—unaffected Marilyn, remaining true to her nature (because she is nature itself), and a monkey, the unknowing inventor of the product, B4 (!). Powers of fiction and of comedy. It was the time when movies still knew—in the mode of playful reinvention—how to integrate social criticism into the development of their own myth, into the American society they mirrored, which had not yet been numbed to the bone by television. Today, this video installation offers Muntadas the angle of a sensuous pedagogy founded essentially on mimicry. Its critical liveliness comes from its capacity to carry out displacements between elements and to make them insistent, so that they seduce by signifying, even by oversignifying; but only if the discourse thus produced also manages to maintain a quality of silence. The journey depends on this. In the catalogue of his recent retrospective in Madrid ("Hybridos"), Muntadas brought three photographs together 28 times on a double page: one shows a motif of urban architecture, the next a board room, or a meeting room or work space. The third frames in close-up, and in a smaller format, one (or two or several) hand(s) caught in the quick of life, with their grain of reality, thus imprinting a circulation between the other two images. As in *The Board Room*, where we go from the screen to the portrait then to the entire room, after having followed the opposite route, if we choose to, 13 times.

1988. Originally translated in 1990 by Alison Rowe.

Antoni Muntadas, *The Board Room*, 1987

The Form My Gaze Goes Through

Marcel Odenbach, *Der Widerspruch der Erinnerungen* (The Contradiction of Memories), 1982

In the silence-shrouded apartments of Marie-Antoinette in Versailles, where Marcel Odenbach was making *Dans la vision périphérique du témoin* (In the Peripheral Vision of the Witness, 1986), those present at the shooting witnessed a strange occurrence. They saw the cameraman, standing on his dolly, attempt to center an adhesive tape across the control monitor, under the ironical, knowing gaze of the director: this "gimmick" obviously was his, and he enjoyed seeing how far it could lead him.

It is always fascinating to watch an artist's involvement with a form, to the point of seeming to master it, because he or she has let it totally consume him or her. In Odenbach's work, it is interesting to watch this form appear, grope its way around, establish itself, reach its peak, and perhaps prepare to disappear. In *Die einen den anderen* (One or the Other, 1986), a tape he shot for German television at the same time he was developing his project for the Centre Pompidou in Paris, he no longer used the geometric partition that for the last five years had appeared—more or less, and in more than one way—to divide most of his shots. To move from one image to another, from one series to another, to stem—as he has always tried to—the excessive plenitude of images, their overwhelming presence, he opted for a new, less constraining form, one more closely bound to circumstances and the setup of the moment. For instance, the shot of a lit chandelier suddenly begins a pendulum swing, and each fan-shaped sweep reveals, as in a new "frame," the shots whose dividing screen it becomes. As always the goal is to conceal, split, divide the image from itself—in order to inhabit "the peripheral vision of the witness."

1

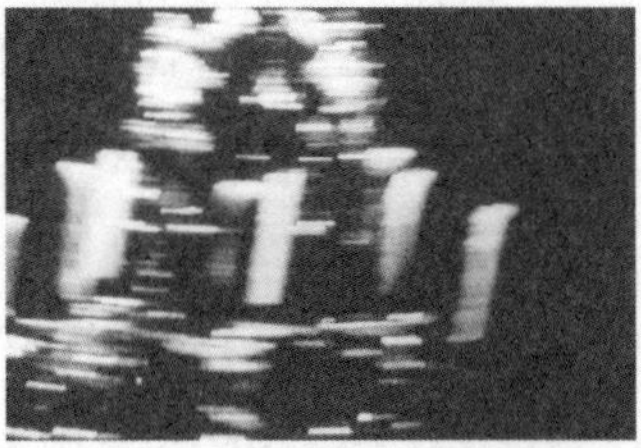

2

3

4

Once Odenbach's tapes went beyond the realm of performance art, the political and critical debates of the 1970s, and the medium's first affirmative gestures toward itself, his main concern became how to divide space: to see, more and less, in a different way—be it as witness, author, narrator, character, protagonist, presence, silhouette (and he is as much one as the other), or the spectator *en abyme*. In the transitional work *Der Widerspruch der Erinnerungen* (The Contradiction of Memories, 1982), the division of space, remarkably enough, is born in the very first shots out of the continuum of the image itself, marking bodies, matter, lines, and lighting. An inner motif of representation exists, or preexists, that will become the dividing strip, receptacle of other images.

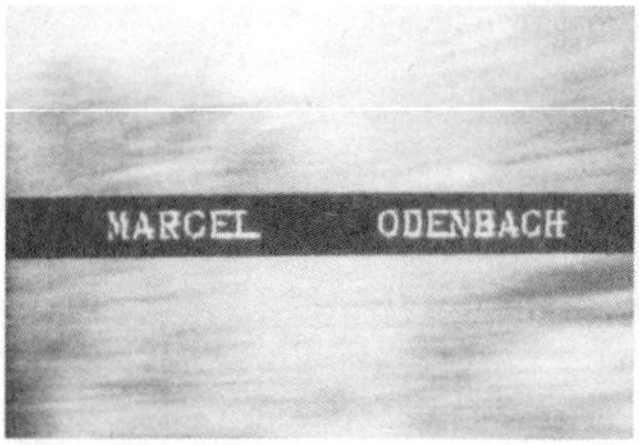

1

2

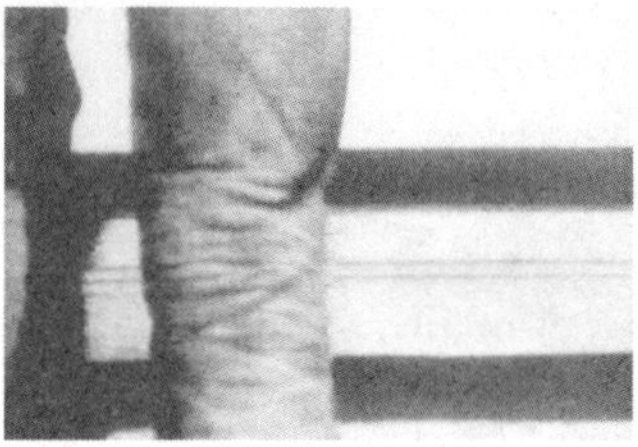
3

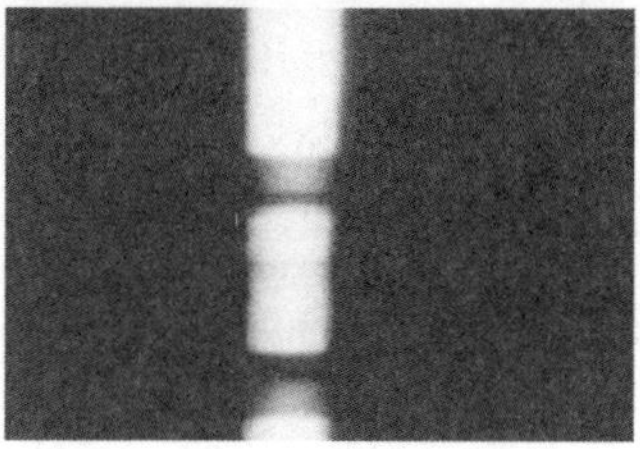
4

Note how it forms between the protagonist's legs; how, when he goes away, the form is immediately replaced by the lines that appear along the stair and under the door. Note too how, more abstractly, the strip carries the author's signature. And how, without yet becoming *imagery*, it is used to mold and modify the frame to ensure the transition from one shot to the next—and not just any shot: seen from behind, facing a screen-like window, somewhere, someone is having a vision. Transition and coexistence, appearance and disappearance—while avoiding both the traditional superimposition of cinema and the too-simple keying effect in video.

The strip appears as such in *Als könnte es auch mir an den Kragen gehen* (As if I Were Seized by the Collar From Behind, 1983). In this commissioned tape, whose original title was *1000 Meurtres* (1000 Murders), Odenbach wanted to be able to actually show two images at once without using a double screen, while still saving the techniques of superimposition and dissolve for more complex combinations. Creating meaning out of the clash of two shots (as Eisenstein did, but in a very different way) by adding a number of off-screen spaces, he invented a new kind of space. For example, after the first shot, which isolates the eyes of the spectator-witness in a smaller frame in the upper right-hand corner, two drawings by Goya appear. Their placement sets up two virtual strips (one horizontal and one vertical), which are quickly divided by a central vertical strip that widens to reveal the face of a frightened woman (Angie Dickinson in Brian de Palma's *Dressed to Kill*, 1980). The film sequence continues at length (an alternating series of shots and reverse shots from the woman's gaze), while art reproductions appear, one after the other, in a variety of layouts (like leafing rapidly through a book). The effect of terror, thus derealized, taken out of context (nothing is revealed of the film to those who have not seen it, and little of what the heroine sees is shown), is somehow attenuated; yet it is also increased by being reproduced in another way, because of the subtle off-screen space created by squeezing the frame. This effect also acts upon Goya's drawings and paintings, consigned as they are to anticipation and the workings of memory. A twofold off-screen space within the composition of the image is thus combined with culturally determined off-screen spaces; together they determine the intellectual and sensory effects born out of a friction of images.

1

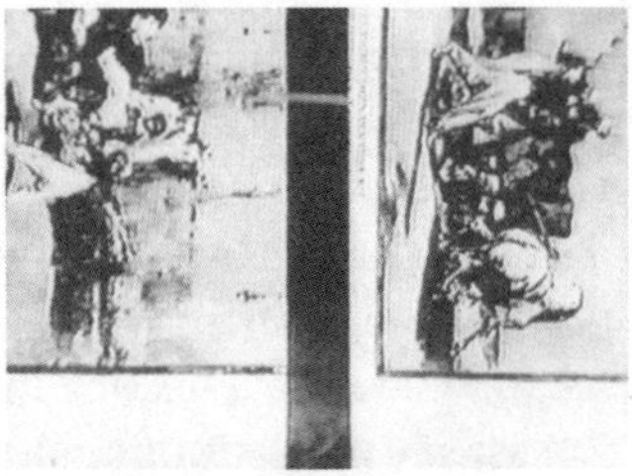
2

3

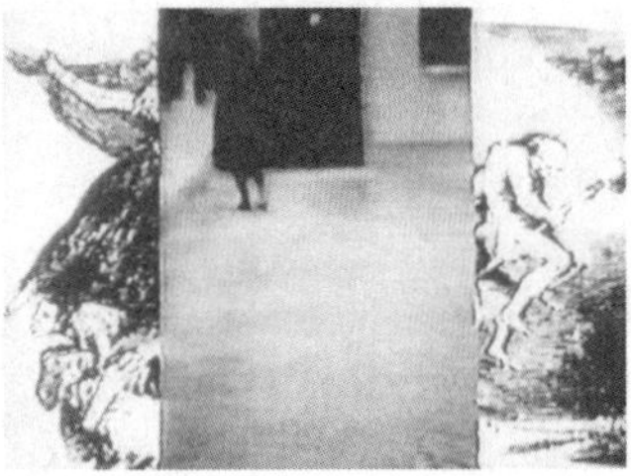
4

Obviously, from the start, the use of the strip form is linked to voyeurism. It creates effects between the different fragments of the frame that resemble point-of-view shots: not only by its own appearance as a slit or edge along which the gaze may rest before gliding toward off-screen spaces, but also because its visual motifs always presuppose the active presence of a gaze. The strip form thus isolates the eye itself: the viewing eye and the viewed eye. In one of the strongest moments of *Als könnte es auch mir an den Kragen gehen*, the horizontal strip—red now and placed near the top of the screen—shows a woman's beautiful, frightened eyes (on a poster) being compulsively shredded by a hand wielding a knife (the gesture, here confined once again to off-screen space, of Pascale Ogier in Jacques Rivette's *Le Pont du Nord*, 1982), while numerous scenes of violence fill up the rest of the screen. Thus the viewer is challenged by relentless visual activity. "Deceived about the enemy, the struggle, massacres... our people work out their problems of guilt in the psychological laboratory of television series." Alfred Hitchcock is the central reference in this ever-present TV-cinema—"for me [he is] the greatest filmmaker," says Odenbach, who experiences, incorporates, and redistributes the "psychosis-neurosis-perversion" of the visual *dispositif*, in turn recycling the frantic recycling of Hitchcock by de Palma and others. Before, in *Der Widerspruch der Erinnerungen*, shots of Janet Leigh (from *Psycho*, 1960), blinded by headlights in

1

2

3

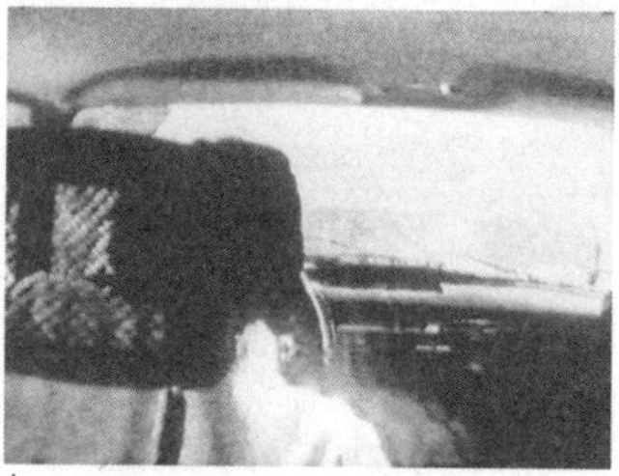

4

a heavy rainstorm, dovetail with those of the hero-voyeur-driver-dreamer; they partake all the more effectively in producing the strip form that the internal layout (placement of the blacks and whites, frame effect of the car windows) sets up. Similarly, in *Vorurteile* (Prejudices, 1984), the few shots quoted from Hitchcock's *Strangers on a Train* (1951) produce a thrilling effect (impossible to capture in a still frame): the out-of-control merry-go-round describes a moving strip that sweeps the screen, suddenly revealing to our fascinated gaze a close-up of a little girl clinging in terror to her horse. And in the tape made from the installation, "the peripheral vision of the witness" suddenly narrows—with the violence and confusion of an underlying text—in the briefly glimpsed images of attacks on women from Hitchcock's *Dial M for Murder* (1954) and *Frenzy* (1972).

The strip form's greatest strength is the crystallization it achieves between the passion of the gaze and the elements of representation. Take *Vorurteile*. To grasp how the form functions, let us try to describe the first minutes of the tape, in somewhat excessive, though necessary, detail. After a few landscape shots (blue-tinted black and white) punctuated by a sequence of music and sound (classical music, construction site noises, Hollywood music, African music), a pale blue strip appears against a background of dark shutters that seem to be slowly opened by it. Against this background the forms of two crosses, reminiscent of the strip, are outlined in the two sides of the image: they are nothing but the beams of light filtering through the shutters' slats. Soon an exotic ritual object appears, taking up nearly all of the vertical space in the strip and held by a pair of barely perceptible hands; it turns upon itself and the strip widens until, on each side of the screen, it leaves two thin black strips, roughly the same size as that of the first clear form. The object turns upon itself, and because of its shape it forms a sort of second strip placed at the center, especially since it becomes divided within itself, casting a shadow. Then the larger strip narrows, returning to its original form; and suddenly,

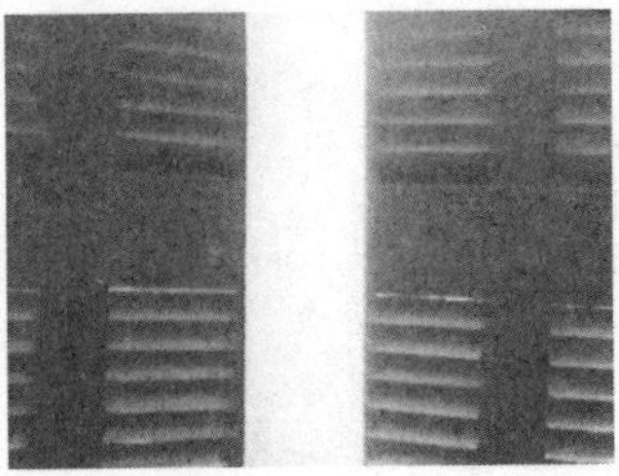
1

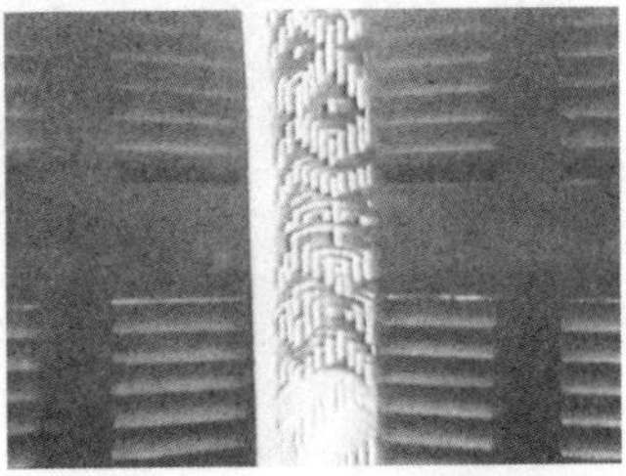
2

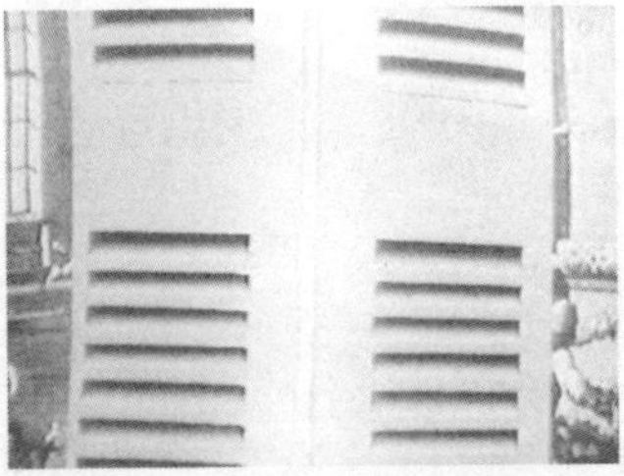
3

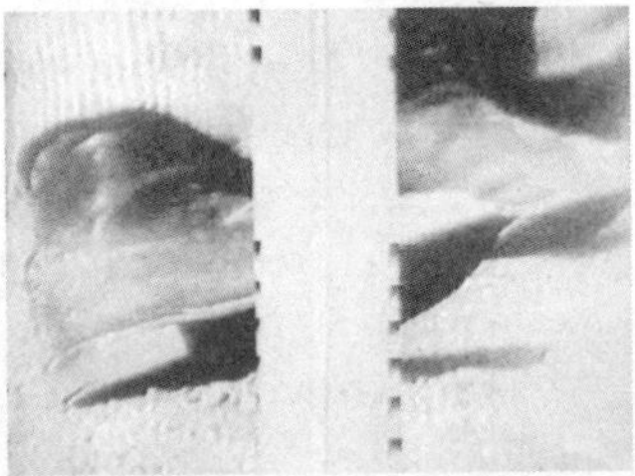
4

by inversion, one of the shutters, bathed in light, takes over the space hitherto occupied by the ritual object. Simultaneously, a still-indistinct image is framed within the narrow margins that previously circumscribed the dark shutters. Something remarkable occurs here: the vertical axis defined by the slats reproduces another sort of strip in the lighted shutter, the same size as the one that separated the two dark shutters, and the cross thus formed with the horizontal strip (itself produced by the slats) reproduces the double black cross in the earlier images. Then this wide central strip formed by the shutter is in turn reduced and ends up in the same confined space it first occupied between the shutters. There is a slight difference, however: the folding in the center and the fine crenulation of the strip's outline recall the visual motif of the shutters that have almost dissolved, in the midst of split yet recognizable images that appear in quick succession—photographs, shots from films and TV series, images of raw materials, factories, wars, offices, mines, active and heavy bodies. Until finally the shutter, still lit, fills up the entire field for the first time.

What is the result of such an arrangement of the strip form? It would certainly be of little interest without the fine, musical quality of Odenbach's work, without his keen sense of the relationship between sound and meaning, of counterpoint and rhythm, and without his highly personal way of getting involved in subject matter to produce not only "present-day chronicles" but also "untimely meditations" (exemplified in the German essay tradition by Nietzsche and Robert Musil, but cast in a new, lighter form in Odenbach). Obviously the strip lends material expression to the gaze as function: its scansions, its off-screen spaces, its excesses, its lacks. Proceeding by variations, it forms and formulates the same, unceasing question: How far can one go in showing less to see more? How much of the visible can be anticipated, guessed, extrapolated, concealed, so that its share of absence can be reconstructed from the fragments of its presence? Its active, multifaceted, mobile, virtual, infinite presence: *beneath* and *within* the image, always already, there is *imagery*—there are *images*. Any image is both form and content for another image, born of a limitless background of images. The arrangement of the strip form in the first part of *Vorurteile* clearly demonstrates that the *represented reality* (in this case the shutters, the exotic object) and the *representing form* (the strip as a variable form) are in a relationship of constant reversibility: they keep engendering each other. This is the energy that sparks and sustains the narration, these are the rules of the game that *Vorurteile* follows—a refined, theoretical, playful work (as are, in varying degrees, all of Odenbach's tapes). The choice of the image of shutters all the more strongly conveys the idea that what reveals is also what conceals. A new relationship is created between the frame and the mask.[1] The off-screen effects created within the image transform and multiply the classic relationship of a shot with the one that follows it (the interesting aspect of this relationship is its ever-present latency) as if to exhaust all possibilities of the film-video *dispositifs* from the same position of the gaze, in a ceaseless process of construction and deconstruction. The rules of this game are all the more apparent in *Vorurteile* in that, between the series of film and television images, the game itself becomes the theme of the tape: after the ritual object, the invisible character's hand manipulates several other objects, in a slightly obsessional manner, within the same formal frame. The effect culminates in the last shot: the hand turns a rattle; in a continuous motion, a cyclical round dance of light displays the masking-unmasking effects of the framing light previously orchestrated by the strip form.

1

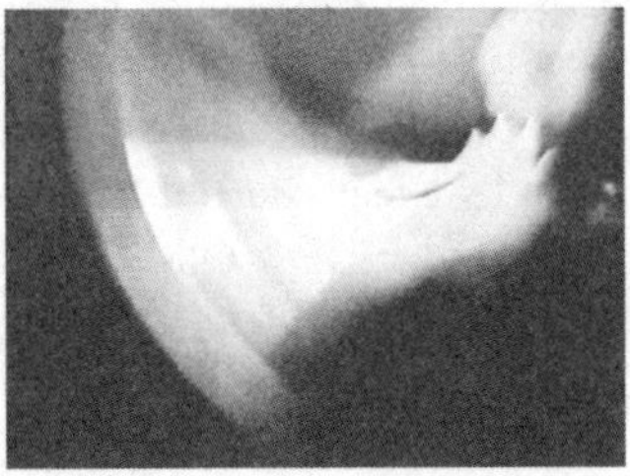

2

Thus there is no element of the "real" that is not itself a function of a gaze *dispositif*. A gaze that is a form as well as an eye. An eye that is a form. Everything becomes derealized, relativized, yet strongly fixed, subject to the variations imposed upon the representation by the strip. The variations follow a twofold movement: critical analysis and poetic drift. They allow for what I earlier called "crystallization," which operates through the substitution, overlap, and interpenetration of signs, organized such that body and sex are always the elements that lead the exploration each work undertakes of perceptible reality and sociocultural memory. Thus crystallization takes on highly symbolic character. It breeds effects of meaning that are both continuous and discon-tinuous: on the one hand these effects are quite free, nearly volatile, due to the extreme mobility, the plasticity of the form, which often seems to exist as if by fluke; on the other hand they are quite clear, even emphatic, because of the trenchant, almost brutal relationship between the signs. For example, in *Die Distanz zwischen mir und meinen Verlusten* (The Distance Between Myself and My Losses, 1983), where the range of variations altering the elasticity of the strip form (via the lighting etc.) is expanded to an extreme, a very interesting moment occurs. In the vertical strip that contains images between two black borders, a series of small silhouettes appears, probably a common deck of cards. By a proven process, which here creates a veritable *mise en abyme* within the triply divided strip, the central part of the small silhouette remains identical while the other two change. An infinite number of unexpected bodies is thus produced according to the same formal principle that structures the whole frame, as well as the entire tape. In *Ich mache die Schmerzprobe* (I Do the Pain Test), a 1984 work partly devoted to bodybuilding, the central strip shows a machine with a piston violently pumping up and down while a man, face down on the ground, raises and lowers his legs in a regular motion. Since the central strip slices up the man's body, the machine seems to penetrate him and perform the sexual act that, thus "framed" and "masked," he seems to suggest all the more by his own movements. Similarly, in *Als könnte es auch mir an den Kragen gehen*, the strip was generated by the protagonist's eye, but all the images and references of the tape—the "1000 murders" of our culture of images—passed between his legs, finally spread wide by the strip form (as they were, at the beginning of *Der Widerspruch der Erinnerungen*, by a ray of light). Thus crystallization spreads from moment to moment, from tape to tape.

Sex-body. Memory-culture. Thus "the peripheral vision of the witness" takes shape. Ever since *As if Memories Could Deceive Me* (1986), the strip form has not only divided the shot by creating one double image split by another; it has often constructed three images through a powerful flicker effect. The two border images are as much two heterogeneous reality fragments as the same space split by two divergent axes. In Versailles, it was astonishing to see Odenbach ask the cameraman to frame and light, one after the other, one of the two (left and right) sides of what might have seemed to be a single tracking shot. This was to prepare for a highly "perverse" editing within the image, since in his new installation he not only twice opposes three images against each other, but also, frequently, two spaces facing and complementing each other, as though in a broken mirror, on each of the monitors that in turn face and complement each other.

1

2

3

4

From one monitor to the other, sitting between the two of them on a *tête-à-tête* sofa that ironically designates his double place, the spectator-witness can only come and go, turn his head, caught "in the peripheral vision" of which he has become the exploded center, causing a perpetual desynchronization between the screen he is seeing and the screen he has seen. On one of the screens (but he could just as easily choose the other) he will first see, in the (black and white) central strip, the protagonist's back as he runs away in slow motion, in the space marked out by white lines drawn between two lanes of cars moving toward the camera, then off-screen—while in the two (color) border images, the camera tracks in on the *Galerie de la Reine*. This layout is soon reversed: in the central strip, shot in Versailles, people first in contemporary dress, then in historical costumes, are shown from the back, walking away through the gallery, followed continually by the camera, while simultaneously, on the Quai des Tuileries, the two lanes of cars advance toward us, on either side of the now-vanished protagonist. At this point, if the spectator turns toward the second monitor to look at the other fiction enacted there, he will see, in the center, two characters in historical costumes having a conversation and strolling back and forth along a walk in a large park; and on both sides of the screen, a series of "views of Paris"—quite varied, combining past and present, architectural motifs and everyday gestures. This layout, like the one described earlier, and occurring simultaneously with it, is inverted in a similar effect of masking-unmasking.

It would be easy, but time-consuming and tedious, to enumerate the full range of forms and forces. These symmetries, desynchronizations, inversions, generated by a finely calculated play of chance, turn the space of this very simple installation into enchanted volume. For me, its essential quality lies in its clarity, its polemical tone. To my mind, Odenbach's intent has never before been so clear. Perhaps this is because it is underlined by a text for the first time, even if, as he tells us, "words die in the presence of images." The tape's dialogue suggests the limited, fragmentary, arbitrary, and personal character of any process of representation; it upholds the inductive quality ideas have, the irreducible value of time and emotion, the accuracy of an intellectual and sensory framework that makes a "field of vision" possible. Thus it ensures the circulation and crystallization that link all the elements together. Let us look at the "look" of the strip form. A *mise en abyme* transforms it, not without irony (through carefully chosen words, tone, situation of cultural masquerade) into a programmatic text: *Dans la vision périphérique du témoin* marks a point of culmination, a break for its author.

Circulation, crystallization. Odenbach's art evolves out of his very personal way of being placed between uncertain chance and absolute planning. Through precise elaboration around and out of the strip form, he has created a peculiar and, in a way, very classical world in which everything seems to answer to and for everything else, and every detail tends to mirror the whole. Elements are deployed in relation to each other, as in a musical score, but they produce meaning, thus causing constant symbolic refractions.

For example, the runner's panting, heard during half of the installation's first tape, is answered throughout the ending of the second tape by a similar panting, issuing this time from scenes of sex and violence whose sound invades the image. This meaning-saturated world, however, grappling with multiple levels of reality, is also without real exteriority; it does not seem to validate or justify itself in any way. It is drifting, expressing the point of view of a sensibility tested and restored to itself through a form. It is an ever-retreating witness to the world such as it is disseminated within it. "I believe less and less that I will ever again come to concern myself with the finiteness of the acts and decisions that are within me. Facts have become alien to me. I live more and more in a world of moods," Odenbach comments.[2] And these words from the "witness": "I am left with nothing but emotions." This world is a crossroads, and Odenbach's work is a series of such crossings. It has its themes, its constants: childhood and games, a fondness for tinkering and for objects; a fascination with culture, both learned and popular—the German soul with its pomp and circumstance, horrors and myths, Nazism, terrorism, all sorts of music and architecture, a strong culture of the image, cinema (mostly from the US, Hitchcock, etc.); television (as vehicle for all images), painting (Goya above all); a disturbing attraction (somewhere between perversion and pornography) toward fragmented and dislocated bodies (there are lots of porn flicks in the strip form and/or the background); a fondness for African or South American exoticism (quite pronounced in the choice of music); an acute sense of everyday gestures and postures; a pendulum swing between past and present, the imaginary and reality, matter and memory. All of this feeds back, more or less, into every work, but it does not really dictate a subject matter, or turn into narration. Neither does it ever become a mere pretext for pristine formal operations, or exhaust itself in anything more than a nonetheless keen attention to the process of creation as such. What is this installation, for example, dealing with, if not many of these things at once, things that "congeal" through the strong cohesion of the formal *dispositif* selected to put them together? Is it dealing with the past and present?

Obviously. With the point of view that someone may have regarding that? Of course. With architecture? Yes indeed. With the body? That too.

If we must finally find one word to describe what Odenbach makes, let us use "self-portrait"—as literary tradition conceived it, as it has been redefined by a certain auteur cinema, and as today's video permits in a clearer, more natural way. The self-portrait is this idiosyncratic literary genre whose logic has been described, and genealogy traced, in a book by Michel Beaujour.[3] Unlike autobiography, which tells the story of a life, the self-portrait tells only the story of an I: it is less interested in events, and its progression is defined by a single movement around the endlessly repeated question, "Who am I?" The self-portrait was born, in Montaigne's *Essays* (1580), from a transformation of classical rhetorical procedures that had organized the representation of the world and discourse and set the rules for invention and memory. All of this, in the self-portrait, is redirected toward the person who writes to know him or herself better—only to discover in the act of writing a mere fleeting proof of his or her identity. The system of places and images and the analogical and encyclopedic functions that are so powerful in classical rhetoric are always at the origin of the text: but they exist autonomously, and the book somehow becomes an end in itself. Even if the self-portrait has changed only minimally (Beaujour dwells on its value as a transhistorical model), it thus becomes a highly modern genre, which, from the 19th century on, embraces all the avatars of the crisis of representation, and triumphs in today's literature from Nietzsche's *Ecce Homo*, to Michel Leiris' *The Rules of the Game*, André Malraux's *Anti-Memoirs*, and Roland Barthes' *Roland Barthes by Roland Barthes*. In a way it even partakes of its own definition: the self-portrait is not really a genre, since it is more than a genre.

Film has been deemed inappropriate for autobiography: it is considered either too objective or too subjective, split between a staged truth and a recorded one, between expression and description. The spectator is forever outside the frame, and the boundary between viewer and viewed cannot be crossed; in short "the autobiographical 'I' cannot survive the move from text to film intact [...] there is no 'eye' for 'I' [...]"[4] It seems, however, that in some of its more marginal efforts, cinema has approached this less straightforward, much more cunning type of subjectivity that speaks through the self-portrait—when the latter remains on the boundary between documentary and fiction, between testimony and narrative, haunted by the insistent, constant, yet intermittent and surreptitious presence of a voice and body. As in the work of Robert Frank, for example. Or in Godard's, more and more clearly. Video by its nature facilitates this particular movement. It makes it much easier for several discourses to be presented at once (this interweaving of voices is one of the conditions of the self-portrait). And the material presence of the author's body is much more natural in video (as an indispensable element in this interweaving).

Many video artists (for example Bill Viola, or Odenbach) have claimed they used themselves as figures or performers in their tapes because it was easier, and that this way they could keep the feeling of intimacy necessary to their experiments. But are we actually—beyond this practical alibi—dealing with a triumph of "the aesthetics of narcissism?"[5] Probably. But more profoundly, this is the way a complex expressive mode strives to find itself (to lose and find itself again) in the world of images and sounds. Someday we will have to draw the map and reconstruct the history of the video self-portrait, pinpointing its similarities to and differences from the self-portrait in literature (or painting). For example, in the video works of Jean-André Fieschi or Thierry Kuntzel, of Juan Downey or Viola—or Odenbach, who seems to come closer than any of the others to the notion of the self-portrait.

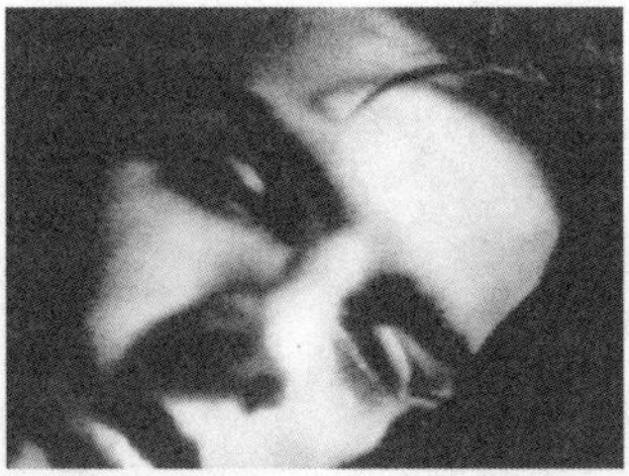

1

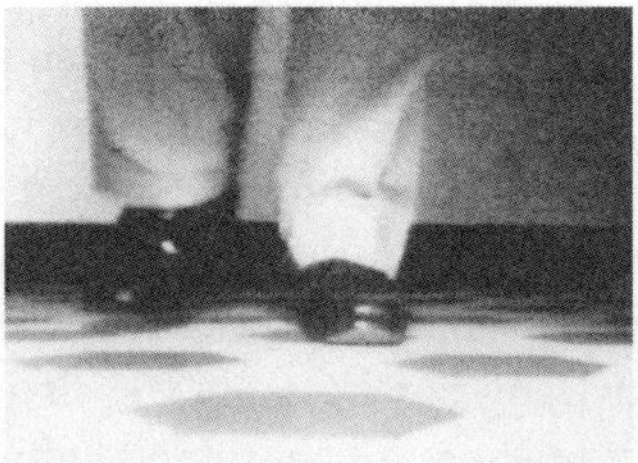

2

I

Fragmented, yet present. Master of the game, yet possessed by it. An all-consumed enunciator. Such is the body of the author-narrator-witness-character-hero-figure-silhouette, born of performance, diffracted in tapes and installations. Seeing eyes; an invisible hand holding the steering wheel; hands playing a myriad of childish and provocative games; feet, legs, a half-body walking, whirling, going through doors; legs again, curled up on a bed and moving rhythmically, under which images of murder and violence are gliding by; a face in sleep, a face awake; a man asleep at a piano; a quick glimpse of a gymnast's body; an ironical guest (seen frontally, in a quick medium shot); a man running away, panting (there is a quasi-imperceptible change, in slow motion, for about three minutes, from a close-up of his arm to a long shot).

The author's body—mingled with other bodies, yet constantly recognizable, apparent—this body follows the function of the strip form. The strip cuts across the body, which in turn is engendered by it; the strip leads the body, and is defined by it. The body punctuates the quest of "Who am I?"; it is the visible part of the situation of *énonciation*,[6] the perceptible aspect of the name with which Odenbach expresses his fascination in the final and/or opening credits. One could consider this sheer narcissism. I would prefer to say that this is in order to overlook none of the avatars of the narcissistic attitude, since Odenbach's practice as an artist is so focused on himself: he reorders the world he displays for us from that very point, frail and perilous as well as unshakable and incisive. Take the signature effects, extremely similar to those created for Hitchcock in the credits designed by Saul Bass. Whereas Hitchcock's name, diffracted into body-gazes, is swallowed up in a story, with the highly symbolic apparition of the Master's figure as a sole reminder, the author's name in Odenbach's work abides in the individualized body that sustains the work's development.

1

2

3

"[T]he self-portrait is first of all an imaginary perambulation through a system of places, around a depository for memory-images."[7] Within this register there are, for Odenbach, two major categories of images. On the one hand he includes in his work material shot here and there, on his travels and in the course of his everyday life: such images thus become so many memory-images, since they follow (or at least, one can imagine they do) the traces of earlier memories; they function like Freudian "screen memories." On the other hand, the use of quotations is the cultural form taken by this imaginary stroll: they blend so well with private images that Odenbach now tends to construct his own quotations, to replay a scene for his own benefit, thus increasing their value in this game, for this fictional double of his (as in *Die einen den Anderen* and *Dans la vision périphérique du témoin*). Paradoxically, the force that draws the self-portrait toward the past is also the mark of its ineluctable modernity: by renewing the energy it has received from a classical tradition, it assimilates the utopian drives that strive for the unification of art and life as well as the recycling of culture, the drifts and diversions that characterize the postmodern condition. The self-portrait would be, as though this were its very essence, always already postmodern.

As for the most intimate mood of such a work, its most accurate reflection might be found in the reference to Musil that Odenbach himself has chosen to capture his sense of "peripheral vision." I perceive his nervous, anxious, precise sensitivity—that of a "witness"—as an oscillation between two opposite poles, the two ages of the Musilian outlook: on the one hand, young Törless in his confusion,[8] eagerness, tenseness, his highly physical identity, his immaturity already permeated with selfish concerns; on the other hand, Ulrich, the "man without qualities." In his lack, as Maurice Blanchot has so brilliantly analyzed, of particularities more than qualities, since he is his own empty, unstable, resonant space, kept open to all possibilities by his own lack of definition.[9] The modern hero, "the possible man." In brief, a being passing through and passed through. Marcel Odenbach: a very personal young man, a "man without particularities."

1986. Originally translated in 1988 by David Jacobson and Bérénice Reynaud.

[1] Bellour alludes here to André Bazin's famous distinction between the frame of a painting and the frame of a film image. See *What is Cinema?* vol. 1 166: "The outer edges of the screen are not [...] the frame of the film image. They are the edges of a piece of masking that shows only a portion of reality" [translators' note].

[2] Marcel Odenbach, *Tip, tip, tip, what is this man supposed to be?* (Stuttgart: Walter Phillips Gallery, 1983) 34.

[3] Michel Beaujour, *Miroirs d'encre: Rhétorique de l'autoportrait* (Paris: Editions du Seuil—Collection Poétique, 1980) [*Poetics of the Literary Self-Portrait*, trans. Yara Milos (New York: New York University Press, 1991)].

[4] Elizabeth W. Bruss, "Eye for I: Making and Unmaking Autobiography in Film," *Autobiography: Essays Theoretical and Critical*, ed. James Olney (Princeton: Princeton University Press, 1980) 298.

[5] Rosalind Krauss, "Video: The Aesthetics of Narcissism," *October* 1 (Spring 1976) 51–64; reprinted in *Video Culture: A Critical Investigation*, ed. John Hanhardt (Rochester: Visual Studies Workshop, 1986) 179–191.

[6] Linguistic theory establishes a difference between *énoncé* (the content of what the subject says), and *énonciation* (the fact of uttering an *énoncé*). When the subject says, for example "I am here," "I" is both the subject of the *énoncé* and the *énonciation* [translators' note].

[7] Beaujour 110 [*Poetics of the Literary Self-Portrait* 104].

[8] Robert Musil's novel *Die Verwirrungen des Zöglings Törless* is translated more accurately in the French title, *Les désarrois de l'élève Törless* (literally Pupil Törless's Confusions), than in the English title *Young Törless*. In his text Bellour uses the word *désarrois*, which is a direct allusion to the title [translators' note].

[9] Maurice Blanchot, *Le livre à venir* (Paris: Gallimard, 1959) 169 [*The Book to Come*, trans. Charlotte Mandell (Palo Alto: Stanford University Press, 2002) 137].

“The Letter Goes On … ”

For Jackie, Takae, André, Barbara, and Tone, who first told me about Video Letter.

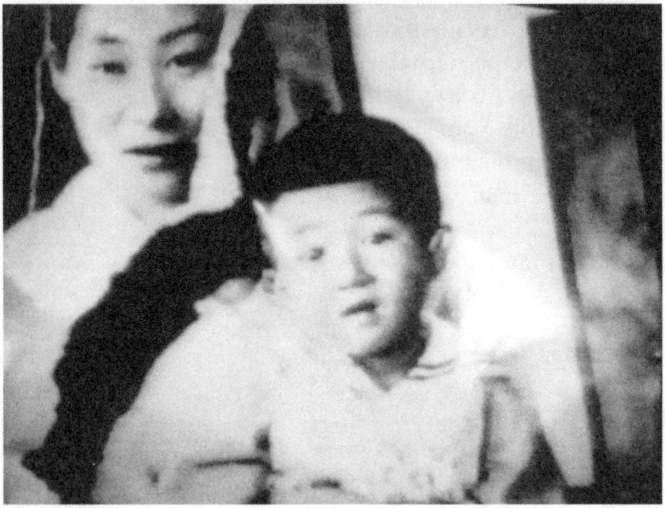

Shuntaro Tanikawa & Shuji Terayama, *Video Letter*, 1982–1983

The letter goes on and on. If it is a real letter, it never stops saying, wanting, wanting to say more.

In film, the letter is often unique. It points relentlessly to one of the essential properties of the letter—that elliptical space of loss around which some of the greatest films have constructed their scenarios: Ophüls' (1948), the ultimate example of a letter driven to vertigo; or Mankiewicz's (1949), where three letters—addressed by one woman to three other women—carve a furrow of secrecy into the placid surface of things. The letter is like a one-way street. Even when it names a
supposedly "real" interlocutor and through this tends to multiply, to become fragmented and thus relative, it always steers toward an ideal vanishing point, an empty place around which its words can come together, because they came into being there (for example, empty bed in Frédéric Mitterrand's

Lettres d'amour en Somalie, 1982). And even when the letter becomes one degree "truer," that is, leads to a real exchange (between a mother and daughter who write and respond to each other, as in Chantal Akerman's *News from Home*, 1977), in the image—and thus in the most vivid point of the "letter" addressed to the spectator—we see only one point of view (in *News from Home*, the geography of New York, where the daughter is thrown off-balance, leading to the correspondence with her mother).

So the advantage of the video-letter (should we see this only as a stroke of luck?) is having permitted (at least once) a "real" exchange. Those vanishing points which are common to all letters are traced unpredictably here, along the lines of an everyday life that is quite obviously simulated, disguised, elaborated (it is not a matter of a simple correspondence, published afterward), but which is no less decisive when it comes to what we might call the inner body of the letter.

For almost two years (Tokyo, 1982–1983), Shuji Terayama—poet, man of the theater, avant-garde filmmaker (of sorts)—and the poet Shuntaro Tanikawa jointly conceived this video-letter that comes sadly but "naturally" to an end with the death of one of the two correspondents. Katsue Tomiyama, producer and cofounder of Image-Forum, pushed these two old friends to experiment in this format popularized in Japan by the extraordinary growth of consumer video (although their attempt also recalls the ancient tradition of *renga*, the exchange of poems, one of the equivalents of the Occidental ritual of literary correspondence). At home, with minimal equipment, each one filmed letters made up of images and sounds that would be sent to the other as they were finished, like so many answers. After the death of his friend, Tanikawa completed the editing and the sound mix. The tape thus consists of 16 letter-fragments that are linked together by a very simple principle of alternation. Each one opens with a heading bearing the names of the sender and the addressee.

And yet the greatest strength of *Video Letter* (1983) is the way it introduces doubt into what would seem to be above question in an exchange of letters: the identity of each of the correspondents.

It is not that we do not recognize them. We see them appear very distinctly, physically, in at least two sequences. Numerous marks of enunciation punctuate the exchange

(Terayama says several times: "Mr. Tanikawa … "). And above all, the discrepancies in the voices, the tones, and even the registers of language, imperceptible to the European spectator, clearly establish who is speaking for the Japanese spectator, to whom this correspondence is initially supposed to be addressed. Two lives are also sketched out here, and through them two styles, two modes of relation to time: for Tanikawa, a kind of zero biography, drier and more disconcerting, seeming to focus on instants; for Terayama, a few fragmented yet very strong signs that develop a story over time—photographs of youth and childhood, of sickness, of a mother's ageing.

And yet a certain uneasiness persists (I hope that I am not the only one to feel it). Now and then, for a brief or lasting moment, we find ourselves in a strange in-between: we are no longer quite sure who is speaking. Even if its modes vary, this effect comes almost entirely from the power of the autonomy of the image, which cannot guarantee in and of itself the separation of identities at moments when it is not made clear elsewhere.

This slipping of identities is made possible from the outset by the fact that, contrary to a published correspondence where each name appears on every page like a running title, here the name is mentioned only once, at the beginning of the letter, making it more difficult to find than in a book. This arrangement is in no way mandatory: we could just as well imagine names inscribed on the page-screen-video and thus given a stability analogous to the one they have in a book. It can happen then that we forget the name. We forget it all the more readily in the letters without words (there are several of them), or of few words (there are many of these) and moments when the image becomes very ambiguous, at once opaque and open to too many meanings. It also often happens that we see fragments of bodies appear in the frame instead of faces or recognizable bodies: legs, a back, mainly hands, doing tasks, holding objects. This is one of the ways we lose the thread of the exchange, hanging onto fleeting names, onto bodies that do not support them. But this fragmentation goes well beyond the bodies and touches the representation as a whole. It contributes to a general uncertainty about what is seen in the image, and above all about the point of view that makes it visible. This, in turn, reinforces the natural tendency of the image to become "objective," to retreat into its opacity—that is, to open itself up to infinity, without being attributed to anyone. The numerous marks of identity that punctuate the exchange conflict with this ambiguity, to the point where we find ourselves in a strange situation: we clearly hear two men who are really speaking to one another, and yet from time to time we do not believe that we are hearing either one of them, and it is precisely this that leads us to doubt the identity of the one writing, as if they were one and the same.

Two sequences are particularly disquieting in this way: the first, where Tanikawa is writing and yet for a long time we see Terayama in a photo album (that Tanikawa has come across, he makes clear only afterward, once the uneasiness is felt); and the next to last, where again Tanikawa is writing, but in the image we see (how is it possible?) Terayama speaking, though we cannot hear him, to an indefinite off-screen space, where a woman's voice cries, louder and louder.

So it is that much more understandable when one of the correspondents tries at a certain moment to define for himself this shifting and mixing of identities unique to this exchange of video letters (yet perhaps going beyond it, touching upon the effect specific to any exchange of real letters). Terayama is writing. In the image we can make out signs of writing, and the voice asks itself: "Is it me? No. Is it my name written in letters?" We see the face of a man, then the camera draws back and the voice says: "No, it is only a photograph." And the question is displaced from one sign to the next as it attaches itself to various identity cards. On some we recognize the name, on others it is illegible (invisible). And the voice asks: "Maybe I'm a poet. Maybe I'm not Shuntaro Tanikawa. Maybe I'm just a man."

As we can see, this confusion of identities implies an essential, haunting, and at the same time very simple questioning of subjective non-identity, which is the second of *Video Letter*'s attributes. Identity is reduced here to what appears, to the questions formulated (in the text) and suggested (to the spectator-reader) by the content of the images, which means at the same time a great deal and very little: signs scattered like grains of sand, oscillating between pure contingency and one or two points of anchorage.

"Am I an invisible man? No doubt," Terayama asks himself, while a camera moves through his apartment.

This implies that Terayama can be both himself and the other to whom he writes (or pretends to write), and it is their shared non-identity that empties itself in the image—the segmentation of the visible, affixed to words in its nakedness. When sheets of paper covered with signs fall to the ground a few seconds later, Terayama again asks himself: "Maybe I have liver trouble. Maybe I'm an earthling. Whoever comes up with the best answer, could you swear that it's me?"

Three sequences surrounding this one (near the end of the tape) provide answers bit by bit that really are not answers at all, dissolving, scattering, reducing the image of self to an essential flatness. In the first, Tanikawa lets the objects that identify him drop one by one to the ground (ending with his left foot), naming them in turn ("This is ... "). He covers all of them with a large piece of plastic and says: "This could be my blue sky." And as the image fades to black he asks himself: "Who am I? Is this my poem?" In the second sequence, this time facing the camera-screen-mirror, Tanikawa recreates one of the gestures characteristic of American video of the 1960s and 1970s ("video as an aesthetic of narcissism"). He takes visible pleasure in the few words he pronounces ("mint tea"—he tells us what he is drinking), illustrating the level of pure denotation that his bodily presence inscribes all the while in the image. In the third sequence, a voice asks everyone in the street: "Who is Tanikawa?" This produces unexpected answers, a scattering of identities that in the end turns absolutely opaque when he questions a flower and then a dog.

The first two of these three sequences are letters from Tanikawa. The third letter is from Terayama, but has Tanikawa as its subject. The uneasiness felt during the other two sequences comes to mind, in which we see Terayama in the image even though it is Tanikawa who is speaking to him and to us. And so by speaking to the other, each man questions himself about the other's identity in order to define—or to undefine—his own. Tanikawa leans more toward the non-person, Terayama toward the nostalgic subject. But both of them, together and separately, aim toward and realize present states that have the effect of reducing the imaginary part of subjectivity. So we find ourselves faced with these localized, successive, fragmented states that are constantly defining themselves, and those that cross their path, by way of this process of indexing life as such—that is, life only insofar as it exists and is maintained. The correspondence of these two men, their dialogue, which is at once very concrete and very enigmatic, holds open precisely this possibility.

The third merit of *Video Letter* is having known how to find, through a rather uneasily dispersed physicality, a way of inscribing inside the image what the two friends are trying so desperately to understand and to evaluate.

A debate drives them on, trite and yet impossible to avoid: the debate between meaning and non-meaning—meaning and non-meaning of words, leading to the question of what is there before them, within the body and in the image, but also (the very strength of the tape lies in this wavering) in the words themselves as body and image.

And so on the one hand the "themes" appear, themes that are obviously just images compelling attention, themes seemingly preceding meaning and non-meaning (even if they do emerge from the conflict between them): the ailing body, unique in its undivided identity; the animal, limit to the definition of characteristic humanness (both Terayama and Tanikawa own dogs that we come to care about—Nietzsche also comes to mind, throwing himself onto the neck of a battered horse, or the "pity" Barthes saw in this gesture that seemed to him the very essence of feeling as both uniquely individual and the degree zero of identity); the mother, the primal body of affect; the affect coming from things themselves, flat and irreducible.

On the other hand, the words display their uneasy presence: a word that is not a "letter" or a "voice," but is a "meaning," a word that has its share of body, its share of logic. The power of the tape is in rendering this never-ending debate visible, like the diagram of letters that is composed in such a way as to make appear in the image (thus at once matter and idea) what is carved out in words between the two correspondents around meaning and non-meaning.

```
        T
        H  L
   W    I  O
  NO MEANING
   R    G  I
BODY       C
```

But the tape's most intimate strength comes from the respiration of the image itself, from its matter, its skin. "I don't hold my camera right and can't focus the right way. Does that prove I'm alive?" This flaw converted into strategy is one of three ways the image has of telling us the same thing while at the same time more than the words. The frequent, emphatic change from focused to blurred, from blurred to focused, translates both the presence of the body and the materialization of the idea (we go back and forth between one and the other "like" the way we move between meaning and non-meaning). An equally suggestive instability between fixity and movement also runs through the tape. Very often—and it is only afterward that we become aware of the effect of this hesitation—we do not know if the image is moving or not, as when someone's breathing is unsteady (which does not mean that the image does not know how to be still or to be mobile when it means to be). Finally, the third point: the numerous fades to black that constantly dissolve and recompose the image, an image confronted every second of its tenuous and stubborn existence with the conjugation of meaning and non-meaning.

Video Letter's fourth great accomplishment is to create fusion—or confusion—between the various means of expression, the same kind as the one created between the variations in the image and between the speakers.

It would seem that the photograph is privileged. And, if anything, it serves "Terayama's side." I know very few images as unsettling as the one where a very small child, huddled against his mother's body, stares at us. This steady gaze seems little by little to become mad, because at the same time, as in faked political photographs, the part of the photograph with the mother's body breaks off, falls away, and slides off screen. The maternal body seems an image of the film-video *dispositif*, the spectator engulfed in the child's gaze. The representation hits us with all the more force because it is coupled with Terayama's emphasis on the photographs of his mother when she was young and beautiful, strewn across the very bed where we next see her, old and sickly, barely alive. What is more, the tape's first images are all photographs. As mentioned earlier, Tanikawa is the one writing, but a series of photographs of Terayama wordlessly appears, photographs taken from an album that go by with a slow and halting movement, like so many still frames, before the camera zooms into them. So the photograph is privileged. It is a sign of the image *dispositif* that shapes the way the letter is written. It is also analogous to the letter as an object of loss, and thus becomes the very index of time, time followed to the letter.

And yet photography does not really play a pivotal, overarching role. It is still only one object among many, one sign among others. Photography mingles with painting, from which it is not always distinguishable (for example, the image that we finally recognize as a painting from the Flemish school, distorted by objects that hide and transform it, tinted blue like the photographs). It is compared with the words of poems written on the screen-page and associated with mixed representations with more or less definable shapes (posters, calendars, books, sculptures, collages). It is at times even difficult to distinguish from the landscape, as is painting itself. Photography is thus part of the general universe of signs that have been tinkered with, doctored up, which is the last and perhaps the most distinctive quality of *Video Letter* (in that it seems to bring together all of the others).

In this, the tape is very close to those literary or pictorial works that function as bridges between the worlds of language and image, where a general process of sign fragmentation, dissemination, confusion, produces a twofold effect of disconnecting and of reconnecting. The sign—fractured, crushed, mixed—loses some of its hardness, its definition, while it gains in coalescence. Everything is endlessly resolved through the use of passageways and *intermediaries*. Klee, Michaux, Barthes, Marker, Godard.

There is one more thing that *Video Letter* makes possible, one that I hesitate to call a quality: the possibility of death as an ending and interruption of the tape, and by the same token death as a sign of life, because the death is real, not acted, as in a real correspondence. When Terayama dies, Tanikawa writes two letters one after the other, thereby upsetting the alternation that had served as rule and rhythm of the tape. The camera wordlessly follows for a long, long time a line, an ECG line which, freely reinterpreted, becomes at once writing and design. We realize very quickly that this is a lifeline. When it runs straight, Terayama is dead. And so we are left with only one possible metamorphosis, that of the poem. In Tanikawa's last letter, we hear Terayama reading one of his poems. As the image goes from blurred to focused, the camera fixes on a sheet of paper covered with word-signs attached to a post in the middle of an empty field.

Postscripts

1. I find a message on my answering machine from my friend Liz Lyon. I have just shown her *Video Letter.* She says: "Look at page 165 in *Roland Barthes by Roland Barthes*, it's incredible." I look, and in fact it is incredible. And yet so normal. Japan, signs, languages, images, poetry, utopia of language. This is what Barthes writes in this fragment (entitled "The Shifter as Utopia"): He receives a card from a faraway friend: "Monday. Returning tomorrow. Jean-Louis."

Like Monsieur Jourdain and his famous prose (moreover, a more or less Poujadist scene), he marvels at discovering in so simple an utterance the trace of those double operators, shifters, analyzed by Jakobson. For if Jean-Louis knows perfectly well who he is and on what day he is writing, once his message is in my hands it is entirely uncertain: Which Monday? Which Jean-Louis? How would I be able to tell, since from my point of view I must constantly choose between more than one Jean-Louis and several Mondays? Though coded, to speak only of the most familiar of these operators, the shifter thus appears as a complex means—furnished by language itself—of breaking communication: I speak (consider my mastery of the code) but I wrap myself in the mist of an enunciatory situation which is unknown to you; I insert into my discourse certain leaks of interlocution (is this not, in fact, what always happens when we utilize that shifter par excellence, the pronoun I?). Which leads him to imagine shifters (let us call shifters, by extension, all operators of uncertainty formed at the level of language itself: I, here, now, tomorrow, Monday, Jean-Louis) as so many social subversions, conceded by language but opposed by society, which fears such leaks of subjectivity and always stops them by insisting on reducing the operator's duplicity (Monday, Jean-Louis) by the "objective" memorandum of a date (Monday, March 12) or of a patronymic (Jean-Louis B.). Can we even imagine the freedom and, so to speak, the erotic fluidity of a collectivity which would speak only in pronouns and shifters, each person never saying anything but I, tomorrow, over there, without referring to anything legal whatsoever, and in which the vagueness of difference (the only fashion of respecting its subtlety, its infinite repercussion) would be language's most precious value?[1]

2. In 1982 Tanikawa wrote a deeply moving book that is like a (solitary) double of *Video Letter*: *Solo* (Daguerreo Press). Having rented an apartment in order to write, he finds himself far from home, alone, and wonders only that much more who he is. He brings together signs, every possible sign (only a few of them as proof) of his fleeting identity: images (mainly photos, numerous Polaroids pinned to the wall, but also a grab bag of what he sees, in his home and outside), words (poems, newspaper clippings, pages from reference books). Images that can be reduced to a few words, and words framed like images.

3. "The Letter goes on ... " ("La lettre dit encore ... ") is a title from *Epreuves, exorcismes* by Henri Michaux (Gallimard, 1946).

1988. Originally translated in 1990 by Alison Rowe.

[1] *Roland Barthes by Roland Barthes*, trans. Richard Howard (New York: Hill and Wang, 1977) 165–166.

1. Ta. to Te.: "I found some old photos of you … "

2. Te. to Ta.: "Thank you for your video letter."

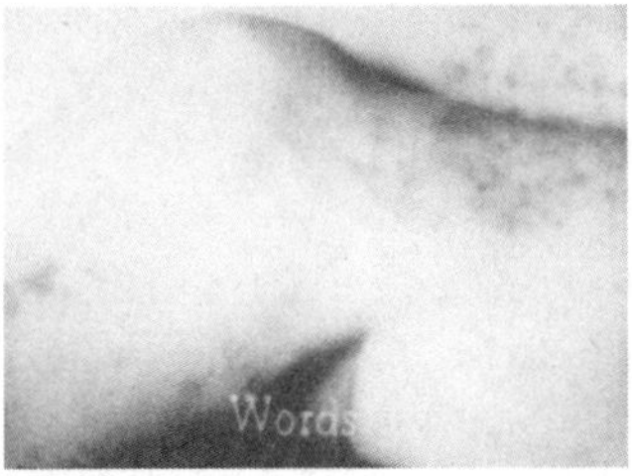

"Words"

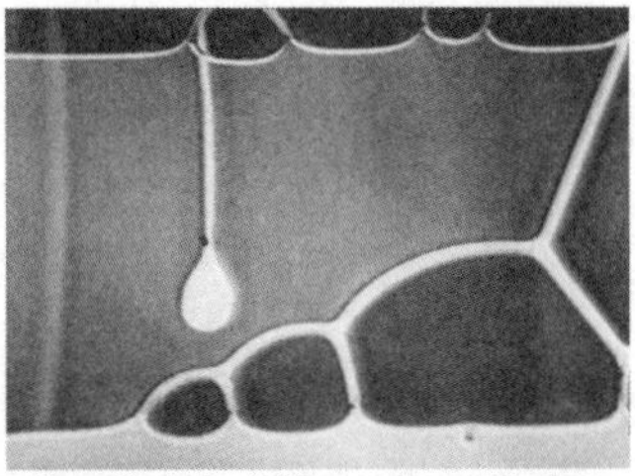

3. Ta. to Te. (voices): "Eventually, yes. In the long run … "

4. Te. to Ta.: "September 15th. Mr Tanikawa, thank you for so many WORDS."

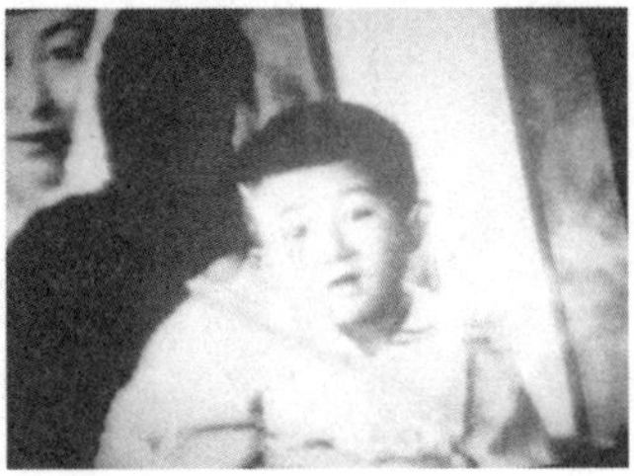

Shuntaro Tanikawa & Shuji Terayama, *Video Letter*, 1982–1983

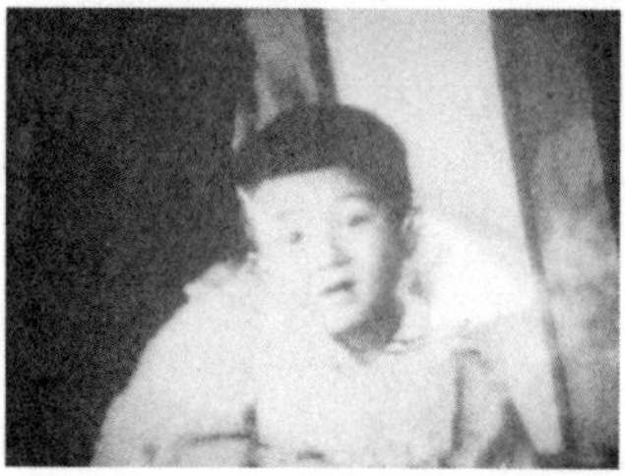

"That is what I would like to think. What do you think, Mr Tanikawa?"

5. Ta. to Te.

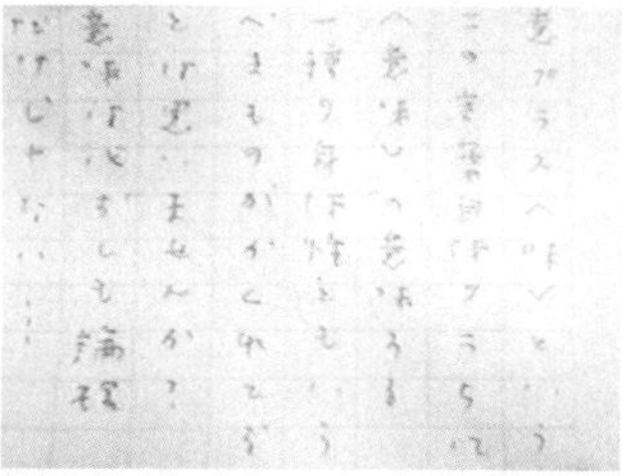

"There is a physical aspect embedded in the word ... "

6. Te. to Ta.: "A lemming."

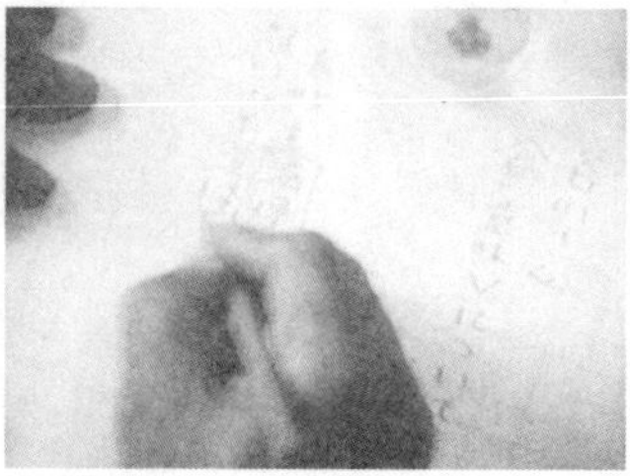

"Mr. Tanikawa … thinking about 'no meaning.'"

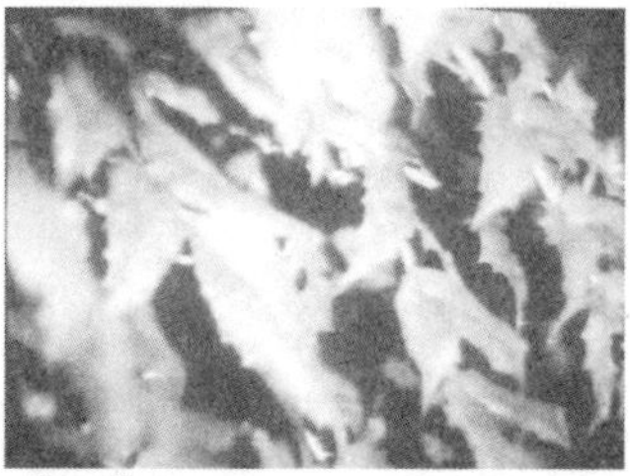

7. Ta. to Te.

8. Te. to Ta.: "September 24th."
(telephone conversation)

"I question what sort of 'no meaning' … "

9. Ta. to Te.: "Do you know what there is between 'meaning' and 'no meaning'?"

10. Ta. to Te.:

"November 1927. My mother."

"October 1982. My mother."

11. Ta. to Te.: "This is my doll ... "

"This is my picture."

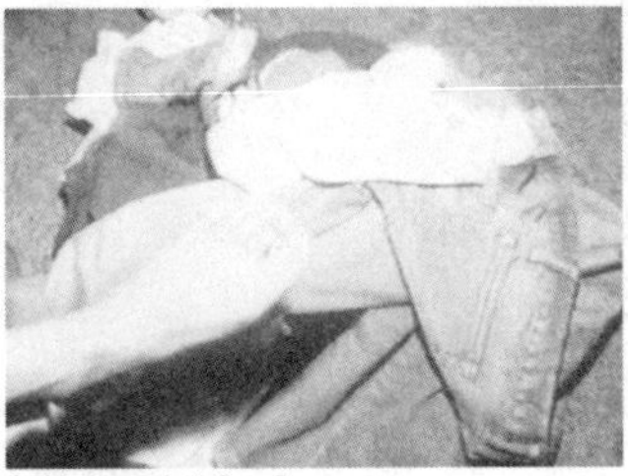

"This is my left foot."

12. Te. to Ta.: "No, it is just a photograph."

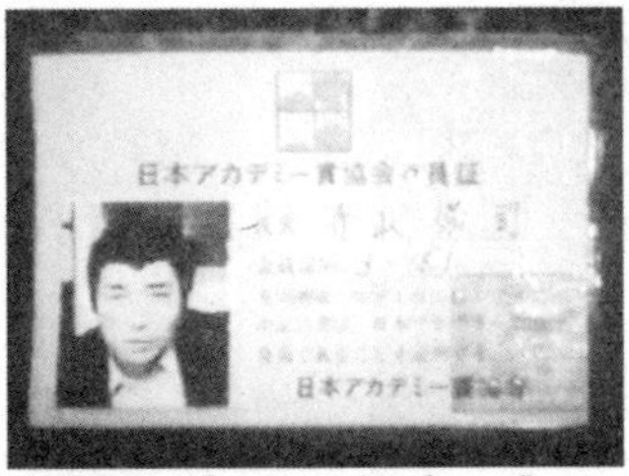

"Perhaps I am from Aomori Prefecture."

13. Ta. to Te.

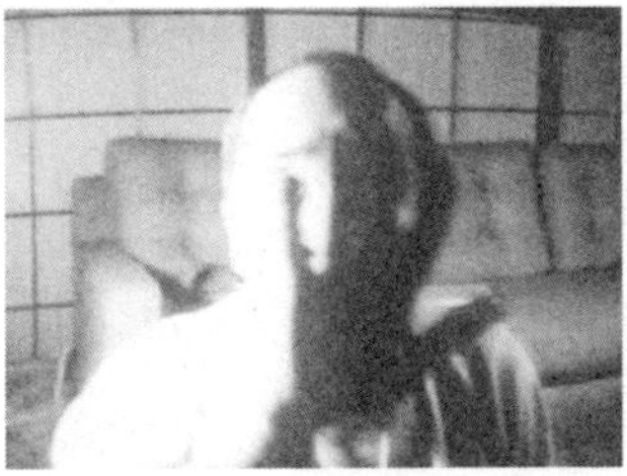

14. Te. to Ta.: (Q) "What is Tanikawa?"
(A) "A poet."

(Q) "What number is he?"

(A) "He translated Snoopy's book."

(A) "I don't know."

(Q) "What is Tanikawa? What food is he?"

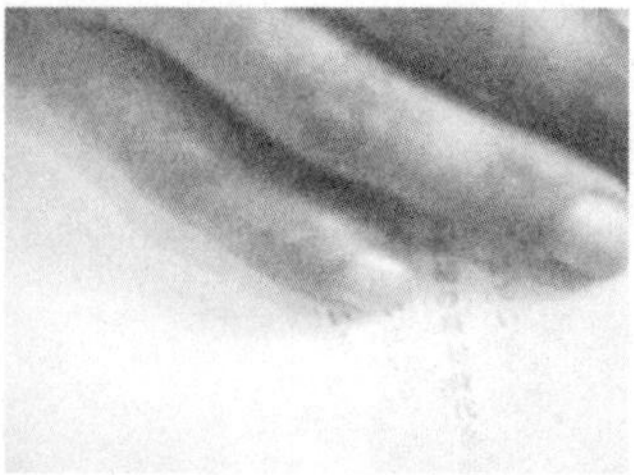

15. Ta. to Te.

"You cannot learn what you are."

"At such a moment the words go to sleep."

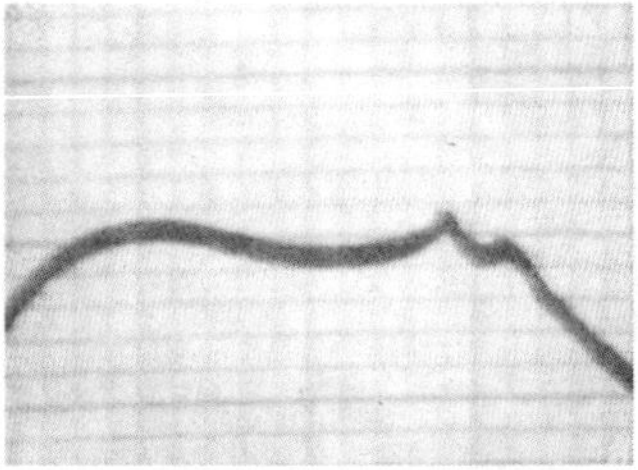

16. Ta. to …

[Tanaikawa reads poems from Terayama]

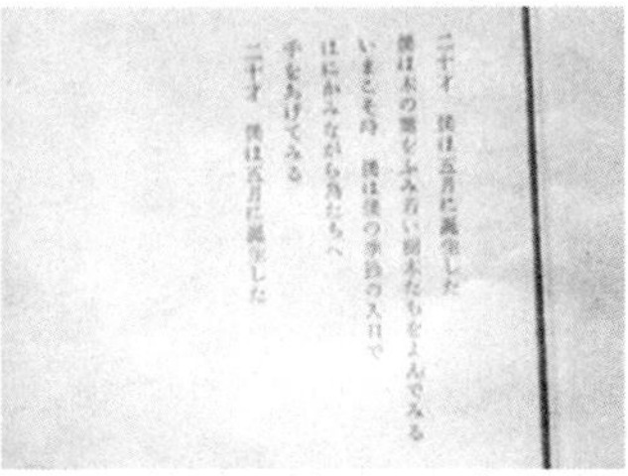

"20 years old. In May I was born … "

Self-Portraits

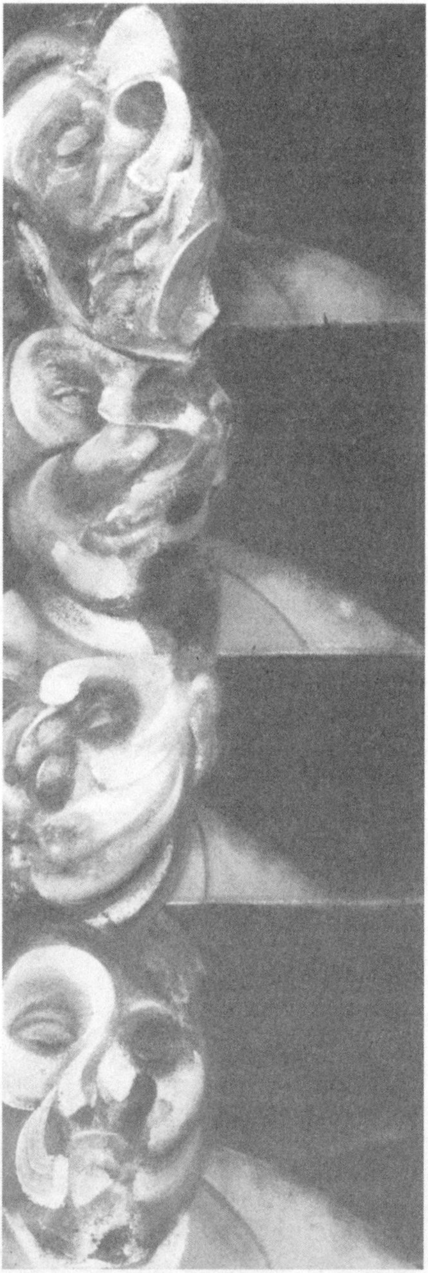

Francis Bacon, , 1967

There is something vertiginous in the video image, in its rationale, in its very being. How can one not see, in the myriad dots that make up its trame, a welter of ideas, drawing in those seeking to recognize themselves in the image and tending to take a lateral course, to join at least some of the dots together? By what it invites us to conceive and allows us to represent, the video image is one of the keenest manifestations of thought, of its jumps and disorderliness. Through thought as image, it gives us an image of thought, vibrant, and unstable.

In Thierry Kuntzel's *Still* (1980), a tiny square at the bottom of the solid blue frame swarms with an indeterminate number of dots; it constantly grows and retracts, disappears and reappears. The few, unsteady, barely recognizable motifs that gradually emerge—the clearest one becomes a landing, a door opening—seem to be programmed by the on-again/off-again miniature frame, pulsating and quivering, an image within the image. It is this little square that I would like to keep in mind and to which I would like to draw the reader's attention while I attempt to trace the trajectory that video seems to have made possible.

I. Fiction

Some books are magnetic, by their fluctuation in relation to and through the image, maintaining between words and images a vibration that may well prefigure that of the small blue square. They swarm with meaning, move, as if beyond themselves, become testaments. Stendhal's *The Life of Henry Brulard* is, to my mind, one such book.[1]

At 52, as we know, Stendhal was seeking a way to say "I." He writes: "What have I been? What am I? The truth is, I would be very hard put to say."[2] With his characteristic insight, he senses here a problem of his time. He also knows that he is taking the phenomenon to the extreme, and he worries, he tells the reader, about this "terrible quantity of *Is* and *Mes*! […] [T]he awful problem of the *Is* and *Mes*."[3] One could always tell one's story (especially pseudonymously) in the third person. "Yes, but how to take account of the inner movements of the soul?"[4]

Thus is Stendhal's autobiographical obsession made manifest: he would like to recover the original truth from moments of experience. He senses a fragile, though precious, assurance of identity that haunts and eludes him. Images appear within, before his inner eye. He says, "I can see the scene,"[5] "I suddenly see myself,"[6] and so on. The power of the images quickens the desire to write, which in turn helps bring them out. He points out that the limpid clarity of the scenes, to which he comes back again and again, often has no relation to the explanations and interpretations that he must give them. For the image, powerful though it be, does not say enough: "It is only an image."[7]

Yet Stendhal is so fascinated with the intrinsic value of these scenes that he trusts neither himself nor any second-hand account—memories, reconstructed or retold, embellished by others or by cultural references—that might come between his visions and the book that springs from them. He also reminds us, as an expert, that, to make sense of himself, there will be no question of "lapsing into fiction."[8]

He will not take his mirror along some highway to produce material for an illusion.[9] For here, on two separate occasions, he writes, "the subject surpasses the teller."[10] He prefers to take a lateral course that would allow him to "describe […] exactly."[11] How then does he proceed? He fills his text with images. Pen-and-ink drawings that become *loci* of fixation, though breaking points as well, points of dispersion that allow his imagination to travel as they sketch out the outline of an autobiography.

There are 167 drawings in *Henry Brulard* (1835–1836), all integrated into the text. Stendhal sometimes adds (explanatory) captions, and nearly always writes, abundantly so, in the drawing itself, specifying locations, places, trajectories, points of view. He situates himself as well, as *H* or *Me*, the subject that writes and sees, stays still and moves. The following examples are fairly representative of his various modes of composition (all that guided my choice of scenes was a preference for a serial effect).

1. *"A year or two before this visit, near the Pont de Claix, on the Claix side, at point A, I had caught a momentary glimpse of her white skin two fingers above the knee as she got down from her covered wagon. For me, when I thought of her, she was an object of the most burning desire."*[12] (He speaks here of his aunt Camille Poncet.)

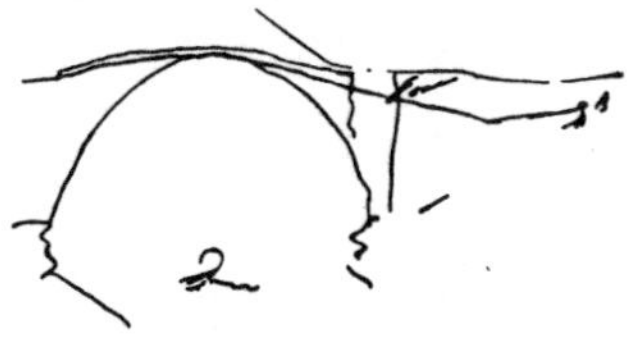

Bridge on the Drac.

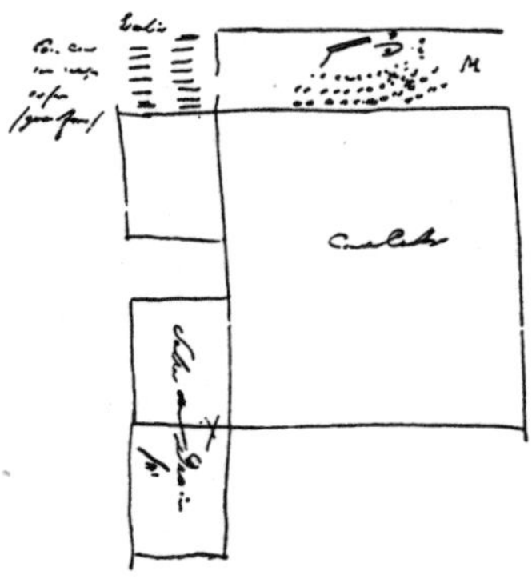

2. *"Death-trap without iron banisters (handrail).—Staircase.—College yard.—Art classroom.—H. My bench. —M. Mathematics classroom.—D. M. Dupuy, a man of 5 ft 8 inches, with his big cane, in his vast armchair.—M. His protégés, the aristocratic pupils.—H. Me, dying with envy to be called to go up to the blackboard, and hiding so as not to be called, dying of fear and timidity."*[13]

2, again. The blackboard scene is repeated in greater detail: "When in my turn I went up to the blackboard in front of the committee, my timidity was renewed, I became muddled as I gazed at these gentlemen […] sitting beside and to the right of the blackboard."[14]

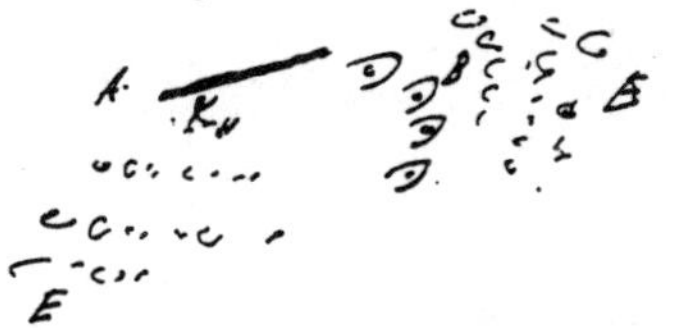

A. Blackboard.—B. Examiners.—E. Crowd of 60 to 80 pupils and onlookers.—H. Myself.

2, a third time. The scene is repeated again, and the motif changes scale (itself repeated three times, with minor differences; I have chosen the second instance). It is a series (and even a two-story series). There are several of the kind in *Henry Brulard*, in various modes.

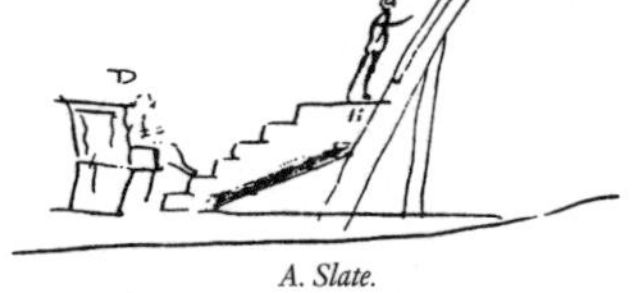

A. Slate.

One of the few times Stendhal figures himself. The narrative comments (in a natural shift from the captions to the body of the text): "I being at the blackboard, H, and M. Dupuy in his huge sky-blue armchair, at D."[15]

3. Stendhal evokes his thoroughly idealized infatuation for a young actress, Mlle. Kubly, seen at the theater: "*One morning, walking alone at the far end of the avenue of tall chestnut-trees in the Jardin de Ville, and with my mind on her as ever, I caught sight of her at the other end of the garden against the wall of the Intendance and coming toward the terrace. I almost fell down and in the end, I took flight, as if the devil were bearing me off, along line of railings F; she, I believe, was at K, and I was lucky enough not to be spotted by her.*"

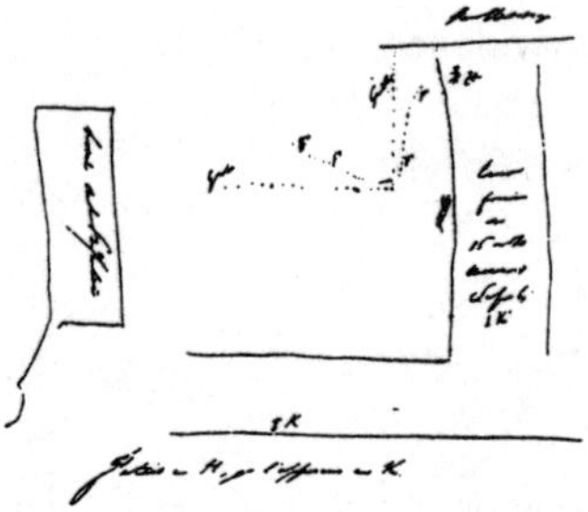

"*(Hôtel de la Préfecture.—Railings.—Railings. – Rue Montorge.—Terrace formed of 15 or 20 superb chestnut-trees.—I was at H, I caught sight of her at K.)*"[16]

4. Stendhal crosses the St. Bernard Pass with troops of Napoleon's army.

"*H. Me.—B. Village of Bard.—CCC. Cannon firing at LLL.—XX. Horses fallen from the path LLL barely marked at the edge of the precipice.—P. 95 or 80 degree precipice, 30 or 40 feet high.—P' Other precipices of 70 or 60 degrees, and endless undergrowth. I can still see the bastion CCC; that is all that remains to me of my fear. When I was at H, I saw neither corpses nor wounded, but only the horses at X. My own which jumped about and whose bridle I was holding with only two fingers as per the order gave me a lot of trouble.*"[17]

5. The scene takes place in M. Le Roy's workshop, where a landscape painting becomes for Stendhal "the ideal of happiness" ("In it, three almost, or not almost, naked women were gaily bathing").[18]

"Staircase of Teisseire house.—M. Le Roy's study.—Screen.—M. Le Roy.—Place Grenette. —Window the bottom of which was draped in green.—Charming landscape hanging on the wall six feet up. H. Me drawing my eyes in red chalk."[19]

On the next page, the hero enters into the painting (and brings the reader along).

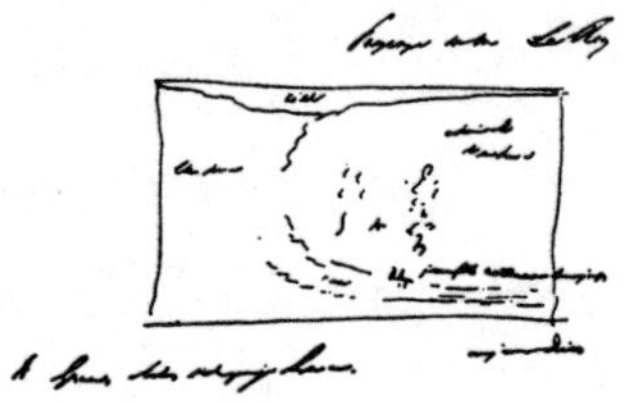

"*M. Le Roy's landscape.—Sky.—Verdure.— Admirable verdure.—Young girls holding up their skirts or young goddesses.—Water.—A. Tall trees such as I like them.*"[20]

These images, which I grab from the text and throw almost haphazardly together here, have a significant effect on the reading, should we pause to consider it. Indeed, they pause one's reading themselves, or suspend it, drawing between the text and the space they occupy on the page as many fault lines as are etched in their schematic diagrams, in their enigmatic connections, and, should we look closely, in the text itself. The narrative Stendhal is attempting to write is less a narrative of his life than of his quest for a truth or, more precisely, for the authenticity of his life, split between the images of the past on which it is based and the time of writing in which he attempts to (re)incorporate them. This is the divide the drawings are meant to bridge, and this the divide they widen all the more, producing a vertiginous sense of distance, of interruption. In this, Stendhal enlightens us on something essential. If he is not really narrating his life but is, rather, trying to catch up with it, it is because he would like to catch up with himself at the very moment in which he is writing, assailed by images, as if in a dream. It is indeed of the imaging[21] connected with any grasp of oneself that Stendhal speaks; that, literally, is what he is staging.

In an article in which he picks up on previous arguments in order to better define the power of this interruption of "images in autobiographical text," Louis Marin effectively shows how Stendhal, in the Saint-Bernard episode (here my fourth example), exhausts himself in a process in which the image that comes up can always stand in for another, one that represents "reality." In particular Marin points out how the danger of real death (baptism by fire), the subject of the narrative at that point, is transformed into the "fatal danger imagination poses to truth" by interposing false images, and how this second danger is materially inscribed in the manuscript with "brief graphical hiatuses" —blanks, that stand as so many withdrawals: "It is the lack of reality for oneself, and with this lack, that of the self where 'I' conceive it […] Hence, in this written text, in this place and this moment, which he writes here and now, this fragmentation of signs that draws out from the page the formless space of what Beyle calls a picture."[22]

I can hardly do justice, even briefly, to the serpentine analyses leading, through two paintings once glimpsed and fantasized about, toward the image of an impossible gaze addressed to a mother in a memory-image that re-stages the very interruption from which all others seem to spring—the premature death of a mother who was passionately loved. Similarly, it would take a long time to show how the autobiographical project is transfixed by two impossible propositions of which one can have neither recollection nor an exact conception: I was born; I died. Yet, one must point out how everything in this process contributes to transforming autobiography ("dying to itself," says Marin) into autothanatography (he said in his book, "autobiothanato-graphie").[23] By which one must understand a presentiment of actual death underlying the writing, the death of the subject to himself in the experience of this writing, and the deficiency of a then-burgeoning literary genre, failing to be the narrative it could be. This movement—and this is its strength—affects both the general arrangement of Stendhal's project and every moment of its progress, in the development of the text as in the lines of the diagrams, and in the gap between the two that makes it oscillate from the one to the other. For it is precisely the lacuna in a text consumed by the image that leads Stendhal to the images, at once more real and more virtual, of the Henry Brulard drawings.

The moment one recognizes and admires in this unique book a cornerstone in the archaeology of the visible-readable, the drawings can present themselves in one of two ways. One could, like Marin, view them as "operators of the image's transformation into a sign," figuring the passage from "image to writing, from the visible to the readable," and allowing us to identify, with extraordinary precision, the point of visuality, at once an illumination and an obstacle, that lies at the foundation of modern writing and subjectivity. One may also, by simply reversing the approach, and at the risk of seeming more virtual, see in these drawings a process that has, from the time Stendhal first conceived them, ceaselessly transformed the readable into the visible, and recognize in them, in their way of setting the text adrift, a harbinger of the sudden appearances and mutations of the image function. From photography to cinema, from film to video, up to our own time's thoroughly contemporary confusion between images and between image and writing, the process invites us to revisit one of its originating moments. One might say that Stendhal's work, by its condensation of narrative elements, can serve as a matrix to fiction.

What is Stendhal doing as he layers these strata between words and images, going from the fixed image to the assorted postures that animate it? He forges a graded trajectory through the mental image. He discovers a space that falls between Freud's screen memory and Sartre's *The Imaginary* (*L'Imaginaire*). He is a kind of proto-Proust but more primitive, for he latches on to his drawings to get at the truth of his sensations instead of transforming the surfacing images into writing. Because of this, he wants to *see*, even if it is through writing and for writing; he writes to see, and this obstinacy of the figure, if one dwells on it, seems to open up three directions.

One is first struck by the fact that this desire to objectify and visualize the decisive moments in one's life coincides, historically, with the advent of photography (Stendhal began *Henry Brulard* in 1835, when Daguerre and Talbot were conducting their first experiments). It is as if drawing were competing with a photograph that might have occurred, virtually speaking. But this desire is also a desire for movement. In this, Stendhal prefigures cinema, like others before him and around him, but with the unique characteristic of being precisely at the juncture of film and photography, to the extent that each of the scenes he attempts to grasp can be said to be simultaneously fixed and moving. For what is he doing, but constantly going *from one shot to another*? Whether through sequences of drawings that vary in scale (the school episode, Le Roy's workshop) or in the movements represented by letters, arrows, dotted lines—all are trajectories that imply (subtle and, especially, virtual) changes of distance, angle, point of view. The narrative fosters this virtuality, urges us to actualize it: it opens up an intermediate space between a series of snapshots and film-editing, a relationship that becomes articulated around the invention of cinema at the end of the century and that has worked upon the twin histories of film and photography ever since. This virtual movement that Stendhal "glimpses" even has the paradoxical characteristic of becoming more and more "real" as photography and cinema come closer together and nearer our time: on the one hand, photography, tending evermore toward movement—through assemblage, text, series, sequences, the book, the system, a distinctive movement gained upon its basic immobility; on the other hand, cinema, variously haunted by a desire to stop, to shed its superfluity of movement, its plenitude and continuity, which have been and always will be its prerogative—such that this off-beat counter-movement has become one of modern cinema's most distinguishing traits.

We can take it further. In our constant mental shifts from the images to the textual coaching, almost physically tracing the inner trajectories toward the drawings, we have the illusion of entering an image that is neither still nor moving but broken down. A series of states. As if this were already the perfect response that cinema, consumed by video, finally gave, via Godard, to images' newfound speed.

But the images that Stendhal proposes, close to the frontier between-the-images, and the additional images that we can project in them, are also of interest in that they prefigure the missing, or lacking, image—*l'image en moins*. These are not merely analog images. The drawing that serves as their medium is not. It was the means available to Stendhal at the time for rendering a basic impression, one he comes back to several times: his visions are often "like a fresco, large pieces of which have fallen away."[24] These images in which the image is lacking are thus much closer to the processed images produced in video, which sheds the film-image's plenitude in an entirely different way than would photography. It brings them closer to mental images or at least to the possibility of mimicking the latter, as Stendhal would seem to be doing with sketches that track the channels of memory. They verge on images one can write as well as draw, with a camera transformed into a brush of light or with a graphics tablet connected to a computer.

We have seen how Henry Brulard is a thoroughly mixed experience of word and image, even generating undecidable relationships between the two. The language constantly refers to the image: first, by the letter's inscription within the drawing, in which it fully participates; and then, within the text, by the author's constant engagement with the mix of figures whose fictional unity he quarries, in view of a new and different space. Here too, Stendhal's projection is closer to video (or to film captured on video) than to the film-image to the extent that video, freely bringing words into the image, enlarges upon the general writerly inclination that it owes to its direct, fly-on-the-wall image quality. It realizes the indistinct dream of the camera-pen, film's soul-searching as filmmaker, and of self-portraiture, especially, such as I imagine it: "the audio-video recording of the twists and turns and slow or frantic unfolding of our imaginary universe, confession-cinema, trials, revelation, message, psychoanalysis, apprehension, a machine for reading the words and images of our personal landscape."[25]

II. Taking Stock

The subject that concerns me has the particularity of having just gained some traction in the world of cinema, where it has appeared through the somewhat explicit adaptation of the findings of a protean literary tradition to the filmic situation. The genre, or rather the field it attempts to delineate (for now, let us call it autobiography), is sufficiently uncertain to be constantly bordering other genres and thus touches the essence of the act of writing. One notes that literary theory has taken a lively new interest in these issues just when they are being intensely explored in film, prompting a flood of new questions. The desire to define a comparable development in video, one almost organically linked to the emergence of the new medium, requires that we engage in a somewhat peculiar unraveling: video brings us back to cinema, which in turns leads back to literature, with which video may very well have a privileged rapport.

In the last ten years then, the ever more weighty and subtle issue of the relationships between film and literature has been enriched by yet another challenge: with the usual disjunction between theory, history, and practice (films and their criticism), we have begun to talk of subjective cinema and of autobiography.[26]

The list of filmmakers appearing, in one form or another, in the first critical appraisals, retrospectives, and programs is a long one: ranging from Maria Koleva and Raymond Depardon to Welles and Fellini, and including Boris Lehman, Jonas Mekas, Chantal Akerman, Chris Marker, Jim McBride, and Joseph Morder. Chosen categories in this diverse group definitely show literature to be providing the framework that brings their works together. The vague, though insistent idea that emerges is *intimacy*, the personal, the private. It seems to be warranted by the notion of writing, as evinced in the circular expression: *l'écriture du Je au cinéma* (or "the writing of I in cinema"). It implies two ideas, two intersecting, though distinct modes of operation. The first concerns filmmakers' choice of keeping close to the subject of themselves, of telling the story of their life, of using their own experience to articulate the question, "Who am I?" with varying degrees of explicitness and all its attendant consequences. The second concerns the private nature—itself quite changeable—of the conditions of production and shooting. It often ensures this promotion of the intimate (though not always so, as Fellini attests); inversely, the intimacy of the shooting does not guarantee intimacy of subject matter (though between the two stances a connection invariably leads by degrees from subjective intimacy to objective intimacy). Such is the necessarily vague background from which autobiography emerges. The vagueness is quite evident on the final page of *L'Ecriture du Je au cinéma*: in one column is a bibliography of the autobiography (reminding us that the week of screenings and the symposium held in Brussels in 1986 was entitled *Semaine du Cinéma et de l'Autobiographie*), and in the other is its filmography. But here the word "autobiography" disappears, giving way to a constellation of substitute words, themselves ordered into six categories: self-portraits, portraits of friends and family; letters, travel diaries, private news; diaries; confessions; childhood memories; filmmakers' journals.

In a highly nuanced contribution, which (given the author's personality) represents the legitimization of autobiography in film, Philippe Lejeune has taken it upon himself to put things somewhat in order, or at least to shed some light on the disorder.[27] He begins by observing the "elasticity" of the concept of autobiography in literature, defined in the 19th century in two quite different ways. In one case, it concerns the story a person tells of his or her life (with the autobiographical pact this assumes). In the other, autobiography defines any text (and not just a narrative) that reveals an author's intention, whether secret or avowed, of sharing his or her own thoughts, feelings, and experiences. Which points—as much or even more than to the characteristics of a writerly endeavor—to an evolution in reading habits that places all the emphasis on the author's person, attributes to the work ancillary productions little considered until then (letters, diaries, etc.), and participates in the general movement toward subjectivization that developed during the 19th century; it would be more appropriate, then, to speak of an autobiographical space. Besides the difficulty of defining the word in a literary context is the particular vagueness, adds Lejeune, produced when one shifts the word from literature to cinema; one may even wonder whether it is entirely legitimate to do so. Two positions then confront each other, one already a little dated, purely theoretical, individual, and pessimistic—that of American poetician Elizabeth Bruss; the other, now attracting film buffs who are both passionately and matter-of-factly seeking to promote the new genre, without too great a concern for definitions, along with a few specialists (I am the one enlisting them in the group) seeking finer-grained understanding.

Elizabeth Bruss' arguments against the existence and even the possibility of autobiography in cinema provides an invaluable framework for defining and discussing these questions. In her view, three parameters define traditional literary biography: *truth-value*, committing the author to speak truthfully, both in terms of verifiable sources and sincerity of intent; *act-value*, recognizing in the author a subject responsible for actions meant to portray his or her own character; and *identity-value*, which ties author, narrator, and protagonist to the same person. Film, says Bruss, conflicts with these three attributes.

1. Even if cinema has managed to establish a distinction between fiction and reality, a film intending to tell the "true" story remains divided between two positions: directly recording the event or recreating the event; it must choose "between staging 'the truth' or recording it directly."[28] By nature, the image is destined either to be too real or not real enough; it is torn, even in its constituent elements, between documentary truth and fiction. It can swing from one to the other at any moment. Such a difficulty is unknown to language, which has no direct connection with reality and has a variety of resources at its disposal for conceiving "true" stories.

Language also has conventional devices for rendering certain emotions, certain inflections (doubt, hesitation, scruple). These resources are absent in filmic language. The image will have as hard a time declaring its "sincerity" as demonstrating its truth.

2. The act-value in literary autobiography encounters two different problems, the first being the division of labor. Whereas the written work (nearly always) assumes a single source, film generally implies a distribution of jobs: a film auteur is never quite the same thing as an author; cinema brings about a transformation in the very nature of "authority." The second and more decisive problem is that of expression, which we encounter from the opposite direction: how does one mark a particular image not only with sincerity, but with a point of view, with subjectivity. Film must have recourse to excessive markers (of which the "subjective camera" is the classic example); it is always divided between description and expression: marks of expressivity, which are an author's prerogative, actually hinder the quality of reality the author seeks to impart to the story.

3. Finally, identity-value is lacking in cinema. While, in literary text, the speaking "I" fuses almost naturally with the "I" spoken of, in cinema, the divide between the seeing and the seen is unbridgeable. Raw presence and utter absence forbid the imperceptible passage, nearly independent of time and place, that allows the subject of language, indistinctly writer, narrator, character (and, in the end, reader) to merge into a fuzzy unity. Language, Bruss reminds us, is neither pristine objectivity nor pure subjectivity. In cinema, the one ends where the other begins. Thus, one could sum up her argument with the phrase, *la subjectivité disparaît devant l'objectif*—subjectivity vanishes before the lens.[29]

To this severe, and apparently unequivocal, position, Lejeune opposes a very pragmatic argument. He points out how much Elizabeth Bruss underestimated the existence of a cinema with which she was largely unfamiliar and which had developed considerably since she wrote her text. He shows how voice-over, used frequently and sometimes abundantly, allows one to retrieve some of language's benefits. He points out how the use of photographs, also quite frequent, can help the filmmaker deal with the difficulty of evoking the past. He evokes the troubling, unprecedented nature of the screening sessions filmmakers have taken to attending, in which they must, in a very intimate context, present the audience with an autobiography from which, when the lights come up, they seem suddenly to emerge, different but the same. Summoning a number of examples, Lejeune shifts, as he puts it, from "problems of vocabulary" to "the reality of a new genre," whose currency, diversity, and intensity he captures adeptly. But we sense his (intentional) hesitation regarding terminology and a return, in the end, to questions from which he began: in his conclusion, he treads carefully between *ciné-Moi* and *autobiographie*, subtly placing the burden of this new genre on the second term, always his domain (and, by the same token, delighting in the new prize).

In the end, however, Lejeune does not respond to Bruss, whose general outlook he nevertheless takes pains to recall: she is concerned with the gradual disappearance, in culture and thus in contemporary society, of the image of the Self, long signaled by traditional literary autobiography and especially called into question with the advent of mass media.

Her tone is not alarmist. She is interrogating, philosophically weighing the pros and the cons in the developments she observes. Lejeune's thoroughly empirical approach does not answer such tersely, though strongly expressed, concerns. In a word, he tells us, cinema was first silent, then learned to speak, and may now be learning how to say "I," in its own way. Everything is in the manner. Elizabeth Bruss is not really saying that it cannot say "I." She only says that this "I," through the problems it encounters in the saying, does not say "I" in the same way and that this supposes a different notion of "I," of Self, or of the subject. Three choices present themselves: (1) either the new works Lejeune mentions substantially change the questions of the *dispositif* and the mode of utterance that Bruss puts forward; or (2) the question that concerns her and the way in which she articulates it remain fundamentally irrelevant to his approach; or (3) he did not want to deal with the issue in the context of this essay. There is certainly some truth in the first point: new works have cropped up, and Elizabeth Bruss was unfamiliar with many of even the earliest examples. But that does not demolish the crux of an argument with which Lejeune appears to be rather in agreement. Such that, notwithstanding discrepancies in word, tone, and attitude, the line between the two grows rather fine: the one declares autobiography to be impossible in cinema, the other sees it flourish there but also suggests that it thus becomes quite different from itself, though he does not so much as hint at what such a transformation might (or might not) contribute to contemporary subjectivity.

His comments on Raymond Depardon's *Les années déclic* (1983), are a case in point. He underlines the effectiveness of the *dispositif* employed: alternating between a close-up of Depardon addressing the spectator to talk about his life and a screen showing first some photographs on which he comments to point out certain motifs, followed by excerpts from several of his films. One shot in particular catches Lejeune's attention, one of the first 30 that the teenage filmmaker produced with his hobbyist's camera: we see his legs framed in a high-angle shot, climbing up and down a stairway. "A long take that is doubly autobiographical: from head to foot, and, in its citation, from present to past." But he leaves out two things. The shot is very strange, forced, its point of view—an actual pov shot—inconsistent; at first glance, one doubts (at least I doubted) that the body one is looking at belongs to the one who is speaking; and the impression of strangeness lingers even when one becomes convinced of it. Moreover, the existence of this prior gaze, as such, a raw, straightforward interpolation, significantly changes the nature of the autobiographical act: answering the clash of bodies is a temporal divide. The nature of the pact is itself strange, if one thinks about it: on the one hand, it is more direct and more "real" than a written narrative could ever be, with that face staring at you and saying, "I am me, and that used to be me"; on the other hand, this former self never seems to really join the self who is speaking to us. Moreover, even if one observes an ordered return to beginnings (from birth), and though snippets of personal life surface here and there, the retrospective movement is focused on one dimension of the author's life: his vocation as photographer and filmmaker. The theme is central, naturally, as would be the telling of a writer's vocation. But here it lags behind the (approximately complete) image of oneself that someone who has chosen to tell his life story is generally seeking to grasp. This may be due to the nature of Depardon's commission for the Rencontres d'Arles. Or to his discretion. But this discretion must itself be examined. I think that the discrepancy is largely due to the fact that the truth here put into play is almost entirely determined by techniques (photography, film) that are bringing about a profound transformation of the autobiographical subject. The cinema *dispositif* has its part to play, though its inevitably divisive effects are tempered by the voice guiding us. Photographs, on the contrary, speed the transformation. They fragment the body of the film into discrete stops, little snapshot deaths: they turn the photographer, and the filmmaker who becomes one through them, into an obscured, intermittent subject.

This precariousness of a subject turned over to the image, and especially to photography (paradoxically cinematic autobiography's indispensable ally), is exacerbated as soon as the narrative form, its only stable point of reference, disappears. This is manifest in the films of Robert Frank. In *Conversations in Vermont* (1971), the most clearly autobiographical of his films, in which Frank speaks with his son of their shared past through a collection of photographs, he opts for a radical division from himself. His presence on the screen explodes in gestures and words; he constructs a kind of hallucinated present in which handfuls of photographs and contact sheets figure as so many fragmented moments of the past, springing up to phantasmagorically shadow the impulses of the moment, its materiality, its space, and its time. The highly accentuated contrast between the erratic, hyper-sensitive motion and the stability of certain shots or framed moments heightens the tension between photograph and film; all the more so in that the contrast has as much impact on the becalmed reality of the present as it does on the fragmented time of past images. The meeting of the two media becomes the basis for the constitution and dissolution of the filmmaker-photographer, telling his story through film after having first done so, of necessity more enigmatically, through photographs.

The best example of the impact of photography on the formation of an autobiographical subject in cinema may be Alain Jaubert's little film *La Flèche du temps* (1982). What appears on screen, for five long minutes, are photographs, lots of photographs, strung together from birth to the moment of shooting. The soundtrack resonates with historical echoes of the years traversed (the war, May '68, etc.). An "I" does appear, though it is composed of a myriad faces, the first having little to do with the last: identity (nearly) nil.

Whichever way we turn, it seems hard to capture the features of a subject that is searching for itself. Take Brakhage, Morder, Cocteau, Fellini. To varying extremes, together with Depardon and Frank, they compose a spectrum of postures, outline an impossible autobiography. Brakhage, following Maya Deren, invents an immense power of saying "I" in the American avant-garde. But what is this "I" that speaks to us, without so much as a word (or, practically, a sound), gathering over the years one of the most impressive collections of images in the history of cinema, instigating an uninterrupted transmutation between the image's charge of reality and its expressive value, obtained through every possible device, modulation of speed, fusion, and distortion? As we know, he filmed his wife, the birth of his children, his house, his family life, put himself on screen in his natural and spiritual environment, and included documentary and cultural images in some of his films. But never has the treatment of autobiographical space prompted such a dispersion of autobiography as narrative (or even as testimony), such a volatilization of the pact of recognition that it implies with the reader-spectator. We are clearly dealing with something else.

Curiously, not going as far as Depardon, yet going beyond him as well (in *Les années déclic*, for there are other Depardons), Joseph Morder's great endeavor nearly instigates as thorough a destruction as Brakhage, even if it is diametrically opposed to his movement. On the one hand, to put it briefly, there is the diary, born, like almost all personal diaries, of boredom, crisis, unexpressed desire, and finally becoming a real journal, kept methodically for years on Super 8 (and because Morder displays it, at least in fragments, it is a distant relative to André Gide's *Journal*, one of the first diaries to be published in its author's lifetime, a practice that has since become quite common). On the other hand, there are films that are spawned from diaries like pseudopods (*Mémoires d'un Juif tropical*, 1988, for instance): they have that rare quality of being at once autobiographies (though partially so, devoted to a particular problem, life fragment, or moment, even when childhood features prominently) and deliberate, perverse attempts at autobiography's destruction. One can see it collapse, structurally and dynamically undermined by fiction, the over-flowing, logical slippage toward fiction, with its traps, divisions, and equivocations, worlds away from any possible preordained truth. Fiction becomes the only place in which to learn, to understand, what "true" stories can tell.

Finally, seemingly at the other end of the spectrum, though in fact quite close, lies the "real cinema" by great "auteurs," undermined from within by the dreamt-of autobiography. *Le Testament d'Orphée* (*Testament of Orpheus*, 1960) is such a creature. Heir to a prior fiction—*Orphée* (*Orpheus*, 1950)—which it incorporates, inhabited by the physical presence of the author, now a character in the fable he is constructing, wholly engaged, as he says in the prologue, on his own behalf but without seeking to summon up and chronicle his life via any retrospective narrative that might refer in the least to its concrete reality (for, rather than tell of his life, he would prescribe the conditions of his death, and so make the work appear to be the condition of a resurrection): such is *Testament*, an autobiography pre-transfigured into a parable of poetic and cinematic creation, with its settings, its images, its symbols, and its gods.

And Fellini, of course. One of the greatest builders of the paradox of Self, along with Pessoa, Pound, Michaux, and a few others (including Pasolini, his alter ego in an archaic and mythic Italy). With his usual finesse, in the famous screen-test sequence in *8½* (1963), he has a friend of the producer speaking with Mastroianni and quoting lines that Stendhal wrote during his travels in Italy. "The solitary ego that feeds upon itself ends up strangled by a great cry or a great laugh." But he goes on, unconcerned with ambiguities of the "I" and the Self or their connection with a reality that might have been his own. In an endeavor irreducible to any tale of origin, and yet haunted by it, Fellini builds the ever more precise and lavish circles of an autobiography without ties, free of any concern for truth or identity. It is simply dreamt, or re-dreamt, confirming the admirable process by which every film can perfect an illusion-machine whose very nature makes such a paradox possible: "I have invented myself entirely: a childhood, a personality, longings, dreams, and memories, all in order to enable me to tell them."[30]

If one had to provide an emblematic image of autobiography in film (I intentionally switch from the grandest of spectacular cinema to an intimate film of the avant-garde), it would have to be Hollis Frampton's *Nostalgia* (1971). A camera peers steadily at us; a series of 13 photographs come to rest, one after another, on the lens; a voice explains the circumstances of the shot and tells the story represented by and recalled from the photograph: fragments of a discontinuous past stretching over a lifetime. What is remarkable about the photographs is that each of them slowly, relentlessly burns to ash, which then crumbles and scatters around the lens—that watches us all the more fixedly—while the voice attempts to conjure the drama of which they were a part. *Nostalgia*, or autobiography consumed, condemned to retreat before the violence of the cinema *dispositif*, the power of the negative undermining it. And cinema, reduced to ash under photography's impossible-impassive eye.

How may I explain the vague feeling that cinema, or at least a whole swath of cinema, has entered an "autobiographical space," just as literature had done nearly two centuries previously? How to assess the state of the "I" in cinema? One could begin to clear things up a little, I think, by distinguishing two major (and often confused) ways of dealing with subjective experience. The first is autobiography: if its conventional definition is to retain at least a modicum of substance, one is obliged to observe that, in film, it has become fragmentary, limited, dissociated, uncertain—haunted by the overarching forms of dissociation that arise from the guises of fiction. The other—its definition often becoming really dubious precisely when it refers to an experience that, though autobiographical in nature, is also its opposite—is the self-portrait. Such a clarification could shed some light on that swath of cinema; but that is not really my purpose. More particularly, one could more accurately assess the transformations that video has introduced into the space it now shares to some extent with film by virtue of its more direct involvement in a certain tradition of literary experience.

III. The Self-Portrait

I borrow the idea of self-portraiture from Michel Beaujour's fine book, *Poetics of the Literary Self-Portrait*.[31] He uses this word, which hardly satisfies him, to delimit a distinct genre, or at least a mode of discourse, that is irreducible to the painted self-portrait, even if it shares a general framework with the latter[32]; and it is profoundly different from autobiography, if one accepts the negative definition given it by Philippe Lejeune in his comments on Montaigne's *Essays*.

Self-portraiture differs from autobiography first by the absence of any sustained narrative. Narration is subordinate to the logical deployment of an improvised assemblage of elements sorted into an array of what one may term "thematic" headings. Self-portraiture is thus nearer to analogy, metaphor, and the poetic than it is to narrative: it "attempts to cohere via a system of referrals, repetitions, superimpositions, and correspondences between equivalent and interchangeable elements, such that it is principally manifest through discontinuity, anachronistic juxtaposition, montage." Where autobiography is defined by temporal closure, self-portraiture appears as an infinite totality, where nothing is given in advance, since its author announces, "I will not tell you what I have done, but I will tell you who I am." The self-portraitist starts from a question that evinces an absence to oneself, and to which anything may eventually answer; where the autobiographer is constrained to a limited plenitude that ties him to the course of a particular life, the self-portraitist goes directly from dearth to excess, without knowing exactly where he is going or what he is doing.

But this totality, this tidal swell of everything and anything, in bits, in fragments, this method that each seeks to invent and employ to contain their memories and fantasies, this dialectic of memory and imagination, is not arbitrary or haphazard; rather, Beaujour tells us—and this is the central idea of his book—it is a variation on the procedures of classical rhetoric, turned to other purposes than the art of persuasion. From Saint Augustine (its point of origin) to Montaigne (its real birthplace) and Leiris (its perfection in the modern era), the structure and rationale of the self-portrait evolves through the works of such diverse writings as those of Jérôme Cardan, Nietzsche, Jacques Borel, Maurice Barrès, Rousseau, Roger Laporte, Malraux, and Michel Butor.

One may briefly define the self-portrait by its five major characteristics:

1. The self-portrait is born of idleness, of withdrawal, it is "the sign of writing's culpability in a culture where all is not well in rhetoric." To writing as action, intervention, and dialogue, it opposes writing as inaction, digression, and monologue. It is a solitary flight of rhetoric, whose heritage it subverts.

2. The subject in self-portraiture is of an encyclopedic nature. It traverses (literally and figuratively) the "places," or *loci*, of which culture and thus the self-portrait itself are made up. It is heir to the Medieval Speculum and to all the *topoi* of rhetorical mnemonics. These *topoi* consist of a set of *loci* through which images pass. The *locus* is permanent, the images come and go. Self-portraiture, which restricts the social effect of rhetorical mnemonics to private space, is first "an imaginary perambulation through a system of places, around a depository for memory-images."[33]

3. The self-portraitist is the hero of the book posited as absolute in a quest for memory and self. The book thus becomes at once utopian (though without closure), corporeal (transforming the writer's body into a glorious body by treating the body of work in which it participates), and sepulchral—a tomb the writer constructs so as to know and transfigure death. Exemplary models are Socrates and Christ, captured in the moment of their death.

4. The self-portrait, governed by that which is most personal, thus becomes the book of the impersonal. It transforms the particular into the general, oscillates between anthropology and thanatography. It is akin to spiritual exercises and to religious meditations, of which the Cartesian Meditations are the secular counterpart. But self-portraiture is ensured neither by God nor by one's own thought. Not quite and yet more than the Cartesian cogito, it hangs in the tension between I think and I am: it is "a cogito of dislocated instances."[34]

5. Finally, the self-portrait is "transhistorical." From the moment it appears, on the ruins of oral culture,

it remains an unfailing demand and sign of the culture of typography and libraries. It varies even as it repeats and reproduces itself, though its history, from the Renaissance onward, closely follows the fluctuations of the evolving modern subject.

One of the problems of this scholarly and somewhat vertiginous study resides in recognizing these fluctuations while articulating the constitutive elements of a consistent model. Without a doubt, self-portraiture develops with absolute clarity during the Renaissance, goes into decline through the long stretch of neoclassicism, and begins to make an uneven comeback in the late 18th century. It then intersects somewhat with autobiography (which, according to Lejeune, begins its development at this time) and becomes one element in the vague though powerful notion of autobiographical space. From the moment any work is enlightened from within, as it were, by this "new sign of value," which Lacan identified so judiciously in what he called *les petits papiers*—shorter writings: letters, diaries, notebooks, etc.[35]—it acquires the dual status given it by romantic-positivist criticism and then by modern criticism. It first becomes the mirror of a life that one can recompose, even if the author has not done so, and thus swings toward autobiography (biography is the genre that answered the critics' obsession); the work also becomes the organic and automatic expression of a subjectivity that is always more or less in search of its own nature, even if it manifests the power of the impersonal, of literature as such (in the sense given by Valéry and Blanchot). One could even say that, from a certain point in time, and obviously to varying degrees, there has been a self-portrait in every work, and that it is upon this basis that writers have by degrees approached the self-portrait as a work. Which introduces a new fluctuation, to the extent that either an entire oeuvre explicitly shifts toward self-portraiture (Leiris and Roger Laporte are such relatively rare cases) or that a single work (or two, or three), but an essential work, attests to the importance for the writer of this formal rapport with oneself—Rousseau's *The Reveries of the Solitary Walker*, Nietzsche's *Ecce Homo*, Malraux's *Anti-Memoirs*, Barthes' *Roland Barthes by Roland Barthes*, and so on.[36]

IV. Rationale

The concerns of this book can obviously contribute to the interpretative analyses likely to be made of subjective cinema and autobiography. It is clear that, where autobiography in cinema is lacking, fractured, transformed, where, for all the reasons that we have seen, it foils and consumes itself, it is largely to the benefit of a process that, directly or indirectly, reactivates the literary self-portrait (even if its transposition to film obviously changes many things). The poetic treatment of autobiographical material in Brakhage—his organization of the material and spiritual elements of his universe through a series of figures that he assembles in a process of shock and derivation seemingly governed by analogical principles—all this comprises a kind of self-portrait (even if the term only half applies, due to the subject's obviously elliptical nature). At the other extreme, the same process is at work in the partial, semi-fictional, and superimposed autobiographies that Fellini constructs (in a kind of reverse archaeology, piling up layers that the critic-cum-archaeologist must excavate in his stead, as in *Fellini-Roma*, 1972). From this perspective, *Nostalgia* presents an autobiography consumed and reduced to a minimalist self-portrait, to a negative trace, to ash.

For reasons that must now be defined, it is video, video art, that would seem to come closest to the transformation of rhetorical tradition in the modern space of subjectivity. But one must understand "video" to be set off in quotes. This is a special situation that will have prevailed only for the limited time in which the two image regimes face off—"Cain and Abel, Cinema and Video," Godard would say—each influencing and displacing the other until, eventually, one way or another, they become one.

There are at least five reasons why video seems more suited to self-portraiture than film. None of these reasons is in itself absolute, yet together they contribute to changing the overall configuration, like the passage from quantity to quality in physics.

1. The first is the constant presence of the image, instantaneously and continually there, like reality's ceaseless double. Bill Viola explained how, whenever he sets out to work, the image is already present: "It's humming, it's

going." The recording merely becomes a second decision, originating from an immersion in "real time," forming a kind of second body.[37] Here is a situation that brings us much closer to language than does film. One should certainly not push the analogy too far or have it say what it hardly intends to say; yet the images one chooses are nonetheless formed upon a constant base that is one of the subtlest equivalents to that verbal foundation upon which all our captivating phrases are formed.

2. The second reason derives closely from the first: in authoring video, one can more easily introduce one's body directly into the image. One simply enters a pre-existing frame, an image that can record as long as desired or as the length of tape allows. It is easier to have private access to one's own image, to connect with the intimacy of one's own gaze: this often gives the image a quality of being, a presence-absence that is hard to reproduce elsewhere. Finally, the camera gaze seems more natural on video. Even the most austere or intimist video art is referred, directly or not, to the *dispositif* of television, as evinced in the conditions of both recording and consumer reception. Clearly, a gaze directed at the camera in a film continues to be felt (somewhat) like a transgression, an extreme transition, while the same gesture seems natural, almost expected, on video (despite all the overlap increasingly blurring the difference).

3. The third reason rests with the video image itself, which one can process and transform much more easily, both while recording (if only slightly, and quite privately) and in post-production (Thierry Kuntzel has produced gripping effects from the combination of the two stages, treating the light in black and white during the shoot in view of further processing afterward). By its nature, then, the video image can more directly translate one's visual impressions (as if more direct than perception itself), motions of the body (as if beyond its surface), and processes of thought (as if beyond its rationalizations). These qualities, which would seem to allow the video image to transform any analogical reproduction, compensate for much of the tension that Elizabeth Bruss identifies between the expression of subjectivity and the objectivization of reality. Since the image is less strictly dependent on documentary truth (what Pascal Bonitzer calls the film image's "grain of reality"), it will

not be as compelled *a priori* to disburden itself of it in order to render the subject's expressive, and excessive, intention (as in the great experimental films, like those of Brakhage or Mekas). The transgression connected with any personal vision is paradoxically suppler and more natural in video than it is in film because the image is by nature more artificial. Here, too, one can express the difference in terms of *dispositif*: film remains the place where every image is one of a kind, unique, even if there are an infinite number of them; television is the place where one image can always be substituted for another. Such are the conditions that both prescribe and authorize the image in video art to be all the more singular.

4. We have seen how the self-portrait transforms the givens of classical rhetoric through a general process of subjectivization, distortion, and digression. In particular, it transforms the system of topics, the encyclopedic and dialectic topoi that govern the operation of memory and invention, the generative relationships between ground and image. If, in our contemporary world, the "mass media" fulfill the positive functions once provided by classical rhetoric,[38] if television, especially, now has the global function of regulating invention and memory, the self-portrait naturally becomes the most subjective expression of video art's specific resistance to television ("contre, tout contre").[39] With the universalization of television (of both its content and its dispositif), the self-portrait embodies the need for a reversal at once utopian and catastrophic: it is the form and the force by which a lone individual reinvents the tentacular and restrictive forms of the universal within the framework of his or her own life. If "self-portrait's original sin is that it perverts exchange, communication and persuasion itself, while denouncing this perversion,"[40] then such, indeed, is the fourth reason lending self-portraiture its rationale.

5. Finally, it seems clear that the coupling of the electronic image and computerized systems is in the process of establishing (via videodisks and databases) a kind of absolute and ultimate version of the artificial memory that classical rhetoric had patiently developed. All the conditions seem to be in place to give rise, on the frontier between video art and the "new images" that will likely take its place, to a new and yet ancient form of the self-portrait. It had first

developed in the wake of the shock wave triggered by the introduction of the printed book; we now see it come into its own among the arts of the image as they gain both in universality and in singularity, saturating in some sense every possible vector of individuation, or of what one should still perhaps call subjectivity.

V. Trajectories

"Ego" is one of the words Jean-Paul Fargier proposes to Paik in his *Arche de Nam June*; Paik answers: "It's our biggest problem, it's Stendhal's problem." Video inherits the problem from film and endows it with a terrible lightness and a new weight. As soon as a body is transformed, its form lightening, nearly vanishing altogether, the question "Who am I?" makes a dual comeback: a few months ago, while waiting for the train in the subway, one could read the question on "Tube"[41] as it captioned the development of a character who changed before our eyes. In it, one eventually recognized a great transformer par excellence, Salvador Dali in person. Paik knew all this, he who first detached the body from its envelope. But he preferred to leave the question hanging, to remain aloof, elliptical, and ethereal. He appeared in his tapes so as to engage in some pure performance actions; he composed these with friends; through them, mingling among them, he stages himself, as in *Allan 'n' Allen's Complaint* (1982), where he drags his microphone across a rock, interviews Ginsberg and Kaprow, and affords a laugh when Kaprow walks on water (it is so easy with video). All this in voice-over, or in short cutaway shots, to show that he is there and that he knows what it is all about (including the fact that anyone can take themselves for Christ), but especially to avoid giving in to the weight of that gargantuan problem to which he gives the name "Stendhal."

Jean-André Fieschi, Vito Acconci, Thierry Kuntzel, Juan Downey, Jacques-Louis Nyst, Marcel Odenbach, Bill Viola. The first question regarding the trajectory that I trace through a collection of works concerns their choice. They appeared to me, each in itself, but especially together, the one related to the other, to be especially representative of an indeterminate though powerful genre, of which they define the various postures, in various cultural spaces. Which is not to say—far from it—that they stand alone. Nor that other works have not contributed to enriching a field, which, by definition, is impossible to enclose (and which I do not pretend to have fully covered). In the United States, in addition to Downey, Acconci, and Viola, one could easily add the names of Joan Jonas, Pier Marton, Doug Hall (not to mention Joan Logue who, after years of exploring portraiture, intends to turn to herself and indeed to engage the self-portrait). In Germany (and in Austria), where the tradition of performance has determined many choices since the beginning of video art, the works of Ulrike Rosenbach, Klaus von Bruch, Rebecca Horn, Valie Export, and, more recently, Gerd Belz would easily join those of Marcel Odenbach. In Canada, the work of Colin Campbell, despite his increasingly forthright inclination toward fiction, would also contribute to such a perspective. In Japan, Shuji Terayama and Shuntaro Tanikawa, with their admirable *Video Letter* (1983), invent both a "real" exchange of letters and a subtle, minimal, and troubling self-portrait *à deux*. Obviously, all this adds up to many pieces of work, to which we can add the partial, though significant, gestures that help accentuate the general sense of video art's natural tendency toward self-portraiture (I am thinking in particular of intense moments of text or/and image in Gary Hill's work: for instance, in his two last installations, *Crux*, 1983–1987, and *In Situ*, 1986, which together compose a fantastic reprise of the crucified body become language-body and television-body).

The seven works I selected for discussion (representing four countries, or five, counting the Chilean connection in Downey's work) hail from different horizons, and the form self-portraiture takes in their work varies considerably. Fieschi's and Acconci's endeavors, for instance, are relatively similar in their adoption of a homogeneous form that developed over a period of several years: thus, Fieschi's *Les nouveaux mystères de New York*, shot between 1976 and 1981, and a series of tapes Acconci produced between 1971 and 1977 may both be considered self-portraits. With Nyst, Viola, and Odenbach, on the other hand, an entire production evolves and shifts toward a more global yet more tenuous form of the self-portrait that is difficult to isolate in any particular tape. One must further distinguish between the two making up the first group. For the moment, *Les Nouveaux*

Mystères remains a unique production in the development of Fieschi's work. First a film critic, then a director of films on art and of television programs on cinema and theater, Fieschi may, thanks to this experiment, become one day a new kind of filmmaker. Acconci, first a poet, then a "performer" and independent filmmaker, conceived an impressive number of tapes in a few short years; among them, *The Red Tapes* (1977), nearly a complete self-portrait in themselves, stand as a masterpiece and a culmination, after which Acconci dropped video (until when?) in favor of sculpture, installation, and environmental works. As for the second group, Nyst shot a few films before turning to video; Odenbach, who began with performance, pursues a career in painting and drawing alongside his video and installations; Downey had long been a filmmaker specializing in anthropological documentaries before taking up video; Viola, considered perhaps the foremost video artist, devoted himself exclusively to the medium from the start; and Thierry Kuntzel took an unexpected route, from film theory to video via a quick jaunt through Conceptual art.

These works haven't all had the same degree of exposure (at least in France). Those of Kuntzel, Fieschi, and Viola have been described and commented upon to some extent; less so those of Odenbach and Nyst; Acconci and Downey are practically unknown in France. In any case, I could not count on the reader's familiarity with their work (and have therefore included some bibliographic references). This is the second issue with which I have had to deal.

A third difficulty resides in the relationship between the singularity of the work and the generality in which it participates. No form, in its particular instances, deviates as much from its model as self-portraiture. But while each work fulfills the contract in its particular way, they all conform to a global conception that helps bring them together.

For these three reasons, then, I was caught between two difficult choices: (1) either engage in the description of each work, if only to present it, and point out what leads it to the self-portrait or (2) give only secondary attention to the works themselves and go straight to the subject, to the articulated positions and cultural forms that lend coherence to video self-portraiture. Either approach seemed unworkable to me; I therefore shuttled between the two, convinced that one could not really avoid the difficulty in a chapter of this type.

Self-portraiture presents the added difficulty that any distinction in levels of discourse appears spurious since its vocation of being *everything*, interlaced and disorderly (as in Montaigne and Leiris), can only mix them up. The strength of self-portraiture in video, as in its written form, lies, says Fieschi, in knowing how to hold on to "the trace of things at the moment when they occurred."

First Movement

In the beginning is the body. The visible body. Yet also a kind of inner body, whose impetus the work translates and of which the visible body is an emanation. Both are made possible through a roaming, available body. The body Blanchot calls *désœuvré*, "idle" or "abandoned."

To begin with, there is Jean-André Fieschi's somewhat magical camera, oft described by Fieschi and others: his *paluche*.[42] Held in hand rather than against the eye, it frees a body unknown to itself: "What I saw in the frame was not what my own human eyes saw, but what was seen by the eye at my fingertips, producing a very strange division of the image from itself, the curious impression of not being before the image, but being traversed by it."[43] This first impression is due to the fact that handling the *paluche* dismantles all the determining codes that have governed the construction of the image since the invention of cinema, and it does so quite naturally; that is, without having to make an effort or produce an effect. The impression becomes clearer when the body of the one filming appears in the image (the insert of the dilated eye, for instance, or the hand writing in "Enfances, une," or the first, lengthy shot of the third episode in the *Nouveaux mystères de New York*—"La fée des images"—where Fieschi films himself in a close shot, advancing down a street that streams by; he would not appear to be filming since we never see the camera, but we can tell from the tension in his body, walking while framing itself, that he has the *paluche* in hand). The peculiar division of a body—the filmmaker's body at work—from itself, showing it to be already inscribed in the flow of what's filmed, produces a dissolution of the mirror effect that invariably arises in some sense when one passes from one side of the camera to the other. Without it, says Fieschi, there would be no image. The dividing line between the one who sees and the one who sees himself is thus not really crossed—that would be impossible—but disjointed, dispersed, disintegrated. Like the tension between expression and description that so preoccupied Elizabeth Bruss, it gives way to the impulse of a manifold vision that proceeds from no assured master-eye, because the eye is everywhere, at every point of a body that refracts the outside (the "real") that it experiences and in which it is itself immersed. Such a process is possible because light is "alive," because the created image appears at once natural and supernatural: it changes with the extraordinary sensibility of a tube as likely to capture very low intensities as to produce high contrasts. Before any thought or any calculation, light becomes an instinct of the body.

Snug within the image, this body films "on impulse," in the open; it accepts the discovery of the oncoming image, and itself becomes a returning image. Fieschi has told the whole story well enough, several times. It arises from disillusionment and a growing scepticism regarding the state of sound and image, of film in the era of mass communications and television. Then comes his utter astonishment before the object, the possibility of an image ("I had a kind of flash. Suddenly imagining a thousand possible films"). Then begins a physical and technical learning process, the baby steps of experimentation ("how to move while filming, how to eat while filming, how to write while filming"). Finally, in a single afternoon, the machine-man and the child reborn in him shoot four sequence-length shots that become, virtually unaltered, four of the six first shots of a work still unknown to him: a celluloid toddler who falls from a baby carriage into a stairwell; a manuscript text in a notebook, written by his companion of the moment, surrounded by photographs, stills from silent films, images of women's suffering; the "speaking shadow," or *bouche d'ombre*, an insert after some whirling shots, where Fieschi, *paluche* in one hand, microphone in the other, films and reads a fragment of text in one breath, on Freud, Caligari, Vienna, and sleepwalkers; a house caught by chance while making adjustments in his window and in which

1

2

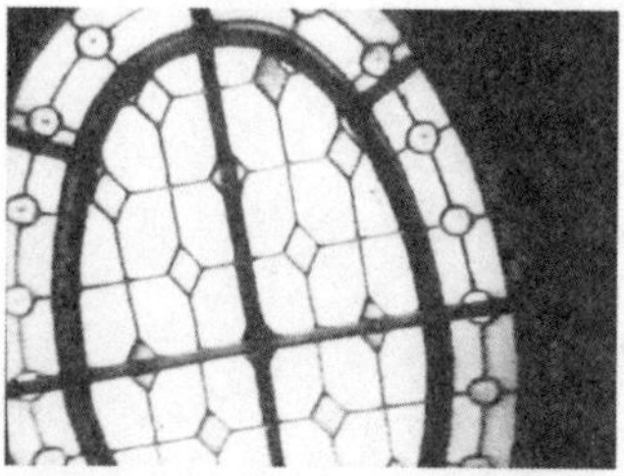
3

4

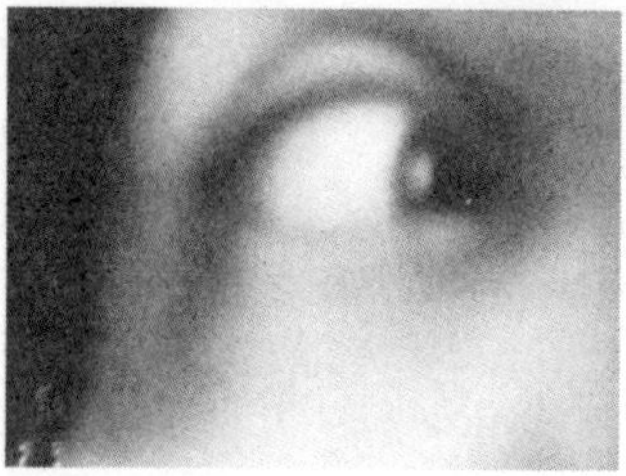
5

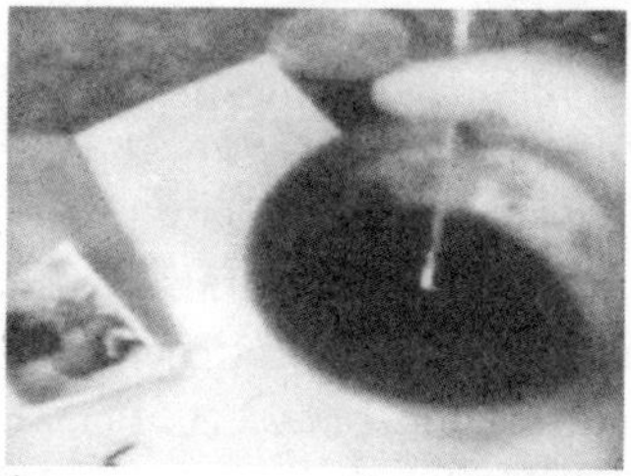
6

7

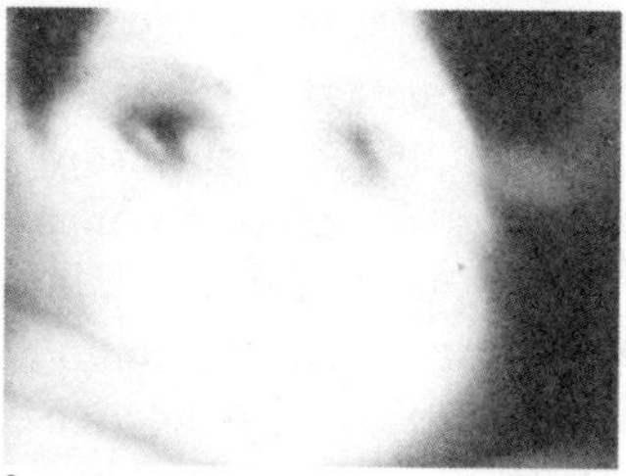
8

9

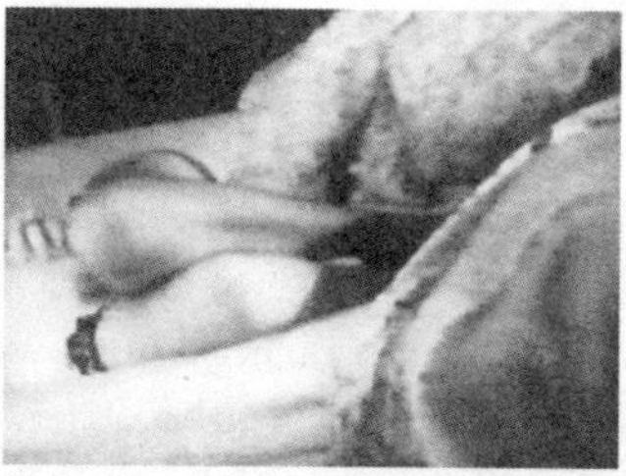
10

Jean-André Fieschi, *Les Nouveaux Mystères de New York (Enfances, une)*, 1977 he sees the house from *Nosferatu* (1922). He shows these shots to Claude Ollier, who by chance was passing by that afternoon and whom he films at once, to listen to him talk about it with him, thus producing the seventh shot for his tape. Of the four sequences, Fieschi would later say: "I had the impression that they sprang up *naturally*, and *from the body*."

Though quite different, Acconci's work resonates with similar intensity. Except for *The Red Tapes*, the 33 tapes he shot between 1971 and 1974 (17 in 1972 alone) are practically all constructed along the same pattern: a single, usually fixed frame, subject to very slight movement.[44] Acconci is nearly always represented in these tapes: from the back, face forward, sitting, standing, lying down, alone or with someone, facing a monitor or projection screen, somewhat fragmentary, once even reduced to a detail (his gaping mouth). He is sometimes silent, or murmuring, though he is usually speaking to an imaginary woman or directly to the spectator. The text is generally focused on the situation, the current (physical) action, the dispositif brought into play, though it sometimes extends toward the autobiographical or refers to times, places, events, contexts. The black and white image is always uniformly gray, sad, soiled. The tapes are repetitive and are all very long in relation to what is going on; their length generally seems predetermined by the actual length of the tape—20, 30, or 60 minutes. Nothing is edited. Everything is in real time, in closed circuit.

Rosalind Krauss' well-known text, "Video: The Aesthetics of Narcissism,"[45] was based in part on two of his tapes, *Centers*, in which Acconci endeavors to keep his finger pointed toward the center of the image, and *Recording Studio from Air Time*, in which, conversing with his own image, Acconci turns the monitor into a pure mirror. He is rooted in the eternal present of a time closed upon itself, without reciprocity or reflexivity or access to anything but reflections of his own image, echoes of his own voice. He is the hero or exemplary victim of the (Lacanian) imaginary. Touched then, to its very core, video would seem to be a purely psychological medium, while painting and film are spared such capturing by the materiality of their *dispositifs*.
The argument is a strong one, and it touches on something profound in the works that Krauss deals with, especially those of Acconci. Still, there is something forced in it as well.

Could we not perhaps say that video's material *dispositif* points up the imaginary structure underlying the cinema *dispositif*, veiled by other, archaic and secondary identifications and by the illusions of deferred time? One might also reconsider what Krauss dismisses too quickly: the finger pointing to the center of the screen is also pointing to another, to the spectator; and the reflection of himself that Acconci contemplates is also the vehicle for a discourse addressed to a woman. Another, exterior, and symbolic instance, then, supports this imaginary position and exaggerated narcissism as it seeks to situate and get a handle on itself. Take *Home Movies* (1973). Acconci, facing a slide show, has his back to us: he projects images of his work, and thus again of himself, of his performances, which are often excessive, aggressive, violently sexualized. We do not know whom he is addressing: an imaginary audience, as in the kind of cultural demonstration one finds in museums, or us, the onlookers. Then suddenly, he leans over to the left to whisper something to a woman, establishing a relationship in which these images of him take on a completely different meaning, until he gets up and takes his third position, placing himself next to the image projected on the wall, while continuing his dual monologue. Here (as in many of his other tapes, particularly due to the impact of the text, in *Pryings*, 1971, for instance), narcissism, first brought to a point of flat neutrality and of incandescence, is reversed. The insistent, often furious materiality of the body contributes to the effect, lending an archaic dimension to an imaginary posture that aims for symbolic import. All this movement, carried forward through hours and hours of tapes over five years, becomes powerfully and clearly concentrated in *The Red Tapes*, where the prior narcissism is transformed: they compose Vito Acconci's true self-portrait. The first shot shows him face on, blindfolded: only if he fails to know himself does Narcissus, beside himself, become the echo of the indescribable totality that informs him without his becoming visible either to himself or to anyone else. The self-portrait, says Beaujour, is less narcissistic than it is Persephonean (thus does the myth of Narcissus figure in the middle of the "Persephone" chapter in Leiris' *Biffures* [*The Rules of the Game: Scratches*, 1948]; but this is also why, "[i]f Narcissus were to write, his writing would be that of the self-portrait.")[46]

Self-portraiture's inky mirror is what eschews solipsistic, speechless narcissism: triumph over death through writing and resurrection.

I will come back to this tape. But we cannot pass up this occasion to immediately show Narcissus falling into the water, the image multiplying (through the effects of digital feedback), obliterating itself in the de-anamorphosed death's head from Holbein's *The Ambassadors* (1533), such that, springing up in its right place, double among the doubles strewn along this trajectory of mirrors (in orde of appearance: a museum director, a seller of mirrors, an artist, a guide, a historian of feminist art, an art historian)—though more thoroughly inscribed, divided, doctored, multiplied than any of them—is the artist's image-body as transformed by video. Such is the beginning of Juan Downey's *The Looking Glass* (1981): an ambling ramble on mirror effects and the gazing-eye in art and culture; a vertiginously poised (fragment of) self-portrait in which the image of the one handling it flows into the mass of signs that he is recalling to himself.[47] His voice is a thread guiding us through the other voices, his body becomes a master of the baroque ceremonies attending these appearances-disappearances. Four of them, among other more elliptical ones, follow. First, Versailles' hall of mirrors, "La Galerie des Glaces": the face is caught in a video strip that isolates the eye or the bottom of the face, a light beats through the strips, and snow replaces the isolated body fragment. Second, the Balzar, in Paris, where Barthes, says the commentary, had his last supper before getting run over by a truck: here a division takes place in the mirror-image, between the real body and its reflection—staggered and projected, however, reverberating with an intense light. This is supported by dialogue reconstructed from a passage in *A Lover's Discourse* (1977): "But I never look like that. / How do you know? […] You are the only one who can't see yourself, except as an image […] I like to see my own eye. / For your own body you are condemned to the repertoire of its images." Third, the Prado, with the narrator telling how, during the summer of 1962, he went to the Prado every day to see Velazquez' *The Maids of Honor* (1656) and would have an erotic experience, almost an orgasm ("I could feel my body disappearing behind the Infanta's bright silky torso: my skin becoming brown ochre and painterly-textured").[48]

The affect then propagates, from painting to painting, from place to place, as led by a repeated sequence in which the narrator-artist strikes with his hands to control the movement of elements. Fourth, the epilogue: Narcissus falls into the water and dies a second time; it is the self-portraitist's dilated eye that is given the initial treatment, as if the fascinated gaze recoiled into itself to translate the impossibility of seeing and of seeing oneself. It is truly by drowning Narcissus in oneself that the self-portrait is constructed.

So it is with the video-body. In Marcel Odenbach, again, we see an idle body, though differently, prey to an indescribable expectation.[49] Early on and for a long time, performance lends space, and images, to this body in search of itself; the images, emanating from a body that exists only through them, can, in the videotapes and installations (often linked), become in fact embodied. Such is the equilibrium this work maintains, as few others do, as it combines the demands of a market (an abundant, polished production, each work thoroughly finished, as if complete in itself) and the vagaries of personal impulse (the tapes borrow from each other, add up incrementally, enlarging the circle of a personal production that remains whole even in its dispersion). To view and imagine itself, the fragmented body awaits the visual form and the points of reference that will allow it not to come together in an imaginary unity but, rather, to appear within the image as a shimmering reflection. Two major postures affect this body: (1) wandering, ambulation, idleness, and tinkering [bricolage] and (2) the gaze that crouches within in order to spring out. Not exactly to set things in order but to make possible, visible, the exactness of disorder, an attitude at once firm and unpredictable. Ensuring an interplay between the two postures is what I have elsewhere called *forme-bandeau*, or "strip form"[50]—a division of the space of the frame such that several shots come into play simultaneously and as many off-screen fields are created. The body, tinkering and tinkered, obsessed with its child's play, its little pebbles, its puzzles, its rattles, and all these fallen fragments from who knows what combination of auto-eroticism and fetishism, become transitional objects, ensuring passage between play and reality: the instinctive-narcissistic body thus opens to the encyclopedia of the world, becomes its mirror, its Speculum.

The Nysts—Jacques-Louis and Danièle (as one may speak of "the Straubs")—take a very similar approach in their work, but here the equilibrium between the elements is reversed. The body, at least Nyst's own, is whole, even if it combines the affected nonchalance of a television game-show host and the worried distraction of a lone wanderer. Yet, this body is literally disseminated and set on an infinite search with respect to itself, to the extent that it follows the lines interconnecting a number of objects and words—objects that seem both very private and yet charged with an intense fictional power, and words that attach (and detach) themselves from them, drifting according to their own logic, functioning as kernels of fictions: kernels so substantial they would also figure as objects if the practice of language did not require it to distinguish between words and things. Under such conditions is the image born, itself programmed by other images: the image the Nysts are searching for and that titles their recent tape (*L'Image*, 1987), anchored between reflection and fiction. Thus does a work come about that is "altogether simple and poetic, autobiographical perhaps, in the sense that it circulates a world (a history) whose central motivation (its origin, its end) remains a mystery."[51] How could one better express what makes the Nysts' work a self-portrait (and better still, that strange entity, never fully identified before, the self-portrait of a couple)?

Finally, there are what I would call the *dispositif*-bodies: Thierry Kuntzel and Bill Viola. Why label them as such? Previous descriptions already expressed the ineluctable transformations of the bodies at work into video-writing *dispositifs*. But we make out something else. With Kuntzel, this something has to do with the dual body his images invent and, through it, with the capacity for integrating and transforming the cinema dispositif into video-writing. Kuntzel only appears twice in these tapes and says little or nothing about himself. Nearly all shot with a *paluche* in an extremely intimate and bare setting (upon which his short texts comment),[52] they outline a self-portrait that verges on self-effacement and the impersonal. In short, a Mallarmean perspective. But the two videotapes we see him in are enough to inscribe (from the body proper, so to speak) the dual image-body I am talking about and around which all his work revolves. First, there is the perforated and scattered body

1

2

3

4

5

6

7

8

Thierry Kuntzel, 1-5: *Nostos I*, 1979; 6-8: *Time Smoking A Picture*, 1980 constantly being reborn and vanishing in *Nostos I* (1979, his first tape), like a pure body of affect; then there is the "real" body of *Time Smoking a Picture* (1980), caught in the play of a double screen and inverted sweep, of variations of light and hue, which, in a single setting (his studio-apartment), simulate an afternoon and evening in real time, when the day is out and the sun goes down. This essentially idle body takes us into unbearable depths of the pure time that consumes the image (differently than in *Nostalgia*), the time, too, in which the hero (as already in *Nostos I*) smokes his cigarette.[53]

As for Viola, to whom I would prefer to come back later, his work generally gives one the feeling of somewhat mysterious correspondences. He has a unique way of making himself a subject while maintaining a real distance. The personal situations in which he chooses so concretely to appear are like stations in a comprehensive exploration of a medium to which he has devoted himself exclusively from the moment he picked up a camera—to the point that one has a hard time situating the subjective dimension whose compelling presence one senses nonetheless, as if a poetics were inventing its rules by adopting the phases of a new form of passion. Viola opens self-portraiture to a singular regime, at once ancient and very new, one that would be inconceivable without a belief in the cathartic virtues of technology, in its capacity to bestow a kind of visible rationale upon the most singular excesses of individuation and the irrational.

Second Movement

What is striking in these self-portraits is how little autobiography they contain. Nor do they develop any consistent, chronological narrative, even in fragmentary form. It is striking, too, that everything that refers to the past, to childhood, which usually accompanies a return to oneself and the search for identity, is so poorly situated and altogether indeterminate in these tapes. And some works are utterly devoid of the reference points without which the literary self-portrait, however different from autobiography, would hardly be conceivable.

Nothing, then, in Viola's work refers in the least to a time prior to the filming itself. Nor is there any reference to childhood whatsoever. And hardly any more in Odenbach, whose entire body of work, haunted by childhood, clearly develops, under the aegis of bricolage, as a transposition of child's play. I can only recall one such reference to a child, very real but entirely fictional: played by an "actor," who falls asleep on the piano in *As if Memories Could Deceive Me* (1986), he then wakes, the dream over, changed into the body of Odenbach. A mysterious micro-excess of fiction, echoing an excess of discretion, or simply the difficulty of recognizing oneself in images as soon as one has to figure oneself as other. That is why the handling of objects usually shows only the hands: one passes more freely from the adult body to the idea of childhood. With Nyst, in *Hyaloïde*, where childhood knocks so insistently at the window, it is fiction that turns it around, allegorizes it: Danièle and Jacques-Louis Nyst, in person, recall shared childhood memories (reconstructed nevertheless) but through the alibi of their characters (Thérésa and Codca). There is one "real" element—a photo of Danièle Nyst as a child eventually coupled with a little pink shovel to form a tableau of childhood fantasy ("a photograph," says Codca, "accompanied by a legend that keeps me alive")—whose situation is highly revealing. As Dubois remarked in his comments on the tape, nothing says this photograph is in fact one of Danièle Nyst.[54] Nor, I would add, of Thérésa (it is not said, though it can be inferred, as the word "photographie" is twice printed on the Thérésa-Danièle shot). Whereas we do not doubt for a moment that the photograph of the woman that opens *Roland Barthes by Roland Barthes* is really a photograph of Barthes' mother (as is that of *Camera Lucida*, hidden from us). Here, critical commentary must point it out: it sets in words that which must remain implicit, such that the image preserves its impact as a private image in the eyes of the one who, while making it public, wants to continue to feel its secret power, all the better to be released from it. Similarly, in *Les nouveaux mystères de New York*, the childhood that one senses so strongly in the first shots and that pervades "L'Ile de la Vierge" (the second episode, mostly shot in Corsica) remains undecidable in the tape itself: nothing indicates either time or place. Fieschi says nothing about it in his text for *Art Présent*[55] (just the word "Corsica," which appears in a short edited excerpt from the manuscript). It takes an outside contribution—an interview with Fargier—for the childhood scene to be clearly recognized as such, localized. This is probably why Fieschi has always wanted to be present at his screenings (a practice that surprised Lejeune with Marcel Hanoun and Joseph Morder), providing references himself, but extrinsically. These nuances only have interest with regard to what they teach us about the encounter between the author (and thus the spectator) and his images, and the Image. Thus Kuntzel (whose self-effacement is extreme), in the original project for *Nostos II* (1984, first meant to be a videotape), tied the appearance of his childhood photos to shots of his own face, then shifted them to another scenography—*Nostos II* as installation—in which he no longer appears (but in which the practiced eye recognizes the same setting as that in *Time Smoking a Picture*).

The reference can sometimes be more explicit. At the beginning of *The Red Tapes*, in the middle of the big theater, in one of the gray intervals in which the image withdraws to give way to the text, a voice murmurs these words, as if to settle an essential contract, the demise of the autobiographical pact in the self-portrait: "Like everybody else he had his story. Born in the Bronx, of Italian descent. Mother living, father dead. I stood, shaking my head in front of my grandfather's front porch that summer. Yes, like everyone else I carried my novel within me. I put everything I had into my novel. It was bursting at the seams, from the first page to the last. I could not get at what I had. I couldn't read the writing, even when it was on the wall. I had to close my eyes and listen. Listen. Don't you hear it? Listen. Something's taking over me, something's taking over me." And the biography fades into the margins of this mythic, illegible novel being renegotiated as themes, forms, obsessions, itineraries, networks.

In one short tape, the self-portrait seems to veer toward autobiography. Juan Downey produced *The Motherland* (1986) shortly after the death of his mother (he had already dedicated his tape on Bach to this event, as an intertitle tells us). He went back home to Santiago. We see a house, and on the screen the words, "I lived in this house for 21 years." We see a woman sitting, the mother, a fiction of the mother. Near her, like a familiar statue, an angel gives her a wing fragment that she sucks. Again, on the screen: "I was born in this bed." The mother is lying on the bed; she spreads her legs and, assisted by an angel, gives birth to a goose. Later, the angel appears at the window, extends an arm toward the mother, gives her a crucifix that was hidden under his clothes. Later still, the angel is lying on the dining room table covered in wounds, which the mother cauterizes in a pagan ritual: he has become Christ, assisted by the Virgin. Meanwhile, among these shots of the Christ-angel, an image presents a man whose face is concealed by a big earthenware plate decorated with the head of demon or god. He reveals himself: it is Juan Downey, the masked author, passing back from autobiography to self-portrait via the myth of origin and its avatars. But there is a second exit: the fable is interrupted from one segment to the next by the abrupt appearance of sequences of current events (the television set located in the home identifies their source [the angel turns the knobs, the goose watches])—military parades, Pinochet hugging junta commanders. This is the second method by which autobiography favors poetic purpose over narrative: by providing memory with places, loci in which to arrange images.

Third Movement

What then are these *loci*, these *topoi*, which the subject of self-portraiture is led to traverse in a movement that prompts it to grasp at all that seems to be a sign of itself, without ever attaining the certainty of identity? To what places does the self-portraitist bring this body, so visibly impulsive yet so enigmatic that one recognizes in the image both the affect imprinted on the image and the words (sometimes) accompanying it?

The fundamental mnemonic metaphor in rhetorical tradition turns backgrounds into tablets and images into a kind of writing.[56] One may see here the origin not only of the book to come but also of the image dispositif in photo-film-video, where video has the privilege of producing an image that is both constantly present and renewable since (in recording and in editing) one image can always be substituted for another. Following the thread leading from ancient tablets to the mystic writing pad, and from the mystic writing pad to the unconscious, Thierry Kuntzel saw in the "filmic apparatus" the truest realization of what Freud sought to show: a material and mental space between the "projected film" and the "film stock" founded on the mnemonic trace, its disappearance and persistence, its effacement and reinscription.[57] The desire, the need to represent this space, is what led him toward video, toward what is likely the most abstract body of work in video art. This "self-portrait by indirection" has three poles, three *loci*: elements of the image dispositif conceived both as theater of visual operations and as memory of past images; the body, which is its vehicle; and the book, which both anticipates and reproduces the properties of the dispositif. We see it in *Nostos I*, its pages endlessly leafed through; and then again in *Nostos II*, where the pages flutter on their own (like the Mallarmean book, it takes place), on one screen, then two, then three, and finally on all nine, effectively reproducing the image of itself as a book of images.

There were places, then, in classical rhetoric, *loci* that were meant to accommodate images in order to memorize them. Such *loci* were usually buildings (house, palace, basilica, cathedral, theater), cities, or sometimes human bodies, that one traced over in one's mind, using natural memory to construct an artificial one. *Loci* were of two major types: (1) "real" or cumulative places, meant to sustain and organize the process of memory following an architectural model (recall that no real distinction existed at the time between individual memory and collective, or encyclopedic, memory); and (2) "analytic" places, built of sequences of logical operations meant to assist in the dialectics of invention. The latter, in rhetoric's very long history, were often reduced to the content with which these operations were meant to deal. Also, from the very beginning, connections and combinations existed between the two types. One could very roughly represent the *topoi* of both memory and invention as formal containers that can accommodate a culture's cumulative knowledge, the commonplaces of society, along with the particulars of personal memory. Such, in a word, is the pattern that self-portraiture adopts, reproduces, and turns to its own purposes. To repeat: "[T]he self-portrait is first of all an imaginary perambulation through a system of places, around a depository for memory-images."[58]

The memory-image is composite; it unfolds on several levels, following associative links that tend either to constitute these levels, as so many autonomous strata or identifiable *loci*, or to pass from one to the other in an unpredictable and constant movement. The path leading from memory to invention is circular, the circles doubling up and inscribing themselves into each other, without coinciding; their progression not progress so much as a controlled drift. Informed by its subject's dread-images, including even the forms objectified through cultural prefabrication, self-portraiture builds upon its own self-revolutions, offering the one who orchestrates the play a detached representation of his or her virtual being, while emphasizing everything that helps it along, all the components of the *dispositif*, the instruments of invention.

This circulation from one *locus* to another, through the images that sustain them, is what makes self-portraits so similar to each other, relative to all the genres they exclude: it is also what makes them so perfectly singular, impervious to reduction and, among themselves, to comparison.

Juan Downey's *The Looking Glass* begins with the following shots: pure digital feedback, with no image; the same feedback accompanying three motifs from *Las Meninas* (the man at the back, the Infanta, the female dwarf); the Narcissus sequence with the interpolated death's head from *The Ambassadors*, ending with a movement that leads from Narcissus drowned to the naked child playing on the rocky beach where the scene takes place, at which point the title "Mirrors presented by" appears; and the series of six presenters, each marked by a particular video effect (revolving image, fragmentation, etc.). Several *loci* or themes emerge: the video *dispositif*; painting; the museum; the mirror; mythology; and the locus of childhood, seemingly divided between the commonplace of psychoanalysis connected with the mirror-child on one side, and, on the other, the plain body of the child at play, prior to all other loci, the very place itself. To explore this childhood space in Downey, we must tie this image with the one from *The Motherland*, already mentioned: the real birthplace and childhood home, which is immediately overtaken by myth (goose-child, Christ-angel), one of the driving themes in Downey's poetics.

1

2

3

4

5

6

7

8

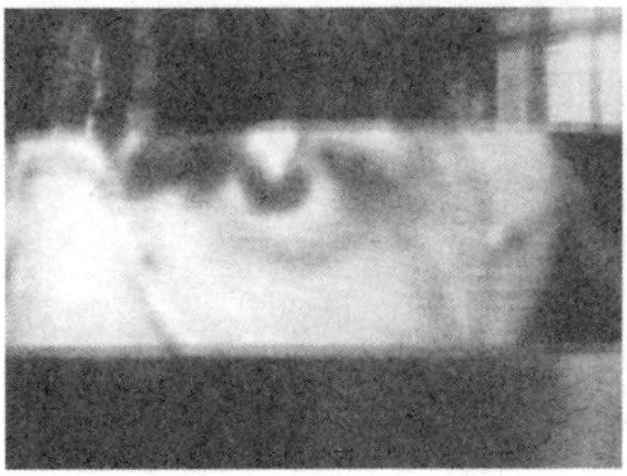

9

10

Juan Downey, *The Looking Glass*, 1982

One does not walk through a self-portrait, one wanders. More than anyone else, Downey transforms this wandering into vertigo—a baroque vertigo already at work in the long (incomplete) series of films and tapes brought together under the title *Video Trans America* (1973–1975). But it reaches an extreme in the series *The Thinking Eye* (1974–1989, of which *The Looking Glass*, was the first installment, with four of the planned 13 completed). Why this prearrangement, which might never be carried through? Because the self-portrait may need to imagine a totality, of an encyclopedic and exuberant nature, to temper the actual, intimate, and profound exuberance that runs through each tape, constantly at play from one place to another, assigning to the baffled spectator the two antagonistic positions the speaker projects: all-seeing God, source and effect of every gaze; and his tortured, Christ-like embodiment. "Culture as an Instrument of Active Thought": such is the subtitle given to this "Thinking Eye" (stolen from Klee). Cultural *topoi*, culled from art history, semiotics, communications systems, mythology, and "mythologies" (in Barthes' sense), deliriously following (through quotation and other devices) the magnetized needle that shuttles them between various poles, all under the purview of a paranoid-narcissistic eye: the eye that would be Juan Downey's, did he not know that the eye was as much (or more) the object of thought as (than) the agent of its own and had it not, by dint of trying to see itself, long since become impersonal.

Marcel Odenbach's encyclopedic approach follows a similar pattern in a minor key. His sure but light-footed vertigo is a perverse version of Austro-German (Musilian) irony, which one could oppose to the logical, South-American baroque of a Borges or a Ruiz. Consider the two sequences devoted to Versailles in *The Looking Glass* and in the video-installation *Dans la vision périphérique du témoin* (The Peripheral Vision of the Witness, 1986). In the first, Downey, leading the game, shot from the front, and clapping his hands, delves into the endless shimmering hall of mirrors, multiplying shots, and proliferating doubles. In the second, Odenbach uses the strip form to divide the space leading to the hall of mirrors while jogging along the Tuileries, his back turned to us; he then mixes past and present by parading an array of historical and contemporary figures, their backs to the

1

2

3

4

5

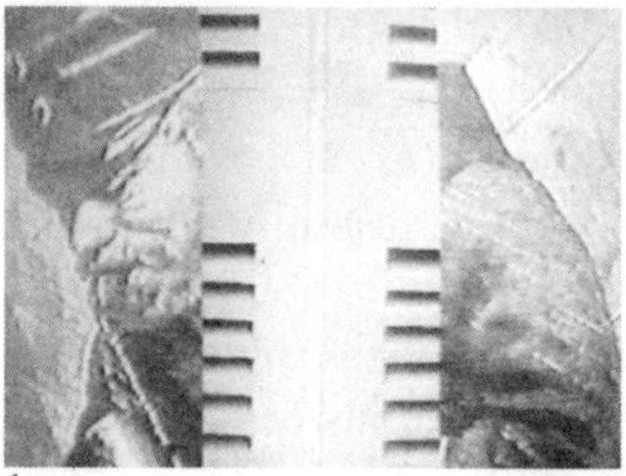
6

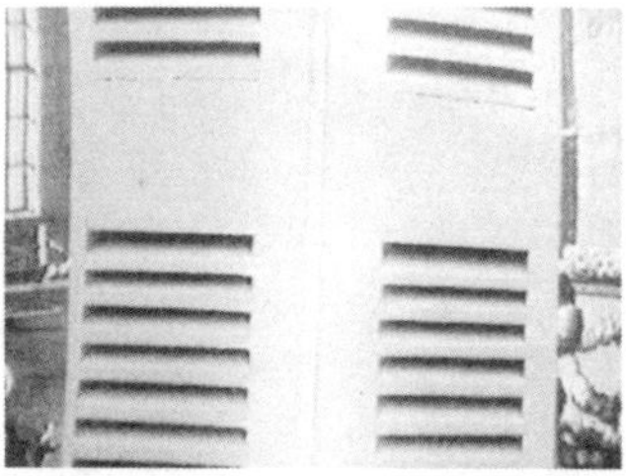
7

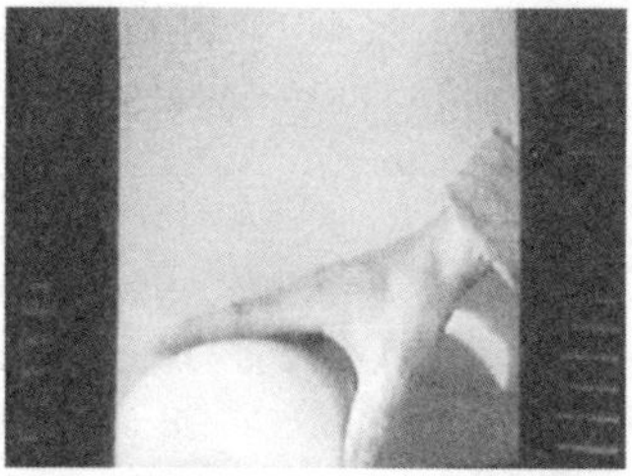
8

9

10

Marcel Odenbach, 1-2: *Als könnte es auch mir an den Kragen gehen*, 1983; 3, 5: *Der Widerspruch der Erinnerrungen*, 1982; 4, 6-9: *Vorurteile*, 1984; 10: *Dans la vision périphérique du témoin*, 1987 camera, through the strip (which reveals a part of the decor that had been hidden in the previous shot).

Four major *loci* of culture are conveyed in Odenbach's images, each of which provides discrete possibilities for citation and reprise (he now admits to taking a liking to reconstructing his own citations): painting (where Goya is the reigning master); architecture (which leads him from Versailles to neo-baroque German chateaux, from the old to the new); photography, as encyclopedia of the world (he makes little use of it); film (Hitchcock, first of all, and De Palma, picking up from him, relying on both of them to construct his machinery of the gaze, but also any movie to speak of, from current events to Westerns, from war movies to skin flicks). And then television, with its singular capacity for reproducing all the other founts of culture, including cinema, which was already reproducing them. But it is through music that Odenbach best expresses his taste for cultural patchwork; as a more pliable medium, it can be treated either with the images from which it originates or in its own right (see the beginning of *Vorurteile* [Prejudices] 1984, with its expansive Hollywood and Brazilian music).

It is through this polymorphic material that history becomes his space, German history in particular—romanticism, Nazism, terrorism. With all this, Odenbach often mixes images of everyday life, whether produced for a particular project or gathered over the years (an informal diary from which he draws as from a personal data bank). And, in the elliptical fashion I have described, the body serves as a junction between these two universes of composite images. With an instinctive flexibility—it is Odenbach's most distinct quality, his artistic quality—he practices an art of admixture that ensures in each work and from one piece to another a constant traffic between these three levels. Manifest, on the one hand, is an acute awareness of formal dispositions and, on the other, a surrender of sensations to emotion. Thus does the most sinuous rhetoric fashion an exemplary self-portrait, too subtle ever to have us believe the portrait to be that of too real a subject.

A concoction that would bear everything about oneself: that is what Vito Acconci strives for in a single, 140-minute black and white tape that crowns four years accumulation of sketches, even while immediately becoming disillusioned

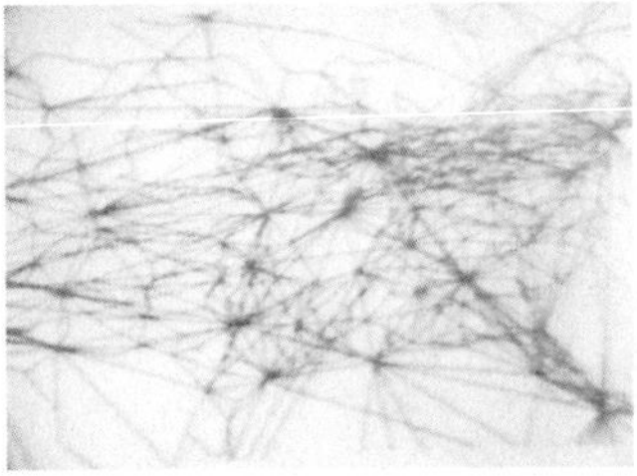

1

2

3

4

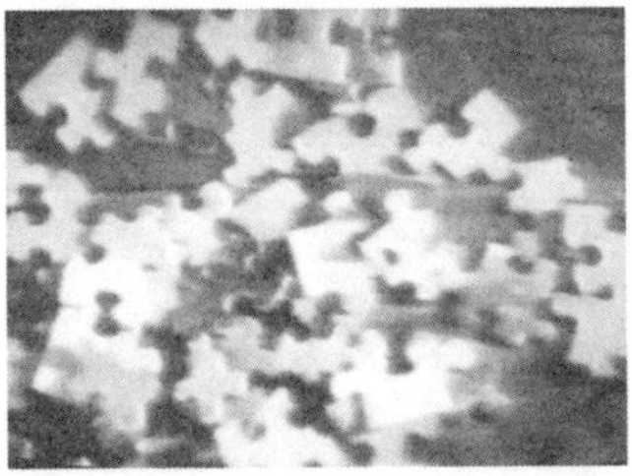

5

6

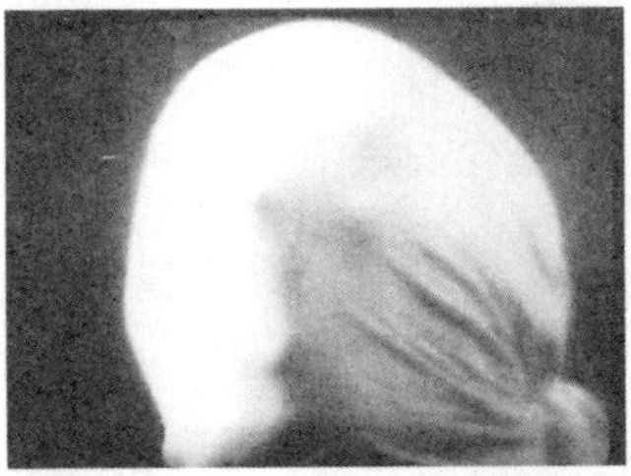

7

8

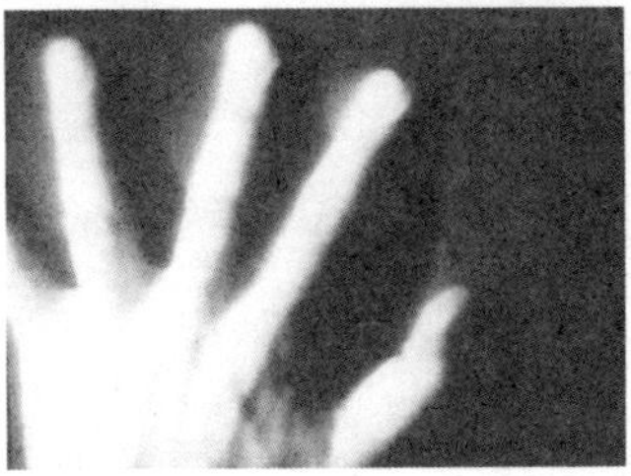

9

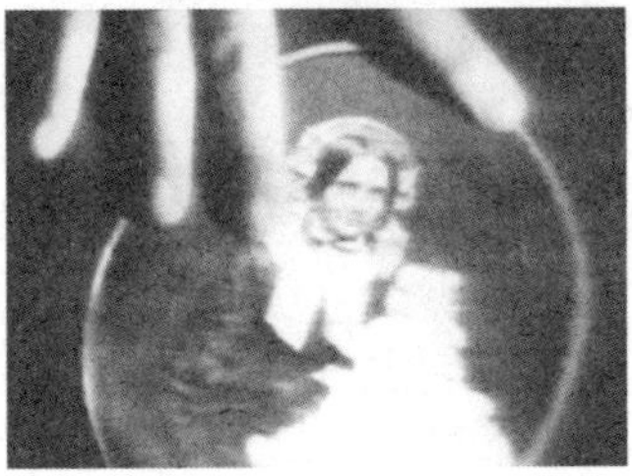

10

Vito Acconci, *The Red Tapes*, 1976–1977

with the imaginary unity of this self and effecting such a complete dislocation that the first utterances suggest he's taking himself at face value.

"I ... I have a statement to make. Yes, I want to say something for myself. For me, there's no more room for feelings. I've entered another room. For now, I have the room for form. No, no, cut, cut, cut ...

"Right, right. Begin again. Begin again. Let's say ... let's say the revolution has failed. Okay. The revolution has failed. Everybody. Long live the Revolution—Long live the Revolution! No, no, cut ...

"Okay. Ready. Start here. Start here. That's him—that's Acconci. But you know that, of course you know that. So it doesn't matter whether or not you look him straight in the eye, it doesn't matter where or when I turn his head."

These words are uttered over a close-up of Acconci, who is blindfolded, and come just before the few autobiographical phrases quoted previously. Then the dislocation begins. It touches the body in different settings, animated by ceaseless, furious, and sometimes fragmentary movement, disconcertingly lodging itself into the image, as if a stranger to it. But it is especially through voice (his voice or voices) that this body sporadically enters another space, a plurality of fragmented spaces. A constant recitation and outpouring of text, proffered in blocks of varied length, matched either to image-sets or to bands of uniform gray that separate and individualize them at regular intervals. Two major principles organize this extensive material. One is the plurality of tones (neutral voices, cries, whispers, etc.) and of speakers ("I," "they")—a plurality that generates a series of fictions. Triggered and released, floating in vaguely defined spaces, they range from lovers' confessions to news bulletins, from private melodrama to science fiction, from the present to the past, from actual to virtual, circulating in generaluncertainty through an array of character paradigms. The other principle is the distribution of series, lists, programs, enumerations, and paradigms of varied nature and extent (note that the second principle overlaps the first). Image and text rarely match but sometimes do so forcefully. The text consists of proper nouns (of people, geographic places, etc.), numbers, letters, colors, temperature readings, conjugations, verb forms, common nouns, even onomatopoeia. Images consist rather of objects: car ads, playing cards, maps, photographs (of people, of landscapes), small object (figurines, both animal and human, buttons, washers, marbles, puzzle pieces). The sequence detailing a number of these small objects exemplifies the interlacing that takes place and what it underlies. Each set is affected by the text of one or more letters, and the camera's movement from one series to another plays out an essential, imaginary alphabet in which Acconci's voice proposes the statement: "Pull myself together." But a second voice intervenes (its voice transformed to a whisper), itemizing a fictional geography that is then transformed into real geography: places and states of the us, soon resonating with historical and political connotations.

Throughout *The Red Tapes*, Acconci explores variations on the locus of the United States (in much the same way that Odenbach did with Germany): furiously, from every angle—history, geography, great figures, literature, film, mythologies. America becomes a cultural parade in seven acts, and the tape an erratic, disintegrated, existential version of Michel Butor's *Mobile*. And, lest we forget, the *Red Tapes* fragment spewing forth a television program. And the ego, searching for itself with a thirst for recognition, disappearing, to its own eyes, into the mass of interconnected *loci* through which it is programmed: points of dispersion that endlessly compose and recompose the imaginary mass of its tortured body.

There are more focused ways of reflecting on oneself. In Fieschi, two major *loci*—childhood and cinema—spawn others (women, psychoanalysis, which spawn others still, and so on). In *Les nouveaux mystères de New York*, deployed in its very title, something unique is produced between childhood and film: a return to cinema's own childhood, to silent film, serials, the age of open, innocent images, still new. But, as Fieschi explains with wonderful precision, this return was such because, as early as in his own late childhood and then in adolescence, he experienced movies as "a search for prior images," of the bodies and landscapes of his native Corsica, "perhaps," he adds, "even for the origin of images."[59] The enveloping concern obviously resides in this pulsation between childhood and film, which the *paluche* transforms into a trembling of the body, a shimmer of black and white, and attempts to put its finger-cum-eye on that improbable moment when the image perches still on the threshold of hallucination. That is what he is attempting to grasp in supreme moments of the cinematic gaze, the anticipation and response of his dilated eye and its concentrated mix of wonderment and terror. Fieschi cites these moments, even as he seeks by his own means to reproduce them. Thus the famous exchange of looks between Nosferatu and Nina in Murnau's film, by which the vampire answers the woman's somnambulist premonition in a purely imaginary space. And Vampyr's errant, non-assignable gaze, which in the end adopts the only possible point of view (Dreyer, 1932): the point of view of one long dead, of Death itself, conjuring the space of childhood terrors. Dreyer's voice, heard over the third sequence (a trajectory over film stills and text) attests the work's debt to cinema, to which it returns so as to progress, by way of culture's "nostalgic appropriation of Paradise," toward archaic childhood.

Such a rapport with cinema as *locus* of oneself is a wholly European, German, and especially French (or Belgian) affair. We can see it in condensed form in Kuntzel. From *Nostos I* to *Nostos II*, one witnesses the reinscription into the video-body of one of the cruelest delineations of the mix of pleasure and destruction attached to the imaginative capacities of the cinema *dispositif*: Max Ophüls' *Letter from an Unknown Woman* (1948). In the video, the hero—Kuntzel himself, decomposed and recomposed—stands near the window of a moving train, like the romantic couple in the fairground train of Ophüls' film. In the installation, the film's soundtrack functions directly as cultural double and as vehicle for the fiction. The film begins with the heroine starting the letter that announces her coming death, and it ends (almost) with the death that interrupts the letter, thus becoming the realization of that death. This beginning and this end of the letter, and its exacerbated romanticism, are heard at the beginnings and ends of the nine tapes; the film's score also serves to punctuate the work, delimiting four acts in which certain motifs are reinscribed in a kind of revisitation. Thanks to the *paluche* and the images circulating between the nine screens, the video actualizes the effects of unconscious memory, or the "mystic writing pad" effect, of the cinema *dispositif* (for this purpose, Kuntzel used a deliberately misadjusted *paluche*, which, at the slightest movement, doubled every captured form with a smoky white trace, producing an embodied reflection of the process of memory). The strongest moment, along with the treatment of the book already discussed, comes with the long sequence in which family and childhood photographs stream endlessly through a window frame that itself seems like a screen memory: they accumulate, one atop another, from one monitor to the next, forming a dual mass, each image eventually becoming the ghost of the next.

Another film, and again a photograph, but this time one taken from the film itself, serves as a starting point for *Hyaloïde* and hastens the appearance of the childhood photograph. It is the photograph of Lucy Holmwood, Jonathan Harker's fiancée, whom Van Helsing is observing in Terence Fisher's *Horror of Dracula* (1958), the first major remake of Murnau's *Nosferatu*. In the Nysts' work (in which other films play a similar role—as *Poltergeist*, 1982, does in their *Thérésa Plane*, 1983) things are fundamentally different: they are watching the movie on television, which, as in Odenbach, becomes cinema's provider, just as it serves the intense encounter that dominates for Fieschi and Kuntzel; it reappropriates its central and natural function in the formation of video self-portraiture. As mentioned previously, the Nysts' work is much more open, playful, freely exploring a variety of places that proliferate with a kind of enthusiasm that recalls the shuffling of levels we observed in Downey, though the process is more intimate, as in Odenbach, and still more explicit. To hint at its operation at a particularly interesting level, one may bring attention to the series of words strung through the images (inscribing and writing themselves into the image) around the idea of writing. They directly become points of anchorage and reference in a video informed by a taste for the spoken word and plays of language; they also testify, on a lighter note, to self-portraiture's attachment to the kind of jumbled series that vaguely recall the encyclopedic taxonomies of the Middle Ages and the Renaissance. Here then, not counting the words that reappear twice on different images, is a dizzying play of associative games haunted by the rhetorical figures crowded around the twin mainstays of metaphor and metonymy: *écho graphie*, *vidéo graphie*, *hagio graphie*, *photo graphie*, *ortho graphie*, *choré graphie*, *mécano graphie*, *calli graphie*, *caco graphie*, *crypto graphie*, *icono graphie*, *historio graphie*, *radio graphie*, *hydro graphie*, *mono graphie*, *cristallo graphie*, *micro graphie*.

One will have noticed the extent to which most of these endeavors are infused with photography: childhood photographs, for Kuntzel and Nyst; film stills, for Nyst and Fieschi; photographs from the encyclopedia of the world, for Odenbach and Acconci. The photograph suspends time, reduces film to a still frame, and the videotape to its basic element. Whatever it represents, it is the exemplary image, at once document, trace, and enigma. It testifies at once to the world's dispersion and to the division of time. It is by definition the first image (both historically and materially); all the more naturally does it become the last, the remainder of a global *dispositif* that it figures, by bringing about a reduction that also testifies to its capacity for inscribing separation and death. This is manifest in Bill Viola's videotape *The Space Between the Teeth* (1976). A section of space, a seated man, Viola himself. He looks at us for a time, then suddenly screams. Several times. The camera backs up, revealing an interminable corridor. It finally stops. The man cries out; and each scream, at regular intervals, triggers the camera's halting, though dizzying, advance, until it is close enough to capture the space between the man's teeth. After each advance, the camera recoils into the corridor, stopping at a position that with each retreat is closer and closer to the man. But each scream, on the conclusion of each advance, after the camera has come up against the man's teeth, introduces a slight disjunction, like a rhythmic hiccup, composed first of one or two blank images. The more we approach the man, the greater the disjunction. A setting quickly appears within this sporadically widening space: a kitchen, a little breakfast table. Soon, the time devoted to each of the two spaces is reversed, as each shot from the camera in the hall, now up against the face, becomes very short, while in the kitchen, time passes, Viola comes and goes, a faucet drips. The shot persists. We go back to the hallway: the camera is back in its original position, at the end of the hall; but the image is now black and white, slightly tilted against a matte, nondescript color background. We hear a scream, the camera zooms out, the image of the hallway collapses: it is a Polaroid, tiny, that falls into the sea. The shot persists until a wave picks up the image and carries it to the left, off-screen.

1

2

3

4

5

6

7

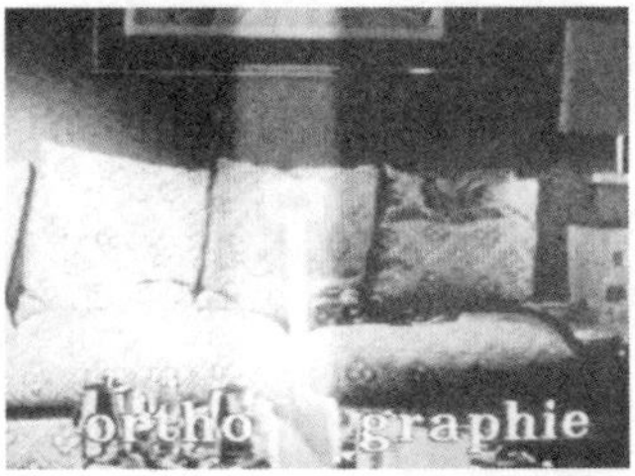

8

9

10

Danièle & Jacques Louis Nyst, *Hyaloïde*, 1985

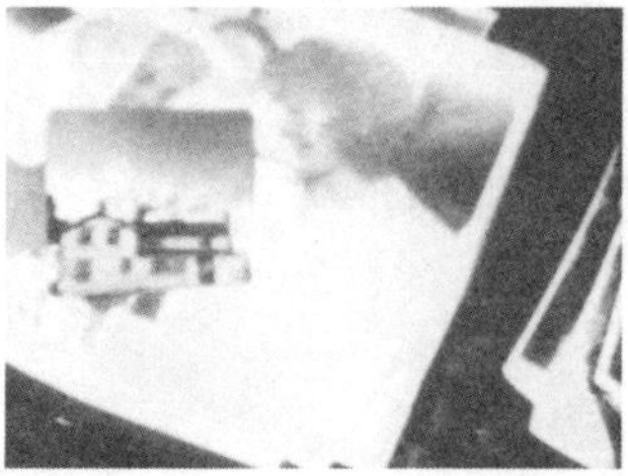
1

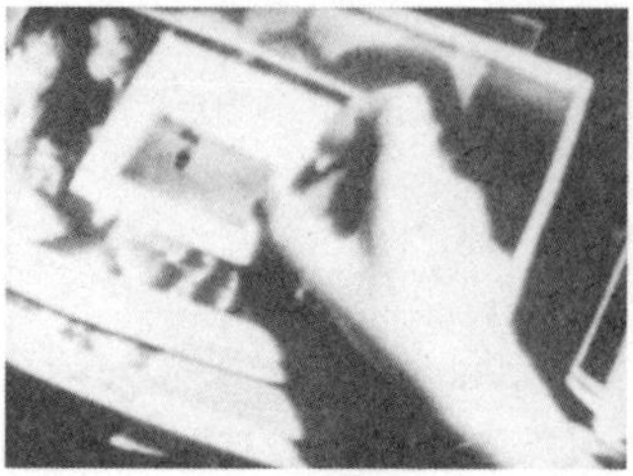
2

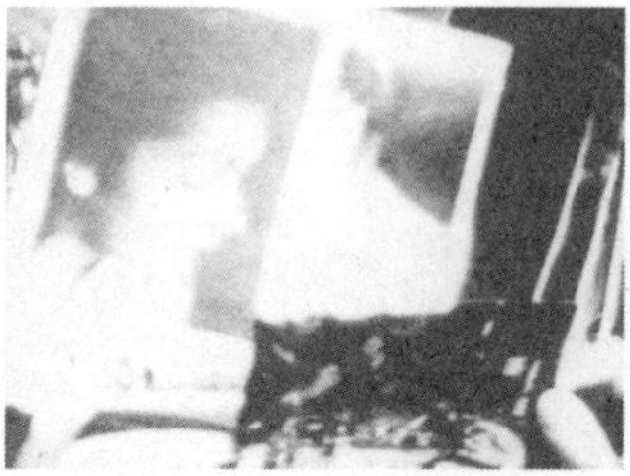
3

4

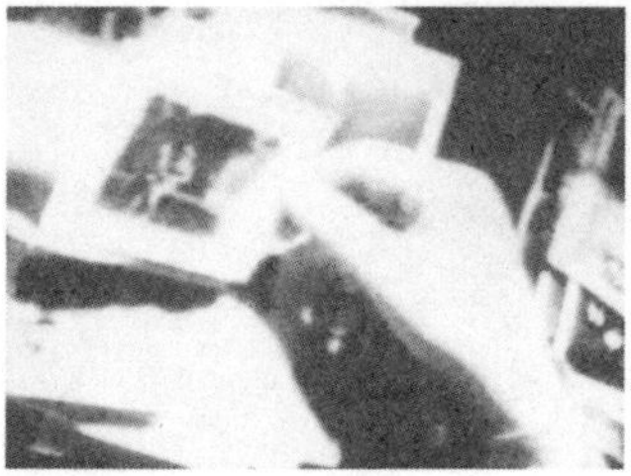
5

6

7

8

Thierry Kuntzel, 1-6: *Nostos II* (installation), 1984; 7-8: *Nostos I*, 1979

What can be said of this dizzying strategy? The predominant and persistent impression is that the entire tape is suddenly reduced to a photograph, glimpsed for the time of a scream—as if an instant summed it up, then disappeared. The photograph thus has a truth function: the vanity of the image. But if we reflect a little more about the interconnection of the two series, we note that, with each scream, the camera goes further into the body, frames an elliptical moment and then, in its place, reveals a scene that seems to appear from between the teeth. This latter scene, first so brief it is almost photographic, gradually settles in and finally becomes more real than the other (which it is already by what it represents). The photograph's abrupt irruption is a call to order: the real is not on the side we think; it is in the interstice, between the teeth, in the darkroom of the body from which the photograph falls.

Fourth Movement

The Reflecting Pool (1977–1980) opens with a man coming out of the forest and standing at the edge of a pool. He faces the camera and we see his reflection on the water. Suddenly, he jumps up and his body freezes in mid-air. The reflection has vanished. In the pool, over time, little by little, a world of sundry movements comes to life. The initial reflection of the body reappears, becomes divided within itself, moves about. When the spectator widens his eyes to figure out how this connects with the suspended body, they see that it has vanished while they were not looking (or that is the impression people usually have).

Again, what can we deduce from such a strategy? In the first place, Viola's work is inspired by a passion for the fixed image or, rather, for a certain fixity in the image: it is an invitation to reflect on what happens with a moving image when, like Viola (one might call up any number of examples), one no longer considers it as such. Let us call such an awareness "the photographic." We then see that such effects are rooted in the body, in the author's own body. They instantly take us beyond narcissism: in *The Space Between the Teeth*, by transcending the image of the manifest body with an irruption from the inner body; in *The Reflecting Pool*, by variously separating the body from its reflection. We also observe that each of these tapes corresponds to a type of place (even if both are loci of experience, for the image as for the body): the one perfectly closed, the other open and outdoors. Finally, Viola clearly demands a particular attention of the spectator, both when things go (too) fast and when they go (too) slowly.

If one asks Viola why he presents himself as an actor-subject in a significant number of his tapes (roughly in two-fifths of his works, excluding his installations, where he appears less frequently), he answers, like Marcel Odenbach (or Kuntzel, Fieschi, and others), that it is a way of preserving the intimacy required for the filming experience and, more generally, for the personal and creative experience as a whole. Increasingly, aided by access to cutting-edge equipment (as that from Sony, in Japan, for *Hatsu Yume*, 1981), and especially by demonstrating (like Godard) an ever-greater unity of production, he has tended to eliminate intermediaries in the various stages of his work. He works increasingly alone (with his wife and partner, Kira Perov). He says: "The work comes from a very personal place for me and it's always a matter of keeping it as close as possible to that source." Also: "there is no difference between what I'm doing and what a writer does." And again: "We create this thing that exists outside of ourselves: the text."[60] Outside oneself but based on oneself: such, precisely, is the interstice in which Viola constructs his singular self-portraits.

On examining these various manifestations, one notices that they are located at the crossroads of two great axes. The body is the vehicle for exploring the possibilities of the medium; it is a *dispositif*-body (the four superimposed bodies in *Olfaction*, 1974, the distorting water-drop-mirror in *Migration*, 1976, the pigeons' slow-motion flight in response to the sound waves emanating from the dish Viola lets fall on Washington Square in *Truth through Mass Individuation*, 1976, etc.). The body is also (and these two aspects often go together) the *locus* of a trial of which he explores the stages, as in yet another ritual transformation of the Stations of the Cross. Its strongest statement is in *Reasons for Knocking at an Empty House* (1982), in both its video and installation versions, both developed from the experience of going three days and three nights without sleeping: in the video, we are in a room in which phases are delimited by bodily movements and variations in light from two windows; in the installation, on a monitor facing the hot seat reserved for the spectator (who participates directly in the sound), Viola appears, disheveled and hit on the back at regular intervals. Here, the *dispositif* is the *locus* of torment and of an experience; it is also the instrument of education and the means for a resurrection. It provides the rule, the consensual discipline that enables the business of living. The gaze is its practice, the world its theater, perception its mode of passage, and memory its condition. Such are the ways of invention.

Viola's self-portrait has the peculiarity that its engagement with memory refers strictly to itself, producing an eternal present in the process of being constituted. Recall *The Space Between the Teeth*, where the camera, advancing through the hallway and into the mouth, passes through a series of positions to which it reverts in decreasing order, then starts over again, and so on. Take *Return* (1975). Viola in a garden, in the distance, a bell and a hammer in hand. He strikes once, twice, a third time, advancing a few meters each time. On the fourth strike, he steps backs in a kind of jump to position 3 and then jumps in the same way to position 4. The process is repeated up to the tenth bell (if I've counted right). Each time, Viola goes through all the stations up to the third then finds himself back at the one from which he struck the bell. He is now in close-up. The camera moves back and discovers a huge barn. Viola enters; in a long shot again. The whole process is repeated up to the 18th chime of the bell (we have long since lost count of prior positions, through which the body seems to scrupulously regress nonetheless, especially since the second part of this movement is now only visible through the barn door). We then only see his white sweatshirt in close-up. He goes backward again, now swept up in a truly dizzying movement, but this time the rhythm is slower, and again, at each station, we hear the striking of the bell. Thus can memory refer to its own operation, the trace of an eternal present.

In this work, where nothing is autobiographical, by its very construction, everything becomes so. And yet,one senses no self-indulgence, nor an excessive confinement (as in Roger Laporte's literary self-portrait, *La Veille*, 1963, constantly brought back to the production of its writing). A phenomenal and infinitely rich world is given us in the singular mode of an exacerbated awareness of the physical and mental conditions implied by its grasp and apperception. Hence the significance, to my eyes, of this striking title: *Chott-el-Djerid (A Portrait in Light and Heat)* (1979). Viola only appears in one very lengthy shot, in which a point, practically invisible on the horizon, advances toward the spectator but remains too distant to be identified. Of whom, then, is this tape composing the portrait? Of the desert, obviously. But of the eye perceiving it as well. A portrait "in light and heat"—that is, in the material components that model the image for the telephoto lens, which is substituting for the eye here and capturing a reality constantly on the verge of a mirage. The tape thus becomes the enigmatic portrait of one who lives and relives the desert experience thanks to the technological possibilities of equipment upon whose functioning he clearly relies. Thus his self-portrait emerges. To the question "Who am I?" he can only answer, *I Do Not Know What It Is I Am Like* (1986). He is none other than the immensity before our eyes, and the singularity of the experience of it, the Stations, the *loci* of experience, which the one living them explores by bringing more and more images into play.

We could draw up an inventory that would give us a kind of table of archetypes, between Jungian psychoanalysis and Vico's sensory *topoi* of the imagination, in which Barthes saw a forerunner of *critique thématique* and Bachelardian criticism.[61] Although the universals of the imagination so dear to Vico, and which Viola discovers in his own way, are here shadowed by an internal reflection on the technology that allows them to be expressed and by a general immersion in a scientific universe. One could simply list them, starting with the *loci* of nature, which are also *loci* of solitude—desert, mountain, forest, plain, garden, stretch of water, and so on. These are followed by all the places of confinement, the flip side of the experience of solitude—corridor, room, cell, any bare room punctuated with windows to ground the vision machine. At their juncture lie the intermediary spaces, inhabited, populous even—streets, halls, roads, squares, and so on—though always imbued with that same quality of solitude, largely due to a complete absence of language in Viola's work to date, which is essentially reduced to an audio environment (having an extraordinary presence).

Finally, there are also the *loci* of culture, manifest as much in the titles and written commentaries to his videotapes and installations as in what they show (discreetly accompanying a body of work that never makes explicit use of citation): Far Eastern cultures, primitive societies, rituals, poets, mystics, scientific references, and finally—because even his work is not immune either to everyday life or to America—television. One could classify and order all of this into opposing dualities of varying magnitude, proliferating and overlapping in a circular logic: nature/culture, closed/open, death/life, shadow/light, animate/inanimate, visible/invisible, mobile/stationary, slowed down/accelerated, human/animal, human-animal/vegetal-mineral. Such are the *loci*, at once material and abstract, through which the image-bearing bodies pass, bodies that become *loci* themselves: Viola himself, then his wife (once only, but memorably, in *Moonblood*), other men and women, children (on two powerful occasions, in *Silent Life*, 1979, and *Songs of Innocence*, 1976), and lots of animals.

But what exactly does self-portraiture mean without autobiography? Three temporal modes successively take effect and overlap in the Viola experience: "real time," shared between the time of his perception as such and that of the camera that shadows it and focuses its image onto the monitor ("the camera's always on, there's always an image"); the time of recording, which effects a selection in this continuous time; and the time of final editing, which seeks to create the illusion that the second time possessed the continuity of the first. Yet there is a fourth time, of which we know nothing but whose presence we sense, and which alone explains the uneasiness that emanates from these works. This time traverses the three others down to the time of perception, of which it takes hold, and opens up another, personal, time below it, unknown and faceless, that sweeps through the specter of past life, such that everything seems to have been "already seen [*déjà vu*]." If each of the tapes is informed by processes of memory, such that images appearing therein seem to be screen memories spawned from each other, it is because these images serve as screens for images of which nothing is told us. Images that Viola intends neither to share the existence of nor even to reveal that he is sharing it with himself. Hence the strange vibration

1

2

3

4

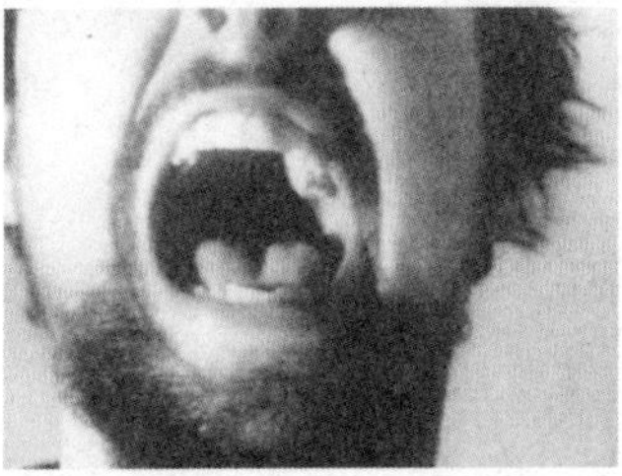
5

6

7

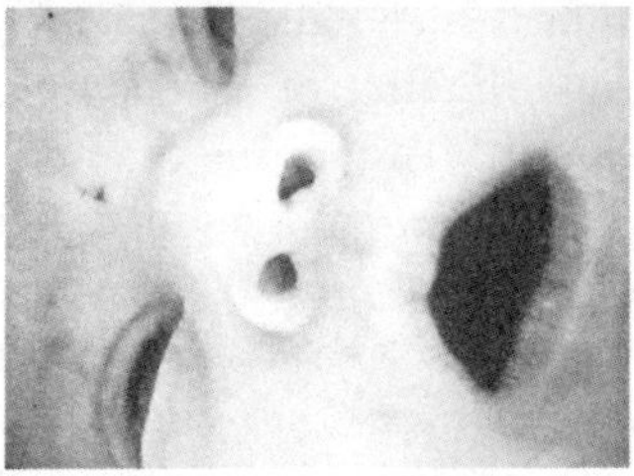
8

Bill Viola, 1-2: *The Reflecting Pool*, 1971–1979; 3-4: *Reasons for Knocking at an Empty House*, 1983; 5-6: *The Space Between The Teeth*, 1976; 7: *Moonblood*, 1977–1979; 8: *Silent Life*, 1979

9

10

11

12

13

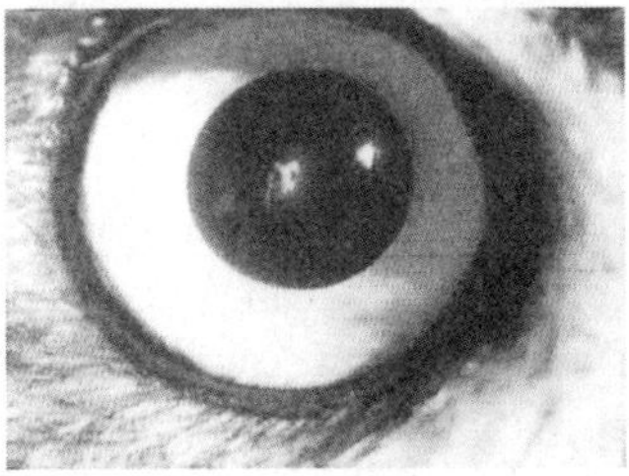

14

15

16

Bill Viola: 9: *Chott-el Djerid. A Portrait in Light and Heat*, 1979; 10: *The Semi-Circular Canals*, 1975; 11-12: *Ancient of Days*, 1979–1981; 13-16: *I Do Not Know What It Is I Am Like*, 1986 that runs through this eternal present, constantly on the verge of self-destruction, this time perpetually regained because it admits of no time lost. As such, this mode is more tragic than it is nostalgic. At the level of the image *dispositif* itself, Viola differs from Kuntzel, to whom he is otherwise so close in the development of corporeal memory.

That, I think, is what makes the central section of *I Do Not Know What It Is I Am Like* so moving. For the first time, Viola shows himself at home, alone, at work, during one of those all-night sessions so conducive to private self-reflection. The four other parts of this long video on animality made human (at 89 minutes, it is the longest) are sort of drawn in by the convergence of motifs streaming by, mostly on the mini-monitor on his work table. We are in an illusion of real time, almost autobiographical, if it were not for the life that is not told but shown, raw and transcendent. Through the very banal actions Viola performs—reading, drinking, eating, strolling—two series of events come to light. On the one hand, the contraction, substitution, fusion of representations by which (as in *The Reflecting Pool*) real time enters a dimension of condensed, magical time, ultra-time. On the other, a shimmering flow of the strange images of his disseminated body that appear everywhere—in a faucet, in a globe, in a water drop fallen on the table, in the plate of fish he is eating. We see him filming in the dilated eye of the owl in a shot that serves as a transition from the second part of the tape to this one: "The color of the pupil is black. It is on this black that you see your self-image when you try to look closely into your own eye, or into the eye of another."[62] But this "I" that sees itself in its own gaze, in eyes of animals, or in surrounding objects, this "I" knows neither who it is nor what it looks like. This thickness that one calls "oneself" owes its reality to the organic depth of the life in which it participates and to the technology capable of (re)producing its complexity and, thus, of including it as a body aware and as image-body. Viola borrows his title, which could serve as self-portraiture's austere motto, from the Rig Veda. But, more than to these ancestral cultures whose heritage he likes to invoke, it seems to me that Viola—through these new states of the self that spring from modern science and in particular from new modes of production of the image—is initiating a return to the very origins of the self-portrait in Western tradition, as Beaujour retraced it. He shares the preoccupations of the *Speculum mundi*, of medieval and Renaissance theaters of memory (he entitled one of his most beautiful installations *The Theater of Memory*, 1985). Apart from Montaigne, and the interiorization attached to oneself, as dispersed and impersonal as one might conceive oneself to be, I also see his work in connection with Bacon and his "method," with Loyola and his *Spiritual Exercises*, or even with Descartes' *Meditations*, which he attempts to reformulate in a contem-porary way, with contemporary means, from a context created by the individuation of the Modern Self. With the difference that the ascetic reasoning of the philosopher's meditations, as of the Saint's exercises, are immersed *a priori* in the body of the sensory world in which the technological operations that make it visible participate. The one I assume myself to be abides in an immersion in which words fail in the telling. The absence of language is fundamental, such that one compensates for it by replacing "I write" by an equivalent "I videograph" (like Kuntzel again, even if the assumptions are different). "The self-portrait stages and dialecticizes the tension between 'I speak' and 'I write,' for the Cartesian cogito does not answer the question: 'Who am I?' 'What do I know?' etc."[63] This indeed is the tension at work in Viola, on the backdrop of the implied relation between techno-science and the Natural Self on which it is based.

This simultaneously logical and mystical (almost alchemical) link with nature is partly what makes this a romantic work, still innervated by the fantasy (discreet yet profound) of an artistic utopia—"le poète […] est chargé de l'humanité, des animaux même."[64] It is the condition on which technology can take God's place to help form a new subjectivity: between its suspension and dissemination in an art of the dérive (drifting or digression)—self-portraiture being one of its forms—and its solidification-dissolution in the cold rhetorical practices of communication. "With the integration of images and video into the domain of computer logic, we are beginning the task of mapping the conceptual structures of our brain onto the technology." "Today, development of self must precede development of the technology or we will go nowhere—there will be condominiums in data space (it has already begun with cable tv)."[65]

Yet this self, ideal and idealized, wishing in a sense to regain its status prior to the great crisis of the Renaissance (in other words before rhetoric definitely lost its hegemony), cannot in the least be said to ignore the austere logic of the crisis from which it was born. The crisis endures, too, as if unchanged, in particular through the self-portrait, which is one of its signs, despite the transformations it has undergone, and whatever transcendence or transmutation with which one might invest it. In the haunting quiet of his California home, Bill Viola at work becomes that image of himself that he projected in his representation of St. John of the Cross. He has entered his cell; there he hears the rumblings of the world, the voices of his mind. And like the saint whispering the *Cantos de la noche oscura* to himself and to God, Viola enters *The Night of Sense* (title of the third part of his tape) and tells himself: "I do not know what it is I am like." And he turns this mandatory passage of self-portraiture into an interrogation addressed to all of creation.

VI. Opening

Even if they do not formulate it as such, the works we have traversed all pose the question "Who am I?" They answer it by making the sometimes barely glimpsed "I" a scattered being of excess, drift, and play, the visible medium for an anonymity that provides access both to a grasp of the world and to the forces of personal angst. Here are subjects drawn from their most intimate selves to a new form of "thinking from the outside," within the limits and possibilities of image and sound. As Elizabeth Bruss pointed out, the difficulties encountered in cinema with the demands of the autobiographical pact show that the medium can "lay bare a more radical mystery beyond the limits of self-awareness"; "[it] can," she explains, "take identity beyond what one consciousness can grasp, beyond even what the unaided human consciousness can encompass."[66] We have seen what the mutation and proliferation of techniques engenders, through video and everything that it involves: the impossible auto-biography is explicitly transformed into self-portraits of a new kind, unfolding with a substantiality, consistency, and logic for which cinema offers no real equivalent.

If I must conclude with Godard, it is because, approaching the issue from the opposite side, he envelops it and gives it a dimension that it lacks: the self-portrait propelled by video into the heart of fiction. Fiction with Godard has always served as decor, for show; it harbors a threefold desire—for myth, for instruction, and for the encyclopedic. A desire that has become progressively more divided with the ever more blatant intrusion of one who unexpectedly asks "Who am I?"

The question requires a revisitation. We see this for example in the way in which Godard is reprojected in a friendly profile of him (for *Cinéma, Cinémas*, when *Soigne ta droite* [*Keep Your Right Up*], 1987 was released) that takes one of the most reflexive sequences in his work and adds playful self-reflection, steering it toward self-portraiture.[67] What is at stake in that scene in *Les Carabiniers* (*The Riflemen*, 1963) where the two heroes come back with a suitcase full of postcards, which they take as a kind of ratification of the realities they depict? Nothing less than the (illusory) possession of the world and its projection as representation. The postcard is indisputably a *locus* of memory: all images pass through it, by class and category, as in encyclopedias, files, thesauruses. Together they compose a mirror of the world. Using the same soundtrack, Godard is slipped into the flow of images through the replacement of certain (black and white) scenes of the film with groupings of (color) photographs of him: thus his images of the world and of cinema—and of himself as agent of these images—circulate among each other. Thus distributed, image by image, in a thoroughly unpredictable and light-hearted concatenation of postcards and photographs, his own image invites us to define this movement through an exploration of his previous work.

In Godard's cinema, documentary traverses fiction: it constructs and runs through fiction in a very peculiar way. On the one hand, cinema returns to itself with an intensity never seen before, such that the work presents itself as a reprise, pastiche, parody, and an homage to its entire history, culminating in Godard's long-held project of a history of film, produced for Canal Plus.[68] On the other hand, a keen eye is cast on the world, engaging a passionate enumeration of commonplaces and cultural loci. This gaze is wild, spontaneous, anarchic, disorderly, like the return journey through film that is its backbone. But it is nonetheless obsessive, systematic, methodological. Very close, globally, to what Vigo had called "a documented point of view."[69] It is the way an "I" declares itself without actually doing so, yet also the way it veers toward the impersonal: an empty place through which all the voices pass and speak. For a little more than a decade, Godard composed, recomposed, and generally novelized Barthes' *Mythologies* and *The Fashion System*; through the fictions that animated his characters, he drew up a portrait—*un état des lieux*—of the contemporary world. These characters had body, voice, fragments of destiny, preserving their singularity and, thus, the fiction, the myth. But they were also woven of citations, voices already formed, aggregates of codes, agglomerations of discourse; fiction reeled back and forth between scrap heap and encyclopedia, navigating between the pleasures of enumeration and those of copying. It fragmented on its way from Rabelais and Don Quixote to Bouvard and Pécuchet, drifting from the Little Red Book to the mail-order catalogue.

During that period, Godard rarely appeared in his own work (though he surrounded it with discourse and allowed himself a few strong moments, as in the voice-overs in *Vivre sa vie* [*My Life to Live*], 1962, and *Deux ou trois choses que je sais d'elle* [*Two or Three Things I Know About Her*], 1967). He remained masked behind as many proxies as there were bodies, voices, characters. The precarious balance was broken during his militant period, a break that translated essentially into a confrontation with video and television. It took two paths: one the rhetoric of persuasion, the other a promotion of the intimate and of what one may call his own "*petits papiers.*" They emerged with *Ici et ailleurs* (*Here and Elsewhere*, 1976) and *Numéro deux* (*Number Two*, 1975), pattern-setting transitional films, and then began to model and modulate all his work, especially from the moment it initiated a return to and through fiction—its third major phase.

The rhetoric of persuasion developed and rationalized the logic of the lesson: provocative, conversational, and ingestive lessons in the work of the first period (and in all his "fictions"); the iron-clad (though ever-ironic) lessons of the militant period. When the pan-political utopia broke down, what emerged was utopian, at once public and private, and found its natural venue in television. The lesson was no longer addressed either to privileged partners in the exchange of fiction or to the dreamt-of masses in the militant films: its target was an assumed, imagined audience. The attempt to persuade here rested on the construction of a critical rhetoric conceived as a search for truth, based on the singularity of a single point of utterance: one person's voice, speech, and (often) body—Godard himself, the auteur-interviewer-reader-improviser-speaker. This private rhetoric countered the "monstrous" rhetoric of mass media; but it presented itself as utopian nevertheless, at the level of communication, seeking with image-words to do the work classical rhetoric once attributed to discourse in a social world whose coherence it partly provided. Godard's rhetoric, contradictory within itself (its singularity and its strength), postulated the world's renewal based on the personal dialogue that one subject seeks to establish with others. Thus, his meanderings have sought to touch children in particular.

In the last ten years, in the wake of this movement, Godard has generated a set of "petits papiers" to accompany his films: project prefaces for *Sauve qui peut (la vie)* (*Every Man for Himself*, 1980) and *Je vous salue Marie* (*Hail Mary*, 1985), a postscript to *Passion* (1982), *Lettre à Freddy Buache* (*A Letter to Freddy Buache*, 1982), *Changer l'image* (in *Le Changement*, 1982), *Soft and Hard* (1985), an interview with Woody Allen, fragments of the "Godard Special" in *Cinéma, Cinémas* and so on. These micro-works (which can be long) have several things in common. Whether addressed to the Centre national de la cinématographie (CNC) or produced for television stations, French or foreign, they all have a public existence; in this they have a lot in common with the two extended television series[70] and fully participate, in their way, in a rhetoric of persuasion. But the subject matter and the confiding tone lend them an intimate dimension. These works seem to lean toward autobiography, as nearly all of them portray moments of a life. But they never attempt to assume the obligations of the contract with that form, even as they touch on the contingencies of everyday life; they focus instead on creative work, the production setting, the processes of invention. They do not tell, they show and demonstrate; they have an absolute sense of presence, regardless of any nostalgic content (for cinema of the past, for instance). The way Godard shows himself, at work (often amid his very machines),

1

2

3

4

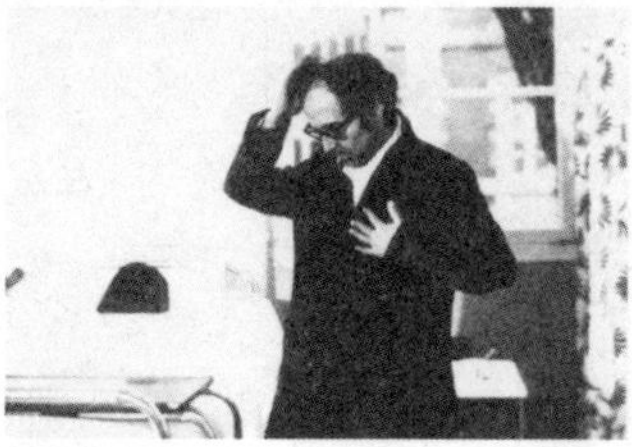
5

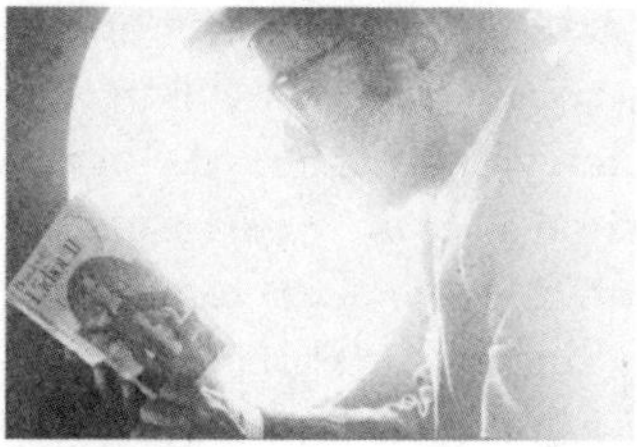
6

7

8

Jean-Luc Godard, 1-2: *Numéro deux (Number Two)*, 1975; 3: *Passion*, 1981; 4: *Lettre à Freddy Buache (A Letter to Freddy Buache)*, 1982; 5: *Prénom Carmen (First Name: Carmen)*, 1982; 6: *Soigne ta droite (Keep Your Right Up)*, 1987; 7-8: *Scénario du film* Passion *(Scenario for the film* Passion*)*, 1982 what he says, what we see, what we feel, everything indicates that these works were shot very freely, by someone in full possession of his own tools, with the freedom to do as he would—*à son gré*, as Mallarmé said of *vers libre*. Finally, the work in the making (sometimes the one being discussed) is often referenced as writing, as text: it attempts to engage a confrontation between writing and the sound-image, sentencing the former to death and attempting to endow the latter with new life, constantly endeavoring, also, to substitute the one for the other, to exchange their qualities, to mesh the one with the other. Quite naturally, as soon as they need to, these works continue the process of merging word with image, partly put into effect through the possibility (after *Ici et ailleurs* and *Numéro deux*) of treating the screen as a page for writing, of establishing a kind of literal screen-writing (again, like television, though in competition with it).

All these public-private pieces, back-to-back with the major private-public television series, form a very new body of work in the filmmaker's apparently fiction-based production. Obviously, fiction is only half the story. Proposed on television, conceived from the expressive possibilities of video, and often very intimate in nature, these works in fact draw his entire oeuvre, past and current, toward its most distinctive trait: representing thematic focal points, increasingly intertwined into a network that accommodates all the loci of artistic production—painting, music, film, and so on—contributing to the making of the work, even as it comes together.

One figure becomes essential in this process: the body, whether manifest as voice or as the body per se. It is ubiquitous throughout the "*petits papiers*" and intimist work. The body, real, factual, everyday, with a familiarity characteristic of television or of home movies, but suddenly, also, the body dramatized to the extreme, prey to creative anguish, experiencing its specific fiction, its daily sacrifice, the crucifixion of image and sound. One obviously thinks of *Scénario du film* Passion, where the body manifests itself such as it is before the blank page-screen to which the film will return. Or of the lesser-known episode, *Changer l'image* (*To Alter the Image*, 1982), which prefigures *Scénario*'s *dispositif*, but where, in addition, a second real Godard alternates with the first, scourged live on the screen for having failed to fulfill his vocation of being humanity's harbinger of new images and new sounds.

In the last few years, the same momentum has led Godard to make significant screen appearances in several of his movies (*Prénom Carmen* [*First Name: Carmen*], 1983; *King Lear*, 1987; *Grandeur et décadence d'un petit commerce de cinéma* [*Grandeur and Decadence of a Small Movie Concern*], 1986; *Soigne ta droite*). And he transposes himself more directly than ever in the impossible *mise en scène* of such variously crucified beings as the Dutronc-Paul-Godard of *Sauve qui peut (la vie)*, the Léaud-Gaspard of *Grandeur et décadence* (1986), and Jerzy of the so well-titled *Passion*. Thus, woven through the Christ-body, are ever more organic and closer ties between his peculiar fictions and the intimist variations of his creative life.

What emerges from all this is that this work, more fragmented and diffuse with every film, seems to be produced from the tension between two underlying and opposing forces (which do not really correspond to the two categories of which they consist—the "great films" and "the rest"—despite the distinction one tends to make). At one extreme, the development of matrices of fiction likely to respond to the world from a documentary point of view by following the logic of an array of *loci*; at the other, a stubborn search for oneself as real body and abstract focal point in which, by a system of analogies and metaphors, places and matrices are composed.

It is in fact strangely difficult in this work to locate the self-portrait that we sense so vividly. It would be easy to place it all in the mass of "*petits papiers*," without which, indeed, it would hardly be visible. As I suggested concerning literary works—and Godard's work is one of the first, perhaps *the* first, to fully translate their movement to film—we could say that self-portraiture resides latently within it. But that is not enough. Both for the truth of the work itself and for its theoretical ramifications, it is much more interesting to see how effort is manifestly expended, not to create a *particular*, localizable, and detachable self-portrait, as per Beaujour's descriptions, but to point the way *toward* the self-portrait. Which is to say that the dimension of self-portraiture unfolds globally, like a kind of constitutive layer, an inner movement, ensuring traffic between two major opposing principles: (1) a rhetoric of instruction, (re)founding the world (as in Rossellini) and (2) a desire for myth and fiction (as in good old movies).

The important thing, here, is that such a movement would not have been possible without the encounter, in the body of cinema as in that of the filmmaker dedicated to embodying it, between the two modes given us by video: (1) television, the only place that can now directly articulate the utopian vision that has long been the prerogative of the Book, which aims, by default, as Barthes put it, for "the transparency of social relations,"[71] and (2) video as such, which is, so to speak, the *locus* for working out a new avenue toward the search for self, which now transpires through an indistinguishable and global amalgam of words and images. In this, Godard responds with great precision to McLuhan, as does Viola on his own wavelength.

But Godard is also responding to Stendhal, who anticipated him a century earlier by approaching the question of self via images when words alone fail. Godard announces—and this may be the crucial point—that the time has come when certain distinctions, and therefore certain representations, have become problematic. After *Henry Brulard*, in which he attempts to grasp the fleeting truth of the Self, Stendhal wrote *The Charterhouse of Parma*, in which the Self is transposed to the novelist's lie, to myth and fiction. He even manages to fully express his love for Italy, which he had failed to properly capture in his travel writings.[72] Today, Godard's response to Stendhal is to say there is no longer a discrepancy but only imperceptible and reversible passages between myth, narrative, and the autobiography of the Self, the self-portrait. This implies that there is no longer any (really) simple past,[73] no real life to tell, no "I," no truly identifiable "Self." Egotism is no longer the stuff of memory but the indelible mark of a perpetual and suspended present, in which, through image-words, before and after, inner and the outer bring to the surface a depth once constituted by the contrasting effects of different verbal modes. Everything is now played out as an intermediate vision, an inter-media language.

1988. Translated in 2008 by Ron Ross.

Jean-Luc Godard, *Scénario du film* Passion (Scenario for the film *Passion*), 1982

[1] These comments on *Henri Brulard* were published in a first version entitled "L'entre-vu," *Photographies* 4 (April 1984) 14–15. I have since read Louis Marin's remarkable book, *La voix excommuniée* (Paris: Galilée, 1981), in which he comments at length on Stendhal's text as well as his study, "Images dans le texte autobiographique: Sur le chapitre xliv de *La Vie de Henri Brulard*," in *Saggi e ricerche di letteratura francese*, vol. 23 (Milan: Feltrinelli, 1984).

[2] Stendhal, "Vie de Henri Brulard," *Œuvres Intimes*, ed. Henri Martineau (Paris: Gallimard/Pléiade, 1955) 38 [*The Life of Henry Brulard*, trans. John Sturrock (New York: New York Review Books, 2002) 5]. He adds ("Vie" 194 [*Life* 197]): "What consoles me a little for the impertinence of writing so many *Is* and *mes*, is that I assume that many very ordinary people in this 19th century are doing as I am. So they will be inundated with *Memoirs* around 1880 […] and, with my *Is* and *mes*, I shall only be like everyone else." [Editor's note: As there seems to have been more than one edition of the *Œuvres Intimes* published in 1955, we will specify that the page numbers here refer to the edition available for consultation at the *Bibliothèque Nationale de France* in Paris.]

[3] "Vie" 40 [*Life* 6, 7].

[4] "Vie" 40 [*Life* 7].

[5] "Vie" 55 [*Life* 27].

[6] "Vie" 347 [*Life* 397].

[7] "Vie" 81 [*Life* 59].

[8] "Vie" 407 [*Life* 461].

[9] His famous definition of the novel in *Le Rouge et le Noir* (Paris: Gallimard/Pléiade, 1952) 557 [*The Red and the Black*, trans. Roger Gard (London: Penguin, 2002) 374].

[10] "Vie" 150, 428 [*Life* 144, 487].

[11] "Vie" 248 [*Life* 263].

[12] "Vie" 149 [*Life* 143].

[13] "Vie" 236 [*Life* 251].

[14] "Vie" 237 [*Life* 252].

[15] "Vie" 307 [*Life* 337].

[16] "Vie" 247 [*Life* 261–262].

[17] "Vie" 420 [*Life* 478].

[18] "Vie" 175 [*Life* 174].

[19] "Vie" 175 [*Life* 175].

[20] "Vie" 176 [*Life* 174]. In the translation, the image of the painting precedes that of the house [editor's note].

[21] To be understood, perhaps, in both an active sense (of rendering into an image) and a sense of manifest appearance; the translation, here, of Raymond Bellour's neologism *imaginéité* [translator's note].

[22] Louis Marin, "Images dans le texte autobiographique," in Marin, *L'écriture de soi: Ignace de Loyola, Montaigne, Stendhal, Roland Barthes* (Paris: Presses universitaires de France, 1999) 204–207.

[23] Marin 204.

[24] "Vie" 136 [*Life* 128].

[25] Alexandre Astruc, "L'avenir du cinéma," *La Nef* (1948), quoted in *L'Art du cinéma* 597.

[26] Specifically:
• The Anthology Films Archives program, *Autobiographical/Diaristic Experience in Cinema*, New York, June 1979, reproduced in *Revue belge du cinéma* 19 (Spring 1987) 18.
• Elizabeth Bruss' essay, "Eye for I: Making and Unmaking Autobiography," in *Autobiography: Essays Theoretical and Critical* 296–320.
• The second edition of "Cinéma et Littérature," organized by Françoise Calvez and Dominique Païni at the Valence CRAC, from October 30 to November 4, 1984, and entitled *Lettres, Confessions, Journaux intimes*.
• *Revue belge du cinéma: Boris Lehman, un cinéma de l'autobiographie* 13 (Fall 1985).
• A show from Frédéric Mitterrand's television series "Etoiles et Toiles," *Le cinéma à la première personne, or Ciné-Je*, with a section by Philippe Venault on "private diaries" [*Journaux intimes*], October 1985.
• An international symposium organized by Adolphe Nysenholc for the closing of *Semaine du Cinéma et de l'Autobiographie* at the Université libre de Bruxelles, March 1, 1986, followed by a publication in *Revue belge du cinéma: L'Ecriture du Je au cinéma* 19 (Spring 1987).
• And let us not forget that, for the last ten years, Dominique Noguez has written several times of the notion of "subjective cinema" [*Le Cinéma autrement*, coll. 10/18 (Paris: UGE, 1977)], which he then developed in connection with the "American underground" [*Une renaissance du cinéma* (Paris: Klincksieck, 1985)].
• Contrary to the editors of *Revue belge du cinéma*, no. 19, I will not include in this list the very good article by Jean-Pierre Chartier, "Les films à la première personne et l'illusion de réalité au cinéma," *Revue du cinéma* 4 (January 1947) 32–41; indeed, it is solely concerned with films of fiction in the subjective voice and not with films in which filmmakers truly express in "the first person."

[27] "Cinéma et autobiographie: Problèmes de vocabulaire," in *Revue belge du cinéma*: *L'Ecriture du Je au cinéma* 19 (Spring 1987) 7–13. All subsequent quotes from Philippe Lejeune refer to this text, pages 7–12.

[28] Bruss, "Eye for I" 302.

[29] Note that the dual sense of *objectif* in French—"objective" and "lens"—underlies the subjective/objective polarity [translator's note].

[30] Quoted in Bruss, "Eye for I" 319.

[31] Michel Beaujour, *Miroirs d'encre. Rhétorique de l'autoportait* (Paris Seuil, 1980) [*Poetics of the Literary Self-Portrait*, trans. Yara Milos (New York: New York University, 1991)]. All the following quotes, unless indicated otherwise, are taken from the first chapter: "Self-Portrait and Autobiography."

[32] I take this opportunity to say that the only work I know of that is devoted to self-portraiture in video refers to the painted self-portrait: Helmut Friedel's "The New Self-Portrait," in *Video by Artists* 2, ed. Elke Town (Toronto: Art Metropole, 1986) 113–124. Likewise, a comprehensive treatment would have to go through the intermediate form of the photographic self-portrait, cf. *L'Autoportrait à l'âge de la photographie, peintres et photographes en dialogue avec leur propre image* (Catalogue of the Musée cantonal des Beaux-Arts, Lausanne, 1985); and Jean-François Chevrier and Jean Sagne, "L'autoportrait comme mise en scène – essai sur l'identité, l'exotisme et les excès photographiques," *Photographies* 4: 47–82 ["Staging the Self—Essay on Identity, Exotism and the Photographic Excesses," trans. C.L. Clark, *Photographies* 4: 132–134].

[33] Michel Beaujour, *Miroirs d'encre*, 110 [*Poetics of the Literary Self-Portrait*, 104].

[34] Beaujour 18 [*Poetics of the Literary Self-Portrait* 13].

[35] Jacques Lacan, *Ecrits* (Paris: Editions du Seuil, 1966) 742 [*Ecrits: the First Complete Edition in English*, trans. Bruce Fink, Héloïse Fink, and Russell Grigg (New York: W.W. Norton & Co., 2006) 625].

[36] Let us clarify a few points:
• Michel Beaujour is not concerned with the implicit development of the self-portrait in the 19th century, which is understandable since his vision is primarily transhistorical. He does not include *The Life of Henry Brulard* among self-portraits and does not even discuss it. Doubtless the autobiographical intention is all too obvious, if one does not pause at the effect of the drawings.
• Philippe Lejeune starts with the word "autobiography" and remains faithful to it, even if he makes it more pliable. He dates the beginning of the genre to the late 18th century. He uses the term "self-portrait" when it suits him,

either off-hand or to adjust his response (but without drawing much significance from the matter) to Beaujour's criticism of him (concerning Leiris, in *Moi aussi* [Paris: Edition du Seuil, 1986] 19–20) or to point out and describe a particular work (Sartre's *War Diaries: Notebooks from a Phony War* [*Carnets de la drôle de guerre*] as opposed to his *The Words* [*Les Mots*], an autobiography examined in *Le Pacte autobiographique* [Paris: Edition du Seuil, 1975]).
• Louis Marin, as we have seen, resolves the question in his own way. He speaks of *autobiothanatographie* to characterize the autobiography's death as it plays out in *Henry Brulard*, largely due to the drawings. His perspective is very close to that of Beaujour, though he does not use the word "self-portrait."

[37] Raymond Bellour, "An Interview with Bill Viola," *October* 34 (Fall 1985) 100. Similarly, Gary Hill says: "I think I was becoming obsessed with the electronic hum. It was like a synapse with the rest of the world" ["'A Manner of Speaking': An Interview with Gary Hill by Lucinda Furlong," *Afterimage* 10.8 (March 1983) 9–10].

[38] In the "*Aide-mémoire*" (or mnemonic checklist) to his *Ancienne Rhétorique*, Barthes recalled how much the "mass media" ensured the degraded survival of Aristotelianism and rhetoric [*Communications* 16 (1970): 223].

[39] Jean-Paul Fargier, "La vidéo contre (tout contre) la télévision," *Catalogue de la 1re Manifestation internationale de vidéo*, Montbéliard, December 6–12, 1982.

[40] Beaujour 14 [*Poetics of the Literary Self-Portrait* 9].

[41] According to the author's recollections, this was a video installation temporarily set up in one of the stations of the Paris métro [editor's note].

[42] Jean-André Fieschi, "Point de vue sur un troisième œil"; "Les nouveaux mystères de New York," *Art Présent* 6–7 (1978) n.d. Anne-Marie Duguet, *Vidéo, la mémoire au poing* (Paris: Hachette, 1981) 165–174.

[43] "Jean-André Fieschi et *Les nouveaux mystères de New York*," in the television show *Vidéo-Babil*, with Raymond Bellour and Philippe Venault, France Culture, April 10, 1983. The following quotes are taken from this interview and from the one with Jean-Paul Fargier, "Rencontre avec un Corse des Carpathes," *Cahiers du cinema* 310 (April 1980) 29–34.

[44] Madeleine Grynsztejn has compiled the best bio-biblio-filmo-video-graphy for Acconci in *Vito Acconci: Domestic Trappings* (La Jolla Museum of Contemporary Art, California, 1987). Only 25 of his tapes were found by organizers preparing an exhibition at the Whitney Museum (*Video Self-Portraits*, 1989).

[45] Rosalind Krauss, "Video: The Aesthetics of Narcissism," *October* (Spring 1976).

[46] Beaujour 161 [*Poetics of the Literary Self-Portrait* 154].

[47] On Juan Downey, the best selection is from the exhibition catalogue, *Festival Downey: Video porque Te Ve* (Santiago, Chile: Ediciones Visuala Galeria, 1987).

[48] Cited in Raymond Bellour, *Eye for I: Video Self-Portraits*, trans. Lynne Kirby, with a preface by John G Hanhardt (New York: Independent Curators Incorporated, 1989) 28.

[49] On Marcel Odenbach, see the catalogue *Dans la vision périphérique du témoin* (Paris: Centre Georges Pompidou, 1986).

[50] I owe this translation of the *forme-bandeau* concept to Lynne Kirby (*Eye for I* 12), who borrowed it, in turn, from David Jacobson and Bérénice Reynaud's translation of Bellour's "The Form My Gaze Goes Through" in this volume [translator's note].

[51] Philippe Dubois, "Les aventuriers de l'image perdue," *IIe Semaine internationale de vidéo* (Geneva: Saint-Gervais, 1987) 58. See also, "La boîte magique," *Hyaloïde*, ed. Danièle and Jacques-Louis Nyst (Crisnée, Belgium: Yellow Now, 1986) (includes the text of the videotape and one still frame per shot).

[52] For Thierry Kuntzel's (brief) texts on his tapes and installations, see *Communications* 48, subtitled *Vidéo*, ed. Raymond Bellour and Anne-Marie Duguet (1988) 149–152.

[53] See "Thierry Kuntzel and the Return of Writing" in this book.

[54] Dubois, "La boîte magique" 47.

[55] "Les nouveaux mystères de New York," *Art Présent* 6–7 (1978) n.p.

[56] Beaujour 87 [*Poetics of the Literary Self-Portrait* 78]. On the "backgrounds and images"—*les fonds et les images*—see pages 86–88, 93–97, 171–178.

[57] Thierry Kuntzel, "Le défilement"; "A Note upon the Filmic Apparatus."

[58] Beaujour 110 [*Poetics of the Literary Self-Portrait* 104].

[59] Fargier, "Rencontre avec un Corse des Carpathes" 32.

[60] From the author's interview with Viola, published in *October* 34 (Fall 1985) 104. One may usefully compare this with what Bruce Nauman has said: "The work isn't autobiographical. It isn't really about me. While I was doing it, it was mostly with images of myself but almost every image is either upside down or the head doesn't show at all or it's only the back. So it was only important to have an image of a human figure, even if I was using myself at the time. A little bit later, when I started using other people, it was easier if there was a face, because it was an actor, an actor being someone who is not anyone." "Keep Taking It Apart: A Conversation with Bruce Nauman," by Chris Dercon, *Parkett* 10 (1986) 56, published in part in *Vidéo: La mémoire au poing*. On Viola, see also: "L'espace à pleines dents" (follow-up to the previous interview with Bill Viola, by Raymond Bellour), in *Où va la vidéo?* 14 (1986) 64–73; Anne-Marie Duguet, "Les vidéos de Bill Viola, une poétique de l'espace-temps," *Parachute* 45 (December 1986–February 1987) 10–15 (French), 50–53 (English). And see the three catalogues: ARC, Musée d'art moderne de la Ville de Paris, 1983–1984; The Museum of Modern Art, New York, ed. Barbara London, 1987; Contemporary Arts Museum, Houston, ed. Marilyn Zeitlin, 1988.

[61] Barthes, "L'ancienne rhétorique," *Communications* 16 (1970) 209.

[62] Excerpt from Viola's text written for the videodisc of *I Do Not Know What It Is I Am Like* (1986), cited in *Eye for I* 46.

[63] Beaujour 19 [*Poetics of the Literary Self-Portrait* 13]

[64] "Humanity, and even the *animals*, are [the poet's] burden" [Arthur Rimbaud, *Rimbaud Complete*, ed. and trans. Wyatt Mason (New York: Modern Library Edition, 2002) 368].

[65] Bill Viola, "Will There Be Condominiums in Data Space?" *Video 80* 5 (fall 1982): 40–41, and in French, in *Communications: Vidéo* 48 (1982): 71–72, 73. Online Portable Document Format (pdf) version from *The New Media Reader*, ed. Noah Wardrip-Fruin and Nick Montfort (mit Press, 2003), available at http://www.cybergrain.com/remediality/viola.pdf, pages 12, 14.

[66] Bruss, "Eye for I" 318, 319.

[67] The episode, entitled "*Les Carabiniers* (revisités)" and broadcast on December 20, 1987, was directed by Pierre-Oscar Lévy. [Editor's note: *Cinéma, Cinémas* was an influential series, produced by French television in the 1980s, on films and filmmakers.]

[68] All this must obviously be taken up again with respect to the two existing episodes of *Histoire(s) du cinéma*.

[69] Jean Vigo's commentary on his own 1930 film *A propos de Nice*: "Documentaire social ou plus exactement, un point de vue documenté" [translator's note].

[70] *Six fois deux* and *France/tour/détour/deux/enfants* [editor's note].

[71] "La transparence des rapports sociaux." English translation from Barthes, *The Rustle of Language*, trans. Richard Howard

(New York: Hill and Wang, 1986), 64 [translator's note].

[72] Barthes, "On échoue toujours à parler de ce qu'on aime," *Le Bruissement de la langue* (Paris: Seuil, 1984). ["One always fails in speaking of what one loves," *The Rustle of Language* 304.]

[73] In French, the *passé simple* is the past tense typically used in narration [editor's note].

Vocabulary and Translator's Notes

It is always a problem, in translating works of an analytical nature, to make the choice between leaving certain terms untranslated, leading to a somewhat artificial result, or to attempt to give terms their closest translated equivalent, often resulting in a dilution of the original intent. The problem is compounded in this case by the collective nature of the translations here and the obviously varied decisions made by each translator for each term. That said, the author and the present edition translator of this book have decided that certain terms are too particular to give them English equivalents that, in some cases, may lead to confusion with other terms that would distance them from their original meaning.

As a result, and with all due respect to the original translators—some of whom are credited here in excerpts from the notes they added to their texts to address this very issue—it was decided to leave the following terms untranslated:

Défilement: Often translated as "unfolding," "unspooling," or "unreeling." For Thierry Kuntzel, "*[d]éfilement* […] means, in the vocabulary of cinema, 'progression, the sliding of the [film stock] through the gate of a projector'[1] and, in military art, the use of the terrain's accidents or of artificial constructions to conceal one's movements from the enemy. In the unrolling of the film, the [frames] which concern us 'pass through [*(se) défilent*],' hidden from sight: what the spectator retains is only the movement hidden within which they insert themselves […]"[2] Bellour makes use of the indeterminate space between these two meanings as he does with *trame* (see below).

Dispositif: The word "*dispositif*" does not have a satisfactory English equivalent, insofar as one must especially avoid the confusion that too often arises when it is translated as "apparatus." The concept of the *appareil de base*, which is correctly translated as "basic apparatus," was introduced in 1970 by Jean-Louis Baudry in his text "Cinéma: effets idéologiques produits par l'appareil de base," in a context, inspired for the most part by Louis Althusser's work, of a critique of cinema's position as the equivalent both of the Lacanian imaginary—the "mirror stage" and its consequences—and of the subjective idealism associated with the Renaissance system of perspective, given new life by cinema. In 1975, when Baudry used *dispositif* in a cinema studies context (in his text "Le dispositif: approches métapsychologiques de l'impression de réalité"), his aim was to take into account the cinematic environment as a whole —in a Freudian perspective, without any critical partiality— an environment that fully incorporates the spectator's psyche, and that is considered an equivalent of the dream state. In *Discipline and Punish* (*Surveiller et punir*) that same year, Michel Foucault used the word, demonstrating its growing acceptance, to describe the series of machinic systems for which Bentham's Panopticon was the historical prototype. Bellour makes free use of this double meaning and its consequences to designate the cinematic environment as well as visual and audiovisual installations belonging both to the history of art and that of techniques.

Paluche: "([L]iterally, a slang term for hand). Invented by Jean-Pierre Beauviala, the *paluche* is a black and white video camera about 20 cm long, often compared to a microphone or a flashlight because it is held in the hand. It is known for its sharp contrast and the minimal amount of light that it requires. Because of its size and mobility, the *paluche* becomes an extension of the hand rather than the eye: 'the most unexpected images become possible, challenging the supremacy of the look in the organization of the visible.'"[3]

Trame: "*Trame*" is the word used in French for what in technical English is called the "raster," the series of lines making up the image on an analog TV screen, or the grid of pixels on an LCD display. The term had its origins in the world of textiles, referring to the woof or weft of a fabric. From this usage came the connotation with which the French reader will be most familiar: what in English would be called the background, the context of a story, *la trame de l'histoire*. Bellour and Jean-Paul Fargier make use of the parallels between these two meanings in their texts on video art: "De la trame au drame"; "Les aventures de la trame." In Fargier's text, "La vidéo, contre (tout contre) la télévision," he even mentions a work by Dominique Belloir and Guy Le Quérec, "Trame nommée désir" (a play on *Un tramway nommé désir*, the French title for *A Streetcar Named Desire*), so the term lends itself to numerous contextualizations. As a result, the decision was made to maintain the usage of the French term.

***

About the titles: foreign films are cited using their original titles followed by their English titles if released in the English-speaking world.

About the footnotes: where applicable, the citations of the French texts from the original articles are followed in brackets by the references to the English versions used in the translated articles.

About gender: as the author of this book is a man, and as the spectator described here is primarily considered to be gradually becoming the individual that corresponds to that man, we have opted to keep the masculine personal pronoun to refer to him.

***

The following works mentioned in this book may be viewed at the *Espace Nouveaux Médias* of the Centre Pompidou in Paris:

Vito Acconci: *Centers* (1971); *Pryings* (1971); *Home Movies* (1973); *The Red Tapes* (1977)

Max Almy: *Modern Times* (1979)

Juan Downey: *The Looking Glass* (1981)

Jean-Paul Fargier: *L'Arche de Nam June Paik* (1981)

Jean-Luc Godard: *Lettre à Freddy Buache* (1981); *Scénario du film* Passion (1982); *Histoire(s) du cinéma* (1989–1996)

Jean-Luc Godard and Anne-Marie Miéville: *Six fois deux/Sur et sous la communication* (including *Photo et cie*) (1976); *France/tour/détour/deux/enfants* (1977–1978); *Soft and Hard (Soft Talk on a Hard Subject Between Two Friends)* (1985)

Doug Hall: *Storm and Stress* (1986)

Gary Hill: *Processual Video* (1980); *Site/Recite (A Prologue)* (1989)

Michael Klier: *Der Riese* (1983)

Thierry Kuntzel: *Nostos I* (1979); *Echolalia* (1980); *Still* (1980); *Time Smoking a Picture* (1980); *Nostos II* (1984)

Thierry Kuntzel and Philippe Grandrieux: *La peinture cubiste* (1981)

Antoni Muntadas: *Media Ecology Ads* (1982)

Jacques-Louis and Danièle Nyst: *Hyaloïde* (1986)

Marcel Odenbach: *Der Widerspruch der Erinnerungen* (1982); *Als könnte es auch mir an den Kragen gehen* (1983); *Die Distanz zwischen mir und meinen Verlusten* (1983); *Vorurteile* (1983-1984); *Dans la vision périphérique du témoin* (1986)

Nam June Paik: *Global Groove* (1973)

Shuntaro Tanikawa and Shuji Terayama: *Video Letters* (1982–1983)

Woody Vasulka: *The Commission* (1983); *The Art of Memory* (1987)

Bill Viola: *Four Songs* (including *Songs of Innocence*, *The Space Between the Teeth* and *Truth Through Mass Individuation*) (1976); *The Reflecting Pool* (including *The Reflecting Pool*, *Moonblood*, *Silent Life* and *Ancient of Days*) (1977–1980); *Chott-el-Djerid (A Portrait in Light and Heat)* (1980); *Hatsu Yume (First Dream)* (1981); *Reverse Television—Portraits of Viewers* (1983–1984); *I Do Not Know What It Is I Am Like* (1986)

The following works mentioned in this book may be viewed and/or downloaded at UbuWeb (http://www.ubu.com):

Vito Acconci: *Centers* (1971); *Pryings* (1971); *The Red Tapes* (1977)

Hollis Frampton: *Zorns Lemma* (1970); *Nostalgia* (1971)

Gary Hill: *Site/Recite (A Prologue)* (1989)

Marcel Odenbach: *Der Widerspruch der Erinnerungen* (1982); *Die Distanz zwischen mir und meinen Verlusten* (1983); *Dans la vision périphérique du témoin* (1986); *As If Memories Could Deceive Me* (1986)

Shuntaro Tanikawa and Shuji Terayama: *Video Letters* (1982–1983)

[1] Maurice Bessy and Jean-Louis Chardans, *Dictionnaire du cinéma et de la télévision* (Paris: J.-J. Pauvert, 1966).

[2] Thierry Kuntzel, "Le Défilement: A View in Close Up," trans. Bertrand Augst, *Apparatus*, ed. Theresa Hak Kyung Cha (New York: Tanam Press, 1980), p. 238.

[3] This note by Annwyl Williams originally appeared in her translation of "Thierry Kuntzel and the Return of Writing." Quoted from Anne-Marie Duguet, *Vidéo, la mémoire au poing* (Paris: Hachette, 1981), p. 166.

About the Author

RAYMOND BELLOUR is a noted film and video theorist and critic; he also writes about literature. He is Emeritus Research Professor at the Centre National de la Recherche Scientifique (CNRS) in Paris. His articles on film and video have appeared in a wide variety of international publications. Among other translations of his work in English is *The Analysis of Film* (Indiana University Press: 2000), *L'Analyse du film* (1979). Raymond Bellour is a founding member of the film journal *Trafic*.

By the same author

All works published in Paris unless otherwise noted.
– *Alexandre Astruc* (Seghers, 1963)
– *Henri Michaux ou une mesure de l'être* (Gallimard, 1966) (enlarged edition, Gallimard, collection "Folio Essais," 1986)
– *Le Livre des autres* (L'Herne, 1971)
– *Le Livre des autres* (interviews) (10/18/U.G.E., 1978)
– *L'Analyse du film* (Albatros, 1979) (reissued by Calmann-Lévy, 1995)
– *Mademoiselle Guillotine. Cagliostro, Dumas, Œdipe et la Révolution Française* (La Différence, 1989)
– *L'Entre-Images. Photo, cinéma, vidéo* (La Différence, 1990) (revised edition, 2002)
– *Oubli* (La Différence, 1992)
– *L'Entre-Images 2. Mots, images* (P.O.L, collection "Trafic," 1999)
– *Partages de l'ombre* (La Différence, 2002)
– *Le Corps du cinéma. Hypnoses, émotions, animalités* (P.O.L, collection "Trafic," 2009)
– *Les Hommes, le dimanche* (Yellow Now, collection "Côtés films," 2009)
– *Lire Michaux* (Gallimard, collection "Tel," 2011)

Books edited by Raymond Bellour

– *Le Western* (10/18/U.G.E., 1966) (enlarged edition, Gallimard, collection "Tel," 1993)
– *Henri Michaux* (L'Herne, no. 8, 1966) (enlarged edition, 1983)

– *Dictionnaire du cinéma* (Editions Universitaires, 1966) (with Jean-Jacques Brochier)
– *Communications* 23, issue *Psychanalyse et cinéma* (1975) (with Thierry Kuntzel and Christian Metz)
– *Lévi-Strauss* (Gallimard, 1979) (with Catherine Clément)
– *Le Cinéma américain* (film analysis, 2 volumes) (Flammarion, 1980)
– *Communications* 48, issue *Vidéo* (1988) (with Anne-Marie Duguet)
– *Cinéma et Peinture, approches* (Coliartco/P.U.F., 1990)
– *Passages de l'image* (Centre Georges-Pompidou, 1990) (with Catherine David and Christine Van Assche)
– *Camera Obscura* 24, issue Unspeakable Images (1991) (with Elisabeth Lyon)
– *Jean-Luc Godard: Son + Image* (New York: MoMA, 1992) (with Mary Lea Bandy)

Critical Editions

– Charlotte Brontë and Patrick Branwell Brontë, *Ecrits de jeunesse* (selections) (Pauvert, 1972) (reissued by Laffont, collection "Bouquins," 1992)
– Emily Brontë, *Wuthering Heights* (Pauvert, 1972)
– Emily Brontë, *Hurlevent* (Gallimard, collection "Folio," 1991)
– Alice James, *Journal*, followed by a selection of letters (Café-Clima, 1984)
– Henri Michaux, *Œuvres complètes* (Gallimard/Bibliothèque de la Pléiade): Volume I (1998); Volume II (2001); Volume III (2004) (with Ysé Tran)

Acknowledgments

Author's Acknowledgments

I would like to thank all those who contributed in one way or another to the making of this book:

– The video artists who generously gave me access to cassettes, documentation, and photographs;
– Those with whom I worked for several years on related and parallel projects: Catherine Sentis and Sylvain Roumette, for "Photo et Cinéma" (Centre National de la Photographie, 1984); Christine Buci-Glucksmann, for the seminar "Entre les images" (Collège International de Philosophie, 1987–1988); Anne-Marie Duguet, for the *Vidéo* issue of *Communications* (no. 48, 1988); Sylvain Roumette, for *Marges de la photo* (Intermedia, 1989); and especially Catherine David and Christine Van Assche, for the *Passages de l'image* exhibition (Centre Georges Pompidou, 1990);
– Jacques Aumont, Erwan Depenanster, Philippe Dubois, Pascal Cuissot (and the Cinémathèque Française), Jean-Paul Fargier, Michel Frizot, Takae Imajo, André Iten, Thierry Kuntzel, Barbara London, Louis Marin, Marie-Cécile Mazzoni, Christian Metz, Paul-Emmanuel Odin, Kira Perov, Sylvie Pliskin (and the DERCAAV group at the Université de Paris-III), Patrice Rollet, Danielle Sivadon, Lori Zippay;

And all the publications where these texts appeared previously:

– "Analysis in Flames": *Diacritics* 15.1 (Spring 1985). First published as "Analisi a la flamma," *Carte Semiotiche* 1 (September 1985);
– "Thierry Kuntzel and the Return of Writing": *Camera Obscura* 11 (1983). First published as "Thierry Kuntzel et le retour de l'écriture," *Cahiers du cinéma* 321 (March 1981);
– "Video Utopia," *National Video Festival Catalogue* (Los Angeles: American Film Institute, 1986). First published as "L'utopie-vidéo," *Où va la vidéo?*, *Cahiers du cinéma* Special Issue (Spring 1986);
– "When the Photo of Cinema is Written." First published as "Quand s'écrit la photo du cinéma," *Cahiers du cinéma* 342 (July 1982);

– "The Pensive Spectator": *Wide Angle* 9.1 (1987). First published as "Le spectateur pensif," *Photogénies* 5 (April 1984);
– "The Phantom's Due": *Discourse* 16.2 (Winter 1993–1994). First published as "La redevance du fantôme," *Le Temps d'un mouvement* (Paris: Centre National de la Photographie, 1986);
– "The Crystal-Duration." First published as "La durée-cristal," *Le Temps d'un mouvement*;
– "I am an Image," *Camera Obscura* 8–10, special issue on Godard (1982);
– "The Film Stilled": *Camera Obscura* 24, special issue *Unspeakable Images*, ed. Raymond Bellour and Elisabeth Lyon (1991). First published as "L'interruption, l'instant," *La Recherche photographique* 3 (December 1987);
– "Six Films (In Passing)." First published as "Six films (en passant)," *Marges de la photo* (Paris: Intermedia, 1989);
– "The Limits of Fiction": *Video by Artists 2*, ed. Elke Town (Toronto: Art Metropole, 1986). First published as "Les bords de la fiction," *Actes du colloque Vidéo-fiction et Cie* (Montbéliard: Centre d'Action Culturelle, 1983);
– "From In-Between the Bodies." First published as "D'entre les corps," *Revue Belge du cinéma*, special issue "Vidéo et Cinéma" (Spring 1990);
– "The Images of the World": *Resolutions*, ed. Michael Renov and Erika Suderburg (Minneapolis, London: University of Minnesota Press, 1996). First published as "Les images du monde," *3ème Semaine Internationale de Vidéo* (Geneva: Saint-Gervais, 1989);
– "The Burning Memory": *Illuminating Video*, ed. Doug Hall and Sally Jo Fifer (New York: Aperture, 1990). First published as "La mémoire qui brûle," *The Luminous Image*, ed. Dorine Mignot (Amsterdam: Stedelijk Museum, 1984);
– "Video According to Saint John": *Illuminating Video*. First published as "La vidéo selon Saint-Jean," *Cahiers du cinéma* 356 (February 1984);
– "The Last Man on the Cross": *Illuminating Video*. First published as "Le dernier homme en croix," *2e Semaine Internationale de Vidéo* (Geneva: Saint-Gervais, 1987);
– "The Art of Demonstration": *Illuminating Video*. First published as "L'art de la démonstration," *A la Virreina* (Barcelona: Ajuntament de Barcelona, 1988);
– "The Form My Gaze Goes Through": *Afterimage* 16.4 (November 1988). First published as "La forme où passe

mon regard," *Marcel Odenbach* (Paris: Centre Georges Pompidou, 1986);

– "The Letter goes on … ": *Illuminating Video*. First published as "La lettre dit encore," *Vertigo* 2 (1988);

– "Self-Portraits": *Precarious Visualities: New Perspectives on Identification in Contemporary Art and Visual Culture*, ed. O. Asselin, J. Lamoureux, and C. Ross (Montreal: McGill-Queen's University Press, 2008). First published as "Autoportraits," *Vidéo*, *Communications* 48 (1988).

The edition translator would like to thank:

The Bibliothèque Nationale de France, the Bibliothèque de l'Université Paris-8, the Bibliothèque de la Documentation Française, the BIFI (Bibliothèque du Film), The New York Public Library.

Index

Imprint

Edited by Raymond Bellour and Allyn Hardyck

TRANSLATIONS, REVISION,
AND CRITICAL APPARATUS FOR THIS EDITION
Allyn Hardyck

COPY EDITING
Clare Manchester

DESIGN CONCEPT
Gavillet & Rust, Geneva

DESIGN
Nicolas Eigenheer

TYPEFACE
Genath (www.optimo.ch)

PRINT AND BINDING
Présence Graphique, Monts (Indre-et-Loire)

The present publication is an English adaptation of *L'Entre-images–Photo, cinéma, vidéo*, first published by Les Editions de La Différence in 1990. It has been published with the support of the Centre National du Livre (CNL), Paris. (*Publié avec le concours du Centre national du livre.*)

PUBLISHED BY
JRP|Ringier
Letzigraben 134
CH–8047 Zurich
T +41 43 311 27 50
F +41 43 311 27 51
E info@jrp-ringier.com
www.jrp-ringier.com

IN CO-EDITION WITH
Les presses du réel
35 rue Colson
F–21000 Dijon
T +33 3 80 30 75 23
F +33 3 80 30 59 74
E info@lespressesdureel.com
www.lespressesdureel.com

ISBN 978-3-03764-144-6 (JRP|Ringier)
ISBN 978-2-84066-513-7 (Les presses du réel)

Distribution

GERMANY AND AUSTRIA
Vice Versa Vertrieb, Immanuelkirchstrasse 12, D-10405 Berlin, info@vice-versa-vertrieb.de, www.vice-versa-vertrieb.de

FRANCE
Les presses du réel, 35 rue Colson, F-21000 Dijon, info@lespressesdureel.com, www.lespressesdureel.com

SWITZERLAND
Buch 2000, AVA Verlagsauslieferung AG, Centralweg 16, CH-8910 Affoltern a.A., buch2000@ava.ch, www.ava.ch

UK AND OTHER EUROPEAN COUNTRIES
Cornerhouse Publications, 70 Oxford Street, UK-Manchester M1 5NH, publications@cornerhouse.org, www.cornerhouse.org/books

USA, CANADA, ASIA, AND AUSTRALIA
D.A.P./Distributed Art Publishers, 155 Sixth Avenue, 2nd Floor, USA-New York, NY 10013, dap@dapinc.com, www.artbook.com

Victor Sjöström, *The Wind*, 1928

Documents Series 6:
Raymond Bellour
Between-the-Images

This book is the sixth volume in the "Documents" series, dedicated to critics' writings.

The series is directed by Lionel Bovier and Xavier Douroux.

Also available

DOCUMENTS SERIES (IN ENGLISH)

Saul Anton, *Warhol's Dream*
ISBN 978-3-905770-35-3 (JRP|Ringier)
ISBN 978-2-84066-200-6 (Les presses du réel)

Christian Höller, *Time Action Vision*
ISBN 978-3-03764-124-8 (JRP|Ringier)
ISBN 978-2-84066-396-6 (Les presses du réel)

Bob Nickas, *Theft Is Vision*
ISBN 978-3-905770-36-0 (JRP|Ringier)
ISBN 978-2-84066-206-8 (Les presses du réel)

Hans Ulrich Obrist, *A Brief History of Curating*
ISBN 978-3-905829-55-6 (JRP|Ringier)
ISBN 978-2-84066-287-7 (Les presses du réel)

Dorothea von Hantelmann, *How to Do Things with Art*
ISBN 978-3-03764-104-0 (JRP|Ringier)
ISBN 978-2-84066-361-4 (Les presses du réel)

DOCUMENTS SUR L'ART (IN FRENCH)–SELECTION

Daniel Birnbaum, *Chronologie*
ISBN 978-2-84066-165-8 (Les presses du réel)
ISBN 978-3-905770-98-8 (JRP|Ringier)

Diedrich Diederichsen, *Argument son*
ISBN 978-2-84066-140-5 (Les presses du réel)
ISBN 978-3-905829-00-6 (JRP|Ringier)

Stéphanie Moisdon, *Stéphanie Moisdon*
ISBN 978-2-84066-205-1 (Les presses du réel)
ISBN 978-3-905829-15-0 (JRP|Ringier)

Catherine Chevalier & Andreas Fohr, *Texte zur Kunst 1990-1998*
ISBN 978-2-84066-235-8 (Les presses du réel)
ISBN 978-3-03764-214-6 (JRP|Ringier)